A SHORT HISTORY OF
ENGLISH LITERATURE

BY

ÉMILE LEGOUIS

Professor of English Literature
The Sorbonne, Paris

Translated by

V. F. BOYSON

and

J. COULSON

OXFORD
AT THE CLARENDON PRESS
1934

OXFORD
UNIVERSITY PRESS
AMEN HOUSE, E.C. 4
London Edinburgh Glasgow
New York Toronto Melbourne
Capetown Bombay Calcutta
Madras Shanghai
HUMPHREY MILFORD
PUBLISHER TO THE
UNIVERSITY

PRINTED IN GREAT BRITAIN

A SHORT HISTORY OF
ENGLISH LITERATURE

King Arthur and his Round Table

PREFACE

THE present volume is a stepping-stone to the larger *History of English Literature* written by Professor Cazamian and myself,[1] and originally designed for French University students. A translation of the same into English having met with a favourable reception in the Universities of Great Britain and the United States, it has been thought that a similar History in an abridged form might prove acceptable in British and American Schools. The modern section of this abridgement has, it is true, lost the advantage of Professor Cazamian's authorship—a great loss if one considers the rare qualities of philosophical breadth and psychological acumen he has revealed in his presentation of the most crowded and complicated periods of literature. The regret can only be alleviated by the consideration that these very qualities, so admirably adapted to mature students, would have been less appreciated by younger minds not yet fully prepared for subtle analysis and intellectual construction.

Here it was desirable that the simple narrative manner should prevail. Abstraction had to be avoided and concreteness must be aimed at. This general tendency of the book is made clear by the illustrations scattered about its pages. It is also attested by a certain number of quotations from poets and prose-writers, though much fewer (for want of space) than both publishers and author would have wished. Their fewness will, I hope, be redeemed by the anthologies, books of extracts, and encyclopaedias of literature, that most schoolboys and schoolgirls have at their disposal.

It is a question whether the living generation of writers should be admitted into a school handbook at all. The present age is moving and perilous ground. Only a provisional account has been attempted of the times since 1900, chiefly since the Great War. The last chapter is, therefore, to be considered as a mere sketch,

[1] *A History of English Literature*, revised edition. J. M. Dent & Sons, London, 1933. Macmillan, New York, 1929.

which will have to be rewritten and filled up after the lapse of some decades.

After due consideration no place has been made for the literature of the United States—a literature now far too rich and original to be relegated, as it formerly was, into a mere appendix to a history of English Literature. It is a world by itself and requires a full and special study. It is no longer imitative as in the days of Washington Irving and Bryant. It has a native impulse, a local flavour; one might almost add, in many of its specimens, a language of its own. It is distinct and creative. It ought to stand apart.

Moreover the author, as a citizen of a country where the 'Unities' were for centuries accepted as the law of dramatic composition, begs to be excused if he has thought fit to retain in this History the only one of the famous three that can be preserved in a book of this kind: the unity of place. The British Isles are the scene—sufficiently roomy and varied—of his narrative. Extreme changes of climate and atmosphere would bring in confusion, or at least cause a break in such harmony as is possible in the work. For the same reason he has, not without regret, omitted the literature produced in the British colonies and dominions, though this is now growing from day to day in volume and value.

He is fully conscious of a sort of presumption in writing a book for the schools of English-speaking countries. Neither would he— even if he could—endeavour to conceal the fact of his being a foreigner. But if his foreign 'citizenship' has not been considered to be a disqualification by University students, may not he hope for the same generous toleration from their still younger countrymen? After all, it may be inspiriting to them to be made early aware that their own pride in their writers is confirmed by critics from other lands who have devoted to the same a lifelong study, to know that men of a different speech can share with them the admiration and love of the master spirits who have made English literature a 'thing of beauty' for the whole world.

There only remains for me the pleasant duty of expressing my gratitude to Professor Nichol Smith, Mr. C. R. L. Fletcher, and Mr. Kenneth Sisam, who have read this work in the proofs and helped me to correct many an error. Had I been able to carry out all their suggestions the book would be better than it is. Their revision has been precious to me. The faults that survive it are my own.

E. L.

CONTENTS

DESCRIPTION OF PLATES

ANGLO-SAXON LITERATURE

Twofold source of English Literature. English literature, in the true sense of the term, scarcely begins before the fourteenth century. For the unity of a literature consists, on the one hand, in the persistence of a language which remains, from first to last, fairly intelligible; and on the other hand in the continuity of written works handed down from generation to generation.

These two conditions were not fulfilled in England until the days of Chaucer. Yet the literature born in his lifetime was no newly found spring gushing suddenly from the earth, but already a fair river formed by the junction of two streams flowing in from widely different lands. As in a biography the study of any available records of his forbears tends to throw light on the hero's character, so he who would know the river must follow each of these two streams back to its source.

The first tributary is Anglo-Saxon literature; the second is the literature imported from France by the Normans. Neither alone can claim to be 'English' literature, but each has contributed its waters to the main flood and influenced its course; just as the intermingling of the two vocabularies—Germanic and Franco-Latin—has formed the English of to-day.

Essentially Christian characteristics. The literature called Anglo-Saxon was that of the Teutonic tribes which from the end of the fifth century invaded Britain, a land inhabited by the Brythons, a Celtic race subdued by the Romans and already christianized. At first the invaders from Engle-land were fierce and terrible —wandering heathen tribes. But when, two centuries later, their writings begin to appear, they were partly civilized. The Angles in Northumbria and Mercia, the Saxons and Jutes in the south-east of the island, had undergone mass-conversion and had become settlers, tillers of the soil, enjoying laws which protected the individual from theft and plunder, and forbade him the right of vengeance. No doubt their annals, like those of all other

B

European nations of the time, show persistent war-fury, violence, and crime; but these are but occasional breaks with Christian morality, which is none the less general and triumphant.

Broadly speaking, Anglo-Saxon literature as we know it is from the seventh to the eleventh centuries the work of clerks, who, if they did not create it, preserved it in its entirety. Not here, therefore, shall we find the true and direct expression of paganism, but rather in continental Germany, where the great *Nibelungen Lied*— in spite of its later date—gives, at least in the Hagen epic, a vivid picture of the bloodshed and fury, the relentless vengeance of pagan times; or in Scandinavia and Iceland, where in the *Edda* and prose sagas are preserved the thought and rites of primitive times. The *Edda* gives us the drama of contests between savage men, and warfare between gods even more savage and unbridled. In its mingling of strange mythology and wild realism Scandinavian literature shows us barbarism both in thought and action. Anglo-Saxon poetry, on the contrary, is generally elegiac in form and edifying in spirit; it is, with some remarkable exceptions, one long lamentation breathed forth by the zeal and fervour of new converts to Christianity.

The Latinist Clerks. The conversion of the Angles by Celtic Ireland and of the Saxons by missionaries from Rome was so thorough that from that twofold inspiration there rose a church which was to rank among the first in Christendom. In the Latin literature of the age there are no more renowned names than those of Aldhelm (640–709), successively abbot of Malmesbury and bishop of Sherborne; of the 'Venerable' Bede (673–735), monk of Jarrow, historian and theologian, one of the most learned men of the day; of Alcuin (735?–804), who towards the end of his life was summoned by Charles the Great to help him restore to his Frankish kingdom scholarship and religion. These great churchmen wrote in Latin, but through their works we learn most about their fellow countrymen—not only their history, ecclesiastical and social, but the very style and thought of their literature. And this whether the writer's native dialect was that of the Saxons, as with Aldhelm, or that of the Angles, as with Bede and Alcuin. All three were learned in English songs and wrote some English verses that are lost to us. But it is not difficult to find traces of their nationality in their Latin; for the spirit breathed by the Latin of Aldhelm or Alcuin is that of the Anglo-Saxon poetry of unknown authors which has come down to us. The taste for periphrasis and riddle is as marked in the one as in the other. Aldhelm in his *Praise of Virginity* speaks of 'the golden necklace of the Virtues', 'the white jewels of merit', 'the purple flower of modesty', &c. Alcuin answers thus the supposed questions of his young Frankish pupil:

> What is the body?—The spirit's lodging. What is hair?—The clothing of the head. What are the eyes?—Guides of the body, vessels of light, an index to thought.

And so on for pages together.

The transition from the Latin of these clerics to the Old English poetry of unknown authorship is easy; the difference is not in thought but in language and metre.

Language and Metre. The most general element of poetry perhaps is language. The qualities and defects of the language predetermine the field of a poem, its successes and failures, almost independently of the genius of the poet who uses it. The sound of a word has a quality of expression outside of and beyond its meaning. The most noteworthy characteristics of the Germanic language spoken by the Anglo-Saxons are the strong stress and the predominance of consonants; and on these are based the laws which govern their old alliterative metre. The line is composed of an elastic number of syllables and is divided into two halves, each half containing two stressed syllables. Two or three of these syllables— one or two in the first half line and the first stressed syllable of the second half line—should be alliterated, i.e. should begin with the same consonant or group of consonants (*sc*, *st*, *sp*, &c.), as in the following line:

> *St*éap *st*ánhlitho—*st*íge néarwe.
> (Steep stone-slopes—paths narrow.)

Sometimes the alliteration is formed not by consonants but by vowels; different vowels may be alliterated with one another, the effect being produced by the gentler vowel-sound, and the absence of the harsher consonants.

Another feature of the language is its sentence-formation. Unlike modern English, Old English was a synthetic tongue, expressing difference of tense, number, and person either by modifying the root-vowel or by different case-endings. Its possession of an elaborate system of declension—each number had four cases, nouns were variously declined, adjectives had two sets of inflexions and verbs many conjugations—allowed a wide freedom in the arrangement of words. Much use was made of detached, disconnected words in apposition, with a cumulative, interjectory effect. This freedom is one of the points in the language of his ancestors which most strikes the modern Englishman.

The faculty possessed by Old English of forming compound words is perhaps what has most influenced its poetical diction. The original sense of each element which forms a compound word is usually clearly visible. Thus *geal-ādl* (gall-disease) is jaundice; *līc-sang* (the corpse-song) is a dirge; *līc-tun* (the town or dwelling of corpses) is the cemetery; a scholar is a 'letter-crafty' man— *stæf-cræftig*. The transition from every-day prose diction to the poetical language used for effect is easy. Alfred's prose has *æfter-genga*, the 'after-goer' or 'successor'; *ærend-gewrit*, 'message-writing', 'letter'; *cyne-stōl*, 'royal-stool', 'throne'. These expressions scarcely differ from other compounds found solely in poetry: *eorth-stapa*, 'earth-stepper', 'traveller'; *brēost-nett*, 'breast-net', 'corslet'; *dēath-reced*, 'death-chamber', 'tomb', &c.

This process passes from language to thought. As we have seen, even when writing in Latin, the Anglo-Saxons developed their ideas by accumulated periphrases; their poets took full advantage of the facility which their own language offered them. They used their compounds not of necessity, not because there was no simple equivalent, but for ornament, either to bring out and emphasize some quality in the subject, or, more often, for effect, or again for the sake of the necessary alliteration. The body becomes 'bone-chamber' (*bān-cofa*); the heart, 'treasure-room' (*hord-cofa*); thought, 'breast-hoard' (*breost-hord*); the breast, 'heart-enclosure' (*fer(h)th-loca*). A soldier is a 'corslet-warrior' (*byrn-wiga*), a 'spear-carrier' (*gār-berend*), or 'sword-hero' (*sweord-freca*); armour is the 'warrior's garb' or 'battle-shirt' (*here-sierce*); man is the 'earth-dweller' (*eorth-būend*).

Many of the compounds bear witness to the enthusiasm of the Anglo-Saxons for war: battle is 'spear play' or 'edge-play' (*aesc-, ecg-plega*), 'tumult of spears' (*gār-gewinn*), or 'crash of standards' (*cumbol-gebræc*); the sword is 'battle-gleam' (*beadu-lēoma*); blood is 'war-sweat' (*heathu-swāt*), or 'carnage-flow'. The elements and natural phenomena supply many metaphors. The sea is the 'pathway of sails', the 'whale-way', or 'swan-path'. The flood is 'waves'-journey'. Mist is 'air-helm' (*lyft-helm*); darkness is 'night-helm' (*niht-helm*). Often the identity of the objects intended by these metaphors must be guessed at: 'head-jewels' means the eyes; 'flesh-coat' (*flæsc hama*) is the body; by 'warrior-dress' (*eorl-gewǣde, guth-gewǣde*) is meant armour. This play on words gave rise to the poetical sport of trying to discover the subject by one of its attributes, a process of wit-sharpening known as the 'kenning', which led naturally to the riddle; and collections of riddles are characteristic productions of Old English poetry.

So uniform is this poetry in accent, style, and metre, that it becomes almost monotonous. There is no light or shade in the song; joy moves as heavily as sadness; irony falls with the weight of a sledge-hammer. The traditional form and unique metre which give grandeur to each poem, at the same time fetter and confine individuality; and in the three centuries of Anglo-Saxon literature there is but little visible movement towards that differentiation of species which is the sign of vitality and progress. The epic unity of form and tone at first impresses, then wearies by its continuous tension; just as the periphrasis inherent in the poetry, often though it enriches, at times obscures and even overwhelms it. Nevertheless it is a strong and impressive manner; its subjects must now be examined.

Pre-Christian and non-Christian Poetry. Although Christian in its spirit and handed down to us by Christian editors, Anglo-Saxon poetry includes lays of pre-Christian times and fragments which are entirely heathen. The clerks who wrote down the lays were the near descendants of warriors and vikings, and beneath their Christianity heathen traditions survived. A battle-cry, a warrior's prowess, quickened the old fighting-spirit within them, and without effort they described the ways of thinking or fighting of a past so near to them. Names, words, were the same. The identical language, the unchanged metre, the inter-play of words and vision inevitably linked by alliteration, flung them back to the days of daring, of venture over land and sea. Deeper even than their new-found faith was the instinct to preserve, though more or less retouched by Christianity, the lay and saga sung and spoken by scōp and gleeman. So have come down to us two short poems dealing with the life of the *scōp*, or tribal poet of continental, heathen Engle-land. The earlier of these is *Widsith*, the Far-Wanderer, who enumerates the noble lords who lavished gifts on him. The later is *The Complaint of Deor* who, less happy than *Widsith*, suffers because he is estranged from his lord, but comforts himself with the thought of fate's habitual unkindness.

But the poem which depicts most vividly the tribal life and rites of ancient days is *Beowulf*, the oldest epic in Germanic literature. The historical element of the story carries us back to the first half of the sixth century. It has nothing to do with our island; there is nothing Anglo-Saxon in its setting or people. The scene is laid in the Danish island of Seeland and in South Sweden, land of the Geats or Götar; the historical Beowulf was himself a Geat. The lays of which the story is composed are probably of Scandinavian origin; in many ways it resembles the Icelandic saga of *Grettir*; on the other hand, it is analogous in some points to the *Odyssey* and to the legend of the labours of Hercules. The Anglo-Saxon poet (probably of the eighth century) who wove the various strands of *Beowulf* into a whole must have been scholar as well as poet, with an imagination which revived and beautified for him the days of long ago. The Christian element, though held in check, yet reveals itself in a certain spirit of nobility and purity. Wild scenes and early times are described with relish, but thought and feeling are chastened and ennobled. The hero is a man of war, strong-armed and daring, developing by degrees into the ideal king who dies to save his people.

Beowulf crosses the sea with a few valiant Geats to help Hroth-

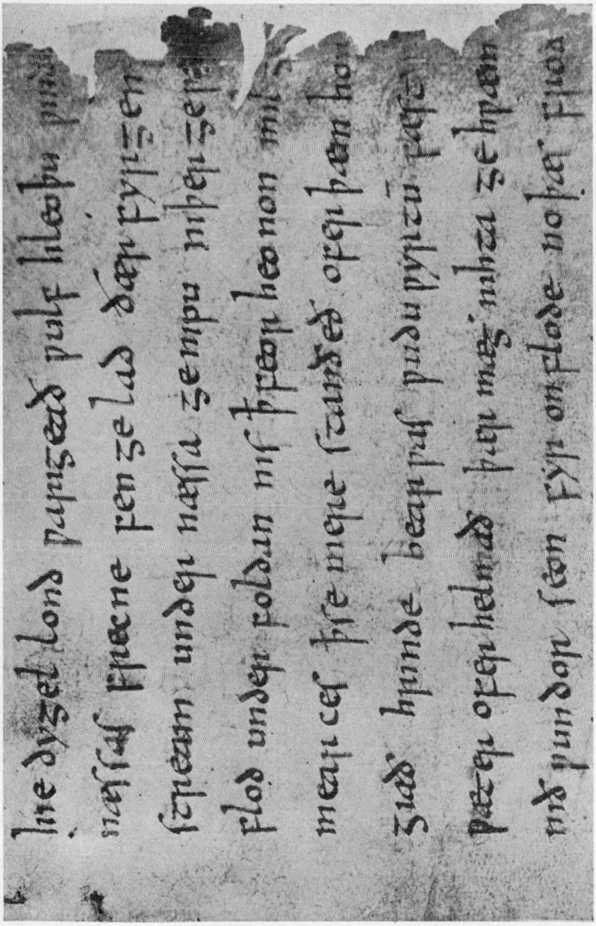

ıne dygel lond warigeað wulf hleoþu wind
næssas frecne fengelad ðær fyrgen
stream under næssa genipu niþer gew
flod under foldan nis þæt feor heonon mil
mearces þæt se mere standeð ofer þæm ho
giað hrinde bearwas wudu wyrtum fæst
wæter oferhelmað þær mæg nihta gehwæm
nið wundor seon fyr on flode no þæs frod

The manuscript of *Beowulf*, ll. 1357 ff. See p. xi

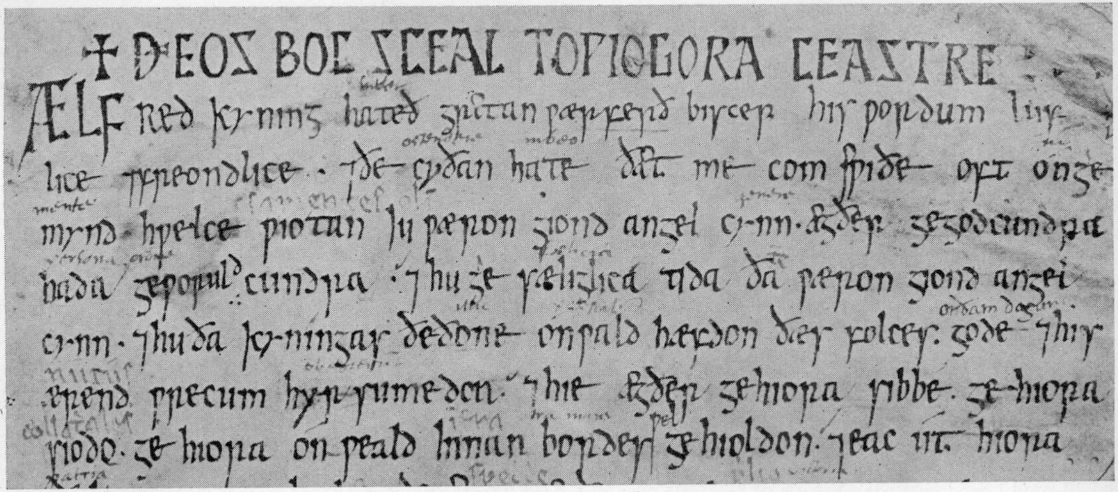

PLATE III

The beginning of King Alfred's preface to his translation of Gregory the Great's *Cura Pastoralis* ||

See p. xi

gar, king of the Danes, whose hall of Heorot is desolated nightly by the monster Grendel, one of the *eotens* or man-eating giants descended from Cain. Each night Grendel comes forth from his den to seize and devour one of Hrothgar's thanes. Beowulf lies in wait in Hrothgar's hall, and in a terrible wrestle tears away an arm from the monster, who escapes to his lair to die. But Grendel's mother comes to avenge her son and kills Æschere, one of Hrothgar's favourite retainers. Beowulf pursues the water-monster-woman to her cave, deep in the dark waters of a dreadful mere; then, wrestling with the monster, who has seized him in her grip, he slays her with a magic sword. Fifty years later, when king of the Geats, he goes forth to fight a dragon which, angry at the robbing of its hoard, ravages his kingdom. He vanquishes his enemy but receives his own death-wound from the dragon's poisonous fang, and dies, happy in the thought that his last fight has saved his people and won for them the golden treasure.

Beowulf consists, as we see, of three successive narratives, and lacks true unity. Moreover the stories are too much alike, just as all three monsters are drawn with the same vagueness. It is a far cry from this to the ingenuity and variety of the labours of Hercules. But a certain grandeur is produced by the very mystery which enshrouds these beings and their loathsome dens. Perhaps the most famous passage in the poem is that describing the misty wind-swept marshland leading to Grendel's lair:

They dwell in a secret place of wolf-haunted slopes, wind-swept headlands, and perilous fen-paths, where a waterfall leaps down underground beneath the shadowy sea-cliffs. Not many miles hence lies that mere overhung with heavy trees: the wood clinging by its roots overshadows the water. There any night may be seen the dread wonder of fire on the water. None of the sons of men is so wise that he knows its depth. Should the heath-stepper, the horned stag, seek that wood, pressed by the hounds after a long run, rather will he give up his life on the bank than plunge in to save his head. No pleasant place is that!

A sombre imagination, inspired by the wild northern scenery, must have gone to paint so dark a picture. But the poem is mournful not in description only but in its general spirit.

The nothingness of life, courage, and renown is emphasized throughout the poem, which is lacking in *joie de vivre* no less than in sunshine. Into a narrative of pagan times, set in a northern frame, the writer has introduced the Christian idea of the vanity of all earthly things.

Elegiac Poems. The same melancholy pervades several short poems distinguished from *Beowulf* by their rupture from the Continent and paganism. They can hardly be called Christian, except here and there, chiefly in their conclusion. They are mostly plaints not unlike the Ossianic poems which in the eighteenth century were so much favoured in Europe, then in love with vague melancholy.

Such, for instance, are *The Ruined Burg*, which mourns the vanished glory of a ruined city, victim of Fate (*wyrd*), very probably the Roman-built city of Bath; and *The Wife's Complaint*, in which the young wife mourns her separation, through false tongues, from her beloved; or the elegy of *The Wanderer*, where a young man sighs for his dead liege-lord. On the ship carrying him afar the Wanderer dreams that he is with his lord again, but wakes to cold and loneliness, to a world of doom and winter-woe and labouring seas.

The most original of these poems is *The Seafarer*, in which are found both the defects and merits of these elegies. The chief defect is obscurity, which is here very marked and has led to more than one interpretation of the poem. Yet, whether the poem be monologue or dialogue, nothing can destroy the picture of those dark northern seas, where the torment of cold is added to the tumult of waves and winds. But all misery is forgotten when the spring returns, the cuckoo's call is heard, and once again the seafarer wanders 'across the sea-flood, over the whale's land'. All through the poem is heard the sound of the sea, the mistress of an island-race. Some ten centuries later Byron, Swinburne, and Kipling were to continue the strain of which the first note was sounded by the unknown author of *The Seafarer*.

War Poems. In the study of Anglo-Saxon poetry chronology is of less importance than subject, and it is in a war-song of the middle of the tenth century that the fierce note of primitive times is heard the loudest; it is found in a fragment of alliterative verse which some monk has inserted into a prose *Chronicle*. The poem chants the praises of Athelstan, king of Wessex and Mercia, who in 937 defeated at Brunanburh the Scots under Constantine and the Danes under Anlaf. There is nothing here of Christian gentleness; the lines have the old heathen ring of exultation over a fallen foe, of rejoicing over the broken invaders. There is more of fierce heathenism in this short poem than in the whole of *Beowulf*. The poet delights to show us the sun rising on the blood-sodden field, from which the old king Constantine fled to his ship, leaving his young son among the broken Scots folk, over whose corpses fought the 'swart raven' and white-tailed eagle, and that 'grey beast, the wolf of the weald'.

About sixty years later another unknown writer described the defeat at Maldon, where Byrhtnoth, chief of the East Saxons, sought to repulse a band of Northmen whose ships had reached the estuary of the Essex river Panta. Although but a fragment remains to us, it is in its way an epic, contemporary with the events it describes, and it has more than one striking resemblance to the *Iliad*. Christians are fighting against heathen invaders, but the spirit of the poem is war-like, heroic, showing the sacrifice of chief for follower and the faithfulness of man to chief. It is the first breath of chivalry, earlier than the French *Chanson de Roland*, which also celebrates heroic defeat and death. Just as Roland makes it a point of honour not to cry for help to Charlemagne, so Byrhtnoth, against his own interests, allows the Danish pirates to cross the river so that the fight may be on equal terms. He meets death on the field and dies rejoicing that he has been allowed to deal mighty blows, commending his soul to the leader of warriors, the merciful Creator. While cowards flee, his thanes die defending their leader. One of them, the old chief Byrhtwold, exclaims as he brandishes his ashwood spear:

Our thoughts must be firmer, our hearts more bold, our courage greater as our force grows less. Here lies our good chief struck down in the dust. May he who thinks now of leaving this battle have remorse for ever.

This heroic fragment differs from *Roland* in its bare severity, as

of a scene witnessed; there is nothing of the ornament and legend
of *Roland*, nothing superhuman or extraordinary in the *Battle of
Maldon*, it is simply an account of men outnumbered fighting to
the last. They play the desperate part to the end, and disaster is
illumined by valour, but not transfigured; for the vanquished
there shines never a gleam of hope. It is perhaps the most heroic
fragment of Anglo-Saxon poetry, and it is strange to find this
great war song at a time when the old verse was declining, weighed
down by the burden of its own traditions.

Riddles. When we remember the enigmatical turn of Anglo-
Saxon rhetoric it is not surprising to find a collection of Riddles
among the national poetry; and these are none the less original
because they are founded on earlier Latin collections. For the
northern poet forgets that his task is merely to describe an object
in roundabout terms so that the quick-witted may name it, and
he throws himself with such warmth into his subject that, in place
of the dry precision of the Latin, we have a lyric. The subjects
of the lyrics—birds, animals, the elements, things in daily use—
are endowed with life and speak to us, so that we have a kind
of encyclopaedia of Anglo-Saxon life. There is, for instance, the
riddle of the limewood shield which describes its sufferings on the
battle-field; or that of the ox-horn used both as trumpet and drink-
ing-cup. The former of these, being short, may be quoted here:

> I am a recluse, with iron wounded,
> With faulchion scar'd, sated with works of war,
> Of edges weary; oft I battle see,
> Perilous fight; for comfort hope not,
> Or that safety to me shall come from martial strife,
> Ere I with generations shall all have perished;
> But they me shall strike with sword:
> The hard of edge, intensely sharp, hand-work of smiths,
> Shall bite among people; I must await
> The hostile meeting: never the healing tribe,
> In the battle-place, might I find,
> Who with plants my wounds would heal,
> But to me the edges' sores become increas'd,
> Through deadly stroke, by day and night.
>
> (Thorpe's Translation of Riddle VI.)

Perhaps the finest of all is that of the hurricane which sings of its deeds and its impersonations, either as a prisoner moaning beneath the earth or as a bringer of terror to earth and sea and sky. Not until Shelley's *Ode to the West Wind* or *The Cloud* do we meet again so deep a feeling for nature wedded to so high a lyrical gift.

Christian Poetry. Except for a few traces here and there Christianity is absent from the preceding poems. It is otherwise with the greater mass of Anglo-Saxon poetry, which is essentially religious. One of its principal monuments is a paraphrase of several books of the Bible—Genesis, Exodus, Judith; or, with more freedom, of Latin poems based on the Bible, like *The Fall of the Angels* of Avitus. A later fragment of Genesis, translated from Old Saxon, together with the occurrence in England of a *Heliand* manuscript with English forms, affords proof of the literary relations still maintained with the Continental Germanic tribes.

The origin of the earliest of these religious poems has been described by Bede in a passage often quoted. A poor herd of the monastery at Whitby in Northumbria one summer night was hailed in his stable by One who bade him sing of the creation. Whereupon Cædmon, although unlearned and with no gift of song, sang of the beginning of created things and of the glory of the Creator; and afterwards wrote down in verse all that he had sung and what others, more gifted than himself, had written. Here is his song, as quoted by Bede:

> Now must we praise the Guardian of Heaven's Kingdom,
> The Creator's might, and his mind's thought;
> Glorious Father of men! as of every wonder He,
> Lord eternal, formed the beginning.
> He first framed for the children of earth
> The heaven as a roof; holy Creator!
> Then mid-earth the Guardian of mankind,
> The eternal Lord, afterwards produced;
> The earth for men, Lord Almighty!

(Thorpe's translation.)

The term Cædmonian has been given to a whole group of Biblical poems, although the paraphrases preserved are later than Cædmon and written by other hands. All, however, share certain characteristics: a fire and earnestness, and a simplicity which sees the Hebrews as the English, Judea as England, and blue southern waters as the grey North Sea. Yet if they read the text incorrectly they endue it with life; the poet is himself one of the Biblical heroes; he is himself adventuring and fighting.

Unfortunately these poems all possess the same defect: lack of conciseness; as paraphrases they cannot render the austere splendour of the original; where the Bible says: 'And God said, Let there be light: and there was light', the Anglo-Saxon has: 'The Creator of angels, the Lord of Life, bade Light appear on the limitless ocean. The order of the most High was accomplished with haste, the holy Light spread over the immensity, as the Creator had required.' Here the action is delayed by prosaic explanation and piling up of synonyms. The Hebrew God creates with one supreme command; the Anglo-Saxon God fumbles awkwardly before He lights up the world. So in *Exodus*, the silent dramatic gesture of Moses over the Red Sea is delayed in the paraphrase while he explains to the Israelites the nature of the miracle. There is the same defect in *Judith*, where the Bible heroine, a woman of action, steely and resolute, becomes a vague, half-frenzied prophetess. It is hard to say whether this defect is due to Anglo-Saxon rhetoric or to the poet's troubled vision.

Cynewulf. The works attributed to Cynewulf leave a similar, if not stronger, impression. A century ago the poet's very name was unknown; since then certain critics have attributed to him nearly all Anglo-Saxon Christian poetry. It is now agreed that he wrote at least Part II of the *Crist*, the lives of the saints *Juliana* and *Elene* (Helena), and *The Fates of the Apostles*, all poems bearing his signature in runic characters. He has by some been identified with a bishop of Lindisfarne who lived in the middle of the eighth century. His lines are flowing and melodious, his style free and easy; but when he is neither translating nor supported by the history he relates, as in his *Elene*, he often becomes diffuse and obscure. The *Crist*, the one original work in which he had some share, seemed at first but dark, tangled confusion. Even after the efforts made by its admirers to disentangle the web, it needs indulgent eyes to discern in it three clear strands: the Nativity of Christ, His Ascension, and the Last Judgement.

The two poems of *Guthlac* are interesting as being the only account in verse of a native saint. Based on the version in Latin prose written by the monk Felix of Crowland, the poems illustrate the way in which Anglo-Saxon verse transforms, and too often deforms, the matter it uses. In the prose the simple faith of early days is full of charm; Saint Guthlac with his love of birds and beasts is the precursor of St. Francis of Assisi. But the pleasant homely details which delight us in the prose are lost in the more ambitious, vague effusions of the poems.

Anglo-Saxon poetry was happier in other narratives, such as the *Dream of the Rood*, where the tree of which the Cross was made relates its story from the time when it was hewn down on the edge of the forest until it received the God-man—'the young Hero strong and brave'.

In its frequent competition with Latin, English verse is seen at its best in the *Phœnix*, founded on the *Carmen de Phœnice* of Lactantius. This time the paraphrase gives warmth and richness to a dry original. The Phoenix which burns itself, to rise from its own ashes, symbolizes Christ and the Christian soul. Very joyous is the Holy Land where the Phoenix dwells; nowhere else, perhaps, in Anglo-Saxon poetry, occurs a description of so fair a scene—sunlit, radiant, flower-strewn.

Anglo-Saxon Prose. Later to appear and slower to develop than the poetry, Anglo-Saxon prose seems unconnected with any past tradition. It first becomes known to us in collections of laws—such as the Laws of Ine, king of the West Saxons, towards the end of the seventh century—and the first pages of the *Chronicle* which was kept up in various monasteries, such as Winchester, Canterbury, Abingdon, Worcester, and Peterborough. The groundwork of the earlier entries may have been fragments of old English lays; they have the force and passion of poetry. When the chronicler attempts to describe an event with precision his style is of the clumsiest; it is but the transcription of a spoken language the syntax of which was still in its infancy. Literary prose does not begin until the ninth century, when Alfred, king of Wessex—'England's darling'—attempted to bring back to his kingdom her lost learning. For this he studied Latin and translated, or had translated for him, those works which he deemed would be most useful to his people. He forms his prose on Latin, making his English follow Latin constructions. Either directly to him or to his encouragement and request, we owe translations of the *Cura Pastoralis* of Pope Gregory the Great, the *History of the World* of Orosius, the *De Consolatione Philosophiae* of Boethius, and Bede's *Ecclesiastical History of the English*. Thus he sought to enrich his countrymen with all that it was given to himself to know. This is how he explains his reason for undertaking the arduous task of editing a translation of Boethius:

I have desired material for the exercise of my faculties that my talents and my power might not be forgotten and hidden away, for every good gift and every power soon groweth old and is no more heard of, if wisdom be not in them. . . . To be brief, I may say that it has ever been my desire to live honourably while I was alive, and after my death to leave to them that should come after me my memory in good works.

If the translations that we owe to him are halting, clumsy, and literal, we must remember that he stood alone and had all to do.

Towards the middle of the tenth century a noticeable advance was made in English culture by the re-establishment of the Benedictine monastery at Abingdon. The Benedictine reform of the monasteries brought England into close contact with Continental learning and did much of the cultural work commonly attributed to the Conquest.

A more refined prose began with Ælfric, one of the pupils of the Benedictine school at Winchester. Scholarly, cultured, and, for his time, a good Latinist, he introduced into his *Catholic Homilies* (990–2), compiled from the Early Fathers, a lighter, clearer, more musical prose. It is poetic in its cadence, and often alliterative without being actual verse. It tends to prove that English prose was attaining high quality when its progress was suspended for several ages by the Norman Conquest. About the same time Wulfstan, archbishop of York (1002–23), fired by the horrors of the Danish raids, inveighed in sermons of eloquence and passion against the immorality and irreligion of the English, proclaiming the advent of the Anti-Christ and the coming Doom.

On the whole, Anglo-Saxon prose is much nearer than the poetry to modern English. The poetry was archaic, retaining obsolete words and expressions, and the alliterative periphrases of the past; the prose was either the speech in daily use or modelled on the Latin which was the universal language of educated Europe, and thus put all scholars on an equal plane. When the revolution came, poetry was to suffer most, being almost destroyed; prose, on the contrary, in spite of changes, remained recognizable and suffered no such break with the past.

FROM THE NORMAN CONQUEST TO CHAUCER

General Characteristics of Old French Literature. With the Norman Conquest in 1066 the literary ideal changes. The conquerors were, it is true, of the same race as the pagan Danes who had so long ravaged Britain, but once they were masters of the French province called Normandy after them, they quickly became gallicized, forgetting paganism, their motherland, its language, and its traditions. At the time of the Conquest they were therefore already French in language and in civilization, and they carried with them many an adventurer from the neighbouring provinces of France. With their laws and administration they imported into England a French literary ideal. Before their supremacy the native tongue drew back, humbled, spoken only by the down-trodden people. Anglo-Saxon literature seemed to disappear altogether; it was silent for a century in which many links with the past were lost. Except Latin the only literature known to scholars will henceforward be that of France. The latter was, at the Battle of Hastings, still in its infancy, but so rapid was its growth that in the twelfth and thirteenth centuries it was the first of European literatures, extending its glory and influence far beyond the confines of France. One of its chief developments occurred in Great Britain, and slowly, drop by drop, it was to permeate the literature of the conquered so thoroughly that when English composition began again it was founded both in matter and form on French works. No knowledge of Anglo-Saxon poetry is needed in order to read Chaucer; but it is impossible to understand the origin of his work without knowing something of the French poetry which preceded it. It is necessary therefore to examine the salient characteristics of the poetry which captured by its novelty and held by its beauty so many an English imitator, known and unknown.

Its most universal trait, and the most striking, is clarity. To pass from *Beowulf*, or even from the *Battle of Maldon*, to the

Chanson de Roland is like coming from gloom into light. This sense of light is everywhere: in subject, in manner, in the spirit animating both and the mind which guides them, and, above all, in the difference in language.

To the predominance of consonants which gives the effect of vigour, as in *strength*, is opposed the use of vowels or diphthongs productive of clarity and melody, as in *oiseau*. In French, vowels play the more important part; their repetition in rhyme or assonance replaces the pleasure of alliteration. The best poems of the *trouvères* are bathed in light by the very word-sounds:

> E Durandal, cum ies clere et blanche!
> Cuntre soleil si reluis et reflambes!
> (O, Durandal [Roland's sword] how clear and white thou art!
> So much dost thou shine and blaze in the sun.)

All, of course, is not due to language only; the joy of the writer in seizing a luminous detail is as evident as is the power of the language to express it. The poets of England evoked sinister landscapes and mournful scenes with such truth and vigour that the corresponding descriptions of the *trouvères* may seem insignificant; but the latter, born under a bluer sky, delighted in the clear bright details of spring, e.g. May with her flower-decked meadows and singing-birds. Such scenes will henceforth appear profusely in English verse, instead of the arctic seas, and battle-fields strewn with bodies torn by carrion birds, of Anglo-Saxon poetry.

French, moreover, had no 'poetic style'; it was bare, unencumbered with family jewels. It used neither periphrasis nor the violence of apostrophe and exclamation, neither brusque metaphor nor obscure ellipse. Instead of its former rhetoric, all but lost in the Conquest, English, when it reappeared, adopted at first the same French style, simple, rather thin, careful only of accuracy of expression. For a long time English was to have no distinctive poetic style. But as a compensation England learned from France to adapt manner to matter. Anglo-Saxon had but one metre—the alliterative, and this served for all subjects, from a riddle on a rake to a poem on the Creation. Compare with this monotony the variety of the French lines, varying from one to twelve syllables, and the limitless combinations of assonance and rhyme—from the long *laisse* of the *chansons de geste* to the short, sparkling line of the *chansonnettes*. Within these extremes lay the whole compass of expression, verses capable in their varying rhythm of producing every step and measure and of translating into speech each fine shade of meaning, from heroism to butterfly frivolity. In Old French will be found, either in bud or blossom, nearly every verse-form, nearly every system of rhyme, nearly every stanza afterwards used in English poetry. This too was henceforth to possess a form which corresponded to its content.

The change which took place was not outward only; the very nature of the versification was to be modified; the accents were to fall, as they did in French verse, before the caesura and on the rhyme; the culminating points were to be the hemistich and the end of the verse. The rhythm was to rise towards the rhyme instead of falling, as before, from the initial alliteration. The pleasure of the echo was to give to vowel-sounds an importance equal at least to that of consonant-sounds. French poetry captivated the Anglo-Saxons to the extent of changing their ear and making necessary the return at fixed intervals of accents and the echo of similar endings; syllabication, measure, and rhyme.

Anglo-Norman Literature. We must now glance at the characteristics of the literature which the Normans produced in Great Britain and which is usually called Anglo-Norman. It is a province of French literature marked by certain traits of dialect and of mind, and it reached its zenith in the reign of Henry II (1154–89).

Anglo-Norman literature added nothing to French epic poetry, which, moreover, almost came to an end in the twelfth century. The great epic legends, of which the *Chanson de Roland* was the most famous, were replaced by chronicles in rhyme. Such were Gaimar's *Histoire des Angles*; Wace's *Roman de Brut* and his *Roman de Rou* (i.e. Rollo); Benoît de Saint-Maure's *Chronique des Ducs de Normandie*, his *Roman de Troie*, and his *Roman d'Énée*; Eustace or Thomas de Kent's *Alexandre*, and Garnier de Pont Saint-Maxence's *Vie de Thomas Becket*.

On the whole these chronicles are prosaic, insensitive, showing neither enthusiasm nor sense of beauty. Intellectual curiosity or utilitarianism dominated the writers. The decasyllabic line and the alexandrine of the heroic epic gave place to the line of eight syllables, which had little rhythm and used rhyme chiefly as an aid to memory.

The Conquest, for instance, did not inspire the Norman *trouvères* with such an epic as *Roland*, but led them to write chronicles. To read of the Battle of Hastings in the *Roman de Rou* causes the same surprise whether one comes to it from the death of Byrhtnoth at Maldon or that of Roland at Roncevaux. Both the epic heroism of the first and the legendary glory of the second are missing. Wace's long narrative is that of a copious and well-informed historian and it is nothing more. He tells us from hour to hour all that took place from the eve of the encounter onwards, the speeches of the combatants in the very language they used; the tactics of the commanders, details of their armour, the slightest incidents of the fight. Of liveliness there is plenty, of poetry none. The narrator may be stirred by the clash of swords, but he does not lose his head; he drives his octosyllabic couplets at an even trot, holding the reins with steady hand.

Many of these chronicles are actual histories, and even when fabulous or legendary, they purport to be historical. Many were written to satisfy the curiosity of the Normans in the traditions of foreign nations past or present. Others tended to gather into a whole Britain's scattered legends, and thus facilitate the fusion of the conflicting races on her soil. Briton, Angle, Norman could unite in praise of the land they lived in, where all that was and had been seemed equally dear to each. Never yet had the island received such praise as in the *Brut*, where the descriptive verses, tinged by the utilitarian mind of the author, pass in orderly review the geography, orography, hydrography, agriculture, and mineral wealth of the country, followed by a history of its population; the whole classified by a mind which never allows admiration to interfere with utilitarianism. Nothing perhaps is more striking than the smiling, fertile, almost 'comfortable' aspect of a scenery which Anglo-Saxon poetry had enfolded in mists and terror. The encircling sea, from 'the pathway of the storm' had become a smooth highway leading to traffic with many distant lands.

Celtic Influence. This practical and prosaic literature includes also a domain in which romance is apparent; this, it is true, is in the matter and not in the manner, which retains its even calm. The touch of the marvellous chiefly occurs when the chronicler wishes to re-tell some Celtic legend. The Normans must have heard continually from their Breton neighbours of their glorious past and hope of revenge on the hated Saxons; of the dreams of love and adventure which charmed away the present. But if some of these legends penetrated directly from Armorica into French Continental poetry, many others came to the Anglo-Normans straight from the Britons in Wales.

Celtic influence—always rather indefinable—had already touched the Anglo-Saxons. The Angles had been converted to Christianity by missionaries from Ireland. Bede himself, though an out-and-out Romanist, came from a monastery originally inspired by the Celtic spirit. Even in the half-heathen poetry of the Anglo-Saxons, kinship with the strange Celtic mysticism was often very striking, although the incurious, exclusive nature of the Saxon limited his borrowings.

United by a common misfortune, Celt and Saxon were brought together by the tyranny of the Normans. The Normans on their side showed a singular interest in the traditions of Britain's first inhabitants. Under such conditions was produced, before the middle of the twelfth century, the Latin *Historia Regum Britanniae* of Geoffrey of Monmouth. Of Welsh origin, and afterwards bishop of St. Asaph, Geoffrey claims to be a true chronicler and pretends to have translated an ancient book in the British language which no one has ever seen. It is impossible to say how much of his book is imagination and how much is based on tradition. He makes Brutus the great-grandson of Aeneas, and brings him to Britain to be the ancestor of the Britons and the founder of Troynovant (New Troy), afterwards London. But the most curious parts of his book are those which treat of Arthur, the heroic defender of the Britons, and of Merlin and his prophecies. Arthur appears as victor over the Anglo-Saxons, the Picts and the Scots. He conquers Ireland, Iceland, Scandinavia and Gaul. He enters into conflict with the emperor of Rome, over whom he triumphs, making the Romans his slaves; and so lives on, ever victorious, until the end of the seventh century.

Clerics might protest, but Geoffrey's fables gained ground and were assimilated first by the Normans, then by the Anglo-Saxons. Both races waxed enthusiastic over an alien hero whom they adopted as a common glorious ancestor—a singular illusion which yet helped to wipe out race-hatred and create English patriotism.

A development of the Arthurian legend was manifested on the Continent in the poems of Chrestien de Troyes; in England the flame was kept alive by Anglo-Norman writers. The *trouvère* Geffrai Gaimar turned it into verse; Marie de France, at the court of Henry II, spread it abroad by her *lais*. Walter Map, who was half Norman and half Welsh, is credited with having welded together the Arthurian legend and that of the Holy Grail. It was he who gave the cycle its religious tone, when he shows Arthur's queen Guinevere repenting of her sin, and her lover Lancelot unworthy to continue his search for the Holy Grail, a quest reserved for his son Galahad. To Walter Map are commonly ascribed *Le Grand Saint-Graal*, *Lancelot du Lac*, and the *Roman de la mort d'Arthur*. The powerful imaginative leaven of this story must not be forgotten; it was the most beautiful and varied of those which were in the minds of the English when they began again to write.

English Literature from 1066 to 1350. Slight as is the aesthetic value of Anglo-Norman literature it is great in comparison with the literature of the same time written in English, a tongue now greatly handicapped by the disdain in which it was held, and by the loss of tradition and lack of culture. Those who used it were often illiterate men, writing for an unlearned people. In fact, the feeling that Anglo-Norman was a French that was becoming increasingly corrupt and that English was not a literary language, led the more intelligent to write in Latin. Latin was frequently employed for learned works throughout Europe, but nowhere was its use so general as in England, and that for works grave and gay, scholarly and popular; and much of this Latin literature of England leaves far behind it the works written either in the English of the conquered or in the French of the conquerors. Chief of the serious works of this Latin literature are: the *History of William I* by William of Jumièges, the *Ecclesiastical History* of Ordericus Vitalis; the *History of the English Kings* of William of Malmesbury, and the *Annals* of Henry of Huntingdon.

The *Historia Regum Britanniae*, already referred to, of Geoffrey of Monmouth is the most famous work in the romantic and mystifying vein. The letters and stories of the Welshman, Gerald de Barri, or Giraldus Cambrensis, the jests and satirical 'Goliardic' verse of Walter Map, the lively *Speculum Stultorum* or adventures of Brunellus the Ass, of Nigel Wireker, are the most noticeable Latin specimens in lighter, and therefore more imaginative and more truly literary, kinds of composition.

Beneath the twofold oppression of Anglo-Norman and Latin writing, English lay prone for three centuries after the battle of Hastings. The few works which have come down to us may be of great interest to the philologist, enabling him to follow step by step the changes in the language, but as literature they are mostly devoid of interest; pathetic, perhaps, by the very clumsiness of their efforts, resulting only in rude translations, lines without music, halting lamely between alliteration and rhyme; at times struggling to obey the rules of syllabic verse and at other times forgetting them. An exception ought to be made for a few short lyrics religious and profane.

If reconstruction was slow, the destruction of Anglo-Saxon rhetoric (except for a subterranean current that was to come to the surface in the fourteenth century) was speedy, almost instantaneous, the two chief causes being: (1) the repeated endeavours made by English writers to translate—almost literally—works from the French; (2) the deep and far-reaching modifications produced in English by lack of culture and by contamination with the language of the conquerors. The Anglo-Saxon vocabulary was being transformed by the disappearance of its old poetic terms, and by the infiltration, drop by drop, of new words imported by the Normans: terms of warfare, of hunting and falconry; terms of courtesy, science, law; abstract and technical words, and those relating to luxury and art. Thus was formed modern English, in which words of French origin, or derived through

French from the original Latin and Greek, are far more numerous than Germanic words, although in current speech, and taking into account the frequency of their use, these last are in the proportion of ten to one.

At the same time Anglo-Saxon words that were destined to survive became modified in form and pronunciation. They were shortened; for, with their integrity ill-defended by ignorant people, and assailed by strangers, either Scandinavian or Norman-French, who deformed them in their efforts at pronunciation, many of them finally retained only their essential part—the accented syllable. Terminations first weakened, then disappeared; Anglo-Saxon became gradually modified into modern English, with its simple grammar. Of the old noun declensions nothing was to remain but the genitive case and the plural form. There were to be no more grammatical genders, but a logical distribution of words into three classes: masculine, feminine, and neuter; article and adjective became indeclinable.

Meanwhile there came into being a regular syntax, in which inversion and ellipse were the exception and not the rule. This process of change was not consummated until the sixteenth century, and in the interval, while loss of inflexion was taking place, the terminal vowels at last became reduced to a single *e*, still sounded at the time with which this chapter deals, but soon to have but an orthographic existence. To this long period of transition philologists give the name of Middle English.

The different stages of the conflict on British soil between the two languages may thus be summarized. At first each speech was separate: the victors spoke French, the vanquished Anglo-Saxon, which lost its twofold dignity of official and literary tongue. French became the language of court, schools, law courts, and, jointly with Latin, of the church and of science. The Normans did not begin to take much interest in the English language until the beginning of the thirteenth century, when the loss of Normandy by John Lackland confined them to the island. Cut off from the Continent, they began to feel insular patriotism. The simplification of English, already referred to, brought about a compromise which resulted in a kind of understanding between the two peoples.

Words that the Normans did not understand or found difficulty in pronouncing were sometimes dropped and replaced by French terms. Or else, to be better caught by mixed audiences, the meaning was often expressed by a couple of synonyms, one Saxon, the other Norman-French, e.g. *meek and humble, odd and strange, grief and sorrow, meet and proper, nook and corner, &c.* The thirteenth century is full of these changes, going on slowly and quietly, and they come to a head in the fourteenth century. By that time the Normans had almost given up French, English in its development was no longer provincial and uncouth, and from thenceforward English triumphed. After 1350 it replaced French in the schools; in 1362 it was used to plead suits in the law courts; and in 1399 Henry IV addressed Parliament in English for the first time. We must now glance at the works written in English before its triumph was assured.

Religious Works. For a century after the Conquest silence remained unbroken. The works in the vernacular which began to appear towards the end of the twelfth century were mostly of a religious nature. To a disinherited people who could no longer read it was before all things necessary to know the words of salvation. Therefore until towards the middle of the fourteenth century the great mass of the works which can be called English literature consisted of homilies, sermons in prose and verse, translations and paraphrases of the Bible, especially the Psalms, rules for the monastic life, and prayers. At first this religious matter formed the whole of the literature, and it predominated until the end of the period. Such works, obviously, contained nothing local but the language. For the most part they were translations, more or less literal, of French or Latin works. If, as generation followed generation, the religious views expressed showed change or modification, it was the result of European, not insular thought, which reflected in turn the asceticism of the cloister, the growing tenderness which arose from the cult of the Virgin, and mystical exaltation. That these writings were in English is due to the fact that they were destined for the poor, the oppressed, the ignorant. The language had therefore to be very simple, with many explanations and matter-of-fact details. Often

the choice of a subject and the manner of relating it were determined by pity for the wretchedness of the faithful. Sometimes the
author excuses himself for employing so base a language as English,
explaining that he is writing for those who know no French and
who have no edifying books. He admits that his style is bad
and his rhymes are poor, but he is justified by his aim.

The earliest of these religious works, the *Poema Morale*, or
Moral Ode, the first version of which probably dates from about
1170, is a solemn exhortation to Christians to turn from the ways
of this world into the paths of holiness and salvation. The chief
argument employed is that of terror, of vivid descriptions of the
punishment to come; over the whole poem, with its sadness and
severity, broods the asceticism of the cloister. There is nothing
new in its doctrine; the novelty is in its form and metre. It consists
of four hundred 'fourteeners', or lines of about fourteen syllables
with a caesura after the first seven or eight syllables, a line which
was to become familiar in later popular ballads, and which was used
in Cowper's *John Gilpin*. Nearly every pair of these 'fourteeners',
rhymed in couplets, contains a well-turned maxim, easy to remember. This concise antithetical style reveals a break with Anglo-
Saxon tradition; the old phraseology has vanished, giving place to
a vocabulary bare of ornaments, precise, enlivened with homely
illustrations, accurate if a little prosaic:

> I am now older than I was in winter and in lore,
> I own more than I did, my wit ought to be more.
> Too long I have child y-been in word and eke in deed,
> Though I be of winter old, too young I am in reed (*reason*).
> *(Modernized text.)*

The *Ormulum*, or work of the monk Orm, written about 1200,
is interesting for other reasons. It consists of metrical paraphrases of the Gospel. In form it is curious and even unique.
The metre is that of the *Moral Ode*, but unrhymed, with a redundant feminine ending. It is always perfectly regular. Orm
was not a poet, but he was a clever versifier and a most conscientious philologist. He used a new spelling, in which he doubled
the consonants after every short vowel.

More poetic are some of the prayers of this time, such as the *Prière à Notre Dame* and especially the *Luve Ron* (or Mystery of Love) of Thomas of Hales, which contains one of the first truly poetic stanzas in the language.

> Where is Paris and Helene,
> That were so bright and so fair of face,
> Amadas and Idaine,
> Tristram, Isoud and all these,
> Hector with his sharp strength,
> And Caesar rich of world's wealth,
> They have glided out of the realm. . . .
> *(Modernized.)*

Very pleasant too is the *Ancrene Riwle* (or Anchoresses' Rule), the best example of the prose of the time ; a treatise written for a community of three anchoresses living in a retreat near a church. A new gentleness and humour permeate these simple and minute instructions, with their sense of devotion to the Virgin and their asceticism softened by the realization of femininity. This Rule exists also in Latin and French, but possibly the English was the original.

There is more appeal to curiosity in the religious works of the early fourteenth century. *The Life of Saint Brendan*, translated from the French, introduced the English to the enchantments of this Celtic legend ; *the Life of Saint Dunstan*, attributed to Robert of Gloucester, is full of homely touches and liveliness, and its prosaic style is forgotten in its swift canter.

In 1303 Robert Mannyng of Brunne (i.e. Bourne, in Lincolnshire) began his *Handlyng Synne*, based on the rather poor French *Manuel des Péchés* of William of Wadington. This was a series of forty-four stories—often dull and colourless—illustrating the ways of sin. Mannyng eliminated Wadington's dissertations, added freely to the original, and wrote his stories and exhortations in vigorous and lively verse.

The need for such edifying works is shown by the popularity of the long *Cursor Mundi* in 24,000 octosyllabic lines, written in the North of England about 1320. It is an amplified version of the New Testament and forms a pendant to the miracle-plays.

Fluent, graphic, full of humanity, this work was a great favourite in its day.

That the taste of the time was often childlike and superstitious is shown by the *Pricke of Conscience* (1340) long attributed to the saintly hermit Richard Rolle of Hampole (died 1349). But he would be a poor poet if he were responsible for these ten thousand octosyllabic lines, formless and uninspired. The author admits that he cares little for beauty:

> For I rek noght, thogh the ryme be rude,
> If the mater thar-of be gude.

His credulity explains Wyclif's reform, and, compared with his poor verses, Chaucer's achievement some twenty-five years later appears a marvel. But the prose tracts which are known to have been written by Rolle, and which were widely read, show on the contrary a writer of real power, whose spirited style is quite modern when one pierces through the crust of his uncouth Yorkshire spelling. He has accents of halting tenderness in his *Nominis Jesu Encomion*, or 'Praise of the name of Jesus'.

> Therefore Jesu es thy name. A! A! that wondyrful name! A! that delittabyll name! This es the name that is abown all names. . . . I yede [went] abowte be [by] coveytise of reches and I fand noght Jesu. I ran be the wantonness of flesche and I fand noght Jesu. I satt in companyes of worldly myrthe and I fand noght Jesu. . . . Therefore I turned by another waye, and I ran abowt be poverte, and I fand Jesu, pure born in the worlde, laid in a cryb and lappid in clathis.

Mystical enthusiasm has no more fervent utterance.

Secular Poetry from 1200 to 1350. By the side of this religious literature there was rapidly springing up a secular literature inspired by French works of chivalry. Its originality was not great; yet a certain dawning patriotism shows itself in its preference for English subjects and English heroes. There is, it is true, hardly one of the cycles of romance and chivalry that was not turned into the vernacular and recited by the minstrels to the people; but those relating to the 'matter of Britain' were the most popular, and in some parts the most original works of the English poets.

At the end of the twelfth century Layamon (or Laucman), a priest of Ernley on Severn, translated for his fellow country-men Wace's *Brut*, which was based on the fabulous work of Geoffrey of Monmouth. Layamon, who was wholly Saxon, faith-fully repeats the recital in which the Britons are glorified at the expense of his own ancestors, whose defeats please him as their victories depress him. Although on the whole he is but a translator, his is not the temper of a *trouvère* amused by good stories, but the passion of a *scōp*. Layamon retains both the accent and part of the vocabulary of the Anglo-Saxon poets. There is something impressive in his work—far removed as it is from Wace's correct-ness, ease, and *courtoisie*—with its blunt appeal to the people, and a return to the massive irony of the national epic. His verse is a blending of the old and the new, halting midway between allitera-tion and rhyme. His best style, swift and bare, is shown in his relation of King Arthur's end:

> When these words were spoken,
> There came thither wending
> A little boat moving,
> On the waters it floated,
> And two women in it,
> Wondrously formed;
> And lo! they took Arthur,
> And swiftly they bare him,
> And softly down laid him,
> And forth 'gan their sailing.
> Then was it accomplished
> What Merlin said whilom . . .
>
> (*Modernized.*)

At the end of the thirteenth century appeared two romances, that of *Havelok* and that of *Horn*, both based on Scandinavian originals but already used by the *trouvères*. Neither is, however, a mere translation from the French. The English authors elimi-nated the interminable scenes of ceremonies and battles, and the analyses of courtly love, which would have wearied their audience, in favour of a more dramatic and more rapid narrative.

Both are stories of adventure, and *Havelok* is the more popular and homely in style. It narrates the adventures of a young Danish

prince, kept out of his rights by a wicked guardian; he is saved by
the old fisherman, Grim, the founder of Grimsby, who was ordered
to kill him, and works for a time in the kitchen of Princess Goldburgh—herself menaced by an unscrupulous uncle. Havelok, in
spite of his ignominious position, astonishes the countryside by
his feats of strength and skill. He is married to Goldburgh by the
latter's uncle, who hopes thus to discredit her. But Havelok wins
back the two kingdoms of Denmark and England, and revenges
both himself and Goldburgh, putting his guardian and her uncle
to a cruel death.

King Horn is more of a love story. Captured as a child by the
Saracens, Horn is set adrift in a boat without sails or oars. The
boat drifts to Westernesse, where he wins the love of Rymenhild,
the king's daughter. When the king discovers their secret, Horn is
chased from the court, after first obtaining a promise from Rymenhild to wait for him 'fulle seuen yere'. At the end of seven years of
adventure and success he returns in the guise of a poor pilgrim,
just as Rymenhild is being forced into an unwilling marriage. In
a curious and moving scene Horn makes himself known to the
young bride, who was intending to kill herself at nightfall.

Havelok is written in rather irregular octosyllabic couplets;
Horn in a ruder, shorter accentual metre, as though it were a lay
to be sung. If the English *Geste of Kyng Horn* be compared with
the French *Horn et Rimenhild,* written by the poet Thomas in the
twelfth century and consisting of five thousand alexandrines, it
will be found that the English poem is seven times shorter, quick,
dramatic, full of life. The long French romance, verbose and
diffuse, here becomes something like a popular ballad, touched
with a happy originality.

There is the same blending of imitation and originality in *The
Owl and the Nightingale,* written about 1220 and attributed to
Nicholas de Guildford. In form the poem resembles the *disputoisons*
then in great favour with the French and Provençal poets. The
'strife' or contention between the two birds on the relative merit
of their song is an allegory in which the Nightingale represents
thoughtless youth, and the Owl the wisdom which comes with
years. Written in regular octosyllabic couplets, the well-turned

rhymes lend point to its thought, satire, and irony. Much of the satire and cynicism of the French *fabliaux* is found in *Dame Siriz* and *The Fox and the Wolf*, the latter an episode from the famous *Roman de Renard*.

The grace of French songs has passed into certain English lyrics of the time of Edward I (1279–1307). Instead of northern scenes they sing of spring and love and flowers. The love-songs *Alison*, and *Spring*, reproduce with ease the lightness and variety of French stanzas, and are marked by a quick eye for the beauties of nature. The following song is wholly English:

> Summer is y-comen in!
>   Loudë sing cuckoo!
> Groweth seed and bloweth mead,
> And springeth the woodë now.
>   Sing cuckoo! cuckoo! . . .

It is, however, chiefly in the political songs, from the thirteenth century onwards, that native genius is manifest. National events gave birth to the songs which express English hopes, anger, hatred, love. Some date from the War of the Barons when the barons in their fight against the king drew to themselves the support of the English people; others, such as the *Song of the Husbandman*, voiced the bitter complaint of the poor against their oppressors; others, again, sprang from national enthusiasm for wars that were truly popular and approved by all the people.

The victories of Edward III caused an outburst of triumph. Attracted by these successes Lawrence Minot, a Northerner, came forward to act as official bard, and he sang of Halidon Hill, of the naval triumph outside Sluis, of the siege of Calais, and other royal exploits. The tone of merciless and heavy irony recalls the war-chants of the Anglo-Saxons. Edward and his men are always incomparable heroes; their adversaries are always braggarts, cowards, false and perjured traitors. Perhaps in such pieces railing is unavoidable. But Minot's chief defect is that he has little else to utter beyond abuse. Yet, poor in substance though they are, his songs have a lyrical turn; they combine alliteration and rhyme in regular stanzas with a strong rhythm, and have thus a swing and an attraction due neither to their thought nor to their vocabulary, which is conventional, unimaginative, often prosaic and full of platitudes and padding.

While London was ringing with the exploits of Edward III and Minot's songs were on people's lips, Chaucer was growing up and beginning to write. Victory in the field was to be followed by brilliance in literature. The long period of fumbling preparation was over.

THE FOURTEENTH CENTURY (1350–1400)

THE literature which blossomed in the second half of the fourteenth century was due in part to the awakening of national pride and confidence, the result of the victories of Edward III. It was not, however, contemporary with these, but came into being afterwards, when the conquests made in France were already lost, and the land was divided by internal strife; its florescence was richest under Richard II, whose reign was one of the most unfortunate England has known. It is a fact that the life of the nation waxed more active and bolder in a time of calamity; the middle classes became wealthier and the spirit of independence gained in strength.

Prose from 1350 to 1400. The conditions of contemporary society are made clearer by a glance at the prose. This prose is scarce and of slight literary value. Its chief interest lies in what information it gives us on the manners and tendencies of the age. Latin still attracted many writers: chroniclers, for instance, like Higden, who wrote his *Polychronicon* before 1363, and Walsingham of St. Albans, whose animated pages often equal those of his famous French contemporary Froissart.

Translation continued. A Cornish parish-priest of Gloucestershire, John of Trevisa, translated (1382) Higden's *Polychronicon* into somewhat awkward English, using the archaic dialect of the south-west. His personal share consists of some additions which include comments on the marked increase in the use of English which had taken place in the last twenty years or so.

Lighter reading was afforded by the *Travels of Sir John Mandeville* (1377). For a long time it was regarded as an original work: in reality it was a translation of an amusing fraud perpetrated by a French physician, Jean de Bourgogne, who attributed to an imaginary knight of St. Albans an account of the latter's extraordinary adventures in fabulous lands.

His account of the Ark on Mt. Ararat will illustrate his method:
And there besyde is another hill that men clepen Ararath, but the

Jewes clepen it Taneez, where Noes schipp rested and yit is upon that montayne. And men may seen it aferr in cleer weder. And that montayne is wel a vii. myle high. And sum men seyn that thei han seen and touched the schipp, and put here fyngres in the parties where the feend went out whan that Noe seyde *Benedicite*. But thei that seyn suche woordes seyn here wille. For a man may not gon up the montayne, for gret plentee of snow that is allweys on that montayne, nouther somer ne wynter, so that noman may gon up there, ne neuere man dide, sithe the tyme of Noe, saf a monk that be the grace of God broughte one of the plankes doun, that yit is in the mynstre at the foot of the montayne.

Chaucer's works include a good deal of prose, among them two of the *Canterbury Tales*: that told by the poet himself—the *Tale of Melibeus*, a translation from Jean de Meung; and the *Parson's Tale*, based in part on a notable French sermon of Friar Laurens. Chaucer also put together various Latin treatises to form his *Treatise on the Astrolabe*, in order that his son Lewis, aged ten years, knowing little Latin, might learn Astrology. But his most ambitious attempt was the translation of the *De Consolatione Philosophiae* of Boethius, which had been turned into Anglo-Saxon by King Alfred and was to be translated again by Queen Elizabeth. Chaucer's prose shows no touch of the originality of his poetry.

The chief prose-writers of the age who did more than translate were the Augustinian canon Walter Hilton and the great reformer John Wyclif (1324–84). Hilton, in his *Scale of Perfection*, gave excellent specimens of terse and clear devotional prose which often anticipates Bunyan's manner. Wyclif, who has been called the first Protestant, wrote at first in Latin; then, towards 1380, that he might appeal to the people in his struggle against the Pope, he used English, and was the first theologian to distribute leaflets and pamphlets to the people. These, however, have little literary worth. His most important contribution to English prose is his translation of the New Testament, on which he was engaged while his disciple Nicolas of Hereford translated the Old Testament. It was a literal translation abounding in Latin constructions, but it nevertheless furnished the foundations of that 'biblical dialect' which is still an important element of English style, and from which was to rise the famous Authorized Version of 1611. In studying the literature of the end of the fourteenth century the stir caused by Wyclif's doctrine and writings must be borne in mind.

The Dialects. English literature at this period is noted for its poetry, not its prose. There yet remained an obstacle in the way of any complete literature. The races were intermingling and the classes drawing more closely together, but the nation's language had not yet reached uniformity. In Anglo-Saxon times there had been much difference—not to enter into smaller details—between the speech of the Angles of Northumbria and that of the Saxons of the south. In the fourteenth century four separate dialects were struggling for supremacy: North, South, East Midland, and West Midland; and each one had its own literature. The growth of nationality enriched each dialect, and thus at first increased instead of lessening the confusion. It may be noticed that the North and still more the West clung to the older forms and were unwilling to adopt foreign words. They returned to the old alliterative line, which was gathering its strength together for a final effort—especially in Lancashire and on the borders of Wales. This revival seems natural if we consider that the new versification had as yet brought in no standard verse to replace it. The alternative was the octosyllabic line, whose thin short rhythm could not satisfy ears used to the strength and substance of the old verse. Chaucer had not yet brought from France the decasyllabic line which was destined to become the 'heroic' line. Moreover the new versification lacked an assured prosody; the accents hovered doubtfully over the syllables, the uncertainty affecting words even of Teutonic origin. It was natural that, where foreign influence was least felt, there should be a reappearance of the old rhythm. As a result there was a return of the epithets and synonyms required by alliteration; archaic terms were revived, the vocabulary became more markedly Germanic. There are lines in the new alliterative romances which are almost as awkward to modern ears as a line from *Beowulf*:

> Schon schene upon schaft schelkene blode.
> (Shone bright upon the spear the warriors' blood.)

But if the manner is old, the matter is new, borrowed from the chivalrous and allegorical poetry then popular. The alliterative line is used for poems of chivalry or allegory; such is *Joseph of Arimathia*, a romance on the Holy Grail translated from a French version in prose; and *William of Palerne* (or *William and the Werewolf*) (1355), a free translation of a French romance, with additional descriptions of nature and naïve, homely details.

Sir Gawayne and the Grene Knight. Pearl. Far superior to these are four alliterative poems found in a single manuscript, which have been given the titles of *Pearl, Patience, Cleanness*, and *Sir Gawayne and the Grene Knight*. They have been attributed to the same author. Despite wide differences in subject and form they resemble one another in feeling and language; in each the dominant idea is the praise of purity.

The only one of the four which belongs to the romances of chivalry is *Sir Gawayne and the Grene Knight*, which owes much to the Arthurian cycle, especially to the *Perceval* of Chrestien de Troyes; but the incident narrated is entirely original.

There is a striking strangeness in the first appearance of the Green Knight—a giant on a gigantic horse—when he rides into the great hall of Camelot, where King Arthur and his knights of the Round Table sit at their Christmas feast. He challenges a knight to strike him a blow with his own great axe, on condition that the striker shall himself stand a like blow a year and a day hence. All hesitate; then Gawayne accepts the challenge and strikes off the Green Knight's head. Unmoved, the latter picks up his severed head, bids Gawayne to meet him at the appointed time, and gallops away.

The year passed, and Gawayne set out over rugged mountains to find the knight in green. On Christmas Eve he reached a splendid castle, the lord of which entertained him hospitably. His host's wife, fairer even than Queen Guinevere, came on three successive mornings to Gawayne's chamber and offered him her love. He very courteously put off the lady, who was none other than Morgan le Fay, Arthur's enemy. By his chastity Gawayne came safely out of the trial, and was not beheaded when the

Green Knight—who was his host in disguise—struck the return blow with his axe.

The hero's character is well drawn. He is no abstract being, like Spenser's Sir Guyon, but a man actually touched by temptation, struggling but triumphant. Nevertheless the scene-painting and descriptions are the best things in this poem: we have an impressive picture of the snow-mountains which Gawayne crosses in winter; in its vigour and realism the scene ranks with the most striking in Anglo-Saxon poetry.

Different in origin, form, and tone is the poem *Pearl*. It is an allegory, like the *Roman de la Rose,* but encloses within the traditional frame a religious fervour analogous to Dante's mystic visions and a refined tenderness which recalls Petrarch's sonnets.

The poet is in the arbour where he lost his pearl—we are to understand that his little daughter, not two years old, is dead—and he comes to her grave to mourn. In his grief he falls asleep and dreams that he is in a fair country, through which flows a marvellous river. On its farther bank sits a little maid clothed in shining white, and he sees she is his Pearl. She gently reproaches him for grieving, since she is safe in paradise—'in this gardyn gracios gaye'—and she leads him along the river which he may not cross, until, far-off, he sees the New Jerusalem. He stands there long, dazed and rapt, until at eventide there streams out the procession of the virgin brides of Christ, and he sees his child among them, the pearl of happiness on her breast. He springs forward to approach her and then awakes and finds himself lying on her grave. He goes his way comforted to know that she is among the blessed.

This moving poem is also very striking in form; the writer imposed upon himself a rigid constraint, by a difficult rhyme scheme, made still more stringent by elaborate alliteration and interlinking of stanzas. It is not only the work of a true poet, but also of a craftsman who seeks rarity.

William Langland and his 'Piers Plowman'. Again from the West came the most popular—if the most inartistic—poem of the fourteenth century: the *Piers Plowman* of William Langland. Except that it is an allegory opening with a dream, and including several different allegories somewhat resembling the moralities and miracle-plays, it is in its form (which is entirely alliterative) and its spirit (which is full of passion and fervour) the work that, in its loose structure and carelessness of beauty, shows the least touch of foreign influence.

There are three successive versions. From internal evidence the first seems to have been written in 1362, after the peace of Bretigny; the second about 1377, after the death of the Black Prince; and the third probably towards 1398, after Richard II, by his violence and extravagance, had alienated his people. It has been questioned whether the three versions are the work of one hand, of two, or even of three; but all are deeply religious, reveal full knowledge of the wretchedness of the people, and burn with the same anger against the vices of a society Christian only in name. *Piers Plowman* is at first a picture of the world as it is, followed by a picture of the world as it might be if the Gospel were obeyed. The poem is written to edify; in intention it is never artistic and is rarely so in fact; but the qualities of thought and heart which inspire it lend the exhortation strength and loftiness. Moreover the writer's rude vitality and irony make some of his scenes intensely alive and full of movement.

One May morning the poet, in shepherd's dress, falls asleep by a stream on the Malvern Hills. He sees in a vision a 'field full of folk', rich and poor, workers and idlers, nobles and merchants, unworthy priests, pardoners, and jesters. In the confusion appears the lady Holy Church who exhorts them all to seek the best thing—Truth. The penitents are anxious to set out and find 'seint Treuthe', but no one knows the way. Then Peter the Plowman makes his appearance. He explains the way they must follow—he himself has for fifty years served Truth by working—and offers to be their guide if they will first help him to plough his half-acre. Those who refuse are forced to work through hunger. The poem in its first form ends here, with the dreamer's awakening.

Within this frame there are, however, two episodes longer than the main narrative and almost independent of one another. They are two moralities, two comedies: the Marriage of Lady Meed (Meed here is both just retribution and prevarication), and the

Confession of the Seven Deadly Sins, in which Langland's satire is allowed full play.

The length of the already overgrown poem was more than doubled in its last version. The sequel is a series of visions, bewildering, sometimes chaotic, with nothing of the vividness of the earlier text, from which it differs, too, in tone. The poem has become loftier, more mystical; and there are some fine passages, especially that in *Passus XXI* on the Passion and the Resurrection. Piers the Plowman reappears, but transfigured, a symbol—now of the true Christian, now of Christ Himself. He is changed from the pilgrim into the pilgrim's goal.

It is a striking work, but misshapen. To the spirit which quickens it nothing but praise is due. To the degenerate Christian of his day Langland offers the essential virtues of work and love. He is not driven by the wish to free his reason, but by the yearning to cleanse and strengthen, and to redeem from its worst iniquities the life of the day. This desire and his choice of a ploughman as his hero make him appear as a rebel against social inequality; but in truth his one desire is that one and all should live a Christian life.

In spite, however, of the *verve* of some of the scenes, and the frank vigour of many of his lines, Langland is neither artist nor musician. His alliterative verse never stirs the aesthetic emotion as true poetry should; and he has had few descendants. English poetry came definitely into its own during his lifetime; but Chaucer's, not Langland's, was the hand that shaped it.

Scotland. Barbour's 'Bruce'. If we turn to the north-east, to that Northumbria which produced the literature of the Angles, we shall find many and increasing changes. South of the Tweed the Northumbrian language was sinking to a dialect, soon to become a *patois*. But, north of the Tweed, Northumbrian was spreading and becoming the language of a nation, a living tongue, 'Scots' or 'Scottish', distinguished from the Gaelic of the Highlands. There arose a distinct literature—the expression of the intense national feeling aroused by the Scottish struggle for independence between 1286 and 1314.

In form this literature is closely allied to that of the practical-minded Normans, in which rhymed historical chronicles in octo-

PLATE IV

The medieval ploughman with his ox-drawn plough. See p. xi

syllabics predominated. It was in this metre that John Barbour, archdeacon of Aberdeen, wrote his *Roman de Troie* and some lives of saints; but it is by *The Bruce*, written between 1373 and 1378, that he has gained his place in literature. It is to Scotland what the *Chanson de Roland* is to France—the national epic. It sets out to be a history, not a work of imagination. Barbour describes in detail Bruce's wanderings, a record in itself stranger than fiction and quickened by the chronicler's fervent patriotism. Nothing is more moving than this story of Bruce, hunted like a wild beast, escaping time and again by his dauntless vigour, agility, and cunning and returning at the head of a force which defeated Edward II at Bannockburn and secured for Scotland her independence.

'King's English'. John Gower. Not one of the dialects referred to was destined to predominate; victory fell to that of the East Midlands—the region which included London, the two Universities of Oxford and Cambridge, and the king's residence—the London dialect, the 'King's English'. In literature it was one of the poorest, and one of its main difficulties was to make headway against the Latin of the Universities and the Anglo-Norman of the Court.

The works of John Gower are a case in point. Gower wrote his first poems—the long sermon against the sins of the time (the *Speculum Meditantis* or *Mirour de l'Omme*) and *Cinkante Balades*—in Anglo-Norman. In Latin he wrote his strongest and most personal work, the *Vox Clamantis*, which deals with Wat Tyler's rebellion, and condemns all grades of society for the sins which brought about the terrible revolt of 1381. It ends with an admonition to all to repent. Its object was to make articulate the voice of the people, which is the voice of God.

Only at the last did he write in English, when, towards 1383-4, he wrote his *Confessio Amantis*, a long compilation of 40,000 octo-syllabic lines. It was written in English at the request of Richard II, for the king complained that

> *fewë men endite*
> *In our Englisshe . . .*

Gower was a cultured as well as a 'moral' man. In order to write a popular work, he sinks the moralist in the lover—a role in which he is obviously ill at ease. It is unfortunate that his best work, and that in which he is most at home, should be in Latin. The *Confessio* is a string of tales within a framework both artificial and ridiculous. On the advice of Venus (who has but little love for him) the poet goes to confess to Genius, high priest of the Queen of Love. In order that the poet may examine his conscience, Genius tells him stories concerning the Seven Deadly Sins, and then cross-examines him on his guilt. In conclusion, after 'confession', the poet returns to the goddess, who dismisses him as unfit for her court of Love, and bids him go back to his 'bokes', in which 'vertu moral dwelleth'.

The connexion between the sins denounced and the stories told is sometimes absurd. But Gower was a great reader and knew many curious tales, which he took from various sources. He can tell a story easily and clearly, and for long his collection was as popular as the *Canterbury Tales*. His English is not unlike that of Chaucer, of whom he was both friend and rival. Learned, fluent, and industrious, he was the typical poet of his day, and his writings are what Chaucer's might have been without Chaucer's genius.

GEOFFREY CHAUCER (1340?–1400)

His life, and the part he played in the formation of English poetry.
It is distinctive of Chaucer that he surveyed with wide, impartial,
and inquiring eyes not only the past, as revealed by books, but
also the life of his own day; he was at once familiar with foreign
lands and, in his own country, at home with every class of people.
The works of his contemporaries show the life of the century
in fragments only; in Chaucer's pages the reflection is whole and
complete. Moreover, beneath the changing customs of the time he
makes manifest the springs which move humanity in every age;
his vivid pictures of his own time and country are no less true of
every century and every land.

Born in London about 1340, the son of a vintner in the City, at
the age of seventeen he was a Court page. Two years later we find
him fighting in Artois and Picardy, where he was taken prisoner.
Ransomed the following year, he returned to London and was in
the king's service, first as yeoman and then as esquire. He also
obtained the patronage of John of Gaunt, Duke of Lancaster.
When he was about thirty he was sent abroad on various diplo-
matic missions to France, Flanders, and Italy. In 1374 he was
appointed Comptroller of the Customs of Wool, &c., in the Port
of London. In 1386 he was elected a knight of the shire for Kent.
A period of misfortune followed under the tyrannous reign of
Richard II, which changed for the better when Henry IV—the
son of his old patron John of Gaunt—usurped the throne in 1399.
But the poet lived but a year longer, dying in 1400. These facts
give some idea of his active life and the multiplicity of his occupations; he was by turn page, esquire, soldier, diplomat, and official;
he mingled with courtiers, soldiers, townsfolk, and city merchants,
with natives of France, Flanders, and Italy, and was at home with
them all; and yet he could reserve leisure for reading, study, and
poetry.

The work, the preparation, which the mastery of his craft

involved, must have been great and prolonged. It is scarcely possible to exaggerate the part he played as the creator of English versification. Except for the thin octosyllabic line already in use, he
had to borrow or manufacture his tools. From France he imported,
and made supple under Italian influence, the decasyllabic line,
which was to become the 'heroic' verse, the metre of England's
greatest poetry. Chaucer used the line in stanzas and in couplets,
for lyric and for narrative.

Bolder than Gower, he risked his all on the London dialect, the
'King's English' so long despised; it should express all the refinement and delicacy of French verse. To wed the native vocabulary
to French courtesy was to be his first task. Unlike the authors
of *Sir Gawayne* and *Piers Plowman*, Chaucer broke entirely with
Anglo-Saxon forms. His face was turned to the south and he
sought his ideal beyond the Channel.

Yet in his days French poetry was languishing, exhausted by
the abundant harvests of the past two or three centuries. The
poet from whom Chaucer learnt his first lessons was Guillaume de
Machaut who, if he lacked higher qualities, was at least a great
artist and a musician; and to a certain extent Chaucer may be
numbered among Machaut's disciples, who included Eustache
Deschamps and Froissart. But Chaucer went further back, even
to the famous *Roman de la Rose*, which by the end of the thirteenth
century had become the model and the fountain-head of all allegorical poetry. Not only did he translate part of this vast composition into good English verse, but it became a companion to which
he turned again and again. The *Roman* was the work of two poets:
Guillaume de Lorris and Jean Clopinel, known as Jean de Meun.
Chaucer was attracted by both. In his youth he was influenced
by the graceful love-allegory of the former poet, in his manhood
he turned to the sceptical philosophy and satirical humour of
the latter.

But his debt to France goes beyond imitation, borrowing, and
echoes of style; he is so penetrated by the spirit of the *trouvères*
that he becomes one himself. The first great literary artist of his
country, his aim—in which he succeeded—was to express in his
mother tongue the beauty which he found in the best poetry of

France; and it was an ideal which was the very reverse of that of the *scōps*.

A Frenchman coming into the clear white light which shines from Chaucer's work will find himself at home; he changes neither sky nor country. Chaucer has the light-heartedness of the *trouvères*, the same pleasure in life; their very tone of voice, neither too high nor too low, very clear if perhaps rather thin. His style is simple, fluent, unforced yet restrained, as temperate in emotion as in laughter. But like the *trouvères* he is too talkative, he cannot condense. His verse borders on prose, but it is always saved by its cheerfulness and simplicity; its very faltering, when there is any, becomes an added attraction and serves to point his most subtle shafts of wit. These features are not mere characteristics of his early days, they were inherent in him and will be found throughout his work.

Lyrical and allegorical poems. His first works, it would seem, were love lyrics; but these 'Balades, Roundels, Virelayes' are no longer extant. The later ballades and roundels which have come down to us show that he had not only acquired great metrical skill, but also could introduce into artificial forms much wisdom, a pleasant homeliness, and a humour which liked to turn the laugh against himself. But of such poems he tosses us but a few—airily, as if in play, just to show his mastery of word-music, while he perseveringly devotes himself to the narrative-verse in which most of his work was written.

At first he was bound by the artifices of his age. From the *Roman de la Rose* onwards, nearly every long poem—such as *Pearl* and *Piers Plowman*—began with a dream, introducing an allegory. For a long time Chaucer submitted to that convention. The first work to which a date can be assigned is his *Boke of Blaunche the Duchesse*, written to commemorate the death in 1369 of Blanche of Lancaster, first wife of John of Gaunt. It is a long, composite work, with a plot more intricate than it need be; yet already the poet reveals himself in the flowers, fresh and delicate, which spring up through the crannies of this flamboyant piece of architecture. Allegory gives way, at times, to realism; a breath of humour blows across this occasional poem, whose prolixity is now and then relieved by passages of sober beauty which approach perfection.

Chaucer turned again to allegory when he celebrated some princely betrothal in the *Parlement of Foules*. The time is St. Valentine's day, and the birds are assembled before the goddess Nature that they may choose their mates. There is a union here of ideas both lofty and homely. Nature holds a full Parliament: there are the Lords—eagles and birds of prey who use the language of chivalry and courts of love; there are also the Commons, such as water-fowls, and gross feeders on worms and grain, who refuse to listen to these chivalrous effusions and are all for bodily comfort, for selfish and rather vulgar common sense. Comedy is allied to high romance; the work is, as it were, a rough sketch for the *Canterbury Tales*.

The same quality is found in Chaucer's most ambitious allegorical poem, the *Hous of Fame*, in which he sets out to describe the caprices of fame, and the strange way in which rumour is manufactured and spread abroad. The poem is incomplete; perhaps Chaucer never finished it, finding it too artificial to satisfy his maturer taste. Yet there are in it passages of delightful humour, in which the poet reveals himself intimately, and tells us very frankly of his own limitations. Caught up by a Golden Eagle and swept towards the stars, the poet admires for a moment the 'Galaxy', or Milky Way, but soon decides that he is too old to study star-lore, and begs to be set down on firm ground once again. The empyrean is not for him.

For similar reasons Chaucer left unfinished his *Legende of Good Women*, written about 1385. In this only the Prologue is allegorical, and it is charming, full of Chaucer's love of spring and his favourite 'dayesye'. He first sees in a dream Cupid, god of Love, who charges him with having written satires against lovers. Then Queen 'Alceste' (Alcestis, who in Greek legend gave her life for Admetus, her husband, when he was stricken with a mortal illness) intercedes for him and bids him expiate his past heresies by writing the 'legends' of fair women who had loved too well. He relates with tenderness the lives of his heroines (many of whom he found in Ovid), the stories of Thisbe, Lucretia, Philo-

mela, and Ariadne being the best; but after a time he tired of
having to show all women equally admirable and virtuous, and
all men without faith or heart, and of the twenty stories which
he set out to write he left the half unfinished.

Chaucer under Italian influence. At the time of his mission to
Italy in 1372 Chaucer was brought into touch with the splendid
contemporary Italian literature, then the finest in Europe. Dante
had died in 1321, but Petrarch (whom Chaucer possibly saw at
Padua) and Boccaccio were still alive. Chaucer knew their work—
at least in part—admired it and was inspired by it, but his debt is
not the same to all. He recognized Dante's genius, but they had
little in common; not for Chaucer the sublimity of the *Inferno*
or *Paradiso*. He borrowed little from Petrarch, who was a humanist too near the ancients and too much in advance of his contemporaries on the way to the Renaissance, for Chaucer to emulate.
But he borrowed a great deal from Boccaccio without direct
acknowledgement, although he does not seem to have known the
Decamerone, the world-famous collection of prose-tales, in which
he would surely have found much to delight him.

From the *Parlement of Foules* onwards there are traces of
Italian influence in Chaucer's allegorical poems; but they are
slight compared with the debt which, in his *Knightes Tale* and
Troilus and Cryseyde, he owes respectively to Boccaccio's *Teseide*
and to his *Il Filostrato* (the young man 'felled by love').

In his *Knightes Tale* Chaucer freely extracted from a sort of
epic a love tale which narrated the rivalry of two young knights,
friends and cousins, made enemies by their common love for the
fair Emelie. He retained all the best of the original, transforming
its stanzas into rhymed couplets.

In the *Troilus and Cryseyde*, on the contrary, he expanded a brief
story, burning with passion and despair, in which Boccaccio had
shown how Troilus loved Cressida and was loved by her, until
absence from him brought about her undoing; she turned to other
lovers and was false to him. About this 'tragedy' there plays in
Chaucer's poem a light of humour which centres almost entirely
on Pandarus, Cressida's uncle, who is favourable to the lovers.
Chaucer makes of him an easy-going, bantering, talkative person-

age, much given to the use of proverbs and maxims; and his amusing chatter constitutes the two or three thousand lines which Chaucer adds to the Italian poem. Admirable as is his translation and adaptation of the passionate scenes of Boccaccio, which he transformed into the first great love-poem in the English language, Chaucer's originality is here shown chiefly in comedy. The emotional, voluptuous pages of the original become in his hands character-studies. He is thus the forerunner of Shakespeare, who was often to deal in the same manner with his originals— when, for example, he took in his hands the romance of *Romeo and Juliet*, preserved the Italian love-story almost unchanged, yet shaped it anew by his humorous development of the characters of the Nurse and old Capulet, and his creation of jesting Mercutio.

The 'Canterbury Tales'. Hitherto Chaucer had spent his strength mainly in translating and adapting; broadly speaking, he was scarcely more than the *'grant translateur'* praised by Eustache Deschamps. His genius had been fettered by restraints in which it was obviously ill at ease, judging from the way he had left two of his chief works unfinished: the one as too artificial, the other as too monotonous. But when he was nearing the fifties he put his hand on a subject which was to allow him—attracted as he was by beauty and ugliness, poetry and prose, piety and scoffing, grace and humour—full and free expression. He had probably ready certain tales, grave and gay, which ran the risk of remaining isolated, without connecting link, when the idea came to him of a pilgrimage, during which each pilgrim might tell his own story. Chaucer, who was then living at Greenwich, may well have seen pass the motley cavalcade of all sorts and conditions of men and women, knights and burghers, artisans and clerks, thrust perforce into temporary fellowship, as they went their way to the tomb of the holy martyr St. Thomas at Canterbury. In endowing with speech so many different people Chaucer was enabled to manifest his own great and varied gifts, and to draw with broad strokes and without bias a picture of actual life.

To begin with he chose some thirty pilgrims and drew a portrait of each one before causing him to speak. These portraits form the *Prologue*, written in entire simplicity and with effortless ease

PLATE V

Chaucer riding

Canterbury Pilgrims

PLATE VI

Chaucer reading to the court of Richard II.
See p. xi

and even seeming carelessness; yet each member of the group stands out distinctly, sparklingly alive, so that he remains for all time not only an individual but a type. In those days each class, trade, and profession had its distinctive dress. Chaucer cunningly seizes on these external differences. He unites the characteristics of a profession and the personal features of his subject to make a life-like portrait. A few more generalities and the result would be a chill symbol; a few more personal details and the outline would be blurred.

Not content with single portraits Chaucer shows us the pilgrims together, the way they react one on another; we hear them talking, arguing, criticizing each other's stories, speaking of their private lives, unconsciously revealing themselves. This they do also in their choice of tales, which are as diverse as themselves. The Knight relates a story of chivalry and love and war. The Miller and the Reeve recall two *fabliaux*, both extremely broad, and the Reeve is careful to tell his against the Miller; just as in the tales of the Friar and the Summoner, the Friar attacks the Summoner and the Summoner the Friar. The Wife of Bath is careful to make clear in her tale that happiness in married life is found in the entire submission of the husband to the wishes of his wife. The *Tales* are some of them very pious, others profane; some full of tenderness, others broadly humorous; some are even tiresome to make them more lifelike and give the hearers an opportunity for inveighing against and interrupting them. They aim at being not only excellent in themselves but plausible and interesting dramatically, in harmony with the character of the narrator.

The religious tales and narratives of romance, often written in stanzas, are as a rule full of poetry and charm; but they are largely translations. Chaucer's originality is best shown when he transforms the *fabliau* into a veritable comedy; or rather in his conception of a great poem which was to represent the extremes and many-sided aspects of life.

Chaucer's amused and tolerant curiosity excludes no one; he is not easily repelled. Loving the world's variety, he is grateful to its defects for their difference from its virtues. He looks at himself without illusion and judges himself without bitterness, in no wise carried away by any desire to excel. Standing on the level of the average man, Chaucer finds the multitude beside him; it is the sense of common failings that makes for fellowship. Of all writers of genius Chaucer is the one in whom we most quickly find a friend. He is the leader of those observers who accept as a fact—without seeking to dye them all one uniform hue—the many-coloured strands which are woven into the web of human life. Some shades may seem to him lovelier than others, but it is on the contrasts of the whole that he founds at once his philosophy of life and the rules governing his art.

THE FIFTEENTH CENTURY. FROM THE DEATH OF CHAUCER TO THE RENAISSANCE (1400–1516)

Chaucer's imitators and disciples. Two centuries were to pass before England could produce a poet worthy to rank with Chaucer. Nothing testifies more clearly to his genius than the inability of succeeding generations to equal or even to understand him. And this is the more striking in that every poet paid him homage. Yet when they thought to imitate him they reached but the lowest step—that on which Chaucer stood when he was at the level of his century; never could they approach him when he moved to higher flights. Moreover the evolution of the language, which was becoming more and more uninflected, made full recognition of his accurate and musical versification increasingly difficult. When the final syllabic *e* became mute, Chaucer's metre, wrongly read, ill transcribed, and, later, badly printed, appeared syllabically uneven and accentually irregular; and this led his successors to think that their own versification might be haphazard.

The decline was immediate, and apparent even in those, such as Hoccleve and Lydgate, who knew Chaucer and acclaimed him master. They were chiefly translators or imitators. Thomas Hoccleve (1370?–1450?) wrote, in 1411–12, for the Prince of Wales —afterwards Henry V—his *Regement of Princes*, based on the Latin *De Regimine Principum* which had been originally written for the instruction of Philippe le Bel. The dissertations, intermixed with examples, are written in smooth and fairly correct verse, but the didacticism is more reminiscent of Gower than of Chaucer.

John Lydgate (1370?–1451?) has the distinction of being the most voluminous poet of the fifteenth century—indeed, of the whole of the Middle Ages—in England. About 140,000 lines of his are extant. This Benedictine monk of Bury St. Edmunds was an indefatigable compiler. His longest poems are his *Storie of Thebes* and *Troy-Book*, retold from two notable French romances; his *Fall of Princes*, from the Latin of Boccaccio; the *Temple of Glass*, a heavy allegorical love-story; the *Pilgrimage of Man*, translated from Guillaume De Guileville; some Lives of Saints, &c. Their retrogression is striking. He takes his subjects back to the state in which they were before Chaucer gave them new life by his humour and his art. Under Lydgate verse decays; his accents are placed at random; he says himself:

> And trouthe of metre I sette also a-syde . . .
> I tooke none hede nouther of shorte nor longe.

Yet in his days he was very popular; unrepelled by his prolixity and by the conventionality of his verse, his readers were grateful to him for narrating so many tales, and for telling them with a certain liveliness.

More attractive than the preceding are a certain number of short poems whose authors are unknown, or little known, and which were for long ascribed to Chaucer himself and included in some editions of his works. Careful study of language and metre has shown that they belong to the fifteenth—or even sixteenth—century. One of these is *The Cuckoo and the Nightingale* written by Sir Thomas Clanvowe (c. 1403). It is a graceful *disputoison* between the two birds, a debate between love and saddened wisdom, similar to that of the *Owl and the Nightingale* of the thirteenth century. Based on the Prologue to the *Legende of Good Women* is the charming allegory of *The Flower and the Leaf*, whose unknown author was apparently a gentlewoman. Its disjointed metre is not Chaucer's, but nothing can be more graceful, more dewy-fresh, than the scene of this morality, wherein is shown the superiority of the Leaf, symbol of work, of a serious, useful life, over the Flower, a type of idle frivolity. There is nothing here of Chaucer's substance, reality, and humour, but something lighter, daintier, more airy; it is the prettiest thing produced in the fifteenth century.

Less freshly coloured, yet with more wit and sense of character, is *The Court of Love*, which of all these poems Chaucer might the most justly claim for his were it not for its 'aureate', rhetorical style. It tells how 'Philogenet . . . of Cambridge, clerke' loses his way in the palace of Cytherea, learns there the laws of the place, enters the service of the fair lady Rosial, and, after a time of trial,

PLATE VII

Lydgate writing in his cell

A medieval library. See p. xii

wins her grace. This little poem is now said to belong to the beginning of the sixteenth century.

We must turn back and see that the terrible Wars of the Roses, which lasted from 1454 to 1485, not only suspended all literary activity, but caused poetry, instead of rising refreshed when the convulsion was over, to lie for a long while sick with a strange languor. This is evident in the work of Stephen Hawes (1475–1523?), another allegorist. Yet, if he is too much attracted to the past, he is, for that very reason, a feeble forerunner of Spenser. When the Wars of the Roses destroyed the flower of England's chivalry, they thrust the old courtly poetry into the dreamlike past; it had become almost as unreal as the scenes and characters of allegory. As a consequence chivalry now assumed the charm of distance, the melancholy of regret, two of the elements of romanticism. It is this vague, romantic atmosphere alone which gives any value to Hawes's platitudes and unmusical verses, to his *Example of Vertu . . .* (1503–4), and to his *Passetyme of Pleasure, or the History of Graunde Amoure and La Bel Pucel* (1503–6).

The two last writers in verse who precede the Renaissance— Barclay and Skelton—show novelty in choice of subject and manner.

Alexander Barclay (1475–1552), in his *Shyp of Folys* (1509) translated the *Narrenschiff* of the Alsatian, Sebastian Brant; he also introduced the classical eclogue to his countrymen, basing his pastorals on those of Mantuan, a famous Latin poet of the Renaissance.

John Skelton (1460?–1529) was an eccentric poet, somewhat difficult to define. A good scholar, tutor to the future Henry VIII, and parson of Diss in Norfolk, he writes frequently like a satirical buffoon, using short, uneven lines, several of which rhyme together—a sort of doggerel. Many of his works are lost; the most interesting of those extant are: *The Bowge of Court* (or Courtrations), the *Boke of Colyn Cloute*, *The Garland of Laurell* and *Why come ye nat to Court?* His satires are often characterized by the coarsest abuse and the worst indecencies. He is, however, capable at times of grace and tenderness, as in his *Boke of Phylyp Sparowe*, an elegy on the death of a sparrow, inspired by Catullus, but its few sweet lines are drowned in a flood of fooling. In this odd work there is everything save that thirst for beauty which the Renaissance was to bring.

Scottish Poetry from 1400 to 1516. It is pleasant in the fifteenth century to turn from English to Scottish poetry, although we do not find anything new even north of the Tweed. The tradition of allegory and the influence of Chaucer still reigned supreme. But the poets of Scotland retained a sense of artistry and of sure rhythm, as well as a vitality, which form a happy contrast to English looseness and languor.

The patriotism which made Barbour write his *Bruce* is no longer dominant. *The Bruce* has but one parallel in the *Wallace* attributed to Henry the Minstrel (or Blind Harry), written about 1461. The fabulous element is far more pronounced than in *The Bruce*, but where Barbour is prosaic Harry is platitudinous. The former's octosyllabic line is replaced by ten-syllable couplets, the only result being a clumsy protraction of the line. It is not poetry. It heightens, by contrast, the brilliance and over-ornateness of other Scottish verses of the period.

The first of the Scottish poets to be inspired by Chaucer was a king: James I (1394–1437). Doubts have been thrown on his literary claims, but have not seriously shaken the tradition that the *King's Quair* (or book) is the personal expression of a romantic episode in his life. At the age of eleven he and the ship which was taking him to France were captured by the English, who held him prisoner for nineteen years. Towards the end of that time he fell in love with Joan Beaufort, niece of Henry IV, and married her in 1424. The poem is a description of his love; it is full of reminiscences of Chaucer, especially of the *Knightes Tale*. The king describes in delightful fashion how the first sight of the young girl, ' beautiful enough to madden the world', came to him in prison to enchant him with love. He inserts in his poem the traditional ' dream', instead of enclosing his poem in it, and his freshness, sincerity, passion, and music give a rare charm to the narrative.

A more original outlook is found in Robert Henryson (1425 ?– 1506 ?), schoolmaster of Dunfermline, who was quite independent even in his imitations of Chaucer, to whose *Troylus and Cryseyde* he

wrote a sequel. This *Testament of Cresseid* describes her wretched
end when, smitten with leprosy, she dies, after Troilus, without
recognizing her, has given her alms as to a beggar. Moral though the
ending is it is touched with deep pity. Henryson laments her fate
even in recounting it; and his stanzas are as harmonious as his
master's. He was influenced also by Aesop, and wrote several
fables, one of which, *The town mouse and the field mouse*, is full of
sly humour. Henryson shows a lively sympathy with the animals,
whose deeds he recounts with gay realism. We owe to him also the
pastoral of *Robin and Marion*, through which seems to blow an
upland wind. Of all the Scottish poems of his time Henryson's
savour most of his native soil.

But it is William Dunbar (1463?–1550?) who is justly reputed
to rank first in this remarkable group. At one time a Franciscan,
later unfrocked, he became a kind of poet laureate in the gay
court of James IV of Scotland. About a hundred of his poems
are extant and they show a surprising diversity of subject and
metre. This fertility bears no resemblance to Lydgate's prolixity,
for Dunbar was an artist, and even a great artist. Not that he
showed much originality either in thought or feeling; he often
kept within the medieval framework; but he possessed to an
extraordinary degree virtuosity of style and metre. No one hitherto had put so much colour into his pictures; above all, no one
had ever written with such a metrical swing and raciness. It
matters not that he has little to say to heart or mind; he dazzles
the eye and charms the ear. Brilliancy is the most striking characteristic of his official allegories, such as *The Thrissill and the Rois*,
symbolizing the union of England and Scotland in the marriage
(1503) of James IV with Margaret Tudor, daughter of Henry VII;
or *The Golden Targe*, a love poem whose glowing descriptions are
more applicable to kingdoms in the *Arabian Nights* than to scenes
in misty Scotland. His metrical *tour-de-force* is perhaps his *Dance
of the Sevin Deidly Synnis*, where in eleven twelve-lined stanzas
he whirls the sins round in a satanic dance. There is equal impetus in his religious poem *Done is a battell on the dragon blak*
wherein he exults over the victory of Easter. The same *verve* is
apparent in his 'flytings', or scolding matches, where he shows an

incomparable command of the vocabulary of abuse; in his court satires, and in the *fabliau* of *The two Mariit Wemen and the Wedo*, written in alliterative verse, and in language carried to the bounds of decency and beyond. His style is at times reminiscent of flamboyant architecture; but so far from being overwhelmed by his wealth of language he carries it with ease; his mere impetuosity sweeps him into lyricism.

A poet of almost equal vigour, Gavin Douglas (1475?–1522), bishop of Dunkeld, intimately connected with Scotland's history, revealed himself as a humanist and a precursor of the Renaissance. He began in the traditional style with an allegory—*The Palice of Honour* (1501), after the manner of Chaucer's *Hous of Fame*; and *King Hart*, with its blend of humour and melancholy, in which he shows marked analytical skill. But the work by which he is best known is his translation of the *Aeneid* into the Scottish tongue (1512–13), the first version in the vernacular to appear in Great Britain, for that printed by Caxton was a translation not from Virgil but from a French romance based on his work. Douglas translated direct from the Latin, shaping the lines into heroic couplets which have freshness and sometimes brilliance. A vivid touch of originality is given by the prologues which he adds to each book of the *Aeneid*. These prologues are personal; in them he talks of himself, of Scotland and the season, with a wealth of description approaching exuberance and at that time unequalled. His vocabulary he gathered from many fields, learned and popular, modern and archaic. Of all his contemporaries he is the most difficult to understand. Few Englishmen and not many of his own countrymen can now read him without a glossary. In short, he stood on the threshold of the Renaissance but never crossed it.

Popular Literature: Ballads. The literature already touched on may be termed the official poetry, Scottish and English, of the fifteenth century. There was in existence at the same time another literature, anonymous, popular, ruder perhaps, but far more alive, to which it is often impossible to assign place or date with precision. It was not altogether of the fifteenth century—it began before and continued long after, but it seems to have been particularly alive at that period, to which the oldest extant specimens belong. The reference here is not to the courtly *ballade*, or short poem with a fixed form, introduced from France and adopted by Chaucer, but to the popular ballad, which is a narrative, long or short, in simple verse; it may be the fragment of an epic, the summing-up in a few stanzas of a love-romance or poem of chivalry, or the relation of some local incident, glorious or nefarious, the hero of which was to the audience a familiar figure. Popular ballads are found all over Europe, but a particularly fertile soil was the 'Border', once the scene of so many sanguinary affrays between the Scots and the English.

It is known that from the fourteenth century onwards there were popular rhymes on Robin Hood, archer and outlaw; but such ballads relating to him as survive are not earlier than the sixteenth century. In short only two ballads exist which can be identified with certainty as earlier than the Renaissance:

'**Chevy Chase**' and '**The Nut-brown Maid**'. *Chevy Chase* (or the hunt in the Cheviots) is the finest of the epical ballads. Its theme is the struggle between Percy of Northumberland and Douglas of Scotland, at the beginning of the fifteenth century; and it reveals manners both wild and chivalrous. Percy wishes to hunt in enemy country, less for love of the deer he covets than to defy his foe and provoke an encounter. He is overjoyed when the fight begins, but when Douglas is slain he weeps over the body of his valiant enemy. The details of the fight are given with a directness and accuracy which make them stand out in relief: the part played by the English archers, the tactics of Douglas, who makes his men advance in scattered formation, the hand-to-hand struggle. The whole breathes a martial ardour which, even at the end of the following century, stirred Sir Philip Sydney's heart as with the sound of a trumpet. The very ruggedness of its metre with its line of seven accents in 4+3, the division always falling in the same place, its halting rhythm and uneven syllabication, were to raise up imitators among the romantics. Throughout literature the strong, homely simplicity of such a poem was able to lead back to nature writers inclined to extravagance and artifice.

The poem of *The Nut-brown Maid*, not strictly a ballad, is very

different. Metrically it is intricate and difficult, written in stanzas
with repeated rhymes and alternate refrains. Yet its complex
versification, evidently the work of a courtly and cultivated mind,
does not preclude an entire simplicity of thought and language.
To absolve women from the reproach of inconstancy levelled
at them by men, a lady and a gentleman rehearse in a lyrical
dialogue the story of the nut-brown maid—'a baron's daughter'—
who insists, in spite of coldness and reproach, on following the
young squire she loves, when he tells her he must flee into the
forest as an outlaw. This, however, is only to try her; the squire is
really a noble lord who will make her the countess of Westmorland.
The value of this poem lies in its sincerity and truth, coupled
with the unforced art of its versification. Printed in 1502, it belongs
unmistakably to the reign of Henry VII.

Miracle Plays. As with the ballad, so with medieval drama: it
neither began in, nor ended with, the fifteenth century. But it
was then that the greater number of miracle plays were compiled,
and this was the age in which they reached their zenith, as yet
unhampered by the beginnings of the modern stage. This century
therefore, offers the most suitable opportunity for an analysis of
religious drama in England before the Renaissance.

Typically English traits are scarce. In so far as religious
matters were concerned the whole of Christian Europe was like
one great nation divided into provinces; development was almost
parallel in all the countries. Therefore, before turning to England
itself, we must note the essential characteristics that were present
everywhere.

Miracle plays grew out of the liturgy itself, with its solemn
rites and the chants alternating between priest and congregation.
They began as short dialogues. There are extant two in use in
England before the Conquest. Recited at first inside the church,
these dialogues developed by degrees into little plays acted in the
church porch. One of the most important was the play of *Adam*,
written in the twelfth century by a Norman, or Anglo-Norman. It
is in three parts, showing the fall of Adam and Eve, the death
of Abel, and the line of prophets announcing the advent of the
Saviour. This play, which lacks neither refinement nor poetry,

was written in French and acted at Rouen, and perhaps also in England. To make these plays really popular it was necessary to turn from French to the vernacular. Therefore their development went hand in hand with the progress of the English tongue, with the rise of the burgher class and the growth of the trade-guilds. In the reign of Henry III began the great cycles of plays in which, on some annual holiday, were unfolded the scenes from Scripture which related to that festival. At first they were the cycles of Easter and Christmas-tide; then the institution of the festival of Corpus Christi in 1311, and its general observance in the fourteenth century, made it the principal holiday. The two cycles, formerly separate, were united, and thus almost all Holy Writ was displayed in one place and at one time, so that the people might be taught, in vivid, concrete fashion, the great truths of religion.

Certain towns, either by reason of the importance of their fairs, or through the more powerful organization of their trade guilds, became noted for the presentation of their miracle plays. The cycle-plays which have come down to us, either entire or in fragments, are known by the names of the places where they were shown. There are the plays of Chester, Coventry (which Shakespeare might have seen as a child), York, Norwich, Newcastle, Wakefield.

Let us imagine one of these vast productions, that, for instance, at York on the feast of Corpus Christi. All the guilds of the city had to contribute to it. The complete festival consisted of forty-eight plays, the substance of which was the whole of the Scriptures. We know the order of the plays and the guild which made itself responsible for one of them. The guild was as far as possible chosen for its appropriateness. The Armourers were responsible for the expulsion from Paradise—because of the flaming sword; the Shipwrights for the building of Noah's ark; the Fishmongers and Mariners for the Flood; the Bakers for the Last Supper, and so on. The stage was a scaffold, stationary at first, then it was set on wheels that it might move from place to place; and it was called the 'pageant'—a name that was afterwards applied to the scene itself. The spectators stood at different stations in the town, marked out with flags. A pageant acted the first play (probably Adam and Eve), then moved on to the next station and repeated it, while the second pageant took its place at the first station. There was no delay, pageant was to succeed pageant swiftly—'without tarrying'[1] throughout the long summer day.

Such knowledge as we have of the English drama in the fifteenth century shows a powerful organization, in which the guilds played an important part, and a vitality and popularity unsurpassed anywhere. The expense and labour entailed in presenting the dramas were more than equalled by the care taken in writing them. Their unknown authors were often hampered by the complicated metre which they used; as a rule it was a stanza of 6, 8, or 9 short lines with rhymes—a difficult metre in which to present a lively, natural dialogue such as we expect nowadays. Their style is often awkward, but simple, bare, unpretentious, and some of the poets have succeeded, in spite of the constraint of the metre, in producing scenes both lofty and pathetic, or, more often, full of boisterous, rustic humour.

One of the most touching plays is that of *Abraham and Isaac*, which shows Abraham torn between reverence for God and love for his son—winding the kerchief about Isaac's eyes, kissing his 'fair sweet mouth' and lifting the sword to slay; and Isaac obedient, submissive, gentle, though shrinking from the thought of death. But, like Chaucer in the *Canterbury Tales*, the writers show more originality in the humorous scenes; indeed, it was only in such interpolations that they could break free. They could take no liberty with the serious scenes from the Bible, but they were free to introduce minor characters, who relieved the strain of too much gravity and made the crowd laugh. It is evident from what Chaucer says that an altercation between Noah and his wife had long been a stock scene. Other humorous figures—in language, dress, and manner English rustics of the day—were the beadle of Pontius Pilate, the Roman soldiers at the Crucifixion, the guards who watched the sepulchre, &c. Shakespeare and his rivals did the same: they preserved the central tragedy of their original source and added a border of comedy of their own.

Nowhere is the humorous side of the plays shown better than

[1] York Plays, XXXIV.

PLATE VIII

An elaborately equipped stage for a late miracle play of the Passion (French c. 1547).   See p. xii

in the Wakefield scenes of goodman Noah and his cross-grained wife, and in the comedy of the stolen sheep in the Shepherds' Play which precedes the march of the shepherds towards the manger. In both the lively, fluent drollery is quite good-natured, without *arrière-pensée* or irony, and in no way incompatible with faith and tenderness. So in the drama of the Renaissance, comedy and tragedy were to blend without destruction of the one by the other.

Moral Plays. To the fifteenth century belong also the earliest extant moralities. Born later than the miracle plays, which represent the epical period, the moralities emanate from allegory. Bible characters are replaced by abstract virtues and vices personified. Their aim, like that of the miracle plays, was primarily the teaching of the Christian faith, but they appealed more directly to the intellect. The miracles were for the unlettered; they were above all a spectacle, appealing to the eyes: the morality exacted more attention to the words; text was more important than scenery; and the construction was more artificial. On the other hand, the morality gave more scope to the author; he could handle his subject more freely, with something of pyschological analysis. To present Avarice on the stage it was necessary first to study a miser's character. The morality led also to a material change in the theatre. In the miracle play each scene, or group of scenes, had a movable pageant; the morality required but one fixed stage. Thus the *Castell of Perseverance* (early fifteenth century), the earliest extant English morality, shows one scene with a castle in the centre, with niches in the corners for the World, the Flesh, God, and the Devil.

The moralities prior to the Reformation—*Mankind, Mundus et Infans*, the *Enterlude of Hyckescorner*—are concerned with wider issues, and show human life wavering between good and evil, between God and the Devil. Finer than all others is the morality of *Everyman*, which illustrates with impressive simplicity the solemnity of Christian death. In a sense all drama, old or modern, seems frivolous by the side of this elemental tragedy, bare and colourless though it may be.

Prose in the Fifteenth Century. The prose of the fifteenth

century is of small account if the name is used only for works
which show originality and artistic value. The reason is the same
as in the preceding period: Latin attracted such writers as were
not merely translators and whose aim was more than utilitarian.
On the other hand, the bold movement of Wyclif and his adherents was checked. The first half of the fifteenth century was a
time of narrow orthodoxy; not until the second half did a few
works worthy of note appear. Yet this scarcity was no sign that
reading and the diffusion of knowledge were arrested—on the
contrary, they were spreading. To this time belongs the first
collection of family letters in English—the 'Paston Letters'; letters
exchanged between three generations of a middle-class family in a
Norfolk village between 1425 and 1503. They are full of information for the historian on the social and domestic life of the time.

Of more worth is *The Repressor of overmuch blaming the Clergy*
(1455) in which Reginald Pecock, the learned bishop of Chichester,
after writing in Latin, undertook to refute in English the charges
brought by the Lollards, Wyclif's followers, against the clergy.
He defended all that they attacked as superstitious, and yet bases
his arguments entirely on reason. To Wyclif and his disciples, who
grounded their faith solely on the words of the Bible, he retorts by
invoking 'the boke of law of kinde writen in mennis soulis with
the finger of God'. This style of controversy scandalized his own
party; many of his books were burnt at Paul's Cross; he had to
resign his see, and, by a strange irony of fate, was looked on by
some as a follower of Wyclif.

In the same way Sir John Fortescue (1394?–1476?), lord
chief justice of the court of King's Bench, forsakes the Latin in
which he had written a treatise to justify by the laws of Nature the
Lancastrian usurpation, and another to the praise of the English
constitution. He turns to his mother tongue in order to write *The
Governance of England*, or *The Difference between an Absolute and
Limited monarchy*, in which he is the first to admire the constitution of his own country and the personal freedom enjoyed by its
subjects.

Prose was still unformed when the first English printer began
his work in 1474. William Caxton (1422?–1491) has himself

PLATE IX

Printing in the 15th century.   See p. xii

Paper-making in the 15th century.   See p. xii

PLATE X

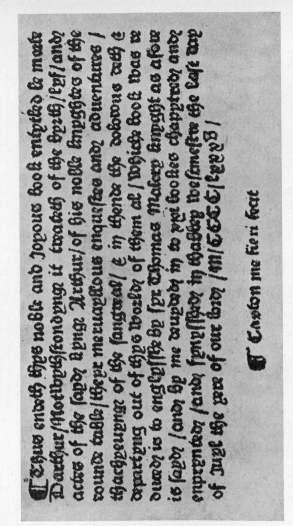

The end of Malory's *Morte d'Arthur*, printed by Caxton, 1485. See p. xii

explained how hampered he was by the fluid state of the language, the differences of dialect, and the rapid changes taking place. He found great difficulty in finding a medium which would be understood by all. He was no classical scholar. The books he printed—works of devotion, prose romances of chivalry, *Reynard the Fox*, the works of Chaucer, Gower, Lydgate—form a medieval library list, but in no way herald the new learning. Thanks to him and his successors the literature of the past was placed within the reach of an increasing number of readers, and remained, even during the Renaissance, more truly popular than anything new.

Caxton was well inspired when, among compilations of less merit, he printed in 1484 the *Morte d'Arthur* of Sir Thomas Malory, a Lancastrian knight who had died in 1471. Doubtless Malory is only a compiler. He has only retold tales narrated many times before; but he has condensed the diffuse Arthurian romances of the later French versifiers, making the whole more distinct by his cutting and compression—in spite of the admission of several lengthy episodes. Above all, he has diffused over the monotonous adventures of his heroes an atmosphere of distance and unreality which works on the mind like poetry. His style is simple, even childish, monotonous, but perfumed with archaisms, and suited to a fairy tale. It is England's first book in poetic prose, the store-house of the one legend of the past which most haunts the English imagination; and it was to keep alive the spirit of chivalry among scholars, poets, and gentlemen.

The next important work in English prose after the *Morte d'Arthur* was another translation—the *Chroniques* of Froissart, the translator being John Bourchier, Lord Berners. It was published between 1523 and 1525. Lord Berners turned again to the Middle Ages for his next work—a translation, in lively prose, of the romance *Huon of Bordeaux*. Then, attracted by the Renaissance, he translated, about 1533, under the title of *The Golden Boke of Marcus Aurelius* (1534), the Spanish treatise of Antonio de Guevara. He is the link between the two ages in prose, as, on very different grounds, Skelton and Douglas are in poetry.

PREPARATION FOR THE RENAISSANCE (1516–78)

The Role of the Humanists. The Renaissance is a European phenomenon. In all literatures in the sixteenth century the same general causes were at work: the liberation of thought from the scholasticism which bound it; the revolt against spiritual authority incited by the Reformers, who were later the bitterest enemies of the same revolt; wonder at the new earth and sky as revealed by navigators and astronomers; perception of greater beauty in the Greek and Latin classics—especially in the former, which had lately been recovered.

But while these characteristics were common to all, the effect of the Renaissance in each country was the formation of a national literature. In the Renaissance as in the Reformation there was a strong element of individualism. The desire for literary beauty led to an intensive cultivation of the language spoken by each nation, to an increased use of its own power of expression. It tended to widen the dividing line between nations previously united by the pursuit of the same ideal—even when royal ambition or material interests flung them one against the other. The spiritual and aesthetic unanimity of the Middle Ages was definitely broken.

As compared with France and Italy the chief peculiarities of the Renaissance in England are the following: the reviving breath came to literature later and more slowly; humanism had for a long time no decisive effect on either poetry or prose, the language having scarcely attained its full growth by the beginning of the sixteenth century. Prose had no precedent, no great tradition. It is a significant fact that the two books published in England which first attained European fame—the *Utopia* of Sir Thomas More (1516), and Bacon's *Novum Organum* (1620)—were both written in Latin. Verse, disordered since Chaucer's days, did not definitely recover its equilibrium until 1579, with Spenser; the intervening years were a time of essay, of advance and retreat. As a result efflorescence in England began when the magnificent

Italian literature had already become decadent, after France had produced Rabelais, Ronsard and his *Pléiade*, and when Montaigne's *Essais* were appearing. Hence it was in a generation enriched with all the substance of Italy and France that England, for the first time, was to realize her high literary ambitions.

Again, the Renaissance here was further divorced from the plastic arts than in Italy or even in France. England was a nation which bought her statues from abroad; a nation, too, in which the more strict among the reformers protested against 'images', and in which the Renaissance had a more inward and moral character. Not before, but after, the Reformation did the Renaissance triumph, when Anglicanism, diffused over the land, had become tinged here and there with Calvinism. In so far as the Renaissance was an aspiration towards beauty in every form, and the development of every activity, it never breathed quite freely in the puritan atmosphere which already lay over the nation. There were doubtless free spirits, but they were rebels and notorious. In the greater number morality was natural and sincere; others assumed it to avoid censure. On the whole there was deeper gravity, more probing of conscience, less serenity; and a more intense preoccupation with questions of faith and conduct.

On the other hand, although England in her Protestantism had broken more completely with the Middle Ages than had France or Italy, yet her literature was linked more closely with the past than that of either. This fact is the more striking since English literature in the preceding centuries had only indirectly expressed national feeling. Much of her literature had been imported from France and was imbued with the French spirit. None the less it is a fact that although the Renaissance and the Reformation beckoned her onwards to new paths, England remained more faithful to the past than did the Continent. This is explained by the increasing influence of the people, later exerted particularly strongly in the theatre; popular taste in literature is for things of the past. This continuity was helped by the growth of an ardent patriotism, at times aggressive and disdainful, which glorified the annals, history, and legends of the nation, her traditions and antiquities. From this patriotism was born the ambition to rival the masterpieces of Greece and Rome, of Italy and France; with an antagonism to any foreign influence which might hinder the growth of the nation's genius. More and more England felt herself —and desired to be—different from the rest of Christendom.

The Beginnings of Humanism (1490–1578). For some thirty years, from 1490 to about 1520 when the religious quarrels began, there blossomed in England a scholarship which, though limited to a few choice spirits, was pure, serene, and full of hope. Drawn to Italy by the desire to learn Greek from the exiles gathered there after the Turks had captured Constantinople in 1453, some young Englishmen, eager to examine the Greek manuscripts saved from destruction, drank deeply of the new learning. Among these English scholars were: William Grocyn (1446?–1519); Thomas Linacre (1460?–1524), physician and scholar; and, above all, John Colet (1467?–1519). They, on their return to England, established so sound a teaching of Greek in Oxford that the famous Erasmus came from the Continent to learn from them. Colet's influence gave a religious bent to the studies of Erasmus and made him devote himself for a time to a reformation which both he and Colet deemed might be accomplished by persuasion, knowledge, and purification of morals, without any break in unity.

But in Erasmus there was a passionate admiration for the thought and form of the Roman and Greek classics; he was also a brilliant wit, as witness his *Moriae encomium* (*The Praise of Folly*), and intimacy with him was to awaken the genius of the only English humanist of the day who possessed the creative gift—Sir Thomas More (1478–1535). More was a noted lawyer and a member of Parliament, when in 1516 he finished his famous *Utopia*, true prologue to the Renaissance. This, unfortunately, was written in Latin. Written in English it might not have brought him European fame, but it would have set him high in the ranks of English literature, in which he now has a place only by virtue of his controversial treatises, his *Dialogue of Comfort*, and his *History of King Richard III*, where the portrait of the tyrant is drawn with a vigour which recalls Tacitus.

The framework of the *Utopia* was suggested by the recent Portuguese and Spanish discoveries. Utopia is an imaginary island set in

PLATE XI

Plan of the island of Utopia from More's *Utopia*, 1518

the newly-explored seas, and inhabited by an ideal people. This fiction, modelled on Plato's *Republic*, gave More an opportunity of expressing his opposition to existing customs and manners. The Utopians are in revolt against the spirit of chivalry; they hate warfare and despise soldiers. Communism is the law of the land; all are workers for only a limited number of hours. Life should be pleasant for all; asceticism is condemned. More relies on the goodness of human nature, and intones a hymn to the glory of the senses which reveal nature's wonders. In Utopia all religions are authorized, and tolerance is the law. Scholasticism is scoffed at, and Greek philosophy preferred to that of Rome. From one end to the other of the book More reverses medieval beliefs. He gives play to his lively and subversive imagination; at times he seems to write against his own deep conviction; for he was himself an ascetic, a fervent Roman Catholic who died heroically, a martyr to his faith. But he was sincere in his fight for the constitution of a society which was not 'a conspiracy of the rich against the poor', and in which cleanliness, comfort, and well-being might be enjoyed by all.

More's English works reveal glimpses of his rich and complex nature, alive to everything, bringing a light-hearted homely vocabulary, a dramatic sense of character, into the driest controversies. Unfortunately, to his English prose he brought neither rule nor measure; his sentences are, at times, interminable. He left to men who were his inferiors the task of shaping English prose.

The Educationists. These educationists are: Sir Thomas Elyot (1490?–1546), author of the *Governour* (1531), a treatise of moral philosophy, imitated from the Italian and full of the spirit of antiquity; Sir John Cheke (1514–57), professor of Greek at Cambridge, who wrote in 1549 *The Heart of Sedition, how grievous it is to a Commonwealth,* a forcible expression of English conservatism, hostile to social change; Sir Thomas Wilson (1525–81), who in his *Arte of Rhetoric* (1553) recommended the use of a pure and simple language, and derided those of his contemporaries who affected 'strange ink-horn terms', 'outlandish English', 'barbarous Anglo-Norman law-phrases', &c.

Standing out more clearly than the preceding is Roger Ascham (1515–68), the most popular of the educationists, and the most entertaining of the group, whether in his *Toxophilus* (1545), in which he tries to keep alive the love of archery and the bow, the national weapon; or in his *Scholemaster*, published in 1570, two years after his death, in which he sets forth his views on the teaching of the classics. A good Protestant, he hated the Rome of his day, papistical and corrupt, as much as he admired the writers of ancient Greece and Rome. His style is penetrated with Latin elegancies and turns of speech. By turns he imitates Cicero's periods and Seneca's nervous conciseness. As a result his English is somewhat stiff and formal; but behind his imitations the man himself is revealed, with his sincerity, good sense, and heartiness. He is one of the earliest among the English 'classical' writers.

These are the better known of the educationists; but in order fully to understand the work then being done, we should add to their number those many unacknowledged, unknown guides who, in school and University, were teaching men to admire and imitate the masterpieces of antiquity.

THE REFORMATION AND RELIGIOUS CONTRO-VERSIES FROM 1525 TO 1578

Translations of the Bible. The Prayer Book. Humanism did not long remain undisturbed. Scarcely had it reached literature when the Reformation crossed and thwarted it. The greater number of the humanists were forced to choose between the Pope and Luther or Calvin. They could no longer follow their own quiet paths to knowledge, but were thrust into the fray. In the year following the publication of Sir Thomas More's *Utopia* Luther nailed his ninety five theses, which opened his battle with the papacy, to the door of the *schlosskirche* at Wittenberg. This changed the course of More's life, which was henceforward devoted to the defence of Catholic unity. The most marked episode of this defence was his controversy with the reformer William Tyndale (1484–1536), the translator of the *New Testament* published at Cologne in 1525. This was followed by Miles Coverdale's translation of the *Old Testament* in 1535. The sacred texts of the Hebrews and those of the early Christians, placed in the hands of all, were to counterbalance the reading of Greek and Latin classics, introducing into English prose the 'biblical dialect' which has tinged so great a part of English literature. What is most striking in these successive translations, and was to be preserved in the authorized translation of 1611, is the adoption of a traditional prose, as far from turgidness as from triviality, simple yet a little archaic, and imaginative, into which have passed, in varying degrees, the beauty of the original texts and a certain magic found especially in Coverdale. Thus was created a type of prose whose influence was unbounded, free to all, instilling into men's minds a sense of holiness, destined to touch with beauty the speech of the rudest and least learned, and to combat the pedantry of scholars. Its effects will be shown most plainly in the seventeenth century.

The translation of the Bible was followed by the compilation in

1549, under Cranmer's direction, of the *Book of Common Prayer* from the Latin missal. Its cadences were to act like poetry on the hearts of believers and to win the admiration of the critical. In it the sonority of the Latin passed into a language which had seemed incapable of assimilating it. The mingling of the Saxon and French elements of the language is perfect. Nothing remains of the harsh abruptness of the pure Saxon. Sunday after Sunday, in every parish church of England, the magnificent phrases were repeated, the rhythm passing from clergyman to worshipper. It may be imagined what an impulse was thus given to a language as yet indefinite, moving uncertainly on its way.

The Dissolution of the Monasteries. Antiquarians and Chroniclers. The dissolution of the monasteries between 1535 and 1539 had also a great effect on national culture. The immediate result was, it is true, the destruction, deplored by the Protestants themselves, of an enormous number of books; the disappearance of numerous schools; and, for a time, a serious diminution in the number of students. But the suppression hastened the end of scholasticism, and brought into the light—to be read and studied —from the seclusion of abbey libraries, such treasures as were saved. The great ardour of the antiquaries dates from this moment. The first in date was John Leland who, in 1533, was appointed to examine the ancient monuments of the country, especially the archives of the cathedrals, colleges, priories, and abbeys; these treasures are catalogued in his *Itinerary*.

Many chronicles, born of the same patriotic impulse, Protestant in spirit, appeared from the middle of the sixteenth century onwards: that of Edward Hall in 1548; that of Raphael Holinshed, a great repertory of national history, used by Spenser and Shakespeare, in 1578–86; that of John Stow in 1580; that of John Speed in 1611. Not one of these chroniclers is a writer of talent, or a reflective historian, but each one is animated by the desire of glorifying the past and present of his native land.

Besides these almost impersonal works, the Reformation contributed to the progress of English prose by bringing religious questions before the people in a vernacular, which, in order to advance the Reformers' cause, had to be strong, clear, and fluent.

One of the most praiseworthy in these respects was William Tyndale, the translator of the Bible, as may be seen in his controversy with Sir Thomas More over this same translation.

Very high, too, are the merits of the preacher Hugh Latimer (1485?–1555), whose vigour and good sense make his sermons some of the most readable prose of the time. His subject was never theology, but morality based on the gospel. Added to his fervour was a genius for vivid illustrations, homely sayings, touches of drollery, apologues striking in their simplicity. He died heroically at the stake under Mary Tudor. With hundreds of other martyrs he is extolled by John Foxe (1516–1587) in his *Acts and Monuments of these latter and perillous Dayes . . . wherein are . . . described the . . . Persecutions . . . by the Romishe Prelates* (1562–3), popularly known as Foxe's *Book of Martyrs*. Written first in Latin, then translated into English by the author, it is a fiercely religious work of stupendous length; and it passed through edition after edition. Shapeless and prejudiced though it may be, its sincerity and enthusiasm for the Reformation, combined with its realistic woodcuts, made it one of the most widely read books after the Bible.

In Scotland: Lyndsay, Buchanan, Knox. In Scotland the Reformation gave rise to a literary movement which showed itself in the verses of Sir David Lyndsay (c. 1490–1555), in the Latin works of George Buchanan (1506–82), and in the treatises of John Knox (1505–72).

Lyndsay was the last of the line of Scottish poets of the fifteenth century. In form he belongs to the Middle Ages, but he is distinguished from his predecessors by his zeal as a social reformer. His attacks on Rome are enclosed in the traditional frames. With prolix liveliness, lacking taste and beauty but with a certain rugged strength, he lashes out at kings and prelates, at their abuses and corruptions. At first his satire was social—we should call him a democrat to-day—but as the years passed it became increasingly protestant. His longest poem is the *Monarchie* (1552), based on a sermon by Knox, written in octosyllables the virulence of which recalls Skelton, but which are distinguished by their even rhythm.

The noted humanist Buchanan wrote almost entirely in Latin,

so that he appears here merely as a cultured Scotsman, in whom the Renaissance and the Reformation met. Celebrated in France, where he was first student, then teacher—one of his pupils being Montaigne—famed for his Latin verses and his tragedies modelled on the classics, from 1560 onwards he became one of the champions of the Reformation in Scotland. First the tutor, then the open enemy, of Mary Queen of Scots, whom, in a violent pamphlet, he indicted for Darnley's murder, he wrote a history of Scotland, also in Latin, and left in the vernacular but two short treatises which are, however, worthy of note.

To John Knox, on the contrary, may be ascribed the honour of being the first great Scottish writer in prose. After a stay with Calvin at Geneva he wrote in 1558 his pamphlet against the Roman Catholic queens of England and Scotland, Mary Tudor and Mary Stuart: *First Blast of the Trumpet against the Monstrous Regiment of Women*. He then returned to Scotland where he tormented and terrified the queen by his audacious preaching. His *History of the Reformation of Religioun within the realme of Scotland* (1564) is not the work of a man of letters but of a man of action who narrates events in which he has himself played a great part. Ill constructed, it is yet full of matter, abounding in passages at once vigorous and picturesque, and enlivened with humour and satire.

In all these men—especially the Scots—something seems to presage a new era, social as well as religious, democratic as well as protestant. The triumph of Presbyterian and Puritan was drawing near. Meanwhile the need of the reformers to reach the people led them all (except Buchanan) to discard Latin for the vernacular, and undeniably they contributed to the progress of that English prose too often disdained by the humanists.

POETRY: WYATT AND SURREY, SACKVILLE, GASCOIGNE

POETRY owed less than prose to the reformers. They held aloof from it as profane and frivolous. Its renewal had its rise in humanism, and especially in the Italian Renaissance. The revival was uphill work: verse had to be drawn from the languor to which it had sunk in Stephen Hawes, and from the disorder in which a Skelton had plunged it; all had to be done anew. Two courtier poets in the days of Henry VIII undertook the task, for which Italy provided both model and stimulus. These two pioneers, whose work was ended by their untimely deaths, were Wyatt and Surrey.

Wyatt. Sir Thomas Wyatt (1503–42), who had stayed in France and Italy, brought back with him from the latter country in 1527 admiration for her lyric poetry and a desire to fashion English verse on the Italian model, or on that of antiquity seen through an Italian medium. His first task was to introduce into English verse dignity, grace, and harmony. Unable to find these qualities in Chaucer, of whose correct pronunciation he was, like his contemporaries, ignorant, he had to build afresh. It is evident from his sonnets how clumsily he moved at first. The first in date is a kind of monster as far as accent and rhythm are concerned; but by degrees Wyatt attained relative smoothness and regularity. He borrowed from Italy forms unknown to England, chief of which was the sonnet, that was to have so high a destiny, to sing so much pain and happiness straight from the heart, unencumbered by fiction or allegory. At the same time Wyatt introduced in his sonnets the new lyric style, rich in images, metaphorical, and subtle, and the impassioned diction of Petrarch and his followers. Truth to say, he is more personal in some of his slighter lyrics, where, instead of sighing and imploring after the fashion of Laura's lover, he turns on the lady with some home truths and declares his freedom. His frank and manly nature is shown best in his satires, based though these are on Horace and Alamanni.

Surrey. The Earl of Surrey (1517?-47), who ended his life on the scaffold when he was only thirty, followed in Wyatt's footprints. The first part of the way was traced for him, he had not painfully to restore the rhythm of verse. Nearly all his extant verse is regular and harmonious. He had not Wyatt's energy and independence, but he is more graceful, more sensitive, more given to elegy and the love of nature; he is, moreover, a finer artist. His sonnet *Of Sardanapalus* . . . is perfect in structure, strong and classical, without precedent in the language. The lines he wrote during his imprisonment in 'proude Windsor', in which he recalls his life there in the past, evoke a brilliant, stirring picture of the life of a young noble.

His metrical innovations are important: he was the first to give to the sonnet its purely English form, less elaborate than the Italian but perhaps more suited to a language with fewer rhymes. This form, which was to be Shakespeare's, was made up of three quatrains with different rhymes, followed by a couplet. But his chief title to fame is his introduction of blank verse in his translation of Books II and IV of Virgil's *Æneid*. This innovation is typical of the Renaissance: who would not blush for rhyme since it was not sanctioned by antiquity? Surrey's blank verse is merely the decasyllabic, or heroic, line without rhyme. Of classical origin, it is scholarly, not popular. Surrey understood that his line should not resemble rhymed verse too closely, and that he should imitate Virgil's breaks and extension of sense from line to line. But he did this too seldom, and without the ease and confidence acquired long afterwards by his imitators. Yet he was possessed of the epic tone, and his metre, such as it is, showed itself better able than the couplet to render the Latin hexameters. Thanks to Surrey English prosody gained a magnificent instrument which, when perfected, was to be the metre for drama as for epic.

The works of Wyatt and Surrey were not published until some years after their deaths. They appeared in 1557 with some inferior verses in the famous collection now known as *Tottel's Miscellany*. Their influence therefore was not immediate; and even after the collection was published a whole generation passed before their initiative was followed.

Sackville. The only poet who has left any memorable verses between Surrey and Spenser is Thomas Sackville (1536–1608), who returned to medieval tradition in his contributions to the *Myrroure for Magistrates* (1563), a continuation of Lydgate's *Falls of Princes*, for which he wrote the *Induction* and *The Complaynt of Henry Duke of Buckingham*. The *Myrroure* is a series of narratives by various writers, each poem relating the 'tragedy' of some great personage in English history. Besides Lydgate, Boccaccio and Chaucer had produced similar compilations. But in the *Myrroure* all the characters are English, a fact which testifies to the patriotism that was leading the English to explore their annals. Otherwise even the best parts of the work, which are Sackville's, show retrogression.

The *Induction* is but a series of allegorical apparitions, but the vigour of the stanzas with their strong scansion was something new. His well-knit lines fall more powerfully than lines had ever fallen before; the language from which, since Chaucer's day, the terminations had almost all disappeared, became in Sackville's hands more nervous, more forceful than in any preceding century. It has been rightly said that Sackville was the link between Chaucer and Spenser.

Gascoigne. Mention may be made of one more poet before Spenser: George Gascoigne (1525?–77), who was remarkable for taking the first steps down the paths newly opened by the Renaissance. He was, in a sense, a pioneer, even if he did not advance very far in any direction. It has been claimed for him that he wrote the first prose tale of modern life, the first prose comedy, the first tragedy translated from the Italian, the first masque, the first satire in blank verse, the first treatise on versification in English. The satire, *The Steele Glas*, is his best-known work. It is a protest against the luxury of the time, an exhortation to return to past simplicity. His blank verse is correct but dull; it has the sound of a hammer striking a wooden anvil.

THE THEATRE FROM 1520 TO 1578

Humanism in the Theatre. No masterpiece was produced during these years, but the English theatrical spirit explored many paths and gained the experience without which Elizabethan drama would have been impossible. The theatre combined the survival of the past with preparation for the future. The miracle plays continued, although viewed with disfavour both by Protestants and humanists. Gradually the pageants lost ground; one by one the cycles of the various towns died away. Theirs was but a prolongation of existence; they did not change, but remained in the form they had assumed in the fifteenth century. Their interest for us lies in the fact that they had still a large public, and that innovations grew up by their side without at once supplanting them.

The moralities, on the other hand, not only continued to be appreciated, but were modified according to circumstances. Those which were produced before about 1520 were merely Christian; they might be described as 'without place or date'. Then they became impregnated with the spirit either of the Reformation or of the Renaissance. Two distinct groups appeared, according as the lesson taught was humanist or protestant.

Skelton's morality *Magnyfycence*, written about 1516, is the first example of a secular morality; its apparent object was not to combat impiety, but to give Henry VIII, in the form of an allegory, a lesson in wisdom and a warning against extravagance.

But the influence of the Renaissance appears more clearly in *The Four Elements* (1519), and the play of *Wyt and Science* (towards 1540). These are not inspired by religion or by ordinary morality, but by the desire for knowledge. They were obviously born in educational circles, which view knowledge as the ideal goal and look upon ignorance as the devil. The first was written under the impression made by the narratives of Amerigo Vespucci, and is full of allusions to the recent discoveries. Theology is set aside: God can be known only by His works, by the study of Nature.

The second is remarkable for the rationalistic convictions which animate it from one end to the other. The comic element is provided by an episode in which Ignorance stumbles through his alphabet to his mother Idleness. She, who represents the old sleepy methods of teaching, is no less ridiculous than her foolish pupil.

The Reformation on the Stage. The Reformation early sought to use the moralities for her own ends; and the attempt was made simultaneously in Scotland and England. Sir David Lyndsay's *Satyre of the Three Estatis*, acted before the king of Scotland in 1540, is both political and religious. The three estates—Clergy, Nobles, and Burghers—are pilloried together. They are led respectively by Sensuality, Oppression, and Falsehood; and the people, in the person of 'John the Commoun Weill', have many weighty grievances against them. But the chief attack is directed against popish ecclesiastics. These last, on the appearance of Veritie, carrying a New Testament, turn on her in anger and threaten her with the stake. An episode shows us Pauper, stripped, fragment by fragment, of his little all, at the deaths of his father, his mother, and his wife, by his landlord, his vicar, and the vicar's clerk.

In England the same virulence was shown by John Bale, bishop of Ossory (1495–1563), who tried to turn the miracle plays themselves to Protestant uses, and embodied his teaching in moralities mixed with history, such as *Super utroque Regis conjugio* (*The two marriages of Henry VIII*), and *Proditiones Papistarum* (*The treachery of Papists*). The most interesting of his dramatic attempts is his allegory on John Lackland, *Kyng Johan*, in which he recasts history to his liking. In his hands the wretched sovereign becomes a great king, hated and slandered by the church because he had dared to turn against Rome. Here historical drama is seen emerging from the morality as from the opening chrysalis. It is history travestied, but it is history; and Bale's morality often anticipates Shakespeare's *King John*.

Heywood's Interludes. Although John Heywood (1497?–1580?) was a devout Catholic and a friend of Sir Thomas More, the works he wrote under Henry VIII are not controversial. His was the spirit of the *fabliaux* of the Middle Ages, in which, without thought of rebellion against dogma and discipline, the clergy were often derided. His originality consists in the fact that he avoids moralizing and aims only at amusement. His *Interludes* are comic dialogues, or slight jesting scenes, based as a rule on French originals. The best known is *The Four P's*, which is a dispute which of the four 'P's', i.e. Palmer, Pardoner, 'Pothecary, and Pedlar, can tell the biggest lie. The Palmer declares that in all his travels throughout Christendom, in which he has seen some five hundred thousand women, he has never once seen any one woman out of patience. He wins with ease. There is no plot, but the liveliness of the disputants recalls Chaucer. If Heywood also wrote *A Merry Play between the Pardoner and the Frere, the Curate and neybour Pratte*, and *A playe between Johan Johan the husbonde, Tyb the wyfe, and Sir Jhān the preste*, true farces in which the incidents are conventional but the action full of life and humour, he showed a keen sense of stage-craft.

Progress of the Drama after 1550. Influence of the classics. Comedy. Not until after 1550 did the influence of the classics make itself felt; in comedy first, and, as was natural, in a scholastic circle. The first comedy written in accordance with the rules of antiquity was *Ralph Roister Doister*, produced towards 1553 by Nicolas Udall (1505–56), who was successively headmaster of Eton and Westminster. Instead of making his scholars at Westminster act Plautus, Udall wrote for them an English comedy in five acts, in which some of the characters were borrowed from the classics, but others were taken from English life. Ralph himself is reminiscent of the bravos of Plautus; like them he is braggart, fool, and coxcomb. Matthew Merygreke is inspired by the 'parasite' of classical comedy. But Dame Custance (Constance), courted by Ralph, is a loyal English matron and her attendants, the one old, the other young, are real English servants drawn with life and gaiety. If Udall has a moral design—to satirize boasters—his chief aim is to amuse. 'Mirth', he says, 'prolongeth life and causeth health.' Although he has only produced a farce on a classic model, he has built up his plot without sacrificing gaiety. His verse is still forced and stiff, but his language has raciness.

There is yet more liveliness in a comedy acted about the same time at Christ's College, Cambridge, which owes to antiquity only its regular construction and its division into acts; in characterization it is wholly English and rustic. This is *Gammer Gurton's Needle*, written by a Master of Arts of the University. Mother Gurton loses her needle ('fayre longe strayghte neele that was myne onely treasure') while mending the breeches of her man Hodge. Diccon, a ne'er-do-well, tells her that her neighbour Dame Chat has stolen it. Then follow quarrels, recriminations, and cross-purposes—the whole village is turned upside down. The curate intervenes, and Diccon takes advantage of the confusion to steal a ham. At last all is discovered. Hodge gives a cry—the needle was in his breeches! The play is not refined, but the dialogue is full of life; the rhymed lines—more nimble than those of Udall—are well-suited to comedy; there is no borrowing from antiquity to mar the realism; and there is a drinking-song (*Back and side go bare* . . .) which can scarcely be surpassed.

Tragedy. Farcical comedies, however, even when cut out after a classical pattern, could not contribute much to the progress of the theatre. Their only novelty lay in the separation of laughter from gravity, which, in the miracle plays, was intermingled with it. National drama and the drama of antiquity met fully for the first time in tragedy. The first English dramatists, like those of France and Italy, took for their model not the Greek tragedians, but Seneca: a dangerous model, for Seneca's tragedies were oratorical, fitter to be declaimed than acted. He eschewed dramatic movement; his tragedies abounded in monologues, with no action. His imitators borrowed from him certain machinery, such as the Chorus, or the Ghost, charged with the explanation of the play. Above all they seem to have been struck with the atrocity of his subjects, associating the idea of tragedy with monstrous crimes, such as the feast of Atreus in *Thyestes*, in which a father is made to eat his children's flesh.

In 1562 a tragedy after the manner of Seneca: *Gorboduc, or Ferrex and Porrex*, was acted at the Inns of Court; the joint authors were two lawyers and members of Parliament: Thomas Sackville, author of the *Induction* in the *Myrroure for Magistrates*, and Thomas Norton, who wrote three of the five acts. Seneca's influence is shown by its sustained gravity and loftiness of style;

in the almost abstract quality of the scenes, where all is told
by messenger and confidant; in the long speeches as well as in
the sanguinary character of the plot. Gorboduc abdicates in
favour of his two sons, Ferrex and Porrex. These two princes
soon fall to dissension—as did Eteocles and Polyneices—and the
younger kills the elder. The queen, who more dearly loved the
elder, having killed his brother in revenge, the indignant people
rise in rebellion and murder both king and queen. Then follows
civil war, anarchy, usurpation, and the death of the usurper.

Despite this accumulation of crimes the piece is cold, lacking in
movement and dramatic feeling. The authors found it easier to
express ideas than to create character. Moved by patriotism, they
wished to depict the misfortunes of a kingdom where the succession was uncertain, a subject which preoccupied the minds of politicians in Elizabeth's reign. This tragedy was Seneca transformed
by lawyers and members of Parliament; but it is the first of a great
lineage, and, in spite of many defects, maintains a high artistic
level. It introduced to the English stage the sense of fatality, and
was the first to be written in the blank verse which reveals the
influence of antiquity. Its lines lack the suppleness which the
action demands, but they achieve strength and dignity.

Formation of a National Theatre. Many other influences were
at work besides those of antiquity. Even under Henry VIII the
famous Spanish *Celestina*, a work at once domestic and dramatic,
drew forth an English imitation. The theatre of Dutch neo-Latin-
ists gave rise to educative plays which may be classed under
the heading 'Prodigal Son group', such as the *Misogonus* (1560)
of Thomas Richards, and Gascoigne's *The Glasse of Government*
(1575). Gascoigne adapted in *The Supposes* a comedy of Ariosto;
an unknown author in *The Bugbears* (1561) adapted another
Italian comedy. From Italy again came several other plays of
which the names alone remain.

The foundation of a truly national theatre was helped by the
formation of companies of professional players. These were at
first 'poor player men', harried by the authorities, apt to be
numbered, if found wandering, with 'Roges' and 'Vacaboundes'.
Their most effective way to avoid this imputation was to place

themselves under the patronage of some powerful nobleman. The first company to obtain the Royal grant of a patent was that of the earl of Leicester in 1574. The performances took place at first in the inn-yards, but in 1576 the first theatre was built, outside the City boundaries, somewhere in Shoreditch.

As the result of the various elements enumerated there appeared between 1550 and 1578 certain plays which were really English, and the forerunners of the higher drama yet to come. Certain of these, such as *Appius and Virginia* (date unknown), John Pikeryng's *A newe Enterlude of Vice, conteyninge the History of Horestes* ... (1567?), are very like moralities; like Bale's *King John* their characters are in part abstractions and in part historical beings.

The most interesting in this respect is the *Cambyses* (1569) attributed to Thomas Preston, fellow of King's College, Cambridge. In form it is a true Shakespearian historical play, the narrative of Herodotus being followed faithfully and merely divided into scenes. The acts of Cambyses are shown in all their variety and incoherence. To enliven matters there are breaks in the drama for scenes of buffoonery, where the chief role is played by the Vice, Ambidexter, a cynical personage who, like Iago, delights in the evil of which he is a witness and in the crimes of which he is the instigator. Horrible punishments are shown on the stage; pathos is exaggerated until it becomes lachrymose—anything was admitted that might draw tears. Yet there is a scene in a flowery garden when a breath of fresh air blows through the ranting melodrama. The play lacks but two things—style and genius. Preston wrote so clumsily and with such ridiculous bombast that his play, for long popular, became the laughing-stock of his successors.

The theatre still needed an appropriate metre (for none had followed the example of *Gorboduc*); or, in default of this, the abandonment of verse for prose. This need is apparent even in plays far superior to *Cambyses*, such as the *Damon and Pythias* (1564) of Richard Edwards, or the *Promos and Cassandra* (1578) of Whetstone, from which Shakespeare was to take the story of *Measure for Measure*. Except for this, the formula for the national theatre was found; the experimental period was over; the great works were drawing near.

FLOWERING OF THE RENAISSANCE 1578–1625

General Characteristics of the Great Period. Original though the great period of the English Renaissance—often somewhat inaccurately called the Elizabethan Age—may be, it had its rise in a multitude of ancient or foreign influences. It was a fertile soil enriched by a thick layer of translations. By 1579 many of the great Classics, both ancient and modern, had been translated into English ; nearly all by 1603, the end of Elizabeth's reign. There were, however, certain surprising exceptions. There was no translation of Plato, although his philosophy was one of the chief sources of inspiration ; nothing from the Greek tragedians, in spite of the passion for the stage ; and only one comedy of Plautus. The *Il Principe* of Machiavelli, the influence of which was then considérable, found no translator, nor did the satirical epic of Rabelais. Nearly everything else was placed at the service of the reader who knew none but his mother tongue ; and many translations enjoyed as great a popularity as if they had been original works. This was true of Plutarch's *Lives*, translated by Sir Thomas North (1535–1601) from the French of Amyot ; and with John Florio's translation of Montaigne's *Essais*. No less popular were the translations in verse ; notably Ovid's *Metamorphoses* by Arthur Golding (*c.* 1536–1605), completed in 1567 ; Sir John Harington's Ariosto—*Orlando Furioso in English Heroical Verse* (1591) ; Tasso's *Gerusalemme Liberata* translated by Richard Carew in 1594, by Edward Fairfax in 1600. But nothing equalled the popularity enjoyed by the *Semaine* of du Bartas, translated by Sylvester between 1590 and 1606, and the *Iliad* turned into 'fourteeners' by George Chapman between 1598 and 1609. These innumerable exercises helped to make supple the prose and verse of English writers as well as to enrich the minds of the people.

Among outside influences that of Italy predominated, although those of France and Spain were considerable. Italy gave the keynote to the new culture, and the Elizabethan courtiers found the principles of refinement in the *Cortegiano* of Castiglione, translated by Thomas Hoby in 1561. The development of the theatre and of the English novel owes much to the stories related by the *Novellieri*, those lively dramatic tales of Boccaccio, Cinthio, Bandello, Straparola, and others. It is difficult to imagine on what the English stage would have been nourished without these narratives, tragic and humorous, often sensual, treating of pleasure, love, violence, tears, and blood; of which so many were translated in various collections between 1567 and 1587.

The encounter of the English with the Italian spirit—which had already enriched Chaucer's poetry—brought to the England of the end of the sixteenth century an added splendour. But by that time the English character had become set in a mould too distinctive and too insular to be a mere reflection of foreign genius. Although the nation was not yet wholly permeated by the Reformation, under its influence a reaction had set in against the country which was the seat of the Papacy, and in which the Renaissance had developed into a sensuality which seemed to threaten a return to paganism. By the second half of the century the question of Italianism had thus become two-sided: against the attraction of Italy's art must be set the new perils which endangered her admirers. Even when depraved, an Englishman felt that he was different from an Italian. Italy, which aroused his passions, became for him by degrees a land of debauch, of crime and poison, of Machiavellianism; a kind of Utopia of dissoluteness. So the very Italianism of the time contains both action and reaction. Finally, Italy, after serving the Englishman both as stimulus and model, came to be for him the antithesis of his national character, which was the more clearly defined by the contrast.

England's guiding force from 1578 to 1625 was not religion but patriotism. To this patriotism all else—even religion—was subservient. To the majority, the Protestantism which was soon to triumph was no more than freedom from foreign influence, and might be summed up as the rejection of papal supremacy. They desired a Christianity which was insular, and sought to monopolize God. The extreme formula of this religious egoism is enunciated by Lyly when, in 1580, he writes 'the living God is only the English God'. He was, moreover, a God who, for many people, limited His requirements to patriotism. Except for a group, small as yet, of Puritans with unquiet consciences, whose energy was applied chiefly to their own salvation, the multitude thrust aside care and austerity and gave themselves up to the joy of living. England was still 'merry England', more eager for plays and pastimes than for practices of devotion, and was reaching forth to that full and free development of every faculty which is the very essence of the Renaissance. The intellectual paganism of the humanists was very largely supported by the instinctive paganism of the multitude.

In this religious tepidity letters had their spring and the Renaissance flowered. To the delayed success of the profound and far-reaching Reformation is due the drama which is England's most magnificent literary title, as well as much of the poetry which was her glory under Elizabeth and James I. The starting-point of this love of letters was the same patriotism which drove England forward to claim the first place in every field of action. She had nearly a century to make up in voyages and discoveries. Yet in one bound she sought to catch up her rivals—Spain, Portugal, and France—to reach and to surpass them. The spirit of imperialism was born. Drake accomplished his voyage of circumnavigation in 1578. Richard Hakluyt celebrated in 1589 the English *Navigations*. In 1588 English seamen destroyed the Invincible Armada. All hearts swelled with confidence and pride.

Literature was moved by the same spirit of conquest and self-praise. England began to reckon up her written works and blushed to find herself poor compared with France, wretched by the side of Italy, humbled before the superiority of the ancients. Yet she, the last comer, was proudly determined to rank with the first, spurred forward by a belief—gradually instilled into her by the Renaissance—in the greatness of letters, particularly of poetry.

On the pediment of her great period was inscribed the definition which, in his *Apologie for Poetrie*, Sidney gives of the poet—'of all sciences . . . the monarch'. And, in his *Shepheardes Calender*, Spenser describes poetry as 'no arte, but a divine gift and heavenly instinct not to bee gotten by laboure and learning, but adorned with both: and poured into the witte by a certaine *enthousiasmos* and celestiall inspiration'. This Platonic philosophy is present everywhere in the Renaissance, but it seems to have penetrated more deeply than elsewhere into the spirit of English poetry. Belief in the necessity for this 'enthusiasm' —the Greek word is translated in many ways, this in itself being a proof of the universal holding of this article of faith— is almost the only dogma. It is this 'enthusiasm' which Shakespeare calls 'fine frenzy', and Drayton (praising Marlowe) 'fine madness', and (praising Shakespeare) 'a clear rage'. Those only are poets whom this *daimon* inspires. Drayton requires of the poet that he shall see 'brave translunary things', and disdainfully bids Samuel Daniel return to prose because of his temperate serenity. Exaltation is required from the candidate for poetical honours. This faith stirred the writers to pride and independence; transformed their innumerable thefts into noble spoils captured from the enemy; and inspired more than one to set at naught tyrannical rules of grammar and versification and attempt new styles and manners. From the whole emerges an impression of intrepidity. In spite of an avowed respect for precedent and in spite of fleeting fashions which, for a while, codified oddness and eccentricity, a wide initiative was left to every poet.

THE LEADERS: LYLY, SIDNEY, AND SPENSER

THE usual distinction between prose and poetry must be laid aside for a time in order to group together the three men who, although furnished with unequal resources, all helped to initiate, towards 1578, the cult of beauty. At the moment poetry penetrated everywhere; the very prose of romances like *Euphues* and the *Arcadia* is poetic. Lyly (with the exception of his dramatic work), Sidney, and Spenser must be presented together.

John Lyly. John Lyly (1554?–1606) was one of the first of those who sought consciously for an artistic style and whose chief desire was to say a thing well. Indeed, it may be doubted whether he had any clearer aim. So opportunely did he reply to the desire of his countrymen for 'finer speech than their language will allow', that his curious way of writing, mannered and affected, set the fashion not only at the Court but almost throughout literature for the next dozen years.

In 1579, at the age of 24, he published his famous romance *Euphues, the Anatomy of Wit*, which contains much moralizing and many attacks upon irreligion and immorality. Its subject was the adventures of a young man (Euphues), well-endowed by nature but not disciplined by education, who, ensnared by the world and the love of a coquette, becomes false to his friend. Withdrawn from Court, an exile saddened by experience, he indites from his cell a warning against women and an exhortation to reform the principles of education.

Nominally, Euphues is a young Athenian, and Naples is the town of temptation. But beneath the disguise is an Oxford undergraduate corrupted by the Italianate society of London. The book was a satire on England, and provoked protests from the Universities and from the ruffled ladies. Of this Lyly recked little. He cared far more for his style than for his matter, and published in 1580 *Euphues and his England*, in which he lavished praises on his country, his queen, the universities, and English women. Although both books contain wit and realism it was not the matter which charmed his contemporaries so much as the mannered graces of his style, which became known as 'euphuism'.

Euphuism is formed of two distinct elements. The first is the principle of symmetry and counterpoise in the prose, emphasized by the use of alliteration in such words as are antithetical. This alliteration is sometimes direct and sometimes crossed, as in 'The *h*ot *l*iver of a *h*eedless *l*over', or 'Let my *r*ude *b*irth excuse my *b*old *r*equest'. A prose thus fashioned becomes almost as intricate as verse. The exaggeration is obvious, but the innovation was useful at a time when it was necessary to give shape to formlessness and art to what was inartistic.

The other element of euphuism belongs more particularly to Lyly. He wished to ornament his style, and how could he do this better than by simile and comparison? He was familiar with books but not with nature. He therefore decorated his prose with similes from mythology and from the natural history of the bestiaries, herbals, and lapidaries dear to medieval minds. They were rich in a fabulous fauna and flora—valuable as subjects for old tapestries —which seemed to him exactly fitted to illuminate his pages. He was seeking not truth but ornament, and since he writes as a moralist the discordance between subject and matter is the more striking. But what may jar to-day was then delightful, and he had his hour of fame.

Lyly is a curiosity of literary history; but the fame of his two great contemporaries—Sidney and Spenser—shines untarnished.

Sidney. Sir Philip Sidney (1554–86) is renowned equally for his person and his writings. He was, in his lifetime, the finished type of the perfect knight, of the scholar-courtier, as defined by Castiglione. But not until several years after his heroic death, when his works were published, did he receive the praise due to him as novelist and poet.

His *Arcadia*, written about 1580 to while away a temporary exile from court and to please his sister the Countess of Pembroke—a romance in which he gave the rein to his fantastic imagination— inculcated a taste for jewels, real and false, which was to last a lifetime after its publication in 1590. It is influenced by the Spanish romance of Montemayor, *Diana*, and has the same mingling of the pastoral and the heroic. The peculiarities of the two styles are combined in passionately romantic stories. The book is a pastoral in so far as the scene is laid in the ideal Arcadia, whose king, Basilius, has retired into the country, where he brings up as shepherdesses his two daughters Pamela and Philoclea. But it is chiefly a romance of chivalry and love, for the peace of the fair land is broken by sanguinary wars. Passion is introduced with the advent of two shipwrecked princes, Musidorus and Pyrocles, who, after strange trials and terrible combats, are united to the two daughters of Basilius.

This is the main theme, but in it are interwoven numerous episodes which break the thread of the narrative. Into the framework of his romance Sidney pours his own thoughts on morality and politics, and on life as he has observed it. Humour is mixed with tragedy. He paints his villains as black as his heroes are flawless, and his heroines are endowed with every virtue. That which chiefly distinguishes the *Arcadia* is its style. This is a curious blend of merits and defects, characterized not by euphuism but by what modern criticism condemns as the 'pathetic fallacy'. Sidney endows with life and will and feeling abstractions and inanimate matter: 'The Ladies . . . drank a little of their cool wine, which seemed to laugh for joy to come to such lips'; blood-stained armour blushes because it had defended its master no better. When ladies come from bathing the water 'by some drops seemed to weep' that it should pass from their bodies. The princesses cover 'their dainty beauties with the glad clothes'; and when they disrobe they impoverish 'their clothes to enrich their bed', and so on. One might dive indefinitely into this sea of preciosity, and bring up pearls either flawed or lustrous, each one testifying to a love of beauty which impresses even when it is lost in excess. Moreover Sidney often achieves nervous vigour by use of bold new combinations of words. His metaphor is abrupt and elliptic. The germ of Shakespeare's energy of style is found in the *Arcadia*, as well as of Shakespearian preciosity. Two brothers dying of their wounds are described as 'each bewailing the other and more dying in the other than himself'. Of Pamela he says that 'she could no longer keep love from looking out through her eyes and going forth in her words'. A lover pities his ears because they would 'never hear the music of music' of his mistress's voice.

But Sidney's real innovation lay, like Spenser's, in the sharpening of his senses by the contemplation of plastic art. He shows a sense of line and colour, of the effects of light and shade, until then unknown in English. He had visited Italy, he had had his portrait painted by Veronese, and had no doubt seen Titian's studio; he had talked with artists and art-critics. Hence he delighted to analyse, and comment on, the intentions of painter and sculptor; and, by the close detail of his own portraits, the precision with which he drew expression and gesture, and noted the correspondence between attitude and feeling, he has enriched the descriptive art of his country.

It needed the constraint of a narrow frame to discipline his exuberant fancy, and the spur of an overmastering passion to turn him from intricate prettiness of style. Passion came when the daughter of the Earl of Essex, Penelope Devereux, whom he might have won when she was a girl, became the wife of Lord Rich. Then, too late, Sidney discovered that he loved her. The bitter sorrow for lost happiness; the unconquerable longing to possess his love; the despair into which he was flung at first through her coldness; the dawning hope when she confessed her own love, although withdrawing from his pursuit; the struggle between honour and passion —all is set forth in *Astrophel and Stella*. For the expression of his love-song he had recourse—as did Petrarch—to the sonnet, neglected in England since the days of Surrey; and, in the straitness of its fourteen lines, he set each movement of his heart and each incident of his love. She is Stella, his star; and he Astrophel, the lover of the star.

He condemned poetic convention and all affectation, although he did not shake himself free altogether, and some of his sonnets are reminiscent of the past. It is true, also, that his terseness is often obscure and his lines when vigorous lack fluidity; but he abounds in expressions both forceful and new, and more than once he attains to sincere and perfect beauty. This is especially true of the songs which follow the sonnets, of which the fourth is a strange and plaintive elegy, and the eighth is the most passionately personal poem in Elizabethan literature.

As will be seen later, the author of the *Arcadia* and of *Astrophel* was also the champion of poetry, and the first, both in date and merit, of the literary critics of his time. His eloquent plea for letters, the *Apologie for Poetrie*, written in fine straightforward prose, without any of the affectation of his *Arcadia*, must also be remembered in order to understand the loss suffered by English literature when, at the age of 32, he met a hero's death.

Spenser (1552?–99). Sidney's works were not published until after his death. Edmund Spenser, therefore, was the first to reveal poetic beauty to his generation. To the England of 1579, belated, humiliated by seeing the Renaissance flower on the Continent while she remained almost barren, the appearance of his *Shepheardes Calender* inaugurated the period of self-confidence and high hope. Spenser was first master of that language whose 'numbers flow as fast as spring doth ryse'. English verse, no longer rebellious, seemed the natural music of his voice; difficulty with the language existed not for him.

He had from the beginning a patriotic ideal similar to that of the French *Pléiade*. The translator and admirer of du Bellay, he aspired to rouse the national muse from languor and make her equal to the highest. But if he turned for his patterns to antiquity and the Continent, he also, unlike the *Pléiade*, based his faith on the former poets of his own land. Chaucer is his revered master— the 'well of English undefyled'; and when he first began to write he took him, he says, as his model. If the contrast between their temperaments is so great that Spenser could resemble him in no other way, at least he became penetrated with his master's language. Instead of breaking with the nation's past, he wished to thrust his roots yet more deeply in the soil. It is true that at first he used his archaism to clothe a form which belonged to the Renaissance, that of the pastoral. It was then the fashion to disguise all characters as shepherds in an amiable and artificial allegory, in which they were either lovers breathing out their joys and woes, or, by a traditional metaphor, priests or pastors whose sheep were their parishioners. In *The Shepheardes Calender* (1579) Spenser united his humanism to his love of the land. There is little that is new in his theme, but he poured into his work much of himself as rejected lover, and as an aspirant, for a time, to the priesthood, indignant at the lack of zeal—and even the simony—of the clergy. He succeeded in making of his imitative 'aeglogues' a national song by his use of the old, racy terms gathered from dead English poets and from the living countryside. He was therefore able to imitate closely Theocritus, Bion, and Virgil, or, more frequently, Mantuan and Marot, without being a mere reflection of any ancient or modern writer.

The merits of the poem are those of style, and, for their time, they are marvellous. Here at last was a poet whose work showed neither negligence nor effort; the pure and tranquil flow of whose phrases gave unalloyed delight. Study of his versification doubles the impression left by his art. Never yet had English poetry seen, never again will she see, a poem in which the union of line and metre is at once so new, so varied, and so rich. Here are lines of every length, in stanzas nearly each one of which is different. Better still, the lines are alternately measured and syllabic, or merely accentual. Popular versification alternates with artistic. And it contains songs of joy or sadness the strophes of which are the poet's own creation. To these merits must be added that of structure. Spenser grouped his twelve eclogues—corresponding to the twelve months of the year—in an harmonious whole, in which consonance and dissonance, purposely blended, gave variety in unity.

About the same time as the *Shepheardes Calender* he wrote *Hymnes in honour of Love and Beautie*, which were an expression of his artist's philosophy, at once idealistic and sensuous, attracted by all beauty, torn between love for woman and a desire of virtue; tossed between paganism and Christianity, between the Renaissance and the Reformation. In order to conciliate the sensuous and the ascetic he sought inspiration from Plato, who identified supreme beauty with sovereign good. With ardent eloquence he embodies in magnificent lines the thought of the Greek philosopher as interpreted by the Italian Platonists: beauty is goodness made visible—'For all that faire is, is by nature good'. To love beauty is thus to fulfil the law.

But within this idealist there dwelt, as often happens, a malcontent. Reality was so far from his dreams! Therefore in Spenser is found also a vehement and bitter satirist. He is a morose judge of contemporary society, which he attacks in his *Mother Hubberd's Tale*, written about the same time as the *Hymns*. It is, in the form of a fable, a denunciation of the intrigues of the court, of clerical inertia, of the fall of chivalry, and, especially, of the great neglect of the arts and letters. Already he concentrates his satire on the Lord High Treasurer Burghley, Elizabeth's favourite councillor and the parsimonious dispenser of her favours and pensions.

The same condemnation of the age is repeated in the *Complaints*, *containing sundrie small Poems of the World's Vanitie* (1591), where, by the side of Virgil's *Gnat*, and the *Visions* of Petrarch and du Bellay, are several personal poems: *The Ruines of Time, The Teares of the Muses, Muiopotmos, or the Fate of the Butterflie*. As a whole the collection is gloomy. The poet's pessimism is caused by the disappearance of noble souls and the triumph of baser natures. The Muses find nothing now to praise in this degenerate time. Favour is shown only to low rhymers with 'dunghill thoughts'. In drama is found only 'scoffing Scurrilitie, And scornful Follie...'. In this sombre series *Muiopotmos* stands somewhat apart; it is a graceful fable in which the poet employs the symbol of the butterfly flitting from flower to flower, to express his own voluptuous nature, before showing the brilliant insect caught in the web of a horrible spider, the fatal enemy in this world of all poetry and love.

Among the poetic forms whose decline is lamented by Spenser is the pastoral, the groves of which are deserted, he says, except by himself. It is in the form of a pastoral that, in his elegy *Astrophel*, Spenser laments the death of Sir Philip Sidney. Yet another pastoral is the *Colin Clout's Come Home again*, in which he describes his stay in London in 1589, after an exile of nearly ten years as an official in Ireland. He is the shepherd Colin Clout, brought by the 'shepheard of the Ocean' (Sir Walter Raleigh) to be presented at the court of the great shepherdess Cynthia (the Queen). All at first was enchanting: Colin was praised and entertained, his poems read and admired; the future seemed full of promise. But soon, forgotten, forced to sue in vain, heartsick at the intrigues and debauchery of which he was a witness, he went back to his fellow shepherds. In other words, Spenser, seeing no chance of advancing his fortunes, returned to Ireland. The end of the pastoral contradicts the beginning: the court is represented first as the temple of virtue, and then as the home of vice, and testifies to the changing humour of the poet, with his moods of enthusiasm and bitterness.

Fortune smiled on him anew on his return to Ireland, for he met there Elizabeth Boyle, whom he married in 1594—a second marriage, for it is now known that he had contracted a former union in 1579. He describes his wooing in a series of sonnets, the *Amoretti*, the most famous, with those of Sidney and Shakespeare, of the Elizabethan sonnets. They are, moreover, chaste and pure, whereas usually the sonnet was used as the expression of an irregular and troubled passion. In them is seen at its best that quality in Spenser which Coleridge excellently terms 'maidenliness'. The finest are those in which he describes the virginal coyness of his beloved. Even more beautiful than the sonnets is the *Epithalamion* which concludes them, and which surpasses in fulness and splendour all compositions of the same nature. It is the commemoration, in vast strophes, of every separate hour in the day from which he awaits all happiness; each strophe frames one of the rites or one of the moments of the nuptial ceremony. A blend of mythological memories and of realistic notations, this great Ode is at once Spenser's most perfect work and the lyrical triumph of the English Renaissance.

For the marriage of another than himself he wrote a harmonious *Prothalamion* (1596), and added to his two youthful hymns two other hymns to celestial love and celestial beauty, to serve as antidotes to the too earthly ardours of the earlier ones.

Even without *The Faerie Queene* Spenser's poems are sufficient of themselves to place him in the forefront of Elizabethan poets. Yet his masterpiece is this same *Faerie Queene*, over which he spent twenty years of his life, and which he did not live to finish. It was his life's ambition and it was the pride of his countrymen, who, from the appearance of the first books in 1591, confidently opposed it to all other epics, ancient or modern.

Its renown, however, is entirely insular, for the whole of it has never been translated. This is not because its subject relates to England and England's glory, for most epics are strictly national. But its complexity and profusion of allegory have discouraged readers, even among his fellow countrymen, most of whom admire him, as in duty bound, but leave him unread. They are deterred from exploring its beauty by the (to them) forbidding letter to Raleigh in which Spenser explains the moral design of his book. It was to be at once an edifying treatise and a sort of double or triple symbol, decipherable only by the initiated. His object was 'to fashion a gentleman by a virtuous and noble discipline'. The characters in the poem are types of virtues and vices. Spenser has, quite innocently, deceived himself and misled his public. It did not occur to him that he was giving the world a book of magnificent pictures; he assumed a preacher's garb which he had to drop before the end. The word-painter, the maker of magical music, posed as a moralist. This misunderstanding would have been avoided had he kept to his original title, one which, better than any other, expresses the nature of his work—a succession of *Pageants*, i.e. of decorative pictures, rhythmical processions, and brave spectacles, such as Elizabethans loved.

In the two first books Spenser, it is true, carries out fairly well his plan of edification; the allegory is continuous and the moral clear. But both fall away in the books that followed; in these, romance predominates. No longer does Spenser soar above his chief model Ariosto, but walks level with him. Moreover he excels neither as allegorist nor as romancer; but as pageant-maker he is incomparable. He lacks the simplicity necessary to a successful allegorist; he has not the dominating central idea, nor the ardour, nor the unity of design necessary for a strong and effective allegory. In place of unity is complication. Each character is created to serve several ends—moral and historical. His King Arthur, in love with the *Faerie Queene* (Elizabeth), is 'magnificence' (according to

Aristotle the prime virtue which enfolds all others) ; he also typifies divine grace; again, he is also the Earl of Leicester, Elizabeth's favourite. At times the reader wanders and is lost if he attempts to understand and interpret clearly; he is reassured only with the thought that to understand is unnecessary; it is enough to see.

The same weakness occurs in the romance, which is intermittent and shines out but fitfully. The poet is hindered from creating living people by his allegory, which requires of him pale abstractions. Britomart is the only one of his heroines who is really, in parts, a living woman. She has been described as another Bradamante, and she bears indeed too close a resemblance to the warlike heroine of *Orlando Furioso* for Spenser to have the entire honour of her creation.

The Faerie Queene is, in fact, a gallery of pictures; and Spenser is a great painter who never handled a brush. Fate set him in a country where the plastic arts were not to flourish for another two centuries. If he had been born in Italy he might have been another Titian, a second Veronese; born in Flanders he might have forestalled Rubens or Rembrandt. Fate made him a word-painter —perhaps the most marvellous that the world has known. Simultaneously through him and through Sidney there awoke in English literature the desire to rival painting. It is as evident in the *Arcadia* as in *The Faerie Queene*. In this last we find, besides numerous descriptions of tapestries and pictures, a crowd of portraits, charming or grotesque, which are masterpieces of painting; large frescoes also such as that of the wedding of the Thames and Medway, everywhere striking effects of light and shade. But immobility alone does not content him ; often he models his art on the pageants, or on the pantomimes, with their expressive gestures, enjoyed by his contemporaries. Yet again he borrows from the masque— ancestor of the opera—then very popular. *The Faerie Queene* might be said to have perpetuated in a descriptive poem the masques of the Renaissance, preserving and reviving the enchantment of such spectacles. The masque, with the help of such old romances as the *Morte d'Arthur*, provided the frame within which Spenser's imagination plays, the faery land in which his many visions move. Composed of unrelated elements, the poem has one unity—the atmosphere. Everything is bathed in this atmosphere, phantasmal, moony; here gloom and whiteness fall in strange deep contrast; here wonders are no wonders, but native to the land.

The reverie induced by his poem required, like the masque, uninterrupted music to lull the soul and bring about belief in unreality. The illusion is accomplished by means of the powerful and monotonous harmony of the nine-line stanza which he used, and which has since borne his name. The fact that the entire poem is written in this one measure is important. We hear a slow music whose ceaseless return rocks the mind, lifting it little by little away out of this world into another, a world of order and harmony, of which this stanza seems the natural rhythm.

The great painter was a no less great musician.

XII

POETRY FROM 1590 TO 1625

I. *Under Elizabeth*, 1590–1603

LYLY, Sidney, and Spenser wrote either for or at the Court. So also did Edward de Vere, Earl of Oxford (1550–1604), the Italianate courtier who was Sidney's enemy; Fulke Greville, Lord Brooke (1554–1628), who was his greatest friend; Sir Walter Raleigh, who helped Spenser. All were courtiers who, in their time, wrote pleasant—or, as in Raleigh's case, bold and spirited—verse. The three just mentioned were contemporary with Lyly, Sidney and Spenser, but those referred to in the following pages were born some ten years later or more, so that the above-named were the real originators of nearly all the non-dramatic literature of the period. The novels bear the impress of either *Euphues* or the *Arcadia* or of both. Pastorals, in imitation of Sidney or Spenser, were abundant. So soon as Sidney's *Astrophel and Stella* was published it brought down quite a shower of sonnets. Towards 1590 the appearance, one after another, of Sidney's sonnets and *Arcadia*, and of the first books of Spenser's *The Faerie Queene*, was the signal for an intense literary activity. The ferment of poetry alone was so rapid that it is difficult to set forth the new works with method. The theatre, of course, attracted the boldest and most energetic writers, but even of these many turned now and then to poetry, and added something at least to the various styles which were the delight of the age. So that one is driven to follow not the individuals but the different poetical forms. Yet mention must first be made of two voluminous writers, who touched drama with ill success, and who—even though they extend into the seventeenth century—are in truth Elizabethans: Daniel and Drayton.

Samuel Daniel. Samuel Daniel (1562–1619) fills an exceptional place in his generation: he was wise and calm in an age of tumult. 'Well-languaged', he carries into his pure and natural verse the qualities of his prose. Imagination, rare in his themes, never disturbs his style. Round his chief work, *The Civil Wars*, may be grouped a fair number of poems in various forms (without counting certain drawing-room tragedies modelled on the classics): sonnets in praise of *Delia*, letters, dedications, panegyrics, elegies, pastorals. He shows deep tenderness in *The Complaynt of Rosamond* (1592), the unhappy mistress of Henry II; a grave serenity in his *Epistle to the Countess of Cumberland*, where, in strong and tranquil lines, he describes the man who has 'built his mind' high above all private passions and political agitations. His *Musophilus*, *containing a General Defence of Learning* (1599) is a fine expression of faith in his mother tongue and its future. Patriotism also inspires him in his *Civil Wars*, a poem in eight books, in which he retraced the events of the Wars of the Roses about the same time as Shakespeare was dramatizing them. But Daniel is more historian than poet; he himself says 'I versify the truth, not poetize'. Step by step he follows the facts, lacking the energy to reanimate the violent manners and deeds of the past. This lack of fire was criticized by his contemporaries. Yet, after the excess and extravagance of his rivals, his calm is restful as a sail in smooth waters after a night of storm. Never harsh or bitter, he is full of good sense and is always master of himself.

Michael Drayton (1563–1631). Drayton's career resembles that of Daniel, and he has treated very much the same subjects, and yet his poetry is the antithesis of Daniel's. To the latter's even movement he opposes a rapid spring, and sudden flights and falls. In temperament Daniel was a classicist; Drayton was as romantic in practice as in theory. His work is considerable. It includes pastorals, such as *Idea, the Shepheards Garland* (1593); sonnets, *Ideas Mirror* (1594); the historical poem *Mortimeriados* (1596), republished with alterations as *The Barrons Wars* (1603); *Englands Heroicall Epistles* (1597); satires obscure and mediocre, odes, collections in which his best verse is found; and finally his *Poly-Olbion*, begun in 1598 and issued in two parts in 1613 and 1622.

His work as a whole shows fancy, fluency, liveliness, but it is nowhere refined. He was a facile versifier. Some of his works, such as his ode on the battle of Agincourt, his verses on the

Virginian Voyage, or the childish fairy-tale of *Nymphidia*, carry one away by their rhythm in spite of their lack of substance and their thinness of thought. His style has vigour and colour, but is wanting in correctness; to him colour was more than line. His phraseology is striking and vigorous, but hardly a period or stanza falls plumb. His *Barrons Wars* has more life in it than Daniel's *Civile Wars*—to which it is a pendant—but it is more vacillating in thought. Out of all his abundance those in which he achieves success, and which survive, are his short poems such as his sonnet, 'Since there's no help', which is a model of a dramatic sonnet: he bids in it a bitter farewell to his mistress, promising to forget her for ever; then suddenly, while he clasps her hand to take leave of her, he addresses to her the loving words by which they may yet be reconciled.

His *Poly-Olbion*, on the contrary, is now only a curiosity. This description of England in 15,000 alexandrines, or lines of twelve syllables, chiefly deserves praise as the expression of a fervid patriotism. County by county Drayton goes through the land, telling the history and legends of every spot. For decoration he uses a puerile mythology, which consists in personifying hill and vale and river. He redeems some of the extravagance and monotony of his subject with his indefatigable liveliness; but in truth he often tends to become ridiculous. If his poem shows the fantasy and poetic ardour of the day, it is also an example of the bad taste and eccentricity which went side by side with the sublime.

Collections of Lyrics and Songs. The public did not read single works so much as collections by publishers of short sets of verses, of which the authorship is often uncertain. Here and there may be found the name of some well-known noble or poet, but more often the verses are signed with initials or are left unsigned. In most of these anthologies lovely fragments will be found side by side with what is mediocre and dull. On the whole the shortest verses are the best and the best of these are the songs.

Never, perhaps, was song so copious, so diverse, and so winged; in song is best shown the fusion of popular genius and the artistic sense awakened by humanism. This fusion is attempted in every type of poetry, but with most unequal success. In many of the

longer poems incongruities jar the reader; excess of disorder or of
pedantry offends the taste of to-day. On the other hand, in many
of the songs and slighter lyrics artifice and nature are so closely
wedded as to be indistinguishable. The rudeness or clumsiness
of the popular muse becomes penetrated with a refined grace of
vocabulary, with a smoothness of versification hitherto unknown.
And this song is everywhere; it resounds in the drawing-rooms,
it wanders along the roads; it is in the town and in the country, it
abounds on the stage and in the novel. Indifferent to the plastic
arts, England was devoted to song. She had her traditional airs
and listened eagerly to what came to her from abroad, especially
from Italy. Her songs were of all sorts: grave and gay, sentimental
and cynical. This England, merry England, was an England of song.

A series of special collections heralded the *Books of Airs*, published from 1601 to 1613, of Thomas Campion, who defended the
national tradition against Italianism and aimed 'to couple lovingly
together words and notes'. His songs are by turns simple and
strange, ancient and modern, sensuous and passionate, bacchic
and pious, worldly and rustic, and all are distinguished by excellence of rhythm and pleasant language.

It is, however, in plays that the best lyrics are often found, and
many of those written by Ben Jonson, Thomas Dekker, Beaumont
and Fletcher, and Webster, are beautiful. But those of Shakespeare are at once the most original, the most spontaneous, the
most varied in rhythm, and the richest in impressions of nature.

In the lyrics of this rich period, by the side of the popular,
unpolished ballad, such as Drayton's 'When captains courageous',
may be found delicate fragments worthy of the Greek Anthology.
The transition from one to the other is insensible and the whole
becomes English by its mastery of words and sounds, or by some
happy bravery of expression. The aroma of antiquity becomes
merged in the odours of the present. It is the essential poetry
of this opulent literature; its fine waving crest, its supreme and
perfect blossom.

The Sonneteers. The vogue of the Elizabethan sonnet was as
brief as it was intense. With a few exceptions it was confined
within the years 1591–7, during which time, after the appearance

of Sidney's *Astrophel and Stella* in 1591, some twenty collections were published one after the other. In these sonnets are found in little the general characteristics of Elizabethan poetry, its blending of convention and independence, of imitation and originality. The influence of Italy and France appears so great that recent criticism has been inclined to regard the whole as artificial, making no distinction between masters and prentices. No doubt the mere fact of writing a sonnet after the time of Petrarch makes one his disciple; but the same might be said of every poet who uses a poetic form which has been used before; yet no one can deny him originality if he be able to give a personal ring to the instrument another has invented.

It must be admitted that imitation predominates in the sonnets of Thomas Watson, Henry Constable, and Thomas Lodge. The chief merit of the sonnets of Daniel and Drayton lies in their style—graceful in the first, lively in the latter. The eccentricity of Barnaby Barnes gives greater originality to his work, but it is at the expense of good sense and clarity.

The glory of the English sonnet lies mainly in the hands of Sidney, Spenser, and Shakespeare. Theirs were no mere rhetorical exercises; here and there, perhaps, they may have borrowed a thought, a *motif*, but, masters of the whole keyboard of expression, they had recourse to the sonnet (in accordance with its original and proper use) to describe their own intimate sentiments, not for some fiction detached from real life. If they give the impression of sincerity it is because they are sincere. The sonnets of Sidney and Spenser have already been referred to. Those of Shakespeare, spoilt as they are by too great subtlety and shadowed in a mystery as yet unpierced, remain the casket which encloses the rarest pearls of Elizabethan poetry. In them Shakespeare sings his devotion to a young noble, whose beauty he celebrates, and to whom he devotes himself entirely, finding in him all happiness, as well as consolation for the miseries of his life. Or he expresses the pain of his love for a married woman, dark-haired, capricious and changeable, who betrays him with his friend. To the latter he is lenient to the point of forgiveness; for the woman he feels an anger which turns to hate. The deep pathos of these sonnets is relieved by the rare beauty of style and imagery, by the perfection of lines whose subtle melody has never been surpassed.

Other Poems of the Time. To the poetical forms already enumerated, others must be added in order to complete the list of Elizabethan poetic forms. Under the influence of Italy there grew up a body of voluptuous poetry which, in spite of passages of beauty, rightly drew down upon it the reprobation of the Puritans. The most remarkable of these works are Marlowe's *Hero and Leander*, left unfinished at his death in 1593, and afterwards completed, in a mediocre manner, by Chapman, Shakespeare's *Venus and Adonis* (1593), and his *Rape of Lucrece* (1594). Marlowe's bold, vigorous couplets, and Shakespeare's rich and skilful stanzas, assured, from the first, success for these works, and had many imitators.

In opposition to the above there appeared certain poems of morality and devotion. The most ardent of their writers was the Jesuit Robert Southwell (1561–95), who sought in Italy an antidote to *Venus and Adonis* and, in his *St. Peter's Complaint*, reproduced Tonsillo's mannerisms. His ardour is shown more purely in the strange vision of *The Burning Babe*, the Christ-child burning with suffering and love.

Moral and didactic poetry included the eloquent quatrains of Sir John Davies's *Nosce Teipsum* (1599), and the edifying reflections in his *Microcosmos* (1603) of the poet John Davies of Hereford.

Better known were the satires, after the manner of Horace, Juvenal, or Persius, produced by Joseph Hall (1574–1656) in his *Virgidemiarum* (1597–8); John Marston, the dramatist, in his *Scourge of Villany* (1598); and John Donne. All were literary exercises based on the ancients, but on each the writer impressed the mark of his own temperament and observations. These satires, full of invectives, sometimes vehement, against society, were but the academic manifestation of a pessimism which was to become sincere and often painful at the beginning of the following century.

II. *Under James I, 1603–29*

There is something arbitrary in separating the poetry of the reigns of Elizabeth and James I. Such a division is only a chronological convenience. The works of many poets—such as Shakespeare,

Daniel, Drayton, Chapman, &c.—were written in equal proportions under the two reigns. It would be childish to attribute great
importance to the change of sovereign, but this break has the
advantage of marking the development which, with exceptions,
makes the last two decades of the sixteenth century distinct from
the first twenty years of the seventeenth.

The reign of Elizabeth was alight with youth, charged with
growth, expansion, and patriotic faith. The victory over the
Armada throws a lustre over literature, which in its keenest satires
and most sombre creations has spring and lightness. The poet
enjoys his ventures into untrodden ways, and his inventions amuse
him. He is intoxicated by the newness of the metre and the freshness of the vocabulary; of morality and religion he has little,
except such a façade as Spenser erected for his *Faerie Queene*.

After Elizabeth, poetry, when it was not imitative and conventional, when it did not follow Spenser's footsteps too closely,
became graver; here, more religious, there, harsher or more
didactic, sometimes more definitely intellectual. Under James I,
even among the Spenserians, there was closely mingled with Spenser's influence that of du Bartas, the earliest Protestant poet, author
of *La Semaine*, the translation of whose works, completed by
Joshua Sylvester in 1605–6, had so great a popularity. Its grandiloquence passed for sublimity, and gave birth to the idea of a high
epic strain, founded not on pagan or romantic fictions but directly
on the Bible. It showed the possibility of a great poetry which
might be truly religious and Protestant. It was to be admired
by the brothers Phineas and Giles Fletcher and by William Browne
before it stimulated Milton's genius.

Increasing desire for realism was to mark Ben Jonson's work,
just as the disdain of conventional poetical forms, such as the
pastoral, the mythological, and the Petrarchan was to give to
Donne's poems their individuality.

The Spenserians: Wither, Browne, the two Fletchers, &c. Among
Spenser's followers were George Wither, William Browne, the two
brothers Giles and Phineas Fletcher, and Drummond of Hawthornden. Their predominating note is either the pastoral, the
allegorical, or that of the sonneteer.

George Wither (1588–1667), a voluminous writer and satirical Puritan, lived on until the Restoration, but such of his poetry as survives was published before 1622. It includes: *The Shepheards' Hunting* (1615), the elegy *Fidelia* (1615), and *Faire Vertue or the Mistresse of Phil'Arete* (1622). He continues the pastoral tradition but gives it a new freshness by his sincere love for the countryside and a faith in the consolatory power of nature, which heralds, centuries in advance, the poetry of the Lake-poets. Ardent Puritan though he was, Wither remained capable of enjoying the simple pleasures of life, and his *Christmas*, full of good humour, is one of the jolliest of the poems inspired by the season of roast turkey and other good cheer. Unfortunately his good passages are interspersed with platitudes; he wrote too much, carried away by the dangerous facility of the octosyllabic line.

The friend of his youth, William Browne (*c.* 1591–1643), confined his work more strictly to the pastoral. Because of the length of his *Britannia's Pastorals* and their patriotic subject, he has become, in a sense, the classic representative of the type in England. He was inspired by Spenser, still more, perhaps, by Sidney's *Arcadia*, for the *Pastorals* is a complicated romance with interlacing episodes. It is attractive because of Browne's love for the West Country (he was a Devon man) whose heroes he sings, and whose manners and scenery he knows well. Although shackled by the artificiality of the romantic pastoral, he knows how to observe, how to see Nature in her reality, and sometimes renders it felicitously. He can make us hear a pretty concert of English birds, can call up a hunting scene, or paint the dawn breaking over a village. His defects are those of youth—nearly all the poem was written before he was twenty-six—but over the whole work plays an air of gentle cheerfulness and sweet temper.

Spenser's influence is more apparent in the works of Phineas Fletcher (1582–1650), who, after having, in his youth, laid on the altar of Love his *Venus and Anchises*, and imitated *The Shepheardes Calender* in his *Piscatorie Eclogs* (in which, instead of shepherds, fishers discourse on love and religion), wrote *The Purple Island or the Isle of Man* under the combined influence of Spenser and du Bartas. The allegory is by turns physical and moral. The

Purple Island which, with its mountains, rivers, dales, is the human frame, is at first a disguised lesson in anatomy; then it turns into a moral lesson, for fierce battles are waged in the same island between vices and virtues. It is a kind of paraphrase of the Castle of Alma in *The Faerie Queene* (Bk. II, cantos 9–11), and sets off, by contrast, Spenser's almost classic brevity. But in *The Purple Island*—especially towards the end—there is a religious fervour, which is scarcely found in Spenser and which foreshadows Bunyan's allegories.

This fervour is still more noticeable in Phineas's brother, Giles Fletcher (1588 ?–1623), whose poem *Christ's Victorie and Triumph* appeared in 1610. It is the work of a young man, as yet immature; but its luxuriance, its vivid imagination, more than redeem its defects. It is a link between Spenser and Milton, between the first two books of *The Faerie Queene* and *Paradise Regained*; it is Milton's subject treated in Spenser's manner. The stanza is Spenser's, with one line fewer; his style has Spenser's harmony and redundancy of epithets. The finest part is the end, with its picture of heavenly bliss. Nowhere perhaps in the whole of English literature (except in certain visions of Shelley) is there such an enraptured description of Paradise. This Anglican priest shows more rapture and hopeful trustfulness than the two great Puritans, Milton and Bunyan. In Giles Fletcher the spirit of the Gospel reigns supreme; to him religion is the source of happiness, not of gnawing scruples and dread.

By the side of these successors of Spenser may be set William Drummond of Hawthornden (1585–1649), the learned Scot, who was familiar with the Greek and Latin classics, as with all modern literature, and wrote in the purest English. His various poems: *The rejoicings of the Forth* (1617), congratulating James on revisiting his native land; the collection *Flowers of Zion* to which is adjoined his *Cypresse Grove* (1623); and his sonnets in the Italian manner, are full of literary reminiscences, yet impregnated with his own melancholy sweetness and his love for natural scenery which overrides all conventions.

Innovators: Ben Jonson. In contrast with the preceding writers, who on the whole followed beaten tracks, are two poets who opened up new ways, and who had the greatest influence on those of the coming age: Jonson and Donne.

Ben Jonson (1572?–1637) was primarily a dramatist, but he has left a fair amount of poetry. It consists of miscellaneous poems included in the *Epigrams* and *The Forest* (1616), and *The Underwoods* (1640). Satire preponderates in them, and Jonson expresses his harsh outspokenness in lines that are often bitter. But where he admires he praises generously, as in the magnificent lines to Shakespeare prefixed to the first folio of 1623.

Many of the poems are in imitation of the Greek Anthology— elegies and epitaphs, lyrics of crystalline clearness, in which the influence of the classics is evident. For Jonson was the staunchest humanist of his day, and was almost unequalled in his knowledge, if not of Greek, at least of Latin. He was little influenced by France or Italy, and the Middle Ages had no attraction for him as they had for Spenser. His culture was fundamentally Latin; his robust genius was attracted by the Latin muse, with its love of form and its tendency to moralize. The neo-classicism which penetrated English poetry in the seventeenth century is mainly owing to him. He makes us feel that we are on the road to Dryden.

He had many disciples and was the centre of a band of wits who met and talked at taverns; many of the younger writers were proud to be his 'sons' and to be 'sealed of the Tribe of Ben'. More than one sought to follow his example and cultivate the epigram, to rifle the Anthology and become a classicist.

John Donne. The other great influence, distinct from Jonson's, is that of his friend, John Donne (1573–1631), who, after a wild youth, took holy orders in 1615, and ended as Dean of St. Paul's. Many of his verses were written in the reign of Elizabeth when he was young, but they were not published until 1633, after his death. It was only then that they reached the public and provoked imitations.

His poetry is revolutionary. When he began to write Spenser was at the height of his fame, and the Petrarchans were producing volume after volume. Donne revolted against both. Pastoral, mythology, allegory, platonism, a taste for commonplace morality, for easy fluent descriptions, were then predominant. He despised

convention and chivalric love, as he did smooth verse and harmonious flowing cadences. He violated all laws of rhythm in his
Satyres, and is often perverse even in his songs and elegies. Ben
Jonson said of him that he held Donne 'the first poet in the world
in some things', but that 'for not keeping of accent he deserved
hanging'. There is the same originality in his style. He thrusts
aside well-worn metaphors and mythological conceits, and will
have no borrowing from Greek and Latin lines; he insists on
being subtle at the risk of being enigmatic.

Passion, sentiment, sensuality—he subordinates all to 'wit'. This
is shown sometimes by preposterous hyperboles: e.g. he excuses
himself for taking his mistress for an angel because to imagine her
other than she is would be profane; sometimes by the juxtaposition
of incongruous antipodal thoughts, mixing the trivial with the
sublime, as in *The Flea*, in which he deduces all sorts of results
from the fact that the flea, after biting him, bites his mistress. He
does not want her to kill it because

> This flea is you and I, and this
> Our marriage bed, and marriage temple is.

In such passages Donne lapses into the ridiculous, or would do so
did we not feel that he is playing with his subject and amusing
himself with his own extravagance. Elsewhere it happens that his
fantasy is combined with genuine passion. By the side of the con-
ventionalities of madrigal-makers his abruptness of thought shows
to advantage:

> I wonder, by my troth, what thou and I
> Did till we lov'd?

he exclaims. Or he attains with the most far-fetched image an
impassioned sincerity of accent. When parting from his mistress
to go to sea, he implores her not to lament. Each tear of hers is
a globe, a universe that reflects his own image. Then suddenly
comes the thought of the moon who draws to herself the mighty
seas, and he exclaims with matchless pathos:

> O more than moon,
> Draw not up seas to drown me in thy sphere;
> Weep me not dead in thine arms, but forbear
> To teach the sea what it may do too soon:

Let not the wind
Example find
To do me more harm than it purposeth:
Since thou and I sigh one another's breath,
Whoe'er sighs most is cruellest, and hastes the other's death.

He is the same in his religious poems, in some of which burns a strange exaltation, and in which wit is still triumphant. All his poems are overweighted with allusions to the doctrines of philosophers and schoolmen, and to the scientific knowledge of the day, even the most abstruse. His sudden transitions from the material to the spiritual, and his strange, obscure speculations caused Dryden to say of him that he 'affects the metaphysics'. It is as founder of the so-called 'Metaphysical' school that Donne is famous in the history of literature.

XIII

PROSE FROM 1578 TO 1625

Romances and Novels. Throughout the Renaissance poetry may be said to have invaded the realm of prose. Simple, sober, clear prose, written to instruct, not to excite, to nourish reason, not imagination, was then rather the exception. Much of the prose written under Elizabeth is either Euphuistic or Arcadian; it is poetical prose, and characterizes the work of the romance-writers and of the novelists.

Robert Greene (1560?–92) began by imitating Lyly's artifices, combining with them Sidney's romantic conceits when he came to know the *Arcadia*. Greene, who was born at Norwich, had some adventures abroad and lived a dissolute life in London. Yet, throughout all his debauches he contrived to remain something of an idealist, and his writings are almost always moral. His principal works are: *Mamilia* (1583); *Arbasto*; *Perimedes the Blacke-Smith*; *Pandosto* (on which Shakespeare was to base his *Winter's Tale*); and *Menaphon* (1589). He then produced the more popular and realistic 'conny-catching' (or dupe-making) series of pamphlets (1591–2), in which he utilized his extensive knowledge of villainy to describe London's underworld, and to initiate the reader into the ways of card-sharpers and swindlers. He ended with confessions, *Greene's Groatsworth of Wit*, published after his death, in which he deplores his wretched state, and laments his vices. He appeals to his friends—Peele, Nashe, and Marlowe—to give up their wicked ways. Then follows an attack on the actors whose fortunes he and his friends had made and who had forsaken them: 'Those puppits (I meane) that speake from our mouths, those anticks garnisht in our colours.' In a well-known passage he denounces Shakespeare's rapid rise to fame, based on plagiarism from himself and his friends.

Thomas Lodge (1558?–1625) was also a writer of Euphuistic 'novels', and wrote the pleasantest of them all—*Rosalynde: Euphues Golden Legacie* (1590)—a mixture of monologues and mannerisms after the manner of Lyly, and including some of the lightest and most charming lyrics of the century. This romance gave Shakespeare the material for *As You Like It*.

The taste of Thomas Nashe (1567–1601) was for buffoonery. He was satirical, reckless, a fighter, and is remembered for his savage denunciation of the Puritans in the Martin Marprelate controversy. As a pamphleteer he was well armed, his style being a kind of grotesque satire, a mixture of broad farce and lyricism. Although he began by attacking Marlowe's grandiloquence, deriding 'idiote art-masters', with their 'swelling bumbast of a bragging blank verse . . . the spacious volubilitie of a drumming decasillabon', and posing as the champion of simple and moderate language, yet to the end of his life he delighted in unbridled extravagance. His is the spirit of Rabelais and Aretino, as witness his pamphlets *The Anatomie of Absurdities* (1589); *Pierce Pennilesse his Supplication to the Divell* (1592); *Christes Teares over Jerusalem* (1593); *The Terrors of the Night, or a Discourse of Apparitions* (1594); and his laughable burlesque praise of the red herrings of Great Yarmouth, in *Nashe's Lenten Stuffe . . .* (1599).

In the same manner he wrote his picaresque novel *The Unfortunate Traveller, or the Life of Jacke Wilton* (1594), a pseudo-historical account of a young adventurer, which carries the reader over half Europe and makes him witness the chief events of the first half of the sixteenth century. The story ends in Italy, of which he describes alternately the magnificence and the abominations. He prepared abundant material for those melodramas of the coming age whose scenes were to be laid in Italy. *Jack Wilton* ends with a story of revenge told with a strength and simplicity unusual in Nashe. His manner as a rule shows truculence, the constant play of striking verbal formulas, and the fury of one possessed. His contemporaries acknowledged his strength, and he had more than one imitator.

Very different are the works of Thomas Deloney (1543 ?–1600?), the silk-weaver. He first wrote popular ballads; then towards the end of his life he began a series of narratives to the glory of the great corporations of the Weavers and Cordwainers. He traced the history of the latter back to fabulous times, beginning with their patron saints Hugh, Crispin, and Crispinian, down to the reign of Henry VIII, describing the lives of those who by hard work rose from workshop and bench to fame and fortune. Into this half-historical frame he introduces familiar scenes from life; we see the journeymen and apprentices at work and at play—singing, talking, making love to their customers (often maids from the inns); or engaging in amorous adventures which recall the *fabliaux*. Or else the author describes the relation between master and man, or between man and wife: the master's hearty good temper in conflict with the vain niggardliness of his wife, and his refusal to agree to the poorer fare that would increase the profits.

Deloney has two styles. When he treats of the romantic and sentimental he is euphuistic at a time when euphuism was forsaken by courtly circles, for he was of the people and not up to date. But for his workshop scenes he uses the clearest, most nimble prose. He was no poet, but he had good humour and the gift of straightforward narrative, so that we owe to him some of the gayest, lightest fiction, and that in years when prose was borne down by lyricism or buffoonery.

Thomas Dekker (1570?-1632) succeeded Greene and Nashe as prose writer, although Deloney inspired his best comedy. His works were not so much novels as social studies. He began with occasional pamphlets like *The Wonderfull Yeare 1603*, which was the year of Elizabeth's death, and a bad plague year. In his narrative rhetoric alternates with homely anecdotes told in lively fashion. As a rule he is more successful in comedy than in tragedy. In *The Belman of London* (1608) he continued Greene's revelations of London's underworld and imitated Nashe's satire in *The Seuen Deadly Sinnes of London; Drawne in seven severall coaches* ... (1606), and in *Newes from Hell; brought by the Divell's Carrier* (1606).

But it was in *The Guls Horne-booke* (1609) that he found himself. At first he followed his model, the *Grobianus* of the German Dedekind; then he threw aside all outside influence and became entirely himself, racily setting forth his own observations. Grobianism consists in offering, in the guise of friendly advice or flattery, a string of observations which show the absurdity and foolishness of the object of them. Dekker undertook the education of the 'Gull' who came up ignorant from the country, desirous of becoming a man of fashion. He shows him to us when dressing, takes him to Paul's Walk (old St. Paul's was then the meeting-place of idle wits and sharpers), then to dine at an 'ordinary', and on to play-house and tavern. Finally the gull returns home at night, escorted by a boy with a lantern. Particularly amusing is the Gull's conduct at the theatre, where he sits on the stage, displays his person, talks at the top of his voice, gets in the way of the actors, snaps his fingers at the audience, leaves before the end—all to attract attention and be thought a connoisseur.

In this book Dekker's prose is excellent; light and graphic, as well as picturesque. Unlike Nashe, who did not draw but carica-tured, Dekker shows a sense of proportion, of outline and form. He is on the road followed by the humorists of the time of Anne.

By the side of these pictures of manners must be placed the first character-sketches after the fashion of the *Characters* of Theophrastus: those of Joseph Hall (1608), Sir Thomas Overbury (1614–16), John Stephens (1615), and John Earle, whose *Micro-cosmographie* appeared in 1628. Each series served to develop the art of portrait-drawing representative either of the individual or of his profession.

Prose of the Theatre. The development of prose owed much to the writers of romances and novels; and it owed much also to the prose of the dramatists. To appeal to a mixed audience the speech used had to be rapid, clear, arresting. The greater number of the prose-writers referred to were also dramatists, and in the plays of the Renaissance prose was largely used. Rarely, however, was it used alone, except by John Lyly, who banished verse from his plays, employing the same antithetical style, enlivened with 'baroque' comparisons, as he used in *Euphues*. Other dramatists used both prose and verse, keeping, as a rule, prose for homely, humorous scenes, and verse for what was tragical and lofty. Shakespeare did this. Very seldom are his tragedies wholly in verse and in not one of his comedies is verse entirely absent. In *Henry IV* all the great historical scenes are in verse, while those in which Falstaff is the central figure are in prose. But Shakespeare was never bound by this convention; at times he used prose for scenes and characters that were poetical. In *As You Like It* Rosalind speaks nearly always in prose, as if Shakespeare felt that prose alone was swift enough for her torrential flow of words and fantasy. So also he has recourse to prose in moments of lofty tragedy, to express spiritual confusion, nature breaking bounds, as when Othello decides, with Iago, to murder Desdemona; or as when Lear, at the height of his madness, wanders away into the fields about Dover. Shakespeare also prefers prose for eloquence that is based on reason, as opposed to the eloquence of emotion. Brutus, appealing to the intellect of the Roman populace, addresses them in prose; but Mark Antony inflames their passion with admirable verse. Henry V, speaking in advocate fashion to his soldiers, to make clear that the king is not guilty of their damnation should they die in their sins, uses prose. Then he turns to verse when he communes with himself on the loneliness of kings.

In such passages of his plays prose reached a level which will scarcely be surpassed. Yet Shakespeare may be defined as a poet who used prose at times. Ben Jonson's less poetical nature found in prose a more congenial medium than in verse. Two of his principal comedies—*Epicoene* and *Bartholomew Fayre*—are written entirely in prose, a prose rich in concrete details, in which wit and humour are rare, but notable for strength, precision, and often for eloquence.

The use of prose in plays was not limited to Shakespeare and Jonson. Thoroughly to examine the subject it would be necessary to pass in review all the dramatists of the day; but for the most part they ranged themselves under these two leaders. This use of prose on the stage tended to knit together the language of every day, at a time when it was formless, or mannered, or unduly learned and pedantic.

Literary Criticism. The prose of the English Renaissance included many works of literary criticism—works greater in number than in value. They were not original, being inspired by ideas emanating from the Continent, which were themselves based on those of antiquity. Rarely did the critics adapt themselves to the peculiar circumstances of their country, or write with a direct bearing on the great English work growing up before their eyes. A criticism which ignores contemporary work is almost an abstraction.

The question which predominated in England was that of the morality of literature. Stephen Gosson, having in 1579 attacked all secular literature, which he called *The School of Abuse*, and especially poetry 'mother of lies', provoked Sidney's fine *Apologie for Poetrie*, written soon after Gosson's attack, although not published until 1595. Sidney's plea is one of the pleasantest and most eloquent books of the time. If he holds contemporary English literature cheap it is not for moral reasons but because he considers it weak, mediocre, ridiculous, and without art. Poetry he exalts to the highest place; the poet is the first law-giver, greater than either philosopher or historian; poetry in its descriptions of battles and of valiant men notably stirs courage and enthusiasm. But Sidney would have poetry respect classical rules; he condemns the literary practices of the time—including his own; his *Arcadia* contradicts his own teaching.

He was not alone in this self-contradiction. When his contemporaries write as critics they are back in antiquity, heedless whether or no their own works conform to the rules they recommend. This is so even with Ben Jonson who, of all the dramatists, wrote most on his art, and who believed he was following classical models in such a series of historical scenes as his *Sejanus* and *Catiline*. As for Shakespeare, he mocks lightly the mingling of styles, the scenes of 'very tragical mirth' the heteroclite works—like his own—'historical-pastoral, tragical-historical, tragical-comical-historical-pastoral'. He makes fun of the clumsy scenery—not unlike that of his own theatre—of the *Pyramus and Thisbe* acted by Bottom and his friends. While he puts into the mouth of Hamlet praise of tragedy in the manner of Seneca, he himself follows a method which had its roots in the miracle plays.

In this literary criticism a good deal of space was occupied by the controversy on the respective merits of rhymed or quantitative verse. The humanists advocated a 'reformed' English prosody based on vowel quality, after the manner of the ancients. William

Webbe, in his *Discourse of English Poetrie* (1586), upheld the classical metre; while the author of the *Arte of English Poesie* (1589) held the balance even. Thomas Campion, himself the writer of so many graceful lyrics, denounced rhyme in his *Observations in the Art of English Poesie* (1602); and his condemnation had the happy result of drawing from Samuel Daniel his *Defence of Ryme* (1602), the first example in England of reasonable, aesthetic criticism applied to a special question. Daniel shows a justice, sanity, and breadth of vision unknown to his contemporaries. He reduces to naught the superstition of the humanists, but in such a way as to show how good a classicist he is himself, and how excellent his prose.

Religious Prose. Before attaining to Richard Hooker's majestic serenity the religious literature of Elizabeth's days was a succession of controversies. The most violent was that known as the Martin Marprelate controversy, which began in 1588 and lasted for at least five years. In their secret presses the 'Marprelates' printed a number of pamphlets in which they denounced the bishops and 'the rest of the swinish rabble', 'the Beelzebubs of Canterbury'. Their attack, in its buffoonery and virulence, appealed to the populace. The counter-attack of the Anglicans was mostly in the same key; it was delivered by writers of the day who instinctively hated the Martinists as the enemies of secular literature. These champions of orthodoxy were not inspired by religious convictions, but they loved a fight; they fought for Episcopacy from the tavern. The best known of these champions was Thomas Nashe, the disciple of Aretino. In 1593 the chief Martinists—including the Welshman Penry, who seems to have been the leader of the revolt—were arrested and hanged. Sermons were censored, orthodoxy was enforced by pillory and gallows.

But Anglicanism also retorted in milder vein; she became persuasive, basing her doctrine on reason. This glorious task fell to Richard Hooker (1554?–1600), who, in 1594, began to publish his masterly work *Of the Laws of Ecclesiasticall Politye*, at once a monument of serious controversy and a masterpiece of English prose. He worked on this book until his death.

With the simplicity of a child and the holiness of a saint Hooker united great intrepidity and originality of thought. Boldly he sets forth as a principle that the *vià media* of the English Church, for which her opponents reproached her, is, in fact, the very proof of her wisdom. To the extremists who based all on the Scriptures he replies that God manifests Himself not only by revelation but also by reason, and that if the two should come into conflict, reason must prevail. Thus he defends Establishment, which he regards as a manifestation of reason, against the revolutionary attacks of the Puritan extremists. His book is remarkable for its massive structure, its arrangement, and its noble prose. For the first time English and not Latin was employed for a work of such lofty generalization. His style is, it is true, modelled on the Latin it replaces; it is Latin both in its vocabulary and in its Ciceronian periods. But the whole is luminous and harmonious, as far from pedantry as from vulgarity; appealing to reason, yet touching the imagination. In truth Hooker was, for Anglicanism, a Father of the Church.

If in the pulpit Hooker was too diffident for his sermons to gain the credit they deserved, there were other preachers of the day who enjoyed a great reputation. Foremost among these were Lancelot Andrewes (1555–1626), bishop of Winchester, and John Donne, dean of St. Paul's, whose sermons were as strange and 'metaphysical' as his verses; both were the favoured preachers of a select and refined congregation.

Yet nothing in the religious prose of the Renaissance equals in beauty and importance the 'authorized' version of the Bible published in 1611, which was the work of fifty-four scholars appointed by James I under the presidency of Bishop Andrewes. A biblical diction had already been wrought by Wyclif, Tyndale, and Coverdale. The revisers rejected those words and forms which had become too archaic, retaining such phraseology as was clear, although already tinged with the past. Thus in the heart of the English language there grew up a religious dialect that was of it and yet distinct from it, recognizable enough when used to bring into daily speech a loftier tone, a breath of holiness. Its beauties are manifest—beauties as absolute as those of splendid verse. This is due in part to the wealth and freshness of the language, which

PLATE XII

JOHN WYCLIF

WILLIAM TYNDALE

MILES COVERDALE

ARCHBISHOP CRANMER

PLATE XIII

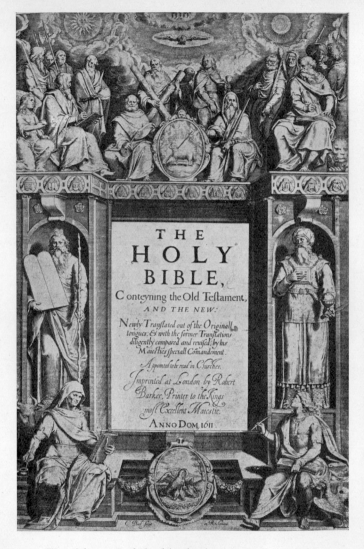

The title-page of the 'Authorized Version' of 1611

had not then become dulled and tarnished, and which is here preserved from its habitual defects. The shortness of the verses compelled restraint and curbed the tendency of the language to overflow in shapeless phrases. It would be difficult to exaggerate the benefit to literature of these pages, read and repeated with so much reverence, keeping the scholar from affectation and pedantry, the philosopher from chill abstraction, and bringing into the speech of the ignorant an element of pure beauty. With the Bible as his chief model a travelling tinker like Bunyan was to write some of the finest English prose.

But the benefit was not unalloyed. The Bible of 1611 had numerous defects which have not been without influence on the mind—and thus on the prose—of many English writers. In part owing to the obscurity of the original texts, in part through its numerous inaccurate renderings, the Authorized Version abounds in unintelligible passages. With its thousand and one strange and obscure expressions, it developed a taste for diction both disjointed and apocalyptical. It is true that the dangers of such a model were counterbalanced by the aspiration towards strict reason, which was to mark the approaching age of classicism. The Bible was to have its counterpoise in Baconism; or, let us say, the practical utilitarianism which led to the formation of the Royal Society for Improving Natural Knowledge was to be diluted by the diffusion of biblical poetry. The Bible was to perpetuate throughout England, even in her prose, an element of poetry, of 'quaintness', here and there of chiaroscuro; just as in thought it was to interpose a barrier of mysticism and imagination against the rising tide of rationalism. When it is remembered that Great Britain is the home of the Royal Society, of Hobbes, Locke, Hume, and Adam Smith, of economists and utilitarians; the nation in which the sense of the practical and positive, implanted by the Normans, is more deeply rooted than in any other land, it will be easier to comprehend the immense importance of the Bible, which kept poetry alive, even though it were sometimes at the expense of perfect intellectual clarity.

Bacon. By the side of religious, there grew up a secular literature, philosophical and moral; not antagonistic to, although

distinct from, the former. Francis Bacon (1561–1626) writes of
religion with respect, but his work is independent of theology,
and even of Christian morality. His was a free mind moving
onwards into new, self-discovered paths. He is the first English
philosopher in date, and one of the most eminent and characteristic ; more, he was one of the pioneers of that modern philosophy
which is not confined within any national limits.

As his character was unsound and his conduct governed by
self-interest, so his intellect was upright and strong. With reason
he declared himself formed for the contemplation of truth. While
yet young he wrote of himself that he had taken all knowledge
for his province. Little by little he elaborated the doctrines which
he set forth in 1620 in his *Novum Organum*. The inquirer was to
turn away from the causes of error—'phantoms of the human
mind'— and devote himself to the study of nature, of which man
should be the servant and interpreter. He should proceed by
systematic experiences, and guard against precipitate conclusions,
passing from particular facts to general laws only by prudent and
successive degrees. His chief care should be the assemblage of
instances, that is, of facts, from which he could rise, by induction,
to the laws which govern nature.

This glorification of facts, the search for them, and their classification, were—especially half a century later— to have a powerful
effect on English thought. The 'Royal Society for Improving
Natural Knowledge' (which began to meet as early as 1645, but
was not named until 1661) was influenced by Baconian principles,
and thus perpetuated Baconian thought in England.

Yet this philosopher who was opening up new vistas before his
countrymen's eyes, breaking with the past and thrusting boldly
forward towards modernity, remained bound to the middle ages
by his language. He did not believe in the future of English, and
was convinced that modern languages 'will at one time or other
play the bankrupts with books'. The first two parts of his chief
work, the unfinished *Instauratio Magna* (1620–3) were written in
Latin. Even of his English *Essayes,* which quickly became popular,
he believed that it was the Latin translation—'being in the
universal language'—which would 'last as long as books last'.

It is, therefore, almost in spite of himself, and through what he may have thought the least of his works, that he takes his place among the great writers of English prose: his *Essayes* (1597–1612–1625), his *Advancement of Learning* (1605), his *Historie of the Raigne of Henry VII* (1622), his unfinished romance of the *New Atlantis*, and several shorter works. His *New Atlantis* is a scientific Utopia, curious in matter, clumsily written, and painfully didactic; its author had not the gift for romance with which Sir Thomas More was so happily endowed. Far more remarkable is Bacon's *Henry VII*, in which he shows his sagacity as moralist. But it is in his *Essayes or Counsels, civill and morall* that he best proves his mastery of his mother tongue. As the title shows, the essays are written to give counsel; they are meant to teach courtiers and statesmen the way to success. They are non-moral and imbued with Machiavellianism inasmuch as in them Bacon describes what men do and not what they should do. He knows that nothing equals goodness, but it is the art of succeeding which occupies his chief attention. Within these limits the essays possess a singular force. In no other writer are found such pithy aphorisms, so pregnant with thought and practical wisdom. Many of his sayings have passed into proverbs. Indeed, in all Bacon's works—Latin as well as English—sentences abound as memorable for their concentrated wisdom as for their brilliance. The *Essayes* are the first true English prose-classic.

Burton. The list of prose-writers of the day closes with an eccentric humanist. All the pedantry of the Renaissance was poured into *The Anatomy of Melancholy* (1621), which is yet vivified by humour. Its author, Robert Burton (1577–1640), though a country parson, spent almost all his life at Oxford. He seems to have lived entirely among books, devouring—and abstracting from—Greek, Roman, and modern writers. He combated the sombre melancholy of his temperament with erudite jests, and by laboriously collecting and summarizing all that had ever been written on his malady. There was nothing of himself in the thick quarto which appeared in 1621, for he had pillaged from every known book; yet there was self-revelation in the choice of subject and in the unity that his temperament infused into it. Melancholy,

his heroine, was not the gentle companion beloved of future
romanticists; to the men of the Renaissance she was Melancholia,
a physical distemper which required medicine. It was no great
distance from melancholy to madness, and Burton draws on a
vast canvas a picture of human frailty and folly. Crowded with
Latin quotations, often redundant—for the author enjoys piling
up synonyms and epithets—his style is that of an eccentric; but
the book exercised a kind of fascination in the seventeenth century,
and in the nineteenth Charles Lamb was to revive its fame.

Something of Burton's eccentricity marks all the prose of those
fifty years. It lacks, as a rule, the even, clear-cut simplicity which
should characterize true prose. As yet it had not completely
severed itself from poetry. Little by little, however, in spite of
the resistance of Latin, English prose gained new ground, reaching
out to include such diverse subjects as theology and philosophy,
literary criticism, moral essays, and 'characters'. It was as
elastic as the novel, which might be either romantic or sentimental, realistic or farcical. Already prose played an important
part on the stage. It had learned to narrate and to discuss;
to be both serious and playful. When it is remembered how poor
and formless a thing it was before 1578, one cannot but be struck by
its progress, scarcely less rapid than that of poetry. The victory
of the Puritans, though it brought about an abundant growth of
pamphlets and journals, interrupted the use of prose for light
literature, which ceased until the Restoration; but in the generation of the middle of the seventeenth century prose was to be
lifted into the high regions of literature; attaining eloquence,
strength, and fullness—all qualities foreshadowed by more than
one of the prose-writers whose work has here been touched on.

DRAMA OF THE RENAISSANCE (1580–1642)

I. *Before Shakespeare*, 1580–92

RICH in all its manifestations though the English literature of the Renaissance may be, the drama is its chief glory, just as it is the nation's most direct and original expression. Outside the theatre, classical or foreign—especially Italian—influences were so strong that they more or less obscured native genius. But the theatre, where all were moved at times by a common patriotism— as they had once been by religion—interested a public entirely English, in plays written solely for them. The lure of applause or gain drew most authors—indeed there were few who did not, at one time or other, write for the stage.

Drama, therefore, is the most important subject for study at this time; it is also the most difficult. The number and diversity of the plays make classification difficult; while the lack of sufficient dates makes it almost impossible to obtain a clear outline of the evolution of the theatrical world. Many plays are lost, and the chronology of those which remain is often doubtful; while the life and character of their authors are frequently unknown to us. Moreover, their habit of refashioning older plays, and the tangle of collaboration—a collaboration that was sometimes successive, and sometimes simultaneous, and sometimes both—add to the confusion. It is difficult to detect with certainty the identity of the playwright, the company of players which produced his works, and the theatre where they were acted. It is equally difficult to attempt a classification of the plays under the various headings: Pure tragedy, Tragi-comedy, Historical drama, Romantic comedy, Comedy of realism, Farce, Pastoral, Comedy of manners, Comedy of character, &c., since such lines of demarcation correspond ill with a drama which habitually mingles many styles in one, aiming at variety and not at unity.

We are compelled, therefore, to search for a central figure, and

Shakespeare being incontestably the greatest, to group about him the constellation of his rivals: his predecessors; his contemporaries; his successors. Moreover, whatever the method adopted, it is important to realize the crowded confusion into which the mind attempts to introduce some order. In the sixty years between 1580 and 1642 London theatres presented almost every day a number of plays both old and new, each one a medley of styles.

It is easier to describe the form of the public playhouse than the evolution of the play. The first theatre was built on the confines of the City in 1576; by the end of the century there were some eight theatres, on both banks of the Thames. They were simple in structure, mostly circular in form; within was a courtyard open to the sky, surrounded by two or three tiers of covered galleries. At one side of the courtyard projected a great platform on trestles, which formed the stage. In the centre, on either side of the platform, two pillars supported the ceiling; at the back, between two doors which served for the entrance and exit of the actors, was another stage overlooked by a gallery with balcony and windows; in front of this rear-stage was a movable curtain. There were neither wings nor back-scenery, and only elementary accessories—a table, chairs, bushes, &c.—to show, or rather to symbolize, the scene of action. At times the locality—for those who could read—was indicated by a placard. The front stage served most purposes, such as needed no clearly defined scene; the rear stage was used when it was necessary to indicate some precise interior. The curtain at the back was raised to show the actors in a particular attitude, such as Ferdinand and Miranda 'discovered' playing at chess in Prospero's cell.

On this bare stage the individuality of the actor was all-important. His dress was as rich as the stage was poor. The attention of the audience was concentrated on his tragic gestures or on his grimaces. Of special importance was his delivery, emphasizing as it did the meaning of the numerous monologues, the many tirades for effect, in the plays of the time. The actor's art—there were no actresses, boys took the parts of women—reached a high level. Although only on the edge of society, actors were not only popular, but often sought after in a flattering manner. Leading actors, if they were steady, and owned shares in their theatre, stood a good chance of making their fortunes. Their public was heterogeneous: from the 'groundlings, who for the most part are capable of nothing but inexplicable dumb-shows and noise', to refined courtiers and makers of intricate sonnets. Between these two extremes lay every variety and type of hearer. The mass of the audience was made up of simple folk out for pleasure, but willing also to be taught and edified; endowed with a curiosity at once ingenuous and ardent, and with an imagination easily moved to laughter or to tears; neither squeamish nor sceptical, taking on trust lyrical flights which were beyond them; careless of rules; ungrudging and swiftly beguiled—the best public to appreciate the essentials of drama: life, pathos, and humour.

The plays were successions of scenes, in the true sense of the word; for, faithful to medieval tradition, they continued to be spectacles in which the incidents of a fragment of history, or of a whole lifetime, were shown to the spectator. To the indignation of scholars like Sir Philip Sidney, the unities of time and space, and even of action, were disregarded; farce alternated with violent tragedy. Such were the popular dramas of the generation preceding the great period, such were to be those of the great period itself, but with this difference, that the plays for the latter would be written by poets, or at least by talented and lively writers, some of whom were masters of style. As was natural, progress was shown at first in the plays written for the queen and her court; but as there was constant communication between court and city, plays and players passing from one to the other, progress soon became general.

John Lyly. Among the plays acted before the court, of which only the titles remain, were several mythological allegories, a mode which, from 1581, took on a new lease of life, thanks to the talent of John Lyly, whose euphuistic romance has already been referred to.

In a series of witty comedies—*Campaspe* (1581), *Sapho and Phao* (1582), *Endimion* (1586), *Midas* (1590)—he addresses Elizabeth in delicate flattery, praising by turns the charms of the woman, the chastity of the virgin, the majesty of the queen. A good humanist, he found in the history or legend of antiquity graceful symbols which took away from his praises the clumsiness of direct flattery. Elizabeth is Alexander, strong enough to thrust back his love for fair Campaspe in order to give himself to his empire. She is Sapho, enamoured for a while of Phao, the handsome ferryman, then mistress of herself, and conquering Venus who had been envious of her beauty. She is Cynthia, loved to despair by Endymion who, overpowered with sleep by the magic art of Tellus, is, by Cynthia's kiss, brought back to life and respectful adoration. She is the queen of Lesbos, against whom fail all the attempts of Midas (Philip II of Spain), whose fatal touch transforms everything into gold.

To these court comedies may be added the more disinterested mythological pastorals: *Galathea*, the subject of which is love; *Love's Metamorphosis*, a lively satire on women; *The Woman in the Moone*; and *Mother Bombie*, a comedy with an Italian plot.

Except *The Woman in the Moone*, which is in verse, the comedies are written in the kind of prose called euphuistic, artificial in structure and language, but refined in manner, witty, and often graceful beneath their artifice. Lyly's plays, with their sparkle and courtly air, are the first artistic plays which have come down to us. They made ready the way for Shakespeare's *Love's Labour's Lost*, and even for his *Midsummer Night's Dream* or his *As you like it*.

Peele. This honour is shared by George Peele (1558–97), who shows in his verse the same taste for fine words as does Lyly in his prose. Like Lyly also he flatters Elizabeth in his graceful pastoral *The Araygnement of Paris* (1581). He used the same ornate manner in his scripture drama *The Love of David and Fair Bethsabe, with the Tragedy of Absalon*, in which he follows closely the Bible record. He seems, in his play of *Edward I*, to have been one of the first to turn to national history; and he parodied the romanticists in *The Old Wives' Tale*. As a dramatist he lacks power, but he is a true poet, although pretty and melodious rather than strong.

But neither to Lyly nor to Peele was due the advance of dramatic art which suddenly revealed its power towards 1586–7 with Kyd's *The Spanish Tragedie*, the drama *Arden of Feversham* by an unknown author, and Marlowe's *Tamburlaine*, three attempts of great excellence, in very different manners.

Arden of Feversham (1586) is surprisingly mature. Whoever was the author, he possessed in an extraordinary degree an almost modern sense of stage-craft. There is nothing romantic about his play. He set before the public the details of a recent crime, the relation of which may be found in Holinshed's Chronicle. In form and subject it is—in spite of its blank verse and some attempts at fine language which recall the Renaissance—a typical middle-class drama, whose merits lie in its psychological truth and delineation of character. The subject is the murder of the rich citizen, Arden, by the tailor Mosbie, the lover of Alice, Arden's wife, who instigates the crime. The characters are forcibly drawn, especially that of Mosbie, coarse-grained and covetous, beneath whose passion broods a sullen sense of class-hatred. Better still is the portrait of Alice, prey to a blind, irresistible fascination, yet energetic and decided, who plans the murder that she may give herself entirely to Mosbie. But the crime accomplished, the spell is broken; she is overcome with horror at her deed, and dies repentant. Although the play lacks poetry and loftiness of thought, and is set in a sordid atmosphere, its striking realism makes it stand out from the productions of a romantic time.

Kyd. For romantic drama was demanded by the great mass of playgoers, and the first playwright to satisfy the demand to the full was Thomas Kyd (1558–94) with his famous *Spanish Tragedie of Don Horatio and Bellimperia*. Kyd owes much to Seneca, the tragedian. Yet what he borrowed was not the latter's regularity of structure and conformity to the unities, but his scenes of horror, the ghost of the prologue who narrates past events, the atrocities, and the soliloquies touched at times with lyricism and grandiloquence.

It is a drama of vengeance. Horatio, son of Hieronimo (or Jeronimo), marshal of Spain, is treacherously murdered while making love to the Spanish princess Bellimperia. She and Hieronimo swear to discover and punish the murderers. The old father, partly mad with grief and partly feigning madness to attain his ends, conceives the idea, when he knows the identity of the murderers, of having a tragedy acted at the wedding of Bellimperia, who is forced to wed Horatio's murderer. The tragedy, however, is played in earnest; every member of the wedding party either is killed or kills himself.

No outline can do justice to the author's skill in interweaving passion, pathos, and fear until they reach a climax. There is no study of character; this would be superfluous when the audience is absorbed in atrocities. Kyd discovered the formula for melodrama; his success was great and lasting, and produced many imitators. Revenge became a favourite subject for dramatists; *Hamlet* is one of the revenge plays. Probably Kyd himself was the author of a *Hamlet* (now lost), twelve years older than Shakespeare's masterpiece.

Marlowe. About the same time as *The Spanish Tragedie*, a drama no less violent—though in a very different way—was attracting the public. This was the *Tamburlaine* of Christopher Marlowe (1564–93). Marlowe was then a young man of twenty-three, and had not long left Cambridge. Without knowledge of the stage, he brought to it an extraordinary spirit of defiance and revolt. Not for him to set forth the horror of crime and its punishment, but to claim admiration for the most sanguinary of men and exalt him as a demi-god. Fascinated by the career of the Tartar conqueror Timurlane, who, from a poor shepherd, became the master of Asia, and was probably the most bloodthirsty butcher known to fame, Marlowe makes of him a super-man beyond all paltry rules of morality. He is a conqueror: therefore in the right. A poet aspiring to the infinite, Marlowe endows his hero with the unbridled ardours of the Renaissance, devoting two plays to his ascension, triumph, and grandiose death.

In his next play—*Faustus* (1588)—Marlowe took for his subject the thirst for knowledge, and the power resulting from it. His Faustus, disgusted with the poor results of human science, sells his soul to the devil in order that for twenty-four years he may satisfy every desire. But to the great questions which haunt him, he obtains no answer. Then comes retribution. In an overwhelming scene Marlowe, the atheist, shaken by his own audacity, describes the deepening agony of Faustus as the hour draws near which is to bring him damnation.

In *The Jew of Malta* (1589) it is the enjoyment of infinite treasure which excites his imagination, as he shows the Jew Barabas exulting in his riches. Then, when Barabas has been despoiled, the same exaltation seizes Marlowe as he describes the horrible vengeance of the Jew against his Christian enemies. Possessed by a very lust of destruction, Barabas falls at last into the pit he has dug for others.

Marlowe came nearer real life—or at least historical verity—in his play of *Edward II* (1593), the finest of the national chronicles which had yet appeared on the stage. It is more human, approaches more nearly to normal drama, and shows more study of character, though his usual lyricism still appears in the delineation of Mortimer, the queen's lover, with his unbridled ambition, and though the author hesitates too much in the apportionment of sympathy among the various characters of the play. But the murder of the king in his prison is one of the most poignant scenes in the drama of the Renaissance.

In technique the stage owes less to Marlowe than to the playwrights just mentioned, but it was quickened by his ardour, inflamed by his passion, and ennobled by the power of his blank verse. He gave to an English audience its first thrill of enthusiasm, filling hearts with a new national pride (although his plays were not patriotic), in the belief—or illusion—that English drama was as sublime as that of the ancients. The fiery declamations of his extravagant characters, joined to the victory over the Armada and the discovery of far-off lands, made the English almost giddy with triumphant strength. His choice of subjects, the heroes he moulded, were but the expression of his exorbitant desires. Like him, his characters sought the impossible, and like him they were never satisfied.

Greene. Marlowe's 'drumming decasyllabon' drowned the voice of playwrights—such as Thomas Lodge and Robert Greene— then in favour with the public, and either silenced them or forced them to imitate his thunder. Greene imitated or parodied the extravagance of *Tamburlaine* in his *Alphonsus* and *Orlando Furioso*. But the tone was unnatural to him, and he returned to his own style in his *Frier Bacon and Frier Bungay*, a rejoinder to *Faustus*, and in the pseudo-historical drama *The Scottish history of James IV slaine at Flodden*. . . . He has neither Marlowe's strength nor his passion, but he has more suppleness and grace; and he can describe an idyll with charm. Whereas Marlowe's women never hold the attention, Greene's heroines are the best characters in his plays: the fair Margaret of Fressinfield in *Frier Bacon*; Ida and Dorothea in *James IV*—all are alive. Dorothea is the prototype of Shakespeare's Julia, Viola, and Imogen, whose love is great enough for self-sacrifice. Certain scenes in Greene's romances foreshadow Shakespeare, but only as a first sketch indicates a finished masterpiece.

SHAKESPEARE'S PLAYS, 1590–1613[1]

THE playwrights already referred to—with the exception, perhaps, of Kyd—were University men and professional writers. But it was from the ranks of the actors themselves that William Shakespeare (1564–1616) emerged, about 1590. He had already spent some years in London, to which he came from his native town of Stratford-on-Avon; and during the intervals of acting he wrote for his company, reshaping the plays in its repertory. His success roused Robert Greene's jealousy, and led him, before he died, to denounce the new writer to his fellow dramatists.

At the outset of his career, Shakespeare's genius is shown by his versatility, no less than by his instinct for the stage. In what may be called the preparatory stage, before 1595, he reshaped dramatic chronicles of Henry VI; he surpassed the horrors of *The Spanish Tragedie* and *The Jew of Malta* in *Titus Andronicus*; in his comedy of *Love's Labour's Lost* he is inspired by Lyly's witty dialogues; his

---

[1] The following is a list of Shakespeare's plays, with the dates assigned to them by Sir E. K. Chambers in *William Shakespeare* (1930).

2 Hen. VI ⎱ 1590–1	*Hamlet* ⎱ 1600–1
3 Hen. VI ⎰	*Merry Wives* ⎰
1 Hen. VI, 1591–2	*Troil. and Cress.,* 1601–2
Rich. III ⎱ 1592–3	*All's Well,* 1602–3
Com. Errors ⎰	*Measure for M.* ⎱ 1604–5
Titus Andronicus ⎱ 1593–4	*Othello* ⎰
Tam. Shrew ⎰	*Lear* ⎱ 1605–6
Two Gent.	*Macbeth* ⎰
Love's Lab. Lost ⎱ 1594–5	*Antony and Cleop.,* 1606–7
Romeo and Juliet ⎰	*Coriolanus* ⎱ 1607–8
Rich. II ⎱ 1595–6	*Timon* ⎰
Mids. N. Dream ⎰	*Pericles,* 1608–9
K. John ⎱ 1596–7	*Cymbeline,* 1609–10
Merch. Venice ⎰	*Wint. T.,* 1610–11
1 and 2 Hen. IV, 1597–8	*Tempest,* 1611–12
Much Ado ⎱ 1598–9	*Henry VIII* ⎱ 1612–13
Hen. V ⎰	*Two Noble* ⎰
Julius Caesar ⎱	*Kinsmen*
As You Like It ⎰ 1599–1600	
Twel. N.	

Comedy of Errors is a free adaptation of a farce of Plautus; and, in *The Two Gentlemen of Verona*, he rivals Greene's romantic sentimentality. He shows that an actor, though lacking academic training, may construct a play and write sparkling dialogue and ringing verse, both rhymed and unrhymed.

For several years, between about 1595 and 1601, owing either to the premature death of his rivals, or their withdrawal from drama, Shakespeare reigned as master, at first with no one to challenge his supremacy. Then it was that he wrote the historical plays: *Richard II*, *King John*, the two parts of *Henry IV*, and *Henry V*; also his fairy play *A Midsummer Night's Dream*; the romantic comedies *The Merchant of Venice*, *Much Ado about Nothing*, *As You Like It*, *Twelfth Night*; the middle-class comedy of *The Merry Wives of Windsor*; the character-farce *The Taming of the Shrew*. These years brought forth but one tragedy—and in this gaiety fights for long against sadness—*Romeo and Juliet*. This was a time of light-hearted and brilliant maturity.

Then came (1601–8), abruptly enough, a series of sombre, violent plays, which are nearly all tragedies. Three relate to Roman history and are taken from Plutarch: *Julius Caesar*, *Antony and Cleopatra*, and *Coriolanus*; one, *Timon of Athens*, is borrowed from Greek history.

Others are based on legends, either Danish, like *Hamlet*, or British (*King Lear*), or Scottish (*Macbeth*). Another, *Othello*, is taken from an Italian novel. At the same time Shakespeare wrote other comedies, but even these have a tinge of bitterness: *All's Well that Ends Well*, *Measure for Measure*, *Troilus and Cressida*. This was the period of Shakespeare's most powerful work, but throughout he views nature and life from the same sombre standpoint. Strangely enough, though his greatest plays belong to this period, he does not appear to have enjoyed the same uncontested supremacy as in the preceding one. The more classical genius of Ben Jonson attracts to itself many of the connoisseurs, and on the other hand, the greatness of Shakespeare's tragical masterpieces does not seem to have been distinguished at once from the productions in a similar vein of Marston, Chapman, Tourneur, or Webster.

The poet's last years (1608–16) have neither the lightness of the beginning, nor the sombre violence of the middle, of his career. They breathe a spirit of serenity, reconciliation, and forgiveness. To console himself for reality he turned once again to romance. It was then that he wrote, or revised, *Pericles*, wrote *Cymbeline*, *A Winter's Tale*, and *The Tempest*. It was a golden, mellow autumn, not untouched by melancholy. Prosperous through his plays, his acting, and the shares he held in theatres, he sought rest in his old home, and died at Stratford in 1616, at the age of 52.

Seen as a whole, his work is distinguished from that of his contemporaries first by its variety. Of the thirty-six plays he has left, no two are alike, or produce in us the same impression. While every other dramatist had his distinctive manner, at once the sign and limit of his personality, Shakespeare handled the most diverse subjects with an ardour almost equalled by his achievement. Alone he shows an equal aptitude for tragedy and comedy, sentiment and burlesque, lyrical fantasy and character-study, of women no less than of men. And these plays, each one of which stands out distinctly, are, throughout his career, intermingled in surprising confusion, as though, in one year, he could range with ease from one extreme to the other, and provide his audience with every pleasurable emotion they were able to enjoy.

As well as versatility the poet has the supreme gift of reviving historical characters or of endowing imaginary people with life; and that not by flashes, like his contemporaries, but constantly; so that they may alter during the play, yet never lose their identity. Abnormally developed though this character-drawing may be, there is nothing in it of strain or effort; it seems spontaneous, natural. Life is in his characters from the beginning, but they stand out more distinctly as Shakespeare moves towards maturity. If, from 1593 onwards, we were to enumerate the characters of any importance in each play, we should find very few lacking the vital spark and signs of individual existence. Differing in age, in sex, in condition, in virtues, and in vices, they possess in common the gift of animation and life. Think, for instance, of the people in the single play of *Romeo and Juliet*, and enumerate those who are alive: there are the two lovers, of course,

but there are also old Capulet, Tybalt the bully, witty Mercutio, the
Nurse, and Friar Laurence. Multiply these by the thirty-six plays,
and the result is a very world of human beings, who stand before
the spectators with a living force greater than that of many of the
creatures among whom we pass our lives. But the words 'life',
'animation', scarcely define the power which places Shakespeare
so far above his contemporaries. Animation, at least, is not
lacking in their characters; some of them are very much alive;
but rarely do they leave the impression of being both living and
true. Neither Marlowe, nor Jonson, nor Beaumont and Fletcher
(to speak only of Shakespeare's most illustrious rivals), satisfy
this need for truth in the delineation of character, by which
alone these exist off the stage. In the plays of Shakespeare's
contemporaries the people are almost always exaggerated, un-
human, arbitrary, or theatrical, aiming chiefly to surprise; in their
feelings we seldom recognize our own; they disconcert us by their
extravagance or their sudden changes of front. Shakespeare's
people, good or bad, in a setting historical or romantic, invariably
maintain their humanity and hold us in a bond of sympathy.

Another radical difference between Shakespeare and his contemporaries lies in the depth and substance of his work. Only
with him does the epic hold an equal place with the romance.
Ten plays are founded on English, and three tragedies on Roman,
history; to these may be added *Hamlet*, *Lear*, and *Macbeth*, based
on more or less legendary chronicles, but accepted by the author
and public as historical; these form a whole found nowhere else—
the solid frame-work of Shakespearian drama. It bears testimony
to a long contact with what he believed to have been really done
in the past; the effort necessary to evoke it implanted in him a
love of truth which is shown even in his treatment of non-histori-
cal subjects, those which he took from Italian tales; or when he
entered the domain of faery. Other writers might render history
unreal; Shakespeare gave to romance the atmosphere of truth.

The Roman plays, which follow Plutarch faithfully enough,
teach a fine lesson of noble simplicity. Yet more striking, perhaps,
are the pictures of national history which relate his theatre to the
religious plays of the Middle Ages, whose object was not pleasure

alone, but instruction and edification. With the exception of *King John*, set by its subject four centuries away, Shakespeare unfolded before his countrymen the great drama of English history throughout the fifteenth century, its glory and its woe, as simply as the miracle plays enacted the scenes from Bible history. Patriotism, not faith, was the theme; and he believed patriotism to be strong enough to hold an audience no less than plays of intrigue and artificial emotion.

In such dramas art holds a secondary place, indeed is barely discernible. Whether Shakespeare was a conscious artist is the question which most embarrassed his contemporaries and has most divided posterity. Genius, imagination, spontaneity, have always been conceded to him; but the idea of firm reason, of a concerted plan, of a will which guided the poet's fire, was long in appearing and is still contested by many. Literary judgements are often based on an antithesis, and it has been the fashion to contrast learned and laborious Jonson with spontaneous Shakespeare. Through the confusion of erudition with artistry, art has been attributed to the one, and genius to the other. But, in fact, unequal though Shakespeare's work may be, his art is no less certain than his genius. Speaking of the actor's art he has himself set forth in *Hamlet* a formula, pregnant with meaning, of the self-control the poet should exercise, even in his wildest flight: 'In the very torrent, tempest, and (as I may say) the whirlwind of passion, you must acquire and beget a temperance that may give it smoothness.'

The recognition of this guiding wisdom best explains the harmony which reigns in almost every one of Shakespeare's plays. Different as may be their elements, each one has its own atmosphere; this could not be the result each time of some lucky chance. The very freedom of the public theatre, the custom of using two, or even three, plots in one play, the mingling of tragedy with comedy, the use in turn of rhymed and blank verse and prose —all contributed to the difficulty of fusing into one harmony so many different tones. The greater the difficulty, the more praiseworthy was the success. And this is never the result of one set code; a different method is employed for each work. Shakespeare's art is not the less real because it is essentially varied, mobile, and difficult to trace. It hides itself behind its own creations.

This concealment was made the easier by his acquiescence—more or less resigned—in the theatrical conditions of the day, which depended on, or resulted from, the needs and manners of the public, the poor scenery of the public stages, and the customs of his fellow actors. His art is essentially empiric, taking account only of realities, and refusing to build on the abstract. Speaking through Henry V he reveals his formula:

> There is some soul of goodness in things evil,
> Would men observingly distil it out.

Shakespeare was not blind to the defects of the stage, to the coarse tastes of the groundlings. He was irritated by the licence taken by the clown, or jester, who interrupted and held up scenes of pathos by his ill-timed fooling; he was annoyed by the over-emphasis of actors who 'saw the air' with their hand, and 'tear a passion to tatters'. Yet there was no attempt on his part at proscription. He made no effort to return to the noble simplicity of the ancients —which would merely have emptied the Globe; but he made the best of matters as they were. The lack of proper scenery did not compel him to place his characters in some abstract place; he relied on the imagination of the spectators to see what he could not actually show them; and he helped their vision forward by rapid, vivid descriptions in his verse. His very text supplies the scenery; people and place are so closely associated in his plays that it is impossible to separate one from the other. In the same way, instead of suppressing the clown he attempts to improve him. He really appreciated the droll figure with his original turns of speech and his puns and play on words. Shakespeare wrote his part for him, and made of him—either in his role of rustic, or court fool, or lord's jester—a kind of popular philosopher, independent, and wise beneath his fooling. Without the clown his plays might gain in noble dignity, but their meaning would be lessened and their philosophy the poorer.

Shakespeare's conservativeness is shown more plainly in greater matters. He seems to have been one of the least inventive among his fellow writers, preferring to refashion subjects already used.

PLATE XIV

WILLIAM SHAKESPEARE
The portrait by Droeshout

PLATE XV

The Elizabethan Theatre : a reconstruction of the Fortune Theatre.
See p. xiii

Half his plays are revisions of works already acted. Nearly all
the others are taken from chronicles or tales which he had read,
and which he merely divided into acts and scenes. There are only
about three or four of his plays of which the plots are his—or rather,
of which no originals are known: *The Merry Wives of Windsor*
(except for a few insignificant details), *Love's Labour's Lost, A Midsummer Night's Dream*, and *The Tempest*. And the three last are
those which, of all others, come nearest to symbolism or most resemble plays with a purpose. As a rule Shakepeare is content to
'hold... the mirror up to nature ; to show ... the very age and body
of the time his form and pressure'. He offers no direct teaching. If
much has been written on Shakespeare's philosophy, it is because
of the striking ideas found throughout his plays. But he had
no code, no system. His own philosophy eludes any attempt to
hold it ; its contradictions and seeming incoherence are those of
life itself ; there is little that we can catch and show as Shakespeare's. The miracle lies in the extraordinary imagination that
invented the ingenious arguments by which the most varied
characters justify their passions or their interests. Each one,
from king to jester, views life from his own standpoint, and often
sets it forth in words which move us by their depth and their
truth to nature. But all this is the outcome of dramatic genius.
Each temperament and circumstance has, in Shakespeare, its own
philosophy. The poet himself lays no claim to a superior and
broader philosophy that includes them all and sums them up.

Where his individuality, hidden behind his work and made
subservient to the stage, asserts itself with irrepressible power is
in the form of his plays, in their style, in their verse. There the
poet breaks forth in his splendour. Marked with the characteristics
of the day, his form is at once unique and incomparable, though
marred by glaring faults. He has caught all the diseases of the style
of his day, as well as its 'happy valiancy' ; and has merged them
into a style which is his alone, and which transforms the elements
which constitute it, fusing into one harmonious whole the dis-
parities—as numerous as though they had been set there for a
wager—within his plays. His dramatic gift alone would have
brought him immediate popularity, but would scarcely have

ensured his fame. The first of dramatists was also the first poet of his time—one of the first of all time. In most instances the fusion of drama and lyricism is unanalysable, perfect. By it a scene is lifted to a higher level, while the proportion of its elements remains unchanged; truth and beauty become blended in a perfect unity.

The defects of this genius are almost as striking as his virtues. A multitude of words and similes flows from him, and it seems no dyke can stay the flood. It was this irrepressible impetuosity which led Jonson to express regret that the poet could not be curbed. Still more often it was subtlety which attracted him. He enters the maze with the confidence of one sure of finding the guiding clue. But the most cunning sonneteer would find it difficult to follow the fine-drawn thread through some of Shakespeare's conceits, where the play on antitheses is so subtle that even the most careful reading can scarcely unravel its meaning. No spectator, even with the finest senses, could disentangle at first hearing the threads of such a skein. The poet is not always restrained by the dramatist. Although many passages—and those often the most famous—of his plays are written with perfect clarity and frank simplicity, Shakespeare had a liking for involved, rare, and somewhat enigmatical expressions, which require something of mental effort from his auditor and even from his reader. This turn of mind required to be checked and repressed by the play's greater need for action.

Another characteristic of his genius is an undefinable energy, something mobile, dynamic, which keeps us ever attentive. His vitality remains undiminished at the end of three centuries and seems to increase with every reading. There is in this something of the mystery which Enobarbus ascribes to Cleopatra:

> Age cannot wither her, nor custom stale
> Her infinite variety. Other women cloy
> The appetites they feed; but she makes hungry
> Where most she satisfies.

There is no work, however fine it be, which does not seem monotonous compared with that of Shakespeare.

SHAKESPEARE'S CONTEMPORARIES AND HIS IMMEDIATE SUCCESSORS

George Chapman. Shakespeare's chief rivals were among the humanists. The hostility shown him at the beginning by Greene and the 'University Wits' was renewed later by Chapman and Jonson. Not that they were his most dangerous competitors for public favour, but it was they who were the loudest in proclaiming their title to write and their classical culture, as opposed to his more slender stock of learning.

George Chapman (c. 1559–1634), the translator of Homer, did not begin to write plays until he was nearly forty. His case is singular. He shows a pleasant wit, a sober manner, and a graceful style in his comedies, of which the chief are: *Al Fooles*, *Monsieur d'Olive*, and *The Gentleman Usher*, all published in 1605 and 1606.

In his tragedies he gives way to romanticism, where heights of lyrical splendour alternate with fustian and obscurity. He seems to have been much influenced by Marlowe, reproducing the latter's exaggerated characters and declamatory tirades, but obscured by a metaphysical jargon and sprinkled with moral reflections taken from Greek and Latin authors, and from the neo-Latin writers of the Renaissance.

His tragedies have this peculiarity about them—that they are founded on contemporary French history. The best known of them are: *Bussy d'Ambois*, written perhaps about 1598, *The Revenge of Bussy d'Ambois*, published in 1613, and the *Conspiracie and Tragedie of Charles, Duke of Byron, Marshall of France* (1608). With the exception of the first, these plays are too long-winded and lack movement. *The Revenge of Bussy d'Ambois* is a kind of *Hamlet*. Bussy d'Amboise is assassinated; his brother Clermont is a philosopher and opposed to violence, and he does not decide to avenge his brother until after careful thought. As to Byron, he is depicted as a braggart, swollen with overweening ambition. The most curious, if the most unequal, of his tragedies is the first, in which Chapman transforms the adventurer Bussy into a super-man, after the fashion of Marlowe, and attempts to draw in Tamyra (as he calls her), Bussy's mistress and the wife of the Comte de Montsoreau, a passionate Puritan, employing the language of virtue even in the midst of guilt.

To sum up: Chapman had nothing of the humanist but his erudition; he was a romantic by temperament. His talent was not governed by reason, he lacked balance, or perhaps good taste, and even good sense; and with all his learning he pushed to the extreme the melodrama of the popular stage.

Ben Jonson. The writer who posed resolutely as the disciple of the ancients and sought to reform the stage according to classical models was Ben Jonson (1573?–1637). He has, moreover, from his own time to this, served as the antithesis of Shakespeare. He deserves his position as much by the value of his work as by the firmness of his attitude. If originality consists in withstanding the flood of popular opinion, then Jonson is more original than Shakespeare. The latter accepted the wretched conditions of the English stage with resignation and a smile; he was not out of sympathy with his public. Jonson, ill-tempered and arrogant, stood out against the Elizabethan drama; to the popular tastes he opposed his tastes, his thoughts, his doctrines taken from antiquity. Shakespeare swam with the tide: Jonson set his massive weight against it.

He was truly learned. Throughout his life he set down in a notebook every passage which struck him in his wide reading. His notes were always there for him to refer to, to use in his works, to be adapted to his needs. He was familiar not only with the best classics, but with lesser writers, the mediocre and the for-gotten, and with critics and commentators; with historians as well as poets. When he writes of antiquity, he does so with docu-ments before him, and with a full knowledge of ancient ways. When he describes contemporary society he does so after careful study, having, pencil in hand (like modern impressionists), taken innumerable sketches from life: picturesque details and descrip-tions of oddities seen or heard—especially if these showed human foolishness.

Of a satirical temper, he put on the stage a succession of eccentrics. Each one has his own particular 'humour', some ruling tendency, habit, or fad. Jonson insists that 'humour' is the dominating feature in man by which all other characteristics are determined. But in fact what he portrays chiefly in his *Every Man in his Humor* (1598) and in *Every Man out of his Humor* (1599), is one exaggerated peculiarity. Character-drawing so repressed and limited was the opposite to that of his contemporaries, who allowed their characters space for full, complex, development and evolution—even to incoherence; and who made fixed oddities only of their supernumeraries.

It is only in the entire absence of romance, in the care taken to remain strictly within the region of comedy, that Jonson shows himself a follower of antiquity. His first plays are loosely constructed; they are more truly reviews of grotesques than well-built comedies. It is remarkable that Jonson only assimilated classical qualities separately, one by one; he never used them all in one play. Moreover, he deceived himself in supposing that he had replaced stage 'monsters' by living men. Inclined as he was to notice only the striking peculiarities of an individual, or the violence of some exceptional character, disregarding the fundamental feelings common to mankind, ignorant of love, he remains apart from nature in the classical meaning of the word. Throughout his plays it is hard to find a normal man or woman; and in this quality Jonson is less classical than Shakespeare.

After a period of Aristophanic comedy—*Cynthia's Revels* (1601), and the *Poetaster* (1602)—in which he attacked his fellow dramatists, Marston and Dekker, he rose to high comedy in *Volpone, or the Fox* (1605), *Epicœne, or the Silent Woman* (1609), *The Alchemist* (1610), *Bartholomew Fayre* (1614), which are among the most remarkable plays of the Renaissance. There is no longer here a mere succession of humorous characters; Jonson's vigour builds up the whole as solidly as a Roman edifice. All is now original: subject, plot, and characters, the last being either creations of his mind or the result of personal study of eccentricities.

There is throughout a cynical outlook, although Jonson's harshness is but unevenly distributed. In the strongest of the plays—*Volpone*—he attacks with violence a cupidity which he sees capable of the most abominable baseness. *Epicœne* is a farce having for plot the 'humour' of a man who cannot bear the slightest noise. *The Alchemist* is an exposure of dupers and duped, of those who raise money by trading on human credulity, and those who let themselves be cheated by the hope of sudden riches. In this last and in *Bartholomew Fayre*, Jonson satirizes the growing Puritanism of the day, in which he sees only hypocrisy and which provides him with curious and amusing caricatures.

After an interval of nine years he returned to comedy in a series of inferior plays somewhat unkindly called by Dryden 'his dotages', in which are found much the same exact observation, the same rich picture of contemporary manners.

At times he attempted tragedy, as in his historical *Sejanus* (1603), and *Catiline* (1611). Both—especially the first—were written with the design of competing with Shakespeare, whose *Julius Caesar* (1599?) had shown to Jonson the possibility of interesting the public in ancient history. He was conscious, moreover, of knowing far more Roman history than his rival. He must have laughed at, or been contemptuous of, Shakespeare's anachronisms. Shakespeare's Rome was London; Jonson meant to show his public ancient Rome. When he published his play he could quote his authorities, and the very editions of Latin authors he had used.

These plays are so strongly built, so close to history, so full of vigour and accuracy, that no one can read them to-day without respect for the author's scholarship and strength of mind. Throughout there is strength, dignity, learning—too much learning, in fact, too many dull and heavy speeches. Too much violent satire as well, for Jonson, more often than not, chose subjects in which he might sound the depths of baseness rather than look for goodness or heroism. His most striking Roman scenes are those which are most like the cynical *Volpone*.

Yet in this robust and bitter writer there dwelt a poet. He may be found in the unfinished pastoral of *The Sad Shepherd*, and again in the numerous masques he wrote for the court under James I. For these splendid entertainments, which were then the luxury of the court and nobles, no one composed better *libretti*, more varied, or written with greater charm, than did Ben Jonson. The rough-tongued dramatist whose stiff blank verse gave forth a muffled sound, moved with grace and ease in these lyrical plays, all rhymed song, allegory, and faery.

John Marston. Among the writers of the day with whom Jonson disputed, none received harder knocks than John Marston (1575 ?–1634). He was himself abusive, 'a ruffian in his style'. At a time when the theatre imposed no restraint, he is the first in coarse and violent speech. He descends at times to extravagance and sheer nonsense, as in his first melodramas *Antonio and Mellida* (1600) and *Antonio's Revenge*, in which, however, there are impressive passages that cause a thrill of horror.

His best plays are a kind of tragi-comedy, from which, through their confusion, obscurity, and gratuitous coarseness, emerge forcibleness and variety, and an originality of which we might be more assured were the dates of his plays better known. It is certain that he presents some striking analogies with Shakespeare, and may have forestalled him in the violent comedy *The Malcontent* (1601 ?), if that indeed preceded *Hamlet*. It might be defined as the first play to set the fashion of inveighing against society in lyrical irony. Whatever may be the truth as regards *Hamlet*, *The Malcontent* certainly anticipates certain points in *Measure for Measure* and *The Tempest*.

Marston's cynicism is less apparent in *The Dutch Courtezan* (1605), a counterpart of Dekker's *The Honest Whore*, and again it is hard to say which was written first. Marston's Courtezan is a passionate woman, potentially a criminal, and no repentant Magdalen purified by sacrifice. In *The Dutch Courtezan*, as in Marston's *Parasitaster, or the Fawne* (1606), are echoes of Shakespeare's heroines Beatrice and Rosalind, but denuded of the poetry with which Shakespeare graced them, and stained with the coarseness natural to Marston.

His best title to fame is his share in that admirable comedy of manners *Eastward Hoe*, where his name occurs with those of Chapman and Jonson. It would be difficult to assign to each author his share, but this picture of the idle and the industrious apprentices (which was later to inspire Hogarth) is one of the most successful in the drama of the Renaissance. A fresh air of reality blows through this morality, which brings before us the life of a tradesman, the interior of middle-class households, the simple honesty of some and the shifty vanity of others. It all moves lightly, easily, without visible sign of artifice. His faults apart, Marston shows a talent at once incisive, nervous, and personal, from which it would seem that more than one of his contemporaries reaped advantage.

Thomas Dekker. (1570?–1632?). Although Jonson associated Dekker with Marston in his attacks, the two are as different one from the other as gentleness from cynicism and good temper from spleen. Dekker reminds us of Robert Greene. He unites everyday realism to irresistable romanticism. Suavity and optimism persisted in him throughout a hand-to-mouth existence and years in a debtor's prison.

Jonson represented him as a poor devil of a 'play-dresser', ignorant and shabby, whose improvisations were choked with folly as with weeds. And it is a fact that Dekker's works show little effort and were written for gain. He wrote much in collaboration, sometimes with mediocre, sometimes with famous, dramatists. Only eight or nine of his own works have been preserved, and but four of these possess real merit. Yet this 'play-dresser and plagiary' has the gift—which Jonson lacks—of grace and freshness. Mere books weigh lightly on him; psychological analysis does not worry him; he is at his best when he writes down scenes from life, describing living people in whose feelings we can share. He represents the popular writer, instinctively dramatic and spontaneously romantic.

The gayest of his comedies is *The Shoemaker's Holiday* (1599), founded on one of the episodes in Deloney's *Gentle Craft*. The hero is Simon Eyre, the jovial London shoemaker, who, with his shrewish wife, his apprentices and journeymen, is vividly described to us. About these lively sketches is twined a rosy thread of sentiment; and this cheerful realism, neither harsh nor cynical, is allied with romance without extravagance, as the simple verse, whether blank or rhymed, is combined with graphic prose.

Elsewhere the poet in Dekker is more visible, as in *Old Fortunatus* (1599?), which opens with something of grandeur in the scene where the goddess Fortune appears with her train of crowned beggars and kings in chains.

The Honest Whore is the best known work of this author. It was published in two parts, of which the first (1604) shows us the courtesan wakening to love and turning from her shame. The second part shows her married to her first seducer—an incorrigible gamester who tries for gain to thrust her back to evil. Loving him, she is willing to sacrifice all for him but honour. By her side watches, all unknown, her old father, Orlando Friscobaldo, disguised as a servant, the most original character in the play. A tender-hearted man under a mask of surliness, he is one of the first 'rough diamonds', in fiction and one of the most successful.

Indeed, the Bohemian Dekker was gifted with liveliness, feeling, and poetry. These qualities are apparent even in his collaborations: in the pleasantest scenes of *The Witch of Edmonton* (written with Ford and Rowley), and in the *Virgin Martyr* (written with Massinger).

Thomas Heywood. The nearest to approach Dekker in pity and gentleness is Thomas Heywood (1575?–1650), who has been described by Lamb as 'a sort of prose Shakespeare'. Perhaps he should have said 'a Dekker in prose', a Dekker without lyricism or fancy, without gaiety; a creator of touching and of dramatic situations rather than of character; on the other hand, because he could at times eliminate romance, better able than Dekker to write a true bourgeois drama.

Like Dekker he kept to the city, and throughout his vast output is perceptible a desire to satisfy the tastes, even the vanity and prejudices, of citizens and corporations. Like Shakespeare he was both actor and playwright; he was also the most prolific of the Elizabethans, and claims to have been the principal author of two hundred and twenty plays, of which only twenty-four are extant. Sometimes he takes his subject from English history, appealing to the patriotism or Protestantism of his public; sometimes he appeals merely to their honest emotion.

In *The Foure Prentises of London, with the Conquest of Jerusalem* there is open flattery of the city. The same note is sounded in his

Edward IV, *The Troubles of Queene Elizabeth* and *The Fayre Mayde of the Exchange*, in which the citizens of London play the chief parts. A wider patriotism appears in *The Fair Maid of the West* (1617; printed 1631), which describes in lively fashion sea adventures and the life in an English port.

Where Heywood succeeds best, however, is in domestic drama in the style of *Arden of Feversham*, with this difference, that crime is softened, and of adultery we see only the moral tragedy— the suffering it inflicts and the remorse it brings, as in *A Woman Kilde with Kindnesse*, acted in 1603. Contemporary drama can show nothing simpler in form and matter, and nothing more moving, than this picture of a happy home destroyed by the wife's treachery, of the suffering of the husband, who for sole revenge banishes his wife; her agony of remorse, and her death at the moment of her husband's forgiveness. When we remember the sanguinary vengeances taken by deceived husbands in other plays of the time, we draw a breath of relief over Heywood's unwonted gentleness. Twenty years later he again took pity and forgiveness as his subject in *The English Traveller* (1633) from which play also shines generosity and kindliness. Heywood was guided by an instinctive goodness, a wide pity, which had nothing in common with Puritan rigour.

Thomas Middleton. As city chronologer and writer of municipal masques and pageants, Thomas Middleton (1580–1627) was no less attached to London than were Dekker and Heywood; and, like them, he sought his subjects in the city. But instead of flattering Londoners, he laughed at them and amused himself in showing up their crooked ways and vices. In this he resembles Ben Jonson, but is less openly didactic. He had a taste for cynicism and licentious quibble, and his chief object was to divert the more frivolous among the public.

One after another, from 1604 to 1612, came a series of highly-flavoured comedies, distinguished by their liveliness, dexterity, and full knowledge of the disreputable side of London life. The best of them are: *Michaelmas Terme* (1604), *A Trick to Catch the Old One, A Mad World, My Masters, Your Five Gallants* (1606), and *A Chast Mayd in Cheape-side* (1612).

The dexterity of these comedies is noteworthy; substance is given to the fooling by keen observation of the swindlers and their dupes, or by sketches taken from life. In *Michaelmas Terme* he describes the knaveries of a usurer who ruins a young man from the country. In *A Chast Mayd* he handles several equivocal plots with nimble deftness, whisking them all at a wild pace to an ending in a roar of laughter. Here and there an original character is drawn with care, but as a rule the people who figure in Middleton's farces are merely types of revellers, vagabonds, gamblers, and thieves. He has little care for morality, yet he does not approve of vice, although he likes to show it on the stage and often refrains from openly condemning it.

Towards 1612 the writer of comedies turned to tragedy, in which he showed unexpected force. It was probably at this date that he produced *Women beware Women*, which deals with the scandalous crimes of the Italian courtesan Bianca Capello. But preceding the horrors is a charming sketch of Bianca as a young wife, pure and loving. The abominations which follow stand out the more darkly against this scene of married happiness.

His other tragedies, or romantic dramas, were written in collaboration with the actor William Rowley (1585?–1642?), and it is not easy to distinguish their respective hands. These remarkable plays are: *A Faire Quarrell* (1617), *The Changeling* (1621), and *The Spanish Gipsie* (1623). Unequal they may be, but at times, they rise to considerable heights, and all are marked by a realism which distinguishes them from the melodramas of the time. *The Changeling* is their masterpiece; it deals with horrible events, but the people, especially the adventurer De Flores, are drawn with a tragic force that might be Shakespeare's. The crimes, the passions, are set down—with a swift, sudden, dramatic restraint, hurrying to the dreadful end—in verse which is disjointed, breathless, nervous, and full of movement.

Cyril Tourneur. Two men of whose lives nothing is known—Tourneur and Webster—turned to stark melodrama, obtaining their effects not, like Middleton, through the illusion of reality, but by throwing a fantastic light on crime and torture.

Cyril Tourneur left two gloomy dramas: *The Revenger's*

Tragaedie, published in 1607, and *The Atheist's Tragedie* (1611). The first, which is the stronger, is a kind of morality in an Italian dress. Vindice, the avenger, recalls Hamlet, in that it is his mission to punish the guilty. Like Hamlet, too, he forces his mother to look her villainy in the face. No other play of the time has a more intense dramatic effect and so clear and rapid a style.

John Webster. John Webster (1575?–1625?), among several mediocre plays, some written in collaboration, has left two, *The White Devil* or *Vittoria Corombona* (*c.* 1611), and the *Duchess of Malfi* (1614), both which reach a high level and possess to a rare degree the faculty of causing a shudder. The first owes its value to the character of the Italian beauty Vittoria Accorambona, whose life scandalized Rome towards the end of the sixteenth century. Webster turns the limelight on her crimes, but he makes us feel also the fascination of her wit and beauty, her unquenchable ambition, and the spirit which faces and fights despair. Superbly she confronts her judges, hurling back at them their overwhelming charges. She is the centre of a plot extravagant in its wickedness, and worked out in scenes of physical horror and fantastic strangeness.

Much the same atmosphere is found in *The Duchess of Malfi*. It is a tragedy of persecuted virtue, of the young widowed Duchess —of whom

> You may discern the shape of loveliness
> More perfect in her tears than in her smile

—driven to madness and death by her two brothers because she has married a subject—Antonio, her steward, who loves her and whom she loves. The play is full of Shakespearian touches, but Webster, if unable to equal the master in character drawing and psychology, yet attains originality by his reliance on the pathos inherent in the situations and even in material things, and by prolonging the sight of almost unbearable suffering. Yet these expedients of an inferior artist are relieved by the poetry of distress and death which dominates the tragedy. For Webster is a poet, and he uses unforgettable phrases—always on the note of death, it is true, and touched with the chill of graveyards—that haunt the mind. Transfigured by suffering, the Duchess shines out from the darkness a lofty, solemn figure.

Webster's genius was strictly individual and was limited to one *genre*. He left but two really memorable plays. His was a slow, painful method of working; but he shows us melodrama lifted into poetry.

John Fletcher and his Collaborators. Towards 1607 began the large body of work which was afterwards inaccurately described in the folio of 1647 as the plays of Beaumont and Fletcher. In fact the volume contains, besides the plays written by the two friends (either separately or together), many others written by Fletcher with various collaborators and produced during the ten years which followed Beaumont's death. There are fifty-seven plays in the folio of 1679, which is the largest collection of plays of the age that has come down to us. Its unity is in Fletcher's personality which binds the whole together.

John Fletcher (1579–1625) came of a good family (although he was left poorly provided for) and was well educated. Possibly need as well as inclination led him to write plays. Possessed of talents which of themselves would have brought him success, he cleverly made the most of his reputation when once he had won it. He organized a kind of workshop where plays might be written, and henceforth made use of collaboration in order more rapidly to meet the players' needs. If it would be incorrect to say that Fletcher introduced joint authorship, at least no one made so much use of it as he did.

With Beaumont. Towards 1607, when Fletcher was twenty-eight, began his friendship with Francis Beaumont (1584–1616), the son of a judge. The two young men wrote at times separately, as when Beaumont produced his comedy *The Woman Hater*, and Fletcher his half-lyrical pastoral *The Faithfull Shepheardesse*. But chiefly they wrote together; either comedies, such as *The Scorneful Ladie* and *The Knight of the Burning Pestle*; or tragicomedies like *Philaster* (1609); or pure tragedy, such as *The Maides Tragedy* and *A King and no King* (1611). All these plays reveal a surprising knowledge of stage-craft; it is impossible to understand the flexibility and, let us say, the modernity of the theatre of the time, without reading *The Knight of the Burning Pestle*. It is a burlesque, a parody, droll, indefinable, a blend of many elements, forming, as a whole, the gayest of comedies, shallow but quick and lively, which might have been written yesterday. The authors pour good-humoured ridicule on the citizens' craze for absurd romanticism, as well as on their conceit and the vainglory induced by the parades and reviews of the city train-bands. This is the English pendant to *Don Quixote*.

Philaster is a tragi-comedy reminiscent of Shakespeare, and it reveals its authors' methods. They skim Shakespearian drama in the hope of producing something better, more refined. But they only succeed in rooting up the flowers, and depriving them of nourishment. They take away reality, yet they do so with undeniable grace; they charm more quickly, if for a shorter time.

There is more of substance in their best work—*The Maides Tragedy*. The plot is of their own invention and treats of the divine right of kings, the unquestioning loyalty of courtiers, and the Spanish cult of honour. The principal character is Evadne, the king's mistress, shameless, fierce, superb; who ends by killing her seducer in the bed to which she has bound him. The characters will not stand close scrutiny, but the scenic effects are admirable, and the play reads pleasantly with its harmonious verse and the ease of a language which has not yet grown old.

With Shakespeare. After Beaumont it seems that for a time Fletcher collaborated with Shakespeare. Many critics attribute to Shakespeare certain passages in *Henry VIII* and also in *The Two Noble Kinsmen*, of which the greater part was written by Fletcher.

Fletcher alone. A certain number of plays bear Fletcher's name alone, and of these the greater number are romantic: *The Tragedie of Valentinian* (1614), *The Tragedie of Bonduca* (1614), *The Loyal Subject* (1618), *The Humorous Lieutenant* (1619). Some, however, are true comedies: *Monsieur Thomas*, *The Pilgrim* (acted at Court, Christmas 1621), and *The Wild-Goose Chase*. Fletcher's hand can be detected in the loosely-constructed plot, the witty dialogue, the substitution of sentimentality for passion, and the free, libertine tone of the lighter parts. It can also be recognized by his metrical style, for his line usually ends with a redundant syllable. This lengthened it out into a sort of effeminacy which will not let the voice rebound, but into which it sinks, as into a soft cushion.

With Massinger. There are few of his contemporaries with whom Fletcher did not write; but his chief helper after Beaumont was Philip Massinger, who collaborated with Fletcher in some ten plays before winging his way alone. As a rule Fletcher assigns to him the subordinate part, but Massinger's conscientious work is manifest in many an act of such tragedies as *Thierry and Theodoret* and *The False One*; or the comedies *The Little French Lawyer*, *The Spanish Curate*, and *The Beggars Bush*. Massinger's intellectualism is often happily combined with Fletcher's lively ease, and it would be unjust to give all credit to the latter for the plays they wrote together.

SHAKESPEARE'S SUCCESSORS.   THE THEATRE
UNDER CHARLES I

Philip Massinger. It is advisable to pursue the study of the drama
without interruption until 1642, seventeen years after Charles I
came to the throne, when the theatres were closed.

After Fletcher the playwright who dominated the stage both by
the number and the quality of his plays was Fletcher's assistant—
Philip Massinger (1583–1639). Eighteen plays remain to us of
the thirty-seven which have been attributed to him, and they
bring before us a clear, distinctive figure: not original perhaps, for
Massinger might be defined as a mingling of Jonson and Fletcher.
In his comedies we find something of the exaggeration of eccentricities and vices which marks the author of *Volpone*; and in his
tragedies something of the romanticism of Fletcher. But Massinger has also individual qualities. His drama is a drama of ideas.
He loves to stage oratorical debates, long pleadings before tri-
bunals. He neither shares Fletcher's aristocratic leanings, nor does
he always care to please the multitude.

His best comedies are: *A New Way to Pay Old Debts* (before
1626), *The City Madam* (1632), *The Guardian* (1633); his principal
serious plays are: *The Fatall Dowry* (1619), *The Duke of Millaine*
(1620), *The Unnatural Combat* (1621), *The Maid of Honour* (1626),
The Bond-Man (1623), *The Renegado* (1624), *The Roman Actor*
(1626), *The Picture* (1629), &c.

The play which had the most lasting success was his comedy
A New Way to Pay Old Debts, in which the chief character, the
usurer Sir Giles Overreach, enlarges on his abominable opinions
with astonishing frankness, and, in his blustering viciousness, is
reminiscent of Ben Jonson's *Volpone*. The same may be said of
Luke Frugal in *The City Madam*, who is a monster of hypocrisy,
malice, and ingratitude. Such beings belong more to satire than
to humour, and check rather than provoke laughter in comedies
otherwise well constructed and written.

Massinger shows his talent best in his serious plays. Those referred to above are all remarkable in different ways. *The Roman Actor*, which he looked on as 'the most perfect birth of my Minerva', may be ranked with Jonson's *Sejanus*, to which it is superior in variety of interest. The hero is the actor Paris, full of enthusiasm for his profession, which he defends with eloquence before the Senate. When the empress Domitia makes love to him, he hesitates to repulse her, knowing that such rejection will mean his death. Then the thought flashes on him—what a magnificent scene it would make: the actor rejecting the empress! That would cause him to go to his death as does the martyr to the stake.

In contrast with this drama of violence, crime, and tumult may be set Massinger's most classical work, *The Maid of Honour*, with its heroine who is the incarnation of virtue, love, and honour. It is true that she is too complacently eloquent and sometimes theatrical, but in spite of pomp and rhetoric she loves and suffers: she is alive.

All Massinger's plays show careful workmanship. Both style and verse are strong and solid; and this at a time when style and metre were beginning to show signs of dislocation. It is true that he is often strained and monotonous, and frequently repeats himself. But if not inspired, he is a conscientious writer of scenes which are massive and often noble.

John Ford. Of the same age as Massinger, and writing at the same time, John Ford (1586–1639?) was the author of work more individual than Massinger's, though of narrower compass. A fatalist, melancholy, disdainful of morality, convinced that passion justifies all things, he was, to judge from his works, morbid and attracted by the perverse and strange, yet a true poet, who wrote with care, harmony, and restraint. He collaborated with Webster, Rowley, and Dekker, and his own works are few. They were all produced between 1627 and 1633. Besides the historical play *Perkin Warbeck*, which is well written but tame, he wrote *The Lover's Melancholy*, *'Tis Pity Shee's a Whore*, *The Broken Heart*, and *Love's Sacrifice*. In all is the same deft handling of emotions and graceful style. In *'Tis Pity Shee's a Whore* he shows the irresistible force of passion. Here, a generation later, are repeated the ardours of Romeo and Juliet, but stained with sin, for the subject is incest between brother and sister. In this painful play melodrama alternates with morbidity, but in the fatalism which dominates it there is undeniable poetry. More harmonious and of unimpeachable morality is *The Broken Heart*, with its unrequited love and suffering virtue. Penthea, unhappily married, repulses her lover, but the resultant stress and conflict within her are so great that she becomes insane, and utters words both sad and strange. Calantha, in a ballroom, hears of a succession of deaths and yet dances on without apparent emotion, but in truth she is stricken to death and dies suddenly of a broken heart.

The impression produced by Ford is as deep as it is painful; the atmosphere of his plays is sultry, motionless, thundery. His persistence in depicting suffering, perverse or exquisite, is a sign of decadence, but as an artist he ranks high.

James Shirley. More prolific and more varied in his works than Ford is the dramatic poet James Shirley (1596–1666), called by Lamb 'the last of a great race'. But his was not a voice strong enough to sound a new note; his plays are skilful reproductions. He is as expert in tragedy as in comedy. In the former his best works are: *The Traytor* (1631), and *The Cardinall* (1641), which show the influence respectively of Cyril Tourneur and of Webster. There is more of novelty in Shirley's comedies; they are more realistic and they describe contemporary manners, modes, and literary styles. Although he could not create, Shirley gives us lively sketches of fashionable life under Charles I. It is this picturesqueness which still keeps alive *The Wedding, Changes, Hyde Park, The Gamester,* and *The Lady of Pleasure*, all written between 1626 and 1635. This last, filled with discussions between husband and wife—she wishing for a life of fashion, and he declaring that she will ruin him—is the prototype of more than one post-Restoration comedy.

Shirley also wrote tragi-comedies, in which he shows himself an apt disciple of Fletcher; his models he found in Spanish literature, the riches of whose drama were then beginning to be known. Of these romantic comedies the best are: *The Young Admirall, The Opportunitie,* and *The Imposture*. Shirley continued a tradition, but he had not the strength to breathe into it freshness or new life.

Closing of the Theatres. There are many other minor dramatists who, now and then, wrote interesting plays, but whom it is
impossible to mention here, so luxuriant was the growth of drama
at the time of the Renaissance. This growth was stopped only
by the closing of the theatres by order of Parliament in 1642.
The contest between the Puritans and the stage had begun with
the popularity of the public theatre; but, protected by the
sovereign and by public opinion, both dramatists and actors had
felt themselves strong enough to flout, defy, and scandalize
their adversaries. When these became masters, they closed the
theatres, which were not reopened until eighteen years later,
at the Restoration.

It would be difficult to trace the evolution of the drama in the
sixty-six years which separate the opening of the first theatre
from the interdiction of plays by Parliament; only the general
changes can be mentioned. More stiffness is apparent in the
beginning; skill, stage-craft, and scenic experience came with
time; dramatic style became increasingly supple; verse, at first
too rigid, relaxed, lost its monotony, then by excess of freedom
finally returned to chaos; prose became more frequent and more
agile. Conventional characters, such as the vice and the clown,
legacies from the morality play, increasingly gave way to beings
who were real or who aspired to be so. Drama moved, if not
towards truth, at least towards realism. Yet if it approached
reality outwardly it grew remote from it in essentials; comedy
showed a preference for eccentricity and anomaly, while tragedy
tended towards romance. Romance, it is true, had been there from
the beginning, but it increased from decade to decade until it
replaced the epical character of many of the first dramas. Plays on
national history ceased almost entirely towards the end of the sixteenth century. In their stead came plays which aimed at sensa-
tionalism, heralds from afar of the heroic drama of the Restoration.

This review of the drama as a whole brings out more clearly
the part which Shakespeare played, set midway in those years: he
humanized the initial violence of the drama, which after his death
tended once more to drift away from the central truth—that of
character and feeling.

THE END OF THE RENAISSANCE

Prose from 1625 to 1660. The years from 1625 to 1660 are filled with the religious and political controversies of the reign of Charles I, and the triumph of Puritanism. Many look on these years as a time when literature shrank from its preceding fullness into something narrower, and in which all thought was concentrated on one book—the Bible. But apart from the facts that the breath of humanism persisted and was nowhere so strong as in Milton's works, and that freedom of mind and morals continued to be shown in the writings of the Cavaliers, it is evident that the religious movement was not solely the product of the zealous Calvinists, who succeeded for a time in establishing Presbyterian discipline, nor of the Independents who rebelled against this discipline, claiming for each individual the right to interpret the Bible according to the light vouchsafed to him. The contest reanimated Anglicanism, which had been lukewarm and indolent under Elizabeth. The religious fervour of the middle of the seventeenth century is due at least as much to the zeal of the Episcopalians—even of those who became Roman Catholics—as to the subversive passion and sombre religion of their adversaries. At no other time in their history did the Anglicans produce, both in verse and prose, works so noble and so fervent. The literature of that time is of far greater variety than would appear at first sight. Yet it remains broadly true that the revival of religion distinguished that generation from the preceding by giving it, as a whole, in place of its partly lost freedom, an air of dignity both grave and severe. The rich humanity, the widespread curiosity, the intermingling of comedy with tragedy in the portrayal of life, were replaced by a passionate controversy on the forms of Christian religion, and a search—which became almost an obsession—for the way of salvation.

Sir Thomas Browne. The contrast is perhaps more apparent in prose. There are no more romances, picturesque descriptions of manners, imaginative entertainment; not even the disinterested meditations of humanists amused by their studies. In this respect the passage from Robert Burton to Sir Thomas Browne (1605–82) is characteristic. Both were equally learned, but Burton was a cleric deeply preoccupied with medicine; Browne, a physician by profession, was by taste a theologian or preacher. Primarily he was a mystic, although he studied science and applied the Baconian method to the examination of the fauna round Norwich and to natural phenomena. His mind is a curious blend. Although in his *Pseudo-doxia Epidemica* (1646) he sets out to rectify popular errors, he is himself credulous enough. In spite of his zeal for, and often deep knowledge of, natural science, he retained a taste for miracles. What struck him most was the little that we know. He poured out his complex soul in the famous *Religio Medici*, published in 1643. In it he declares himself 'inclined to that which misguided zeal terms Superstition'. He loves 'to lose himself in a mystery, to pursue his Reason to an *O Altitudo!*'. Far from rejecting religion for the concessions she exacts from reason, he would have her more exacting. His subjects are, as a rule, those of the preacher: the vanity of earthly glory and the nearness of death. But he breathes new life into these topics with his singular erudition, which rekindles the ashes of a long lost past, and also with his constant reference to the cosmos. And the result is a curious strangeness coupled with a lofty magnificence which is entirely his own.

He gave rein to his imagination in *The Garden of Cyrus* . . ., a treatise on quincunxes, or the disposition throughout nature of the mystical number five. His *Hydriotaphia*; *Urn Burial, or a Discourse of the Sepulchral Urns lately found in Norfolk* (1658), treats of the oblivion which covers the traces of men, even though famous; and with this subject he plays as a dilettante. For in him the artist is greater than the thinker, and the writer more seductive than the man who is somewhat inclined to place himself upon a pedestal. His prose is admirable; nobly built up and already modern in form. What dates it is its Latinity. His lofty thought clothes itself in sonorous words chosen for their cadences, for he believes in the music of his periods as the poet in that of his verses. The interweaving of his harmonies offers an enchantment to the ear scarcely less than that of the finest lyrics.

The Anglican Clergy. Jeremy Taylor. Religious as was Sir Thomas Browne, he was, in a way, an eccentric and a dreamer. But the revival of religion was to bring forth memorable prose from the very heart of Anglicanism. George Herbert, poet of *The Temple*, left in prose but a few pages, *The Country Parson*, which are, however, limpid and full of charm. It is to Jeremy Taylor (1613–67) that we must turn to find Anglican prose in its most harmonious fullness. The Anglicans, once persecutors, were now the champions of religious freedom. Taylor, tolerant by nature, became their interpreter in his *Liberty of Prophesying* . . . (1646). His most famous works are *Holy Living* and *Holy Dying* (1650–1), but above those works must be placed his sermons.

He is distinguished less by logic than by fancy or imagination, fed by reading and by a store of classical culture on which he drew largely, the whole made fresh by a close contemplation of nature. Jeremy Taylor is a prose-poet closely allied to the Elizabethans. He has been called the Shakespeare of English prose and the Spenser of the pulpit. He conceives an imaginative interest in the subjects he describes, to which he has been drawn at first by the desire to make his thoughts clear. As he follows and develops his metaphors, he recalls the fancy, even the mannered curiosity, of some poet of the Renaissance. The thought of a rose leads him to paint it in detail; an allusion to the rising sun develops into a description of its successive phases. If he compares prayer to the song of a lark, he follows its flight lovingly. Such delicate fancy gives grace and freshness to his sermons, at the risk of hindering their argument; the logician becomes lost in the poet. Yet he has moments of strength and dignity, as when he dwells on death, shorn of its 'solemn bugbears', and shows how easy it is then to die. He is not only an observer of nature but a psychologist who knows the heart of man. No one has spoken so wisely and so tenderly of married love, of its first fragility, and of the strength acquired 'by a mutual confidence and experience' through the years, as does this cleric in his sermon on *The Marriage Ring*. A charming anthology may be compiled from his works.

To obtain an idea of the Anglican activity during these years, to the above must be added the following names: Robert Sanderson, the preacher; Thomas Traherne, author of *Centuries of Meditations*; John Hales, with his *Golden Remains*; and especially William Chillingworth, who, in 1638, wrote *The Religion of the Protestants, a safe Way to Salvation*; and John Gauden, the probable author of the famous *Eikon Basilike: The Pourtraicture of His Sacred Majestie in his Solitudes and Sufferings* (1649), a book which shed a halo of romance and martyrdom over the House of Stuart.

The Puritans: Baxter, Milton, &c. The Puritans were no less active than the Anglicans. On the whole, it was they who from the beginning took the offensive. Violence and coarseness had marked their pamphlets in the reign of Elizabeth, and these characteristics recurred in Prynne's *Histriomastix* (1632)—an immense denunciation of the stage—and in many an attack on the episcopacy; above all in several of Milton's tracts. An exception must be made of the moderate Presbyterians like the five parish ministers who signed their treatise against Episcopacy with their united initials, which formed the word 'Smectymnuus'. There is the same moderation in the prolific Richard Baxter (1615–91), author of *The Saints' Everlasting Rest* (1649–50), which is simply written, but neither nervous nor brilliant; and in the rather dull and uninviting prose of John Owen (1616–83).

It is, however, a fact that the Puritan side of the contest appears violent and fierce because it is dominated by the genius of Milton. The numerous pamphlets which he wrote from 1641 to 1660 form the most extraordinary monument of the prose of the middle of the seventeenth century. His case was peculiar. He was a poet and looked down on prose, using it only to perform what he considered to be his duty. He said that in prose he had only 'the use of his left hand'. Yet he constrained it to be the instrument of his passion and lyricism. Forbidding as they may be in parts, narrow in subject and out of date, these prose works are kept alive by the fire and passion that were in him, by his numerous self-revelations, and also by many magnificent bursts of eloquence. At first he fought with the Presbyterians against the prelacy, then he broke from their ranks to write, one after another, four pamphlets in favour of divorce (as he wished to dissolve his marriage with his first wife); and, in 1644, in defence of the freedom of the press, the most eloquent of his prose works, *Areopagitica, a Speech for the Liberty of Unlicensed Printing*. In the same year he published his *Tractate on Education*; then he abandoned English for a time in favour of Latin in order to justify in the eyes of Europe the execution of Charles I. He turned, too, in the end to Latin to express his personal thoughts, heterodox and bold, on Christian doctrine and morality, in his *De Doctrina Christiana* which remained in manuscript at his death.

The remorseless length of his sentences renders them formidable at first to the reader, but from their troubled vehemence breaks forth at times a scathing irony or a sudden splendour. They reveal the impetuous idealist, unpractical and thorough-going.

Philosophy. Thomas Hobbes. Very striking is the contrast between these religious controversies and the contribution to rationalism of Thomas Hobbes (1588–1679). Bacon's secretary and Descartes' correspondent, Hobbes entered boldly into new ways with his *Elements of Law, Natural and Politic* (from 1640), his *De Cive* (1642, English text 1651) and his *Leviathan* (1651). Empiricist and realist, Hobbes asserts that sensations and ideas are bound up with physical causes. Man is a being of appetites, the satisfaction of which would result in a state of incessant war between individuals if a social pact were not reached under a sovereign protective power. The irreligion of the system was atoned for in the eyes of its contemporaries, especially under the Restoration, because it favoured the absolute right of the sovereign. Hobbes's *Leviathan*—to which James Harrington replied with his work on a Utopian Commonwealth (*Oceana*, 1656)—is written in strong, logical, massive prose, exempt from the oratorical vehemence and the ornaments of his great contemporaries, and heralding the prose of the classical period. It is antipodal to that of the Cambridge mystics, or Platonists, such as Henry More (1614–87) and Ralph Cudworth (1617–88), who, towards the same time, wrote in reaction from the philosophy of reason, and the former of whom lived in a spirit of exaltation, becoming almost a visionary.

The Eccentrics. In spite of Hobbes, eccentricity marks most of the prose writers of the middle of the century. Among them must be noted Sir Thomas Urquhart of Cromarty (1611–60), who, happily inspired, turned his verbal virtuosity to use in a translation of the first two books of Rabelais (1653); and witty Thomas Fuller (1608–61). The latter's 'points' and conceits show that he belonged to the 'metaphysical' school. His pleasant optimism and kindliness shed a light over his works: the *Church History of Britain* (1655–6), *Holy and Prophane State* (1642), and *The History of the Worthies of England* (1662).

Izaac Walton (1593–1683) holds a place apart. Of all the writers of the time he remains the most popular; his long life prolonged to mid-Restoration days the spontaneity of the Elizabethan age. He serves as a link between Marlowe and Dryden. A plain ironmonger of Fleet Street, he had all his life a love of culture and an admiration for good literature. His biographies of Donne, Wotton, Richard Hooker, George Herbert, and Sanderson are filled with intimate details and perfumed with sympathy. But his best known work is *The Compleat Angler* (1653), which is at once a technical treatise and charming idyll, written on the morrow of the Civil War by one whose friends were all in the camp of the vanquished, but whose serenity remained unruffled. Walton loves the 'silver streams' in which he fishes; the ale-house where he sups off his trout, and falls asleep in a bed that 'smells of lavender', with his 'scholar' who shares his tastes and, like him, enjoys old songs such as that 'made by Kit Marlow'. He describes these healthful pleasures in a prose limpid, if a little slow; still redolent of the artificial pastoral here and there, but wherein lies mirrored the witchery of the English countryside.

POETRY FROM 1625 TO 1660

IF an attempt be made to classify the poets of the middle of the seventeenth century, they will divide themselves into two principal groups, conformably to the events of those troubled times: the secular poets—those from among the Royalists, and known as the Cavaliers; and the religious poets, subdivided into Anglicans and Puritans. This division is more social than literary, but it is handy and simple, and corresponds fairly well to the difference in inspiration.

Carew. The first poet to show of what spirit the Cavaliers were to be, and to combine in himself the influences of Jonson and Donne, was Thomas Carew (1598?–1639). He was a courtier and a love-poet, writing, his rivals said, his polished verses with great difficulty. His lines have a classical shapeliness. He can isolate a thought and follow it up, and give to every particle a nice proportion. Those of his poems which find their way into anthologies are usually: *Ask me no more*; *When thou, poor Excommunicate*; *Read in these Roses the sad story*. His work is fine-drawn, thin, and a little cold, yet still retaining an Elizabethan glow of imagination. Style and line are shaped and polished with a care that neither Denham nor Waller—the acknowledged pioneers of the classical school—could much improve upon.

The Cavalier Poets. Sir John Suckling (1609–42) is the typical Cavalier poet, with his loyalty, dash, petulance, lightness of heart and of morals. He laughed at 'the trouble and pain' Carew gave to his verses, himself dashing off his unequal lyrics often with irresistible impetuosity. His characteristics are swiftness and audacity. When he rallies woman on her caprices and himself on his inconstancy, he is reminiscent of Donne, but retains only the master's hyperbole, leaving the metaphysics alone. He lets fly his mockery in slight, free, smart verses, in which at times the madrigal assumes the voice of irony (*Out upon it*). He wrote an original wedding-ode in the form of a ballad—*A Ballad upon a*

Wedding—in which a farmer is supposed to describe in picturesque language a grand wedding he has seen. Suckling is king among the 'mob of gentlemen who wrote with ease'.

Yet the cavalier lyric at its highest is found in two little songs by that very imperfect, often mannered and obscure writer—Richard Lovelace (1618–58). One, written from the Gatehouse at Westminster, is *To Althea from Prison*, and contains the famous lines:

> Stone walls do not a prison make,
> Nor iron bars a cage;

the other, written before joining the royalist army—*To Lucasta, on going to the Wars*—contains the no less familiar

> I could not love thee, Dear, so much,
> Lov'd I not honour more.

In contrast to Lovelace, John Cleveland (1613–58) was a satirist. His most successful work is *The Rebel Scot*, a vigorous attack on the nation which had delivered Charles I to the Parliament. Although his lines are full of conceits, and he was a close imitator of Donne, he could write a biting epigram and a couplet that Dryden could not have bettered, and he made ready the way for the poetical satires of the Restoration.

Herrick. Midway between the Cavalier and Anglican poets stands Robert Herrick (1591–1674), the most gifted, the most delicate of all. He belongs to the first through the Anacreontic flavour of his youthful poems; to the latter because, presented when thirty-eight to the vicarage of Dean Prior in Devonshire, he attempted to convert his muse and bid farewell to frivolity. The only collection of his writings is the *Hesperides*, or *Works both humane and divine* (1648), and the former are in the proportion of five to one.

He began as Ben Jonson's disciple—his 'son', meeting 'my Ben' in the London taverns frequented by the wits. Like Jonson, Herrick had a taste for diminutive poems after the manner of the Greek Anthology; but his verses are endued with a sparkling lightness of which Jonson was scarcely capable. With the exception of certain longer pieces, such as *The Hock-cart or Harvest Home*, and *Corinna's going a-Maying*, which has become a classic, most of his verses are songs airy as a breath, pretty madrigals, love-fancies, apostrophes to flowers, light epitaphs. Here is the song of a light heart rejoicing in grace and beauty; there is the melancholy of a sensuousness which knows that all beauty is ephemeral. Everything with him is transposed and lightened. He has no weight of thought or morality; he never swoops, but hovers gracefully, and is the most epicurean of moderns. He was, in his day, the perfect artist in light poetry, while Milton was imposing his sovereign art upon the epic.

Anglican Poets: Herbert. Herrick represents the easy-going Anglicanism of the age. By his side were developing Anglicans whose poetry was infused with religious fervour while it retained something of Elizabethan fantasy. Even more than the Cavaliers did they show marks of Donne's influence and his taste for subtlety.

The most popular of the Anglican poems is the *Temple* of George Herbert (1593–1633), which appeared after the author's death. His lines are the expression of the edifying performance of his priestly duties during the last three years of his life, after he had renounced the worldly career to which he was destined by his birth and brilliant scholarship. His *Temple* is a singular work, full of faith and fervour, and, at the same time, of affectation and conceits. The subtlety is natural to him, in his very spirit, in the unexpectedness of his association of ideas and of the images he strings together. He is the saint of the metaphysical school. If he startles the reader at times, at others he gives the impression of a kind of sublimity. His characteristic is the expression of everything by means of images or symbols; he will have nothing but the concrete. It is his merit; it is no less his defect, for it seems at times to belittle his thought. At times also he is subtle to obscurity, strange to the point of enigma. Although he was an accomplished and versatile versifier, working in intricate stanza and metre, his lines have no easy melody; they are often too closely packed; but they are, as a rule, nervous, original to the point of oddness, sharpened with humour, full of homely sayings, often forming aphorisms and proverbs.

Crashaw. Younger by some twenty years than Herbert, Richard

Crashaw (1612–49), a devout admirer of *The Temple*, became a Roman Catholic when he was thirty-three. But before this he had been strongly attracted by the Spanish mystics and the Neapolitan poet Marino. Theirs, rather than Donne's, are his metaphysics.

His flow of words is astonishing, as in *Music's Duel*, where he reproduces with a virtuosity without parallel the trills of the nightingale; and in his *Wishes to a supposed Mistress*, where he enumerates the incredible perfections of the woman he will love. To this gift was added in his religious poems a rare warmth of enthusiasm, as in his litany of praise to the tears of Mary Magdalen, *The Weeper*, above all in his hymn to St. Teresa, *The Flaming Heart*. The rush of sacred love which ends this latter poem is perhaps the most ardent that has been produced in English religious literature.

His faults are surprising, and not one of his poems is free from defects; but his poetical gifts outweigh them. Less intellectual than Herbert, less simple and precise in diction, he has more colour, warmth, and harmony. In lyrical impetus Shelley alone is his peer.

Vaughan. Unequal also are the poems of Henry Vaughan (1622–95), the doctor-mystic of Wales, who, after some secular verse, published in 1650 and 1655 a series of pious effusions—*Silex Scintillans*. He is perhaps of all the lesser poets of the seventeenth century the one who, after being the most disdained, has become the most admired. For long he was looked on as the type of obscurity, platitude, and inharmoniousness. There are, in fact, but a few of his poems which are of value, but these are real pearls. In them he reveals himself as more musical than Herbert, less reasoning, with a mysticism more fluid, a warmer imagination. He does not pray, like Herbert, within a church, but beneath the sky. His feeling for nature comes from his own picturesque country-side, and this feeling, mingled with his Christian meditations, gives a modern romantic accent to his best verse. His lines have nearly always an air of improvisation and often of awkwardness. But he finds new images in the sights of nature for his meditations on life and death. He has strangely anticipated Wordsworth

in several poems, in particular in the retrospective vision of his
childhood, *The Retreat.*

Quarles. To this list of Anglican poets must be added the name
of Francis Quarles (1592–1644), who, in his *Emblems* (1635), wrote
what can be described as a rhymed commentary on a volume of
biblical illustrations. He abounds in conceits and is often absurd,
but he is also often lively, and he has a shrewd and homely wit.
His *Emblems* were extremely popular; and he may be called the
people's metaphysical poet.

Marvell. The Puritans also had their poets, less numerous, it is
true, but they included one who was among the most pleasing, and
the one who was the greatest, of the century—Marvell and Milton.

Andrew Marvell (1621–78) who was tutor for a time to the young
daughter of Lord Fairfax, the Parliamentary general, then Milton's
assistant as Latin secretary to the council, and, at the Restoration,
the champion of religious and political freedom, wrote poems
which are distinguished by their love for nature. Most of them
were written between 1650 and 1652, while he was at Nun Apple-
ton House, the Yorkshire estate of Lord Fairfax. He gives
expression to his enjoyment of the contemplation of fields and
woods and gardens; he knows the aspects of bush and bird and
blossom. He likes to read 'in Natures mystick Book'. He anticipates the Lake-poets in his almost pantheistic love of the countryside. Another time his imagination shows him a magical picture of
the Bermudas, those islands where some of his Puritan friends had
sought refuge for conscience' sake in the days of the Stuarts. He
also wrote some love poems, the most striking of which—*To his Coy
Mistress*—repeats with a passionate force the Anacreontic precept:
'Gather ye rosebuds while ye may'. He had yet another vein, that
of the ardent patriot, for it was more love of country than religion
which inspired the memorable lines on Cromwell's Protectorate
and death. After the Restoration he turned to political satire, in
which he showed himself a precursor of Dryden. But he is best
known by his earlier poems, in whose fancy the extravagance of
the 'metaphysicians' is checked and humanized. He lacked but
continuity of effort and a more exacting art to attain a place in
the highest rank.

Abraham Cowley. There are certain poets of the mid-seventeenth century who serve as links between the Renaissance and modern times. Among them was Abraham Cowley (1618–67), who took the highest place in the estimation of his day. He closes the list of the 'metaphysicians' and anticipates the English classicists. He resembles Donne in his search for conceits and subtleties; but, the friend of Hobbes, an admirer of Bacon, and one of the founders of the Royal Society, with a taste for physical science, he is above all an intellectual.

As a poet he was ambitious. In his *Pindarique Odes* he attempted to introduce Pindar's manner, an attempt which brought into fashion an irregular ode, a deformation of that of Pindar. Desirous of giving to his country an epic, he wrote his *Davideis* (1656); the structure of the first part of this has some resemblance to that of *Paradise Lost*, but, being written in epigrammatic couplets, it is nearer to *The Rape of the Lock* than to the Bible.

If he lacked imagination, he possessed ingenuity. His best poems are the lyrics in his *Miscellanies*. He shows genuine feeling in his elegies on William Hervey and on the poet Crashaw. The wit which is his characteristic is shown with brilliance in his verses on Wit and on Hope, as is his rationalism in the *Ode to the Royal Society*, which contains a fine tribute to Bacon.

His lines are animated, but they are jerky and dry, wanting in melody, while his forced elisions are disturbing. He was not, therefore, regarded by the classicists as a precursor, an honour which they reserved for Waller and Denham. To-day Cowley's graceful prose *Essays* are more read than is his verse.

Waller. By his long life Edmund Waller (1606–87) links together two periods separated by political troubles and a literary revolution. He has left chiefly occasional verse. His aim was not to be original so much as to smooth the irregularity of English poetry. 'English verses', he said, '... want smoothness; then I began to essay.' Ease and polish characterize his short poems—panegyrics on Cromwell and on king and queen, love-lyrics, verses to other writers, epigrams, and his later *Divine Poems*, which include the lovely lyric, written at 82: *The seas are quiet when the winds give o'er.* His images are clear and felicitous, and there are times when he attains a noble dignity. 'He first', said Dryden, 'made writing easily an art; first showed us to conclude the sense, most commonly in distichs.' He possessed the qualities, or rather absence of defects, corresponding to the tastes of a new era, less careful of originality than of smoothness and correctness.

Denham. In one line of Pope was praised 'Denham's strength and Waller's sweetness'. Sir John Denham (1615–69) is best known by the descriptive, didactic poem *Cooper's Hill*, first published in 1642. It is a meditation on the view from a hill near the forest of Windsor where the scenery is filled with historical associations. Here, as elsewhere, Denham shows himself skilful in formulating his moral reflections and literary judgements; and his concise, well-turned couplets served as models to his successors.

A new era was, indeed, approaching in literature, a time of understanding which would take no pleasure in the exuberant fantasy of a Spenser, and would be repelled by the *tours de force* of the 'metaphysical' poets. This new literature was to be called 'classical', and yet it found in antiquity a curb rather than an inspiration. If, indeed, it was study of the ancients which deserved this name, of all English writers it would be best bestowed on the author of *Paradise Lost* and *Samson Agonistes*. Nothing in the following century bore so deep an impress of the influence of Greece and Rome on the form of poetry; nothing showed a comprehension at once so precise and so high of the beauty of ancient art.

PLATE XVI

RICHARD LOVELACE

From the painting in the Dulwich College
Picture Gallery

JOHN MILTON

From the engraving by Faithorne in the
National Portrait Gallery

MILTON (1608-74)

MILTON alone attempted seriously to fuse into one the spirit of the Renaissance and of the Reformation. Spenser's attempt was half-hearted and only served to show the incompatibility of the two elements. But Milton conceived from the beginning the idea of a work which should unite with the art of antiquity the moral ardour of the Bible. In his own person he had felt the conflict of the opposing forces,—paganism and Christianity, nature and religion,—and had himself found a solution. The intermingling of the two elements may vary with his passing years, but from the first the union was made harmonious by the impulse of a powerful will. No other English poet has been at once so deeply religious and so great an artist.

Born in London, of a family in easy circumstances and Christian without undue strictness, from adolescence he dedicated himself to poetry, to a work as yet undeterminate, but which should be sublime. He was only twenty one when he wrote his first master-piece—his *Ode on the Morning of Christ's Nativity*—in which his mastery is as apparent as in the poems of his maturity. A series of incomparable stanzas celebrates the end of paganism and 'the death of Pan': the oracles are dumb; the Lares and Lemures disappear; the gods of Phoenicia and Egypt vanish. Now shines the day which routs all the evil phantoms of the night. For the evocation of these figures the young poet employed all the resources of a knowledge already great, and of a language richly plenished with Elizabethan treasures, of which he availed himself warily, using only the best and the richest.

He was still at Cambridge when he wrote this ode. He left there to live for a time with his father at Horton in Buckinghamshire, giving up the thought of a business career and deciding also not to take orders and enter the ranks of a clergy which Laud, in his tyranny, seemed to be leading back to Rome. Between 1632 and 1638, in the studious quiet of Horton, he wrote the lovely poems of his youth.

He shows his feeling for nature in the early *L'Allegro* and *Il Penseroso*, short poems in part expressive of the poet's emotions; they are not so much landscapes as moods of his mind. They show Milton seeking for the highest of pure pleasures, or rather, painting as in a diptych, the two aspects under which enjoyment appeared to him according to his mood; the alternation in his heart of pleasures joyous and grave. Each poem evokes a distinct figure: the first, that of Mirth, fresh, rosy, and vigorous, dancing on tiptoe, and the second, that of divine Melancholy like a pensive nun 'devout and pure, . . . with even step and musing gait'.

It is in the following poems that he confronts the moral problem before him, expressing in veiled and allegorical manner his inner conflict. In outward form he adheres to the Renaissance, writing either masques or pastorals. But the form only is of the century; the spirit, the thought, are Milton, austere and grave.

After the fragment of a masque—*Arcades*—Milton wrote an entire masque—*Comus* (1634). It is simple as an old Morality, for Milton lacked all dramatic sense and feeling for the stage, and its didactic tendency is so obvious that it smothers emotion or any thrill of suspense. But it was both new and admirable. It is a hymn, white and immaculate, to chastity. The young heroine, assailed in a wood by the magician Comus, god of wine and sensuality, disdains his attacks and emerges unspotted from the trial. If the poem is ill-fitted for the stage, it is enchanting to read, whether it be for the discourses which make up most of the play, the descriptions which abound in learned reminiscences of the classics, or for the crystalline lyrics, which are to those of the Elizabethans as carefully reared flowers to wild blossoms of the hedgerow. All reveals Milton; the morality of *Comus* is that of Milton, high, disdainful, and solitary. Shakespeare was in communion with the multitude; Milton with the few elect. The whole poem is poised on a snowy height, as narrow as it is lofty.

Less indirectly Milton describes his mental conflict in the elegy *Lycidas* (1637) which is the last English poem of his youth. Under cover of lamenting the death by drowning of a college

friend, Milton returns on himself. This untimely death of a young
and gifted man makes him raise the question 'what avails?'
Why not give oneself up to easy pleasures and 'sport with Amaryl-
lis in the shade, Or with the tangles of Neæra's hair?' But the
call of fame resounds, and Milton, for the sake of honour and
virtue, repudiates the invitations of Pleasure.

Already he perceived that the duty was urgent, for the Church
lay beneath Laud's despotism, and he held it to be the task of all
true reformers to try to free her. This, however, Milton did not at
once attempt, for he left England to travel for fifteen months in
Italy, where he was to hear the voices of the Renaissance mur-
muring their precious memories, and speaking to him of beauty
and of love.

The beginning of the conflict between Charles and his people
brought Milton back to England. He held it his duty to put aside
his poetical projects. For twenty years he was to write in prose,
working, as has already been said, as it were with his left hand.
The sole exceptions to the prose were a dozen 'occasional' sonnets,
among which are some of the noblest in the English language.
Of these is the sonnet on his blindness; that which describes his
vision of his second wife after death; and especially that in which
his indignation bursts forth against the Piedmontese for having
massacred the Vaudois. This last may be regarded both as the
explosion of a great and sincere anger, and as an example of
supreme art.

The Restoration of 1660, in forcing Milton back into private life,
allowed him to return to the high aims of his youth. From
poverty, blindness, leisure, rose his chief works: *Paradise Lost*
(1667), *Paradise Regained* and *Samson Agonistes* (1671). In these
a new Milton is revealed to us. Personal unhappiness and a
nation's agony had darkened his thought. Long and vehement
controversies had given him a habit of dialectics from which he
could not now break free. He felt something like disdain for the
lovely rhymed verse of his youth. From henceforth he turned to
loftier harmonies, founded on rhythm only and on the very
articulations of the thought. He wrote in blank verse only, except
in some choruses in *Samson*. Blind, he turned his back on the

Renaissance as upon trivialities, to fix his inward sight on the Bible. He sang of the Creation, the fall of the angels, the fall of man, the reconquest of Paradise by Christ, or of the sacrifice of Samson who chose death that with himself he might destroy his country's foes.

Milton's greatest work, *Paradise Lost*, is the most Hebraic of all English poems. It is the fruit of a Puritan's meditation on the Bible, in which he believes whole-heartedly, between which and himself he admits no intermediary, while he claims entire freedom in his interpretation of it.

His was not the imagination which can rise beyond self and time, and bring from the far-off past primitive beings. He could, it is true, conceive of the universe as an immensity which contrasts with Dante's manifold grotesque descriptions. Milton's hell is a vast indeterminate space where, in 'darkness visible', on 'the burning marle' are stretched gigantic beings, the vanquished angels changed to demons. But the arch-rebel, Satan, is the poet himself. In Satan's arrogance and revolt may be read Milton's vindictive hatred of the crown. The story of Adam and Eve is the drama of conscience, hesitating between good and evil, exposed to temptation, liable to fall. In the Bible story he found the elements of his own life. Love had come near to being his own undoing. He had married at 35 the 17-year-old daughter of a royalist cavalier. A month of marriage had been followed by the return of the young wife to her father's house, while the poet wrote pamphlets angrily claiming the right of divorcement for 'contrariety of mind'. Although she afterwards returned to him, and Milton was subsequently twice happily married, the first bitterness remained. Woman imperilled man's soul. Hence, in opposition to the code of chivalry, Milton held that woman should be held in subjection. Supreme morality and true felicity were to be attained in a union where the husband is the head and the wife his submissive helpmate. His famous apostrophe (*Haile, wedded love*) sounds the knell of the ancient conception, and replaces love, true and total, as distinct from lust as from asceticism or Platonism, at the centre of human life.

The constant return of the poet on himself which occurs in his epic may diminish its objective value, but communicates to it an emotion, a continuous eloquence, a lyric ardour, which reach their height when he invokes the Holy Spirit at the beginning of his work, or when he laments his blindness; and which are present wherever the sacred text causes to vibrate within him the chords of memory. The central force of the poem is his absorbing personality; its beauty lies in his art, more austere than in the days of his youth, but not less supreme; an art always that of the humanist. The rejection of rhyme is in the spirit of those poets of the Renaissance who were in closest communion with the ancients. The form of the epic, Hebraic in its subject, is cast in an antique mould; it has the look, the style, the divisions of the *Iliad* or the *Aeneid*. In style it is the most Latin of any English poems. The value of words, the syntax, the pauses, the very use of the ablative absolute, ceaselessly recall the classics to the scholarly reader. Milton's periods, the unrhymed verse, beautiful in its cadence, with its enjambment and inversions, possess a solemnity, severity, unbending strength and nobility, inherited from ancient Rome.

Paradise Regained is the complement of, and reply to, *Paradise Lost*. Its subject is St. Luke iv. 1 13, where Christ, after His fast of forty days, resists the three temptations of Satan and thus ends the reign on earth of the evil one. When we pass from one epic to the other, the impression first made by the second is one of greyness, of diminished brightness, of a lower tone. Satan reappears, but he has become smaller, faded; he is no longer splendid and indomitable, but a trickster and a hypocrite. The poem is entirely human, its interest lying in the temptation of a soul. Milton, great heretic as he really was, saw Christ not as divine but as a superman. In this light he describes the thoughts and mental struggles of Christ, who seeks to determine and accomplish His mission. The resemblance between Milton's Christ and himself is striking. The temptations which assail Christ are those which assailed Milton, sorest of all being Satan's offer to Christ of Greece, her literature, philosophy, arts, and eloquence. But this offer, like the others, is rejected: all learning is vain compared with true wisdom; the very poetry of Greece falls before the Bible.

As personal, and more beautiful, is *Samson Agonistes*. Here, the contemner of the Greeks shows himself a more devoted disciple than even in *Paradise Lost*. *Samson Agonistes* might be a tragedy of Sophocles, so close is it in form to Hellenic drama, the strophes of the chorus relieving the dialogue. The whole of the action occurs in one day, at one place. But it lacks movement and development which are both essential to tragedy. The meditative genius of Milton, whose thoughts were for ever turning inward, has achieved a powerful lyrical poem rather than a dramatic one. Three-fourths of the tragedy pass before there is any sign of progress or hint of a climax. All is taken up with Samson's mournful recitative; a Samson blind, betrayed by Dalila, captive in the hands of the Philistines. Here we see Milton in his old age: blind, a survivor of the lost Republican cause among the alien triumphant Royalists. The poem is an expression of the desolation of failure and of his anger against, and contempt for, woman, by nature inferior to man, deceitful, and untrustworthy, whence God's law that she should be subject to man.

This drama with its noble bareness of style forms a fitting close to Milton's life. It confirms what has already been stated: his work is the product of an egoism which is heroic, of a pride so high that it is often sublime; the product also of a matchless art, the delicate rhymed poems of his youth being equalled, with a difference, by the mighty blank verse of his maturity. His epics broke strangely on a dissolute and cynical age, mostly incapable of appreciating either great poetry or religious exaltation. Milton was the last survivor of the great period.

RESTORATION LITERATURE (1660–1700)

THE year 1660, when the attempt to establish a Puritan republic in England ended in failure and the Stuart monarchy was restored by the return of Charles II to his capital, is commonly, and justly, regarded as the initial date of modern literature. There are few moments in history when such a sudden and decisive break is evident, when a country displays such general delight in throwing off a spiritual yoke, and revolting from the religious doctrines or imaginative outlook of the preceding generations. But it is to be understood that as always, so even now, something of the past had survived into the present as truly as something of the future had been anticipated and prepared by men who wrote before the Restoration.

Surviving Puritanism. Bunyan. Indeed, as we have seen, it was after the return of Charles II that Milton composed and published his great religious poems. Still later appeared the most popular of the books which expressed the Puritan faith, those of John Bunyan (1628–88). This man of humble birth, the son of a craftsman, himself a craftsman turned baptist preacher, was over 30 when the Republic came to an end. It was in a hostile, sceptical, and cynical generation, which persecuted and imprisoned him, that he produced the book in which he describes his conversion, *Grace Abounding* (1666), and those in which he sets forth in an allegorical form the life of man as it is viewed by the true Christian: *The Pilgrim's Progress* (1678), *The Life and Death of Mr. Badman* (1680), and *The Holy War* (1682), to cite only his chief works. In these, better perhaps than in any contemporary writings of the Commonwealth, the spirit that had fired the best of the religious enthusiasts is revealed. But Bunyan had no concern with politics; his thought was entirely taken up with religion. He seems to have lived with the Scriptures alone, indifferent to every production of the human mind, occupied only with the quest for means of salvation. The deeply sincere, profound, and passionate searchings of conscience to which he devoted

himself in *Grace Abounding* make it one of the books which penetrate furthest into the mystery of conversion. But this book remains supremely personal, while in the *Pilgrim's Progress* Bunyan
became sufficiently detached from self to describe in the guise
of an allegorical novel the progress of every Christian soul, with
its aspirations, its struggles, its weaknesses, its recoveries, along
the path of life. He accomplished it with the aid of a host of
familiar symbols taken from the personal impressions of a simple
man, who without ever freeing himself from his preoccupation, was
nevertheless able to observe many of his fellows, and to note the
courage of some, the vacillations, the evasions, the various egotisms,
and the hypocrisies of others. A natural talent enabled him to
impose on his thousand observations the unity of an allegory with
a lucidity and lifelikeness which learned authors like Spenser had
been far from attaining. To express them he hit upon a unique
prose which has at once the tang of popular speech and a dignity
derived from the noble translation of the Bible, the simple and
sober narrative portions of which Bunyan had absorbed.

While he was the single dissenter of his time who had an instinctive genius for writing, Bunyan yet testifies to the current of
mysticism which ran all through his age, and which re-emerged
here and there, as in the *Journal* of George Fox (1624–90), the
founder of the Society of Friends, or in the naïve autobiography
of his disciple Thomas Ellwood (1639–1713).

The Anglicans. The dissenters were not the only representatives of the religious thought of the period. The Church of
England, restored to the parishes and pulpits of which she had
been dispossessed under the Commonwealth, achieved a certain
lustre in the theological works of Isaac Barrow (1630–77) and the
sermons of John Tillotson (1630–94) and Robert South (1634–
1716). The last is still tinged with the imaginative glow of the
Renaissance, but on the whole one finds among these Anglicans
chiefly a truthful and utilitarian presentation of religious questions
and a power of clear exposition, sometimes close-knit and eloquent,
in correct, regular and well-balanced prose: qualities which relate
them to that 'age of understanding' inaugurated by the Restoration.

PLATE XVII

The Valley of the Shadow of Death, an illustration
to Bunyan's *Pilgrim's Progress*

The Scientific Spirit. Henceforth it is the scientific spirit which clearly tends to prevail. The impulse given at the beginning of the century by Bacon, although at first checked by years of political and religious quarrels, was strongly renewed on the return of the king. Its most apparent result was the foundation of the 'Royal Society of London for the Improvement of Natural Knowledge'. The patient and detailed study of nature tended to occupy the best minds. Up to this point, apart from Roger Bacon, English science had been able to take pride only in the name of William Harvey (1578–1657), famous for his discovery of the circulation of the blood. Now there was a galaxy of learned men of every order: the mathematicians John Wallis and Seth Ward; the astronomer Halley; the physiologists and physicians John Mayow, Thomas Sydenham, Francis Glisson, and Robert Boyle; the economists Sir William Petty and Locke. Towering above them all by his genius, Sir Isaac Newton (1642–1727) was the discoverer of the law of gravitation, of the decomposition of white light in the spectrum, and of the theory of fluxions. His *Principia*, written in Latin, was published in 1687. It is in this scientific work, rather than in literature properly so called or in any theological or philosophical production, that the period reaches its supreme height.

Historians and Biographers. Research into the precise facts of ethics and sociology characterized most of the prose writers of this period. It is evinced in the composition of numerous memoirs of widely varying kinds, ranging from history proper to mere journals.

The History of the Rebellion and Civil Wars in England by Edward Hyde, Earl of Clarendon (1609–74), begun in 1646 and continued till the author's death, is doubtless a piece of Royalist apologetics, but it abounds in pictures, and especially in studied and often shrewdly life-like portraits. It is transitional in form; the long sentences are indefinite in outline; the passage from the Latin period to the short and concise modern style is in progress but is not yet achieved. From this results a certain awkwardness, relieved, however, by the vivacity of the narrative.

Clarendon, Lord Chancellor to Charles II until 1667, represents the Cavalier spirit which was soon to be that of the Tories. The

Scotsman Gilbert Burnet (1643–1715), Bishop of Salisbury, expressed in his books and particularly in his *History of My Own Time*, published posthumously, the feelings of the Whigs who relied on Parliament; more impartial than Clarendon, almost as penetrating in his portraits, he is inferior as a writer. To him we owe a picture of the reigns of Charles II and James II, and this he subsequently extended to the Peace of Utrecht (1713).

By the side of these general histories must be mentioned such biographies as *The Life of Colonel Hutchinson*, a Republican who died in prison in 1664, written by his widow, and the *Life of William Cavendish Duke of Newcastle*, a good Royalist, by his wife the Duchess. These two works form a striking contrast: the life of the Puritan is traced with a constant dignity, in a slightly strained and oratorical style; the life of the noble lord has more freedom and ease, but the frequently affected prose reveals the eccentricity of its author. Both biographies are remarkable for the conjugal fervour and admiration which inspired them.

Still more valuable are the *Diaries* of Evelyn and Pepys. John Evelyn (1620–1706), a Fellow of the Royal Society, kept a record of his impressions from 1641 until his death. He travelled in France, Italy, and Holland, and found especial pleasure in observing places, gardens, and public edifices, whether abroad or at home. His pages are full of information about the life of the second half of the seventeenth century.

The diary that Samuel Pepys (1632–1704), Secretary to the Navy, kept during the first nine years of the Restoration, is something unique. It was, indeed, not meant by the author for any eyes but his own. Written in shorthand, it was not deciphered until 1825. It is a day-by-day account of the acts and deeds, the good or bad impressions, of a man of the middle class who reveals himself with the utmost frankness, without, however, any other aim than that of heaping up the petty details of every day. He had neither literary nor historical purpose. But no deliberate description permits us to penetrate nearly so far into the intimate life of a man or of a particular period. The family life of Pepys, his irregularities, his friendships, his worries as an honest official and a good patriot, his tastes as a man of the world and a lover of music and the theatre, his aesthetic prejudices, which were exactly like those of his contemporaries, live again in these notes, jotted down every evening without any attempt at style. Although he had no premeditated plan, he worked, in this faithful collection of exact details of one human life, in the same spirit as that daily more numerous band of observers who were facilitating the progress of the natural sciences by minute and persevering research. It was by importing into fiction the same method of accumulating the simplest and apparently most insignificant facts, without passion or any apparent bias, that Defoe was to provide so many models for the realistic novel.

The Essayists. The professional prose writers of the same time, with a more exacting artistic consciousness, have in common with the foregoing an easy familiarity which is more reminiscent of the *Essais* of Montaigne than of the oracular pages of Bacon. In Cowley's *Essays* which appeared in 1668, the likeable temper of a learned and moderate moralist is expressed; in the various writings of Sir William Temple the diplomat (1628–99), the learning is often superficial but the balanced and common-sense wisdom already anticipates the attitude and tone of an Addison. On a foundation of moral pessimism, there is a superstructure of the same tolerance, the same search for the right medium, in the work of George Savile, Marquess of Halifax (1633–95), the champion of political opportunism, whose views are best expressed in his *Character of a Trimmer* (1688), in which he defines the doctrine of compromise.

John Locke. Throughout the Restoration period the cynical philosophy of Hobbes was predominant, but there was also being elaborated the new philosophy which was to be supreme after the Revolution of 1688 and to dominate the eighteenth century. Its principal exponent was John Locke (1632–1704), in his *Essay concerning Human Understanding* (1690), *Some Thoughts concerning Education* (1693), *The Reasonableness of Christianity* (1695), &c. This philosophy is above all that of common sense; it is eminently empirical, practical, and utilitarian. It discards intuition and sees in intelligence the mere product of sensation and experience. On the political side it is liberal and, one might say, parliamentarian. On the religious side it respects existing beliefs and draws from the Bible an entirely reasonable Christian teaching. Religion is a personal affair and should be left free, due regard being had to the security of the State. Dealing with education, Locke protests against scholastic exercises, recommends the cultivation of the mother tongue, and insists on the formation of character as the chief object to be attained; all of these are ideas which for several generations were to guide English thought and to obtain the approval of Continental philosophers. Voltaire was to be one of the disciples—the most famous—of 'the wise Locke'. This moderate rationalism, with no strong desire to systematize, is profoundly expressive of certain inward and lasting tendencies of the English mind.

The New Literature. The writers whom we have just discussed illustrate the intellectual activity of the end of the century in its most serious aspect. They reveal the qualities of study, of reflection, and of thought which form, as it were, a foundation for the literature of the same period. But they do not constitute literature proper, and it is with this that we must now deal. Almost wholly centred about the dissipated court of the Stuarts, and designed to please a frivolous, sceptical, and worldly society, it conceals the solid acquisitions of the time behind its often profligate exterior, rather than reveals or expresses them. It was born of an inevitable reaction against Puritan oppression, and proclaims itself especially by the rejection of too severe moral laws, and indeed often of all moral discipline and all decency, the observance of which is henceforward commonly stigmatized as hypocrisy.

It is usually defined as being under French influence, and this is true of certain tendencies in form, of a growing taste for disciplined verse and prose, of the desire for clearness and correctness, and of the effort to keep separate the types and moods which had been so often commingled in the spacious Elizabethan period. But at bottom there is a striking contrast between the elevated tone of literature under Louis XIV, the habitual nobleness, sometimes too consistently sustained, of the writers, the dignity of the great French classics of the century, and the profligacy of the greater part of their English emulators.

In fact Restoration literature derives chiefly from pre-Common-wealth national literature, but with a preference for its most licentious elements, a loss of almost all it had held of freshness, of fantasy, and of the essentially poetic. The writers of the Restora-tion turned the full-bodied, often turbid, wine of their forbears into vinegar, their lyricism into satire. It is, upon the whole, the satiric spirit which predominates, and with it the new age obtains its least-contested successes. The exuberance of the Renaissance gives way to an embittered criticism of every religious, moral, or chival-rous code, sometimes crudely mocking, sometimes refined by the influence of classical precedents. The excuse is that of depicting human nature truthfully with its instincts exactly as they are; of replacing the fictitious ideal by the naked reality.

Samuel Butler. The first work of the Restoration, one which characteristically opens the new era, was the *Hudibras* of Samuel Butler (1612–80), a product of the revolt against Puritanism. Begun during the Civil Wars, it was published in three parts (1663, 1664, 1678). Butler had acquired a learning as curious as it was varied, and as secretary to a puritan justice of the peace had been initiated into the manner of living which his poem was to ridicule. It was at once a resounding success. The author, inspired by *Don Quixote*, represented the Presbyterian in the grotesque person of Sir Hudi-bras, and the Independent in the guise of Ralph, his squire. Truth to say, Butler did not excel either in the recital of adventures or in character-drawing; as a romance his poem is of the worst. It con-sists wholly and solely of an account of how Hudibras one day began a campaign to prevent a bear-baiting, a profane and pagan amusement. The fight with the crowd of revellers is in the pseudo-heroic mode. Though he is the conqueror in his first onslaught, the knight is afterwards overcome and put in the stocks. Mean-while, he is wooing a rich widow who, to put his love to the test, makes him promise to submit to a whipping. After long shuffling, and after having discussed the matter with his squire and con-sulted Sidrophel the astrologer, Hudibras goes to the widow with a lying tale, but is soon reduced to confessing all his heinous offences.

Except for the amusing contrast between the Presbyterian

Hudibras, top-heavy with learning and loaded with scholasticism, and Ralph the Independent, scorning all written knowledge and believing in the sole power of inspiration, we must not look for character studies in *Hudibras*. But the poem is valuable for the vein of satirical comedy which runs through it from end to end and fills everything, portraits, dialogues, and narrative, with moral and ironical reflections, and with an endless string of the absurdities which infected much of the learning of the Renaissance. This was a heritage from the Middle Ages, the jumbled confusion of which they augmented with vast accretions from antiquity. Thus the poem is something more than a satire on Puritanism. It is a mine of human folly almost as rich, if not as cheerful, as Rabelais's burlesque epic, which largely inspired Butler; almost as complete and final as Swift's *Tale of a Tub*, which was in many respects a continuation of Butler's mockery.

However, Butler is distinguished from both of these, as well as from Cervantes, by the form of his work. He wrote, not in prose like them, but in verse, in octosyllabic couplets which have not a trace of poetry in them, but which allow him to coin numberless aphorisms, short and piquant formulas, often set off by the humour of the rhymes, which are true plays upon words, and sometimes also maliciously distort the sound of the words, as puns might do. In this kind of exercise, Butler was more than an initiator; he remains the supreme master.

Satirists and Court Poets. Although he was profoundly sceptical and devoid of all enthusiasm for the monarchy or the Anglican church, Butler chose the men of the Commonwealth as the butts of his satire. The survivors of the republican age, like Andrew Marvell, whose lyrical work has previously been noticed, retorted in their turn with mockery and satirical buffoonery. Marvell now produced only prose pamphlets and satires in verse, in which he scoffed at the religious intolerance, the autocratic tendencies, the lack of patriotism, and the vices of the new order. He here displays, in prose and verse, an abundant and biting, but turbulent, humour. He allows his attacks to become too personal, and is too prodigal of allusions to the petty happenings of the day for this part of his work to have an interest as enduring as the rest.

John Oldham (1653–83), on the other hand, a faithful disciple of the ancients and especially of Juvenal, shows a tendency to generalization in his *Satires against the Jesuits* (1681). He had vigour and ardour, but he died too young for his gifts to have had time to ripen or his still unpolished verse to become supple. For various reasons these poets yield the first place to Dryden, whose superiority is nowhere more evident than in the satiric mode, as will shortly appear.

It is true that there also blows a lively wind of satire through the verses of those who have been called the Court poets, the great nobles who often scandalized a very broadminded age by excessive licentiousness. But here satire is mingled with other elements, gallantry, trifling, and often obscenity as well. As a whole it is not always easy to analyse, and it may be misrepresented in the attempt. The common basis is cynicism, the desire to shock, but its best verse is also a true expression of temperament, and hence certain of these effusions have the advantage in spontaneity over those of Dryden himself, which are often felt to be the clever exercises of a cold-blooded versifier. The most characteristic of all the 'Court poets' is John Wilmot, Earl of Rochester (1648–80), whose short life epitomized all the vices and all the follies of the Restoration. His sarcastic insolence blazes out in *The Session of the Poets*, his ironic pessimism in his *Satyr against Mankind*. He is conscious of the vanities to which he has devoted his life and redeems the enormities of his conduct by a clear-sighted frankness, a rare strength of line and expression, an instinctive elegance, and some touches also of sincere tenderness. Charles Sackville, Lord Buckhurst, later Earl of Dorset (1638–1701), extravagantly praised in his generation, is distinguished by the bitterness of his irony and the harshness of his realism. Sir Charles Sedley (1639–1701) recovers better than any other the gallant vein of the Cavaliers; voluptuous and elegant, he produced graceful songs as facile as theirs and of a more sustained correctness.

The desire for correctness is equally marked in the didactic poems which were beginning to appear and which were inspired by Horace and Boileau: the Earl of Roscommon (1633–85) translated the *Ars Poetica* of Horace into blank verse and wrote a rhymed

Essay on Translated Verse. The Duke of Buckingham and Normanby, John Sheffield (1648–1721) wrote an *Essay on Poetry*, in which he gave expression to counsels of prudence and common sense without troubling to make any place for imagination.

John Dryden. But in a brief literary picture of this period all other names might be omitted and a study of the various types and the various poetic species of the time founded solely on the work of Dryden, who sums up and excels the other writers in nearly every respect. There was hardly any kind of composition to which he did not turn his hand and which he did not carry to greater heights of strength and beauty than his contemporaries. The very changes of his manner were almost always caused and supported by the obscure development of public taste.

Born in 1631, Dryden was nearly 30 at the Restoration. The descendant of a family which had pledged itself to the Parliamentary cause and the Commonwealth, he had written *Heroick Stanzas* in Cromwell's honour on the death of the Protector. In them he showed himself to be, as well as a good Cromwellian, a good disciple in style of the metaphysical poets, seeking out far-fetched images and conceits, and nowise restrained by the fear of extravagance or bad taste. The accession of Charles II produced a sudden transformation in his political opinions without as yet changing his manner, and he is just as much tainted with preciosity in the *Astraea Redux* with which he saluted the return of the king. He stood well at court, had cemented friendships among the nobility, and practised not ingloriously in the theatre, but had still not greatly reformed his manner when he wrote in 1666 his *Annus Mirabilis*, in which he commemorated the Great Fire of London and the war with Holland. Nevertheless, among many strained conceits there are to be found vigorous touches and forceful and dignified stanzas or even sequences of stanzas.

After an interval of fifteen years devoted to the theatre, he reappeared as a poet, but this time as a satiric and didactic poet. The couplet succeeded the stanza. The lyrical effort, in which was displayed an often artificial ingenuity, gave place to a ceaseless rain of biting observations and weighty maxims. Dryden had found the tool best suited to his genius. He availed himself of it to defend the causes which he successively favoured, or to attack the enemy of the moment. His veerings were so strictly subordinated to his interests as a courtier that some have seen in him a sort of mercenary who, free from all personal convictions, fights for any power that hires him. Anyhow the mercenary has his code of honour which compels him to fight valiantly, and Dryden puts his lively mind and his talent for reasoning and expression entirely at the service of the party he happens to side with. This was the moment when England was dividing into Tories, or champions of the royal prerogative, and Whigs, who desired to limit that prerogative. Dryden was a staunch Tory, or rather became one once he had breathed the atmosphere of the Court. In the rising led against his father by the Duke of Monmouth, Charles II's natural son, Dryden took the side of the king, who becomes David in his poem *Absalom and Achitophel* (1681-2), while Monmouth is Absalom, incited to rebel by the evil counsellor Achitophel (the Earl of Shaftesbury). In this biblical disguise Dryden stages contemporary happenings and characters very felicitously. He excelled in the art of portrait-painting; his 'characters' of Achitophel and Zimri (the Duke of Buckingham) are masterpieces of satire, unfair certainly, but terse and incisive.

He continued his campaign, after Shaftesbury's acquittal by a jury, in *The Medall*, in which he ridicules the popular delight and the medal struck by the triumphant Whigs. He had also turned upon his rival Shadwell, the Whig poet, and pilloried him with pitiless humour in *MacFlecknoe* (published 1682).

Meanwhile, what had been a political quarrel tended more and more to become a religious one. Now followed a series of poems in which the sceptical writer undertook the defence first of all of the Anglican religion, in *Religio Laici* (1682), a panegyric on the happy mean, praising a faith equally removed from the fanaticism of Catholics and that of dissenters. He believed that he was thus up-holding the court and serving the interests of a state threatened by religious enthusiasm. He was ignorant of Charles II's secret conversion to Catholicism. But on the accession of James II in 1685, when the sovereign was an avowed Catholic, Dryden not only made his own conversion public but expounded and defended the religious policy of the new king in his great allegorical poem *The Hind and the Panther* (1687). Here Catholicism is the gentle and stainless white hind which asks only freedom to drink at the spring of faith; the panther, beautiful but spotted, is Anglicanism. As for the dissenters, they are a troop of evil or grotesque beasts: the bear, the boar, the fox, the monkey, and the hare. The hind is gentle and asks little, but talks a great deal, displaying in orderly fashion the arguments which justify its doctrine and show the innocence of its intentions. After this decisive allegory, Dryden never retracted again; the former Poet Laureate did not bear his incense to the new king when James II was hurled from the throne, dragging Catholicism down in his ruin. He contented himself with abandoning political and religious controversy and turning all his activity to purely literary ends; returning to the theatre which he had neglected; translating the classics, chiefly Persius and Juvenal, or Virgil whose *Aeneid* he turned into brilliant couplets; remodelling Boccaccio's and Chaucer's tales; or again, producing several fine lyric pieces like the ode in honour of St. Cecilia, the patroness of musicians, which he called *Alexander's Feast*. The hostility he had brought upon himself by his polemics died down little by little; his great talent was recognized; he became a sort of literary oracle, and when he died in 1700 he was universally acknowledged the prince of the poets of his generation.

He deserved this pre-eminence by the unceasing zeal with which through all his political or religious waverings he had served poetry and literature. Meanwhile, through his admirable prefaces and his various essays, he had taken his place at the head of the prose-writers. He had proved himself the first English critic, not because he was always consistent but because of the intelligence which informed his opinions, even when they were mistaken, and his judgements, although these were sometimes falsified by partiality and prejudice. Above all he had succeeded in giving to poetry the new qualities to which it aspired and which it had not yet attained except in brief moments. He had gradually freed his verse of the last traces of metaphysical eccentricity. In his satires and didactic poems he had fashioned it massive, clear, and virile. He had given the maximum of strength and effectiveness to heroic verse in

couplets. He had made the couplet the weapon of logic and judgement. And although he had thus broken with the national past
and joined the school of the Latins or the French poets, he had
never lost the true English qualities inherited from his great forerunners of the Renaissance. These are to be found in the daring
combinations of familiar words, in the sonority of the verse, and
especially in the cadences of the songs scattered through his plays.
Although he was an innovator and paved the way for the future,
he preserved much of the previous era. His misfortune was that
he devoted his genius to occasional pieces whose interest was bound
to wane with the controversies that had given them birth; or else
to translations and adaptations which, although remarkable in
themselves, must be acknowledged to have hindered the production of the original poetry of which he was capable. He left no
considerable work which was to be as permanent as a true masterpiece. Nowadays to realize all his power we must study him in
relation to his time. But such an examination reveals an alert
and versatile mind of rare energy, apt for all immediate poetic
exercises—in short the most vigorous journeyman of letters that
had yet been born in England.

The Theatre. This same Dryden was for nearly forty years one
of the most abundant purveyors for the stage, although he had
been attracted to the theatre less by his own taste than by the
great favour it enjoyed after the Restoration. The public returned
to it with what seemed almost a pang of hunger after long priva-
tion. It is true that it was not altogether the same public as under
Elizabeth and the early Stuarts; it was not the motley crowd in
which all sections of the population were represented. The Puritan
attacks had left in pious people and even in those who merely had
some regard for moral decency, a horror of those unhallowed
places, where the impropriety of the plays was aggravated by the
disorderly scenes for which the performances gave occasion, and
by the attitude of the hangers-on who haunted the theatres. The
respectable middle class was compelled to stay away. The Restoration theatre was almost wholly an amusement for the corrupt
court and for pleasure-seekers. To good royalists, no less than to
rakes, it was a way of carrying on the war against the Puritans

to hold up to ridicule the moral code which they had imposed on the country, and in which most men now refused to see anything but lies and hypocrisy. Thus there was extreme licentiousness in the dramatic works of the Restoration, not because the times were coarser than those of Marston, Middleton, and Massinger, but because there reigned a fundamental cynicism which regarded the virtues as suspect or ridiculous, and associated the vices with the qualities of open-heartedness and plain-speaking. An obstinate disparagement of human nature, into which there usually enters less of indignation than of malicious pleasure, characterizes comedy. In tragedy virtue indeed exists and is glorified, but it is extravagant, unnatural, unreal, and rhetorical, as if the author, unable to find a model in real life, had been constrained to seek one in the realm of fancy.

Although on the whole the Restoration theatre continued the tradition of that of the Renaissance, the progress of time introduced external and internal changes which gave it a special aspect. The scenery, which had always been poor on the popular stage, and which formerly only displayed its splendour and illusion in that species of opera, the court masque, now played an important part and was often the decisive factor of success. Movable scenery began to be used and stage machinery was more and more employed. Female parts, previously played by young boys, were now entrusted to actresses, and these by their amorous intrigues often contributed to the evil reputation of the theatrical world.

As for the repertory, recourse was had again and again to earlier plays. Davenant, who was a link between the two periods, was a great admirer of Shakespeare, whose godson he was. It is true, however, that Jonson because of his classical qualities, and Beaumont and Fletcher because of their more romantic inspiration and their easy and already modern style, were often applauded even more than Shakespeare by the new public. But the success of the Elizabethan plays was usually obtained by means of a remodelling which appears now both astonishing and unseemly. The final catastrophe of the old tragedies seemed too painful to more frivolous audiences, and *Romeo and Juliet* and *The Maid's Tragedy* were given happy endings. Dryden added many indelicacies to *The Tempest* to bring it into line with contemporary taste.

The theatre, however, was not content with these revivals and adaptations. It had an originality of its own.

Heroic Plays. In serious drama the plays called 'heroic' replaced tragedy, and Dryden himself was particularly distinguished in this *genre*. 'Heroic' plays were not the result of classical influence. They preserved in their composition the usual freedom and overloading of the national theatre. They took their rules from neither Latins nor Greeks. They owed much to France, but more in content than in form. They reproduced the extraordinary adventures typical of such seventeenth-century French novels as those of la Calprenède, of the two Scudérys and of Gomberville, for whom it appears that *Don Quixote* did not exist. Here are superhuman feats, sentiments refined to absurdity, magnificent or execrable passions. There are no characters, only extremely effective situations allowing of high-sounding pompous speeches. The heroes are models, as heroes should be, but their code is not the ordinary code. They are unequalled in valour, they scorn pain and danger, but their actions are guided by knightly punctilio. In the same way they are incomparable lovers by the standard of the 'Courts of Love'. Spanish grandiloquence has infected these plays through the medium of the French novel. In them may also be recognized the example of the great French tragic poet Corneille, who based his drama on the struggle between love and duty, and for whom honour was the peak of virtue. But the really strong and noble quality of Corneille's tragedies is superseded by vague and empty prowess. Here is Corneille run mad.

This type of play flourished during the first twenty years of the Restoration. Davenant with his *Siege of Rhodes* and Sir Robert Howard with his *Indian Queen* had already opened up the way when Dryden entered it in his turn. He seems to have retouched Howard's verse, and he wrote a sequel to the play, *The Indian Emperor, or the Conquest of Mexico by the Spaniards* (1665). He eclipsed his rivals by the ease with which he handled the rhymed couplet, now substituted for blank verse. He used the same type of verse in the other heroic plays which followed: *Tyrannick*

Love, or the Royal Martyr (1669), *Almanzor and Almahide, or the Conquest of Granada by the Spaniards* (1670), and *Aureng-Zebe or The Great Mogul* (1675). It is impossible to exaggerate the improbability of the situations and characters of these plays, the most brilliant of which is *The Conquest of Granada,* or to overpraise the magnificent rhetoric of many of their declamatory passages. Although he was later to write more restrained and more truly human dramas, it was through his heroic plays that Dryden made his personal impression on the theatre of his day. At this period he took great pride in his use of rhyme, and it was indeed in order to defend this practice that he now turned literary critic. He had been inspired in this respect by the French drama, and it was the energy of Corneille's verse that had appealed to him. He might indeed have relied upon the frequent practice of the English dramatists of the Renaissance, including Shakespeare himself, who had employed rhyme a great deal before finally showing a preference for blank verse. But it was the didactic quality and rhetorical splendour of rhymed declamation that attracted Dryden, especially since he was rather deficient in true dramatic talent, which always tends to reproduce natural dialogue and to express the variety of life itself.

Dryden and his contemporaries debated the problems of composition and dramatic style; they knew all the pros and cons. In his *Essay of Dramatick Poesie* (1668), Dryden imagines a conversation between four people, each of whom expresses his own idea of the theatre, with plausible arguments. The fact that he was familiar both with French ideas as revealed in Corneille's *Examens* (analyses of his own plays) and with the practice of the Elizabethans, which he admired, gives Dryden a signal advantage over continental critics; for these were not able to weigh classical precepts against works of genius sprung from a national tradition. Nothing equally intelligent, or better worth pondering even to-day, had been written on these questions. The heroic plays that Dryden defended are now, in spite of brilliant passages, no more than a memory; the pages of clear and vigorous prose in which he justified them remain fresh and living, preserved by their reasonableness, judgement, and searching analysis.

Tragedy. But the extravagance of the heroic plays did not become any the less flagrant, and in 1671 provoked an amusing parody, *The Rehearsal*, produced by a group of wits headed by George Villiers, Duke of Buckingham. The satire was facile and effective. Dryden did not yield immediately; but he was too sensible not to have his own doubts, and he pondered them long enough to realize that he had been worshipping a false idol. When he returned to dramatic composition in 1677, it was with tragedies in blank verse, resembling Shakespeare's in choice of subject, like *All for Love, or the World Well Lost* (1678), a very independent revision of *Antony and Cleopatra*, or *Don Sebastian* (1690), or *Cleomenes the Spartan Hero* (1692). This time the versatile poet proved his possession of the very qualities his heroic plays lacked: he returned to the realm of the historic or at least of the probable; he presented plausible people and simple emotions in fitting language and without bombast. He had drawn nearer to nature, and thus both to Shakespeare and to French tragedy, which itself had in the interval descended from Corneille's heights to the less superhuman level of Racine.

Nevertheless, despite the merit of these last plays, it was not Dryden who recovered the strong tragic emotion of his predecessors. His plays are primarily products of conscious will and artistic talent. The man who at this period succeeded best in stirring the feelings of his audience was Thomas Otway (1652–85), who produced in his short career, besides various comic and tragic works and adaptations of Racine and Molière, two powerful plays, *The Orphan* (1680), and *Venice Preserved* (1682). The former is a domestic drama steeped in that romantic atmosphere of which the secret seemed to have been lost with Heywood and Webster; *Venice Preserved* is a moving study of passion and character against a background of history (the Spanish plot against the Venetian republic in 1618). The hesitations of Jaffier, one of the conspirators, between the political cause he is pledged to forward and the appeals of his dearly-loved wife Belvidera, the daughter of a Venetian senator; the struggle between friendship and love; the betrayal of the conspirators which he decides upon; the curse he draws upon himself from his bosom friend Pierre; his despair when the Senate violates its promise to spare the conspirators he has denounced; all these form a series of closely-knit scenes of increasing emotion which (in spite of a highly indecent underplot) earned for this tragedy a part in the theatrical repertory until the middle of the nineteenth century, an honour which did not fall to any of Dryden's plays.

The names of two other tragic authors, inferior to Otway but exploiting the same vein of emotion, deserve to be remembered. Nathaniel Lee (1653-92), after producing rhymed heroic plays like Dryden, reverted to blank verse in *The Rival Queens or the Death of Alexander the Great* (1677), *Theodosius or the Force of Love* (1681), *The Princess of Cleve*, and *The Massacre of Paris* (1690). Lee is famous for his declamatory passages; he could give points to the fieriest of the Elizabethans. He was unbalanced, and his highly sensual imagination was dissipated and lost itself in mere verbal fury. Some years later Thomas Southerne (1660-1746) won applause with his *Fatal Marriage* (1694) and *Oroonoko* (1696) in which, together with a little of Lee's ardour, is to be found more skill in construction, more judgement in language, and more talent in choice of situations. But in the absence of high intellectual and artistic value, his ways are the ways of melodrama.

Restoration Comedy. The serious plays of the Restoration are in the main as far removed as possible from reality. They represent the factitious ideal of heroism which pleased an entirely unheroic age, and the interplay of noble passions as imagined by a generation more sceptical than passionate. It is in the comedy that one finds, if not the faithful mirror of society, at least a reflection of the gay intrigues, and an echo of the cynical and frivolous conversation, which were the reality of dissolute worldlings. There has been much discussion of the question whether this comedy was artificial or realistic. It was in fact both; artificial in that it made great use of traditional theatrical methods: caricature, the exaggeration dear to farce, and the exclusion of aspects of character which did not accord with its design. It is realistic because it overflows at the same time with lively sketches taken straight from contemporary life, and with the sort of libertinist philosophy which was that of a large part of society. Its abundance of vitality, therefore, is as marked as tragedy's lack of it. If it were not tainted with an astonishing grossness or hinted obscenity, it would be one of the glories of the English theatre. In comparison with Elizabethan comedy, it displays in the best examples many felicitous innovations. It is on the whole surprisingly modern.

Comedy had broken with the romanticism in which it was steeped in Shakespeare. It had broken with the verse tradition, and showed its realistic tendency by the habitual use of prose. If it looked for models, it found them either here in England, in Ben Jonson, who taught it the satiric portraiture of contemporary society, or in France, in Molière, who furnished themes and motives in plenty, and instructed it in the art of throwing individual characters into relief in the dialogue. Ordinarily free from any element of tragedy, it acquired a liveliness, a grace, and a zest of its own. It became brisker through the advance of prose towards clarity and brevity. It was satirical without being didactic, since it was rarely inspired with the desire to correct. Its sole aim was to amuse.

Many writers took this path to popularity. In addition to those on whom special stress must be laid, mention may be made of Dryden with his *Wild Gallant* (1663), *An Evening's Love* (1668), *Marriage à la Mode* (1672), *The Assignation* (1672), *The Spanish Friar* (1680), and others, in which he achieved brilliant effects in dialogue, though he seldom gave the impression of spontaneous *vis comica*; Thomas Shadwell, with his *Sullen Lovers* (1668), and *Epsom Wells* (1673); Sir Charles Sedley, with his *Mulberry Garden* (1668), and *Bellamira* (1687); Aphra Behn, with a series of licentious comedies presented between 1671 and 1689; John Crowne, an author usually mediocre, who once almost achieved talent in his *Sir Courtly Nice* (1685); Thomas D'Urfey, who supplied the stage with facile improvisations between 1676 and 1698; and Mrs. Manly and Mrs. Centlivre in their early work.

But the following are more truly representative, and their work demands more attention.

First, Sir George Etherege (1634–91), earliest in date of the innovators, who from the beginning of the Restoration set the tone of the new comedy, and whose chief work, *The Man of Mode* (1676), blazed a trail which Congreve was triumphantly to follow twenty years later. He was one of the society of rakes which included Rochester, Dorset, and Sedley, and he gave expression to their bent and his own in his easy, natural, and spirited dialogue. He made no visible effort at construction; he relied on his temperament and experience. His comedies have the attractiveness of unforced plants in a favourable soil.

Wycherley. Very different from him was William Wycherley (1640–1716), who for his part had power and constructive aptitude, and who might, moreover, pass for a moralist in that age of pleasure-seekers if he had not jeopardized his moralizing by a grossness and brutality of language which reached and even passed beyond all limits. By the complacency with which he depicts the very vices he flagellates, he recalls John Marston. The cynicism of some scenes is carried so far as to leave a doubt concerning the sincerity of his attacks. His plays are few in number: *Love in a Wood* (1671), *The Gentleman Dancing Master* (1672), *The Country Wife* (1675), and *The Plain Dealer* (1676). The two last, which are the most remarkable, are adaptations of Molière, the first of *L'Ecole des Maris* and *L'Ecole des Femmes*, the other of *Le Misanthrope*. Comparison of Molière with Wycherley is very suggestive. Wycherley overloads Molière's always simple themes, doubling and re-doubling the intrigue, and producing in this way effects of stirring and bustling movement which are not to be found in the originals. He also deforms the characters, making of Molière's Agnès an un-bridled libertine, and of the gentleman Alceste a sea-captain, brutal in language and uncontrolled in his raging outbursts against lies and hypocrisy. In addition, he mingles with the recollection of Alceste that of Shakespeare's Timon; and he introduces romantic elements into his comedy, setting beside Manly, the 'plain dealer', a Fidelia disguised as a page who is a replica of Viola in *Twelfth Night*. Not all these changes are advantageous. Admirers of Molière are justified in crying out upon the profanation. But the result is a work free from narrow imitation, which has become the expression of a different man and a different country. The vigour of Wycherley's handling of the whip of satire is all his own; his also the conception of the characters, which he drives to the verge of caricature by exaggerating their traits. In his humour he has undeniable power, which happily does not manifest itself entirely in scabrous scenes and speeches. Wycherley's prose is solid and virile; in it his concern for his art is very clear. He had none of Etherege's lazy negligence, and bestowed on his comedies all the correctness of form and style of which he was capable. Nevertheless his art remains as crude as his temperament.

Congreve. To appreciate all the artistic nuances of the new comedy, we must go to William Congreve (1670–1729), who twenty years later gave the English stage a series of masterpieces at once essentially perverse and essentially refined. It is to Etherege and not to Wycherley that Congreve is related by his *Old Bachelor* (1693), *The Double Dealer* (1694), *Love for Love* (1695), and *The Way of the World* (1700). He has neither the brutality nor the satirical violence of Wycherley. He depicts a self-satisfied corruption, enjoying its elegance and easily ranging itself with a licentious and egotistical society. He takes pleasure in making all his characters formulate their own doubtful moral code. Congreve was a clear thinker and had at his disposal a most lucid prose, beautiful in the aptness of its words, the natural elegance of its phrases, the neat conciseness of its sentences, and its balance unemphasized by exaggerated symmetry. He dowers with this language such of his characters as are in sympathy with his temper, being of his world. Here is not only brilliant wit like Sheridan's, but words of distinction brought into the service of refinement of thought. A single one of Mirabel's sayings will serve to display its essential quality: 'I had rather be his relation than his acquaintance.' This elegant perfection of expression is habitual with Congreve. It is the very fabric of his witty style, which is embroidered here and there with livelier arabesques and more vivid flowers, but never in such numbers as to conceal the ground. Moreover, it is supple, and although it makes plenteous use of picturesque comparisons, it maintains a sufficient distinction between the various characters according to their social position and intelligence. Its wit does not grow tiresome in the end.

The ideas expressed by this wit are not in truth very edifying: virtue is only a lure, vices are mere trifles. Congreve's lovers are not perhaps more boldly outspoken than Rosalind bantering Orlando, but we are much less convinced of their inner purity. An exception must, however, be made for the Mirabel, and especially for the Millamant of *The Way of the World*, the supreme achievement of the age in comedy. Congreve has succeeded in depicting a pair of lovers completely absorbed in the world, a man of free morals and a supremely coquettish woman, and yet giving the illusion of two hearts capable of true feeling, which beat for one another. In these two at least raillery and cynicism have not entirely killed all tenderness.

In the portrayal of elegance and distinction of manners, Congreve has no superiors, and it is doubtful whether he has an equal. His prose has affinities with verse, and produces in the reader an aesthetic emotion almost as great as that induced by genuine poetry.

Vanbrugh. Sir John Vanbrugh (1664–1726) was distinguishing himself almost at the same time, though for very different qualities, with his three comedies *The Relapse, The Provoked Wife* (1697), and *The Confederacy* (1705). He is very far from having Congreve's elegance and refinement, but he possesses *vis comica* in a rare degree. His humour is as truculent as Wycherley's, but it is never clouded by moral preoccupations; he is always near to farce, and excels in caricature. His touch is broad—as Flemish as his ancestry. He was an architect by profession and he builds his plays solidly, yet without seeming to be troubled by artistic scruples. He is one of the most daring, but also perhaps the most rollicking of the comedians of the day.

Farquhar. George Farquhar's dates (1678–1707) take him out of the scope of this chapter. But his inspiration relates him too closely to the foregoing authors for him to be separated from them. This Irishman displays a good humour more facile and less harsh than theirs. There is more sympathy in his laughter, he gives his plots and characters more air. He is not so narrowly cooped up in the drawing-rooms and pleasure resorts of London. He leads some of his characters out on to the high roads and into inns and villages.

The four comedies: *Love and a Bottle* (1698), *The Constant Couple* (1699), *The Recruiting Officer* (1706), and *The Beaux' Stratagem* (1707) reveal a rapid progress; the last, and by far the best, was staged in the very year of his premature death at the age of 29. Although his plays are still very free, it is pleasant to find them purged of the worst scurrilities and most vicious portraiture of his immediate predecessors.

The alteration is commonly attributed to an attack by a clergyman, Jeremy Collier, which appeared in 1698 under the title of *A Short View of the Immorality and Profaneness of the English Stage*. It is certain that this pamphlet enjoyed an extraordinary celebrity, and the stir it produced among the dramatists is shown by the number of their replies. Collier was in the right, for the theatre had taken delight in mocking religion and morality, had riddled ministers of religion with sarcasm, and had scoffed at their teaching. But Collier could not distinguish between the personal convictions of the writers and those they had given to the characters in their comedies. He held the former responsible for the sentiments of the latter. He did not admit that a rake should speak in character; he would make no allowances for satiric realism. Much more pertinent answers might have been returned to him than those that actually appeared. But on the whole the authors had uneasy consciences, and the best among them were not free from remorse for their indecency and cynicism. Dryden distinguished himself by his *mea culpa*, though he was content to throw the blame on the taste of the court and the courtiers.

Indeed, however unjust it was in detail, Collier's pamphlet was timely, and he well expressed the feelings of every element in the country that was not identified with the rakes, the idle, and the gay world. The greater part of the respectable middle class had remained untouched by profligacy. They held cynicism in horror and liked to see presented the trials and triumphs of virtue. They desired a sentimental drama, and such a drama was just beginning its career at the moment of Farquhar's death, when Congreve and Vanbrugh had forsaken the theatre which had brought them fame. A more seemly theatre was succeeding that which the Restoration had brought in its train. But from an aesthetic point of view, it was immeasurably inferior. Indeed, with the exception of Goldsmith and Sheridan, it was two centuries before England saw the birth of new dramatic compositions able to compete in liveliness and originality with those that had flowered in the reign of Charles II, James II, and William III.

XXII

THE EIGHTEENTH CENTURY (1700–40)

THE eighteenth century viewed as a whole has a distinctive character. It was very definitely the age of understanding, the age of enlightenment, when a literature which had become clear and pellucid began to diffuse knowledge among a growing public. The supremacy of reason was scarcely challenged; there reigned a general belief in the advancement of the human mind. No doubt there was evolution within the limits of the century, and none would maintain that it was the same at its close as at its beginning. Nevertheless, throughout all changes and innovations, its literature kept a sort of general unity, so much so that, even if it be convenient to make divisions in a period so vast and prolific, it would be mistaken to regard them as anything but boundary lines serving to mark off successive generations between which there are no abrupt breaks. 'Sensibility', which bulked larger as the century advanced, was present in germ during its earliest years. Steele had more than one of the traits shown later in an accentuated form by Rousseau in France and by Sterne and Mackenzie in Great Britain. Addison, Goldsmith, and Jane Austen are borne upon the same stream of humour. Crabbe would have been able to agree with Pope on almost all points of poetic technique and practice. Farquhar and Sheridan would have understood one another immediately, and exchanged quips and jokes. The proportions of the ingredients vary, no doubt, in these different writers, but they are the same ingredients. The writers are all in communion. If they could have conversed together, they would have disagreed on many questions, but all would have understood the discussion. The same atmosphere envelops the whole century. The three divisions of this chapter, therefore, should be regarded chiefly as aids to memory and to the classification of the numerous authors according to their respective dates.

Poetry

The new literature, still tentative and undecided under the later Stuarts, gradually established itself after the Revolution of 1688, from which England emerged in its final shape as a constitutional monarchy. It attained its perfect equipoise at the beginning of the eighteenth century. It is customary to give to the period of its purest expansion the name of the 'Age of Queen Anne' or the 'Augustan Age of English Literature'. It is quite true that the twelve years of Queen Anne's reign saw the most famous authors of their generation come to full maturity; and her reign was equally remarkable for the prestige and protection afforded to men of letters who were patronized by ministers as were Roman authors by Maecenas. But it was so brief that most of the great writers overstep its narrow limits, and many of their masterpieces fall outside it. If for a time they knew a Golden Age, they passed from it immediately to an Age of Iron with Walpole and the first Georges, who were indifferent or hostile to everything literary. The title of Classic Age is therefore the most suitable, for, while it defines the dominant characteristic of the literature, it permits of greater latitude in date. The Classic Age includes the whole lifetime of the chief poets and prose-writers. It possesses a sort of harmony which it would be a pity to interrupt for mainly external reasons connected with the circumstances of politics and the succession of rulers, when close spiritual relationship and essential similarity have conferred an undeniable unity on the first forty years of the eighteenth century. The name of Classic Age is justified by the new literary ideals and still more by the realization of these ideals. The previous period had doubtless moved in the direction now taken, but it had not wholly freed itself from the influence of the Renaissance, and in particular from the romanticism of the Renaissance in England. This can be seen in the career of its most illustrious representative, Dryden, and in the success, as dazzling as it was fugitive, of one part of his dramatic work, the heroic plays. But by this time the afterglow of Elizabethan romanticism had faded; and though praise of the *Faerie Queene* is still found here and there in Steele and Pope, youthful Addison,

PLATE XVIII

JOHN DRYDEN

ALEXANDER POPE

who had not yet read Spenser, expresses the prevailing opinion of his time when he calls his poetry both childish and barbarous and declares that nowadays it has become tiresome to the modern reader:

> But now the mystic tale that pleased of yore
> Can charm an understanding age no more.

It was indeed an age that rejected fancy and desired to be guided by reason. It wished to understand, not to imagine. If there was one emotion which seemed to it suspect, out of place, bordering on madness, it was enthusiasm, whether that of faith or that of metaphysics.

Its immediate model was the age of Louis XIV. We have seen that French influence had already grown great at the end of the seventeenth century, but it could not be so powerful and so decided then as it was later. For Dryden the great French authors were mostly contemporaries. They were still at work when he began his career, and had not acquired all the prestige which a certain remoteness now gave them. By this time they had achieved European fame, and their belief in sound literary equipoise founded on the example of the best ancient writers had been accepted by the English, who now appear steeped in French literature. Corneille, Racine, and Molière in the theatre, the moralists La Rochefoucauld and La Bruyère, Boileau with his satire and his principles of poetry, critics like Le Bossu, were for ever in their thoughts. This imitation tended to limit the scope of poetry, but to encourage the development and refinement of prose to a degree of perfection hitherto unknown. Nevertheless, English creative force survived even in imitation. England added to and transformed what she borrowed, and with the new method produced some of the world's masterpieces. She had the satisfaction for the first time of seeing these works circulated throughout the world: she became of account because she had accepted the French standard, which had become the standard of Europe. Her poets and still more her prose-writers were taken notice of and admired in their turn. France accepted them and honoured them, translated them, imitated them, and spread their fame among the continental peoples. Great Britain had become a member of the literary commonwealth, and Europe began to study her language, which had been until then almost unknown.

Another considerable change to be noted is the widening of the reading public. To the court literature designed for the idle and pleasure-seeking succeeded a literature reared on a broader basis. If poetry remained chiefly aristocratic, prose was no longer written only for the lettered. The middle class demanded of writers not only more seriousness and decency but also instruction and information. It wished its books and newspapers to serve some useful end, less to introduce new ideas to the mind, than help to establish some practical rule of conduct. The necessity of appealing to a larger number of readers drove writers to use an increasingly clear and simple style freed from complicated syntax and purged of the pedantry and eccentricity that had marred so very many Renaissance pages.

The link between Restoration literature and that of the true Classic Age is nowhere so evident as in poetry. There was a gulf between Milton and Dryden; nothing is easier than the transition from Dryden to Pope. Alexander Pope (1688–1744) was Dryden's disciple and successor from the outset of his career. Their names are inseparable in the history of English classicism, and in satiric talent and mastery of the couplet there is a close relationship between them.

Matthew Prior. The succession, however, was not direct. Pope was under twelve when Dryden died. Between the two came several poets; the best known is Matthew Prior (1664–1721), who belongs equally to both generations. He made his debut with a parody of *The Hind and the Panther* written in collaboration with Charles Montague, and was at odds with Dryden to the last, but he did not escape his poetic influence. Like Dryden, he used his verse to comment on the events of politics, like him wrote many occasional pieces, complimentary or satirical, and like him cultivated moralizing verse—in a strain, it is true, suggestive of flippancy, and, in *Alma or the Progress of the Mind*, where he denounces worldly vanities, even verging on the grotesque.

Again, like Dryden imitating Chaucer, he borrowed from old poetry a theme which he hoped to freshen and improve by the resources of a better-informed mind and a more literary style. Thus he turned the *Nut-Browne Maid* into the poem *Henry and Emma*. This poem, which was much admired in the eighteenth century, might serve as text for a study of the blunders of neo-classicism. Prior's adaptation reveals a profound misunderstanding of the old ballad's beauty, its truth of sentiment, and its unadorned passion, no less than of the lyric charm of its stanza and refrain. He replaces them by embroidered trimmings, by a narrative made up of satire and sprightly reflections decorated with mythological similes, and by the effects of antithesis which are the usual product of the heroic couplet. For any one nowadays who knows the original poem, the result is intolerable. If a comparison between fifteenth-century poetry and that of the eighteenth century were to be based on this piece of remodelling, it would end in an absolute condemnation of the poetry of the classical school: and if we retraced the stream to its source, we should have to admit that even Dryden sins frequently in the same way when he reshapes Chaucer, in spite of the vigour and real zest of his renderings.

But there is something better than this in Prior. His *vers de société* show a light touch and a pleasing turn of expression. His skilful use of anapaestic metres is a well-timed protest against the growing uniformity of versification. In graceful ease he recalls the cavalier poets, from whom he was descended through Rochester and Sedley, and being unhampered by 'metaphysics' he adds to this ease the gift of lucidity, which his age had acquired at the cost of more than one sacrifice:

> What I speak, my fair Chloe, and what I write, shows
>   The difference there is betwixt Nature and Art;
> I court others in verse, but I love thee in prose;
>   And they have my whimsies, but thou hast my heart.

When he treats a fable instead of aiming at sentimental poetry, he becomes a brisk story-teller; and with a subject demanding wit or raillery he achieves real success. His gay little trifles add a fringe of charm to the too consistently weighty and learned productions of the day.

Sir Samuel Garth. Addison. Before Pope again, Garth and Addison showed themselves good disciples of Dryden in their use of the heroic couplet. Sir Samuel Garth (1661-1719) produced in his *Dispensary* (1699), which he imitated from Boileau's *Lutrin*, a quite respectable example of the mock-heroic manner; he cele-brated in it a quarrel between doctors on the subject of furnishing a dispensary with medicines. Addison first drew attention to him-self by the poem in which he celebrated Marlborough's victory at Blenheim, *The Campaign* (1704), an academic exercise which revealed to a wider public the former Oxford student already ad-mired by a few for the fine rhetoric of his Latin verses.

Alexander Pope. But here is Pope, and with his appearance neighbouring poetical luminaries are rapidly eclipsed. Pope took up Dryden's sceptre and was the inheritor of his genius, but impor-tant differences in the careers of the two poets show the difference between their generations. Dryden, still bathed in the afterglow of the Renaissance, had long known and long admired the conceits of the 'metaphysical poets'; he had preserved a lyrical ardour; he spent half his energies in the theatre; his work had a variety that Pope's was to lack. From the outset Pope was able to profit from the advance Dryden had brought about in the new versification; he took over his predecessor's couplet and with it, except very occasionally, he remained content. The task to which he devoted himself was the polishing and furbishing of this splendid instru-ment. Instead of having to forge and shape it by long labour, he had it perfect in his hands from his youth. The *Pastorals* which he began to write at sixteen are as finished in this respect as his *Essay on Man*. The subjects of his poems were to be of less importance than their form. While Dryden had taken an active share in political dispute, Pope, who, as a Catholic, was excluded from public affairs, usually held aloof from the strife and gave himself up entirely to his task of literature. His aim was to reach absolute correctness; England, he thought, had had several great poets, but not a single correct one. Starting with these premisses, Pope, even when imitating Dryden's heroic verse, exercised his own judgement. He pruned everything which seemed to him irregular, he filed down what was still rough and rugged, and he ended by giving the couplet its greatest possible finish and brilliancy. In so doing, it is true, he restricted the possible vari-

ations of the caesura; and instead of subordinating it to the
demands of the subject, he forced the subject into a prepared
mould, in which each line kept its separate identity sharply
distinguished; the continuation of the sense from one couplet to
another was proscribed, and an evenly balanced rhythm made
itself constantly felt within the line itself. The couplet thus became
a bright and sharp-edged tool, excellent for satire or for turning
aphorisms, but less felicitous in description or narrative, which it
splits up into a multitude of details of equal weight and value,
with no shading or background. This results in a certain monotony,
even in comparison with Dryden. Dryden in his rude onslaughts
fought with every kind of weapon, and wielded a club or a rapier
according to the needs of the moment. Pope's only weapon was
the stiletto. Thus equipped and sure of his mastery over verse and
style he was to essay various genres, but to win his greatest successes only when there was complete harmony between form and
matter, between the chosen theme and his own temperament.

After four elegant and smooth, but frigid pastorals, the young
poet set himself to lay down rules at once of criticism and of
poetry. Hence his *Essay on Criticism* (1711), which reflects his
desire to rival Boileau's *Art Poétique*. This emulation persisted
throughout Pope's career; his satires, his epistles, *The Rape of the
Lock* are all inspired by it. From the start Pope had the advantage
of the French poet in brilliance and incisive force, but he was
plainly less serious at bottom. Boileau had pondered long before
proclaiming the laws of the art of writing, and his code was the
fruit of his experience. In the *Essay on Criticism* Pope sought
chiefly to sharpen terse phrases and shafts of wit. He had no plan,
and progressed rather haphazard, but he coined by the way an
astonishing number of sayings that have become proverbial:

> For wit and judgment often are at strife,
> Tho' meant each other's aid, like man and wife . . .

> Like kings we lose the conquests gain'd before,
> By vain ambition still to make them more . . .

> A little learning is a dang'rous thing;
> Drink deep, or taste not the Pierian spring . . .

When elegant mockery alone is attempted, as in *The Rape of the Lock*, Pope regains the advantage. There is nothing in English poetry more sparkling than this little mock-heroic poem which sings the wrath of Miss Arabella Fermor, from whom Lord Petre had ravished a lock of hair. Pope had exactly the qualities required for evoking scenes where the passions play no part, where all is coquetry, worldliness, ease, and trifling. And there is poetry too in the introduction of the sylphs charged with the care of the toilet and person of Belinda (Miss Fermor). Though borrowed from the Rosicrucians, they have a distant relationship with the fairies of *A Midsummer Night's Dream*; but Shakespeare's little people, at home in the woods and the moonlight, have been replaced by drawing-room sprites, exquisite but artificial, the children of candlelight and lustres.

There are similar gleams of poetry in *Windsor Forest* (1713); Pope knew the Forest well, and he has several admirably exact and elegant descriptions, like that of the pheasant killed by the hunter. But a more robust feeling for nature was needed to hold the poem together, and short though it is, it tends to break up into episodic fragments.

Pope was not more than twenty-six but already at the head of the poets when he conceived the idea of translating Homer. He would be paying a splendid tribute to humanism, which was based on the cult of the classics; and he would be following in the steps of Dryden who had translated Virgil, but he would have the advantage of a more glorious, if more difficult, task. He would recall the achievement of Chapman in Elizabethan times, and a comparison of the two versions would illustrate the progress of English poetry during a hundred years. The 'heroic couplet' would outshine Chapman's old 'fourteener'.

As a matter of fact Pope did not permanently oust Chapman, whose ruder force was once more to find favour with the romantics. But he gave complete satisfaction to this age which acclaimed a translation not merely of vocabulary but of sentiment, manners, and spirit. All that is primitive in the *Iliad* vanished in the brilliant rhetoric and impeccably regular verse of the English poem, which enriched its author, made him independent, and assured his poetical supremacy.

Pope was further to increase his reputation with two poems of passion and sentiment which were greatly admired in his day: *Eloisa to Abelard* and the *Verses to the Memory of an Unfortunate Lady* (1717). He was capable of sensibility, and in these two poems emotion is unmistakable even through the too numerous and too evident artifices of style. Nor did he lack tenderness. The beautiful and touching lines are often quoted in which he expresses his wish to prolong the life of his aged mother:

> Me let the tender office long engage
> To rock the cradle of declining age,
> With lenient arts extend a mother's breath,
> Make languor smile, and smoothe the bed of death,
> Explore the thought, explain the asking eye,
> And keep awhile one parent from the sky!
>
> *Epistle to Dr. Arbuthnot* (ll. 408–13).

Nevertheless, his emotion generally took the form of irritability. He felt bitterly every sneer at his own deformity, every criticism of his verse. This characteristic dominated the latter part of his life, when he became almost entirely a satirist. It was then that he wrote the four books of the *Dunciad* (1728) which castigated bad poets, the *Moral Essays*, and the *Imitations of Horace* (1733–9).

The *Dunciad*, in which the famous translator of the *Iliad* pilloried the miserable writers of Grub-Street, certainly lacks generosity. Inspired by personal resentments rather than any principle of literature, it is sometimes startlingly unjust; it displays in turn as ruler of the realm of Folly, the excellent Shakespearian commentator Theobald, and Colley Cibber, the author-actor, who wrote lively and valuable memoirs. It suffers also from being cumbered with the names of obscure authors whom scholars alone can restore to a ghostly life, for they are no longer read. For this reason the *Dunciad*, in spite of vigorous passages, is to-day one of the most neglected of Pope's works. On the other hand his *Moral Essays* and especially his *Imitations of Horace* remain the most appreciated. The *Imitations* consist of complete and very ingenious translations: Pope modernized Horace while following him closely, but applying to his own times and his own country all the Latin poet's allusions to the Augustan age. The adaptations are admirably well done, and display Pope's acuteness and irony in their most refined form. It is cultivated poetry, meant to amuse cultivated persons, and both its public and its influence were accordingly restricted.

In this final period Pope attempted a more ambitious theme. In the four epistles inspired by Bolingbroke's deism and Shaftesbury's optimism, which bear the collective title of the *Essay on Man* (1733–4), he tried to scale the heights of philosophic poetry. He does not seem to have had any personal philosophic inspiration; he had neither the enthusiasm of the Renaissance poets nor those flashes of metaphysical vision that were to visit the great Romantics. He accepted the contemporary system of thought which appealed most to his mind, and was content to express it in those couplets which he excelled in turning into apophthegms and maxims. The *Essay* lacks that strong progression of connected thoughts that lays hold upon and kindles the mind; but few poems contain so many generalizations expressed with such surprising conciseness and energy:

> Hope springs eternal in the human breast:
> Man never *is*, but always *to be* blest. i. 95–6.

> Man like the gen'rous vine, supported lives,
> The strength he gains is from th'embrace he gives. iii. 311–12.

> An honest man's the noblest work of God. iv. 248.

To sum up, Pope was above all things an artist, one of the most conscious, most persevering, and most finished his country has produced. We do not go to him for really original modes of thought or feeling; he has contributed no wisdom, instruction, or intuition of his own. But he never failed in the handling of his style or his verse. The stamp which he set on poetic form after Dryden was so neat and clear-cut that his manner was widely adopted, and thought by many to be final, throughout the remainder of the century. The part he played in literature is therefore considerable, and if the romantics were implacable against him, it was because they recognized his supreme prestige as the representative of the classical school.

Swift. Pope's superiority over the poets of his generation is as marked as Dryden's. Until the appearance of Thomson in 1726–30 his is the only great name. Pope's contemporaries are now for the most part curiosities of literary history, and few indeed of their verses have lived. The most remarkable are certainly Swift's, not for their strictly poetic qualities but for the energetic personality they reveal, and because they furnish the most striking example of what rhyme and rhythm can add to a deliberately plain style and deliberately prosaic thought. Swift, having begun with free Pindaric odes in the manner of Cowley, and convinced himself of his complete incapacity for the lyric, discovered that his true medium of expression was the 'short (octosyllabic) couplet', eschewing epithets and producing artistic pleasure by its clearness and pith. Thus he made for himself a domain, on the borders of prose, where he reigned without peer. The peculiar talent for versification of this great prose-writer was revealed in *Cadenus and Vanessa* (written in 1713), in which he describes under a classical disguise his relations with Esther Vanhomrigh; in his little poems to his other friend Stella; and particularly in the poem called *On the Death of Dr. Swift* (1731):

> Poor Pope will grieve a month, and Gay
> A week, and Arbuthnot a day.
> St. John himself will scarce forbear
> To bite his pen, and drop a tear.
> The rest will give a shrug, and cry:
> 'I'm sorry—but we all must die.'

John Gay. One of the most popular writers contemporary with Pope and Swift was John Gay (1685–1732), the spoilt child of the Tory coterie and a careless and indolent man of the world. He made for himself a sort of speciality of realistic poetry in the six pastorals of his *Shepherd's Week* (1714), substituting for the artificial eclogue a coarse picture of rustic life with a comic bias. *Trivia, or the Art of Walking the Streets of London* (1716) applied the same process to the city. Gay won popularity with his *Fables* (1727) in 'short couplets', inspired by the French poet La Fontaine; but he did not achieve La Fontaine's sure touch, his delicacy, his variety, or his finish. Some of his fables however, like *The Hare with Many Friends*, are pleasing and individual. It is by this collection and the clever songs of his *Beggar's Opera* (1728) that Gay is chiefly remembered nowadays.

Parnell, Tickell, Philips. To the same circle of friends belonged Thomas Parnell (1679–1718), who was patronized by Swift and Pope and had rather more lyrical inspiration than the rest of the group—witness *A Night Piece on Death*; but his best-known poem, *The Hermit*, is an oriental tale in heroic couplets of an unbearably artificial kind. On the other hand Thomas Tickell (1686–1740), who survives by his fine elegy *On the Death of Mr. Addison*, one of the rare pieces of the period in which sincere emotion raises the verse above the level of the dry wit then prevalent, was a member of the Whig group of which Addison was the centre. The political rivalries of the time made Ambrose Philips (1675–1749) also an adherent of Addison and therefore an enemy of Pope and the Tories. Philips was the Whig pastoralist praised in *The Guardian* and parodied by Gay in *The Shepherd's Week*. His little compliments in lackadaisical and sugared verse not devoid of charm have given the language the ironical epithet 'namby-pamby' (Namby being a diminutive of Ambrose).

Allan Ramsay. In the pastoral manner, which had become more and more artificial, the only poet who succeeded in animating the convention with some rustic realism without resorting like Gay to coarseness was the Scotsman Allan Ramsay (1686–1758). His *Gentle Shepherd* (1725) is a dramatic pastoral, with descriptions enlivened by his happy use of his native speech. Ramsay's verse is racy of the soil. He had a taste for popular poetry, and by his collection of old songs, *The Ever Green* (1724), helped forward the poetic revival in Scotland.

Prose

Daniel Defoe. Pope notwithstanding, the beginning of the century is primarily a prose-writing period and its most memorable works are in prose. The art of circulating facts and ideas among an ever-increasing public had by now made considerable progress. The work of Daniel Defoe (1660–1731) is very characteristic in this respect. Defoe was a journalist whose genius is the more astonishing because he had to invent almost the whole of his craft. Before him there had indeed been several more recent publications, besides many papers in the Civil War times, which corresponded to the newspapers of our day. Sir Roger L'Estrange with his *Observator* (1681–7) and John Dunton with his *Athenian Gazette* (1690–6) have the credit attached to precursors, but it was Defoe who really widened the new path in 1704 with *The Review*, which he conducted until 1713. He had not indeed waited until then to address the public. He was both a man of letters and a man of action. The son of a dissenting butcher, he received a modern education, completely practical and quite unlike that supplied by the Universities; dead languages were replaced by living; scholasticism and metaphysics by history, geography, and politics. Defoe began his career as a hosier; he was an ingenious but rash tradesman and ended by going bankrupt in 1692. He obtained his discharge, however, and continued in business as manager of a tile-works. But he was already tormented by the itch to write. The revolution of 1688 put William III, a Protestant king after Defoe's own heart, on the throne. He was a completely devoted subject, and it appears that the king recognized his zeal and sometimes had recourse to his sagacity. It was to defend this king, of whom many were suspicious because he was a foreigner, that Defoe wrote his first really popular work: *The True-Born Englishman* (1701), a long satire in prosaic but clear and vigorous verse in which the author showed how the English nation was itself made up of the most diverse elements, and that it was ungraciousness on its part to condemn the king for not being of pure English stock. Already Defoe was showing himself skilful in the handling of arguments likely to appeal to the multitude.

His second widely known production was *The Shortest Way with the Dissenters* (1702) in which he took upon himself to defend the dissenters against the rigorous measures advocated by the Anglicans. To produce a greater effect he made his attack obliquely, putting his words into the mouth of a distinguished Anglican, an imaginary personage who demands outright that the dissenters shall be suppressed by being sent to the gallows; and such was the imperturbable gravity of his irony that his co-religionists read it with terror and his enemies with approval until they discovered that they had been fooled. The outcome was disastrous for Defoe, who was thrown into prison and set in the pillory; the people, however, regarded him as a hero.

Ruined once more and undesirous of running further risks, Defoe became a journalist and was patronized and secretly paid by the Tory minister Harley. He was looked upon, apparently with justice, as a secret agent of those who had been the bitter enemies of his party. Nevertheless he seems to have continued to express the moral and economic ideals so dear to him. His knowledge of foreign countries and his travels through every part of England and Scotland made him a very prudent counsellor who was well acquainted with the state of mind of the people.

It was only late in life, in 1719, when he was near his sixtieth year, that he began the series of imaginative stories that constitute the first English novels, *Robinson Crusoe* heading the list. They all took the form of memoirs or pretended historical narratives, in which everything was designed to give the impression of reality. Even where extraordinary adventures abounded, Defoe succeeded in avoiding any appearance of the fantastic, of invention, or of artistic arrangement on the part of the author. The total suppression of art—that is, of apparent art—was made easier for him because he had no taste for beauty. As a rule, even the most indifferent writer aspires to beauty or to what he conceives to be beautiful. Defoe took no account of it. His only purpose was to make his stories so lifelike that the reader's attention would be fixed solely on the events. These would, moreover, be the more readily accepted in proportion as they were vouched for by a greater number of details and as these details looked at one by one were more ordinary, more everyday, more completely stripped of aesthetic significance. It was in this way that Defoe carried to the highest perfection the only art he cultivated, the art of lying. In this respect he presents a striking analogy with the author of *Gulliver*, but if Swift deceives for a moment he is in the end betrayed by his humour, and indeed he does not seek to deceive indefinitely. Defoe, on the contrary, hides his own part so well that the illusion persists to the end, and it was for a long time impossible and is even now difficult to distinguish in some cases between his false reminiscences and his true ones. For his multiplication of details Defoe fell back on his varied experiences of trade and of everything connected with the practical conduct of life. He justified the boldness of his tales by his design of reporting faithfully and also of inculcating a moral lesson. At bottom his books were meant to satisfy the same curiosity about out-of-the-way adventures and the disreputable careers of thieves and prostitutes as Robert Greene's 'cony-catching' pamphlets. The chief change is in the manner and in the style, which rejects all ornament and all subtlety, content to be perfectly precise and practical.

These characteristics are common to all Defoe's fictions: *Moll Flanders*, the life of a prostitute, *Roxana*, the life of a great courtesan, *Memoirs of a Cavalier*, *The Life of Captain George Carlton*, *The Life of Captain Singleton*, *A Journal of the Plague Year* (i.e. 1665), *The Life of John Sheppard*, the highwayman, *The History of Colonel Jacque*, another highwayman, and the rest. *Robinson Crusoe* is one of those numerous accounts of imaginary voyages in which Defoe delighted. Crusoe's sojourn on a desert island, which has become a tale of universal appeal, occupies the middle part of the work. Without relaxing his workaday manner, Defoe was fortunate enough to hit upon a theme that teases the imagination—the life of a man separated from his fellows and obliged to provide for his own physical and spiritual needs. No invention of a poet could operate with such irresistible effect on the imagination of all ages and of all times.

There was no contemporary writer who so broadened the basis of literature as Defoe, or appealed to so wide a circle of readers— to all, in fact, who were able to read. But he himself, in the eyes of men of letters, was outside literature. Neither Pope nor Swift looked upon him as a literary man. This disdain was justified by his career, equivocal to say the least, as a pamphleteer, but it was founded also on his rejection of the whole tradition of humanism to which the other prose-writers of the period, Steele, Addison, Swift, Arbuthnot, and the rest, were attached. Even when they aspired to popularity, they still respected the literary code bequeathed by antiquity and revived by the Renaissance. They obeyed principles of composition and conventions of style derived from their classical education. Instead of reproducing, like Defoe, the modes of speech and writing of common people with intelligent but uncultured minds, they introduced into their style even at its simplest an elegance and art which raised their writings a step above the language of every day. They chose their words, they preferred certain turns of phrase for their distinction, they adorned their pages here and there with some figure of speech or comparison. Even when they renounce all artifice one feels that they have studied rhetoric with profit. And all these things determined the limits of their public. The common people, to whom Defoe addressed himself, formed no part of it. They aimed rather at instructing the middle classes, the honest citizens who wished to cultivate both their intelligence and their style, who demanded decency of conduct and a certain amount of elegance of expression.

The periodicals of Steele and Addison do not rely for their attraction on news of political happenings; they are so many pleasant essays on practical moral questions, reflecting the manners of the time by means of numerous anecdotes of the most varied kinds.

Steele. To Richard Steele (1672–1729) belongs the credit of having taken the initiative. Temperamentally he was of the stock of the Cavaliers; he was a man of the world and a lover of gaming and wine who led a dissipated life. But he had none of the cynicism which had characterized the breed, particularly under the Restoration. He was full of remorse for his failings. He had virtuous and sentimental aspirations and a fund of sincere piety, as is proved by his first book, *The Christian Hero* (1701), an edifying work which establishes the superiority of the biblical code over that of the ancient philosophers; his lesson is that conduct should be regulated not by the desire for glory but by conscience, and he extols chivalrous respect for women. He obeyed the same impulse in his plays, where he tried to break with the tradition of comedy which puts wit on the side of vice and debauchery; he was the founder in England of sentimental comedy.

In a similar spirit he launched his journal *The Tatler* in 1709, under the pseudonym of Isaac Bickerstaff, the nickname of the astrologer Partridge recently made notorious by Swift's mockery. He began by dating each number or section of a number from one or other of those London coffee-houses which were in effect clubs, each one frequented by this or that profession or section of society, men about town, poets, scholars, newsmongers, or politicians. Steele did not at first know very clearly what he was aiming at and progressed at random. But from the beginning he sought to mingle instruction with amusement. He would reform morals by laughing at frivolities. He expressed, often in the sprightly manner of comedy, the moral ideals of orderliness and due seriousness which were so dear to the still half-puritan middle classes. His intentions were excellent, but his talent, which was more lively than persevering, versatile rather than sustained, only rarely succeeded in producing essays of real substance; everything of his suggests haste and improvisation. The collaborators to whom he applied did not succeed any better than he in giving a definite character to this thrice-weekly journal. The poverty of the matter was poorly disguised by the diversity of the forms— dissertations, character-portraits, tales, letters—until Addison came to the rescue.

Addison. Joseph Addison (1672–1719), a clergyman's son, had been Steele's schoolfellow at Charterhouse. He was a much more brilliant and painstaking pupil than Steele, and later distinguished himself at Oxford by his Latin verse and his literary culture. He was a true humanist and at first seemed destined for a purely academic career. He wrote in Latin; he travelled in France and Italy and during the course of his journeys what chiefly interested him was numismatics. The necessity, however, for making sure of patronage had induced him to ally himself with the Whigs as early as 1693. The alliance became still closer when he celebrated Marlborough's victory at Blenheim in *The Campaign* (1704), an epic fragment in the pseudo-classical style which made him famous, and opened for him the way even to the highest political office. He turned his attention, previously concentrated on classical antiquity, to his own time and country. He applied the judgement of a scholar and his literary talent to the criticism of manners. He had the scholar's poise, and, although a party man, detested the violent tone of politics and the excessive partisanship of men in whom the cynicism of the cavaliers or the sombre austerity of the puritans still survived. He showed how ridiculous was either extreme, and could put his whole social teaching in a nutshell, as in the following anecdote:

My worthy friend Sir Roger, when we are talking of the malice of parties, very frequently tells us an accident that happened to him when he was a school-boy, which was at the time when the feuds ran high between the Round-heads and Cavaliers. This worthy knight, being then but a stripling, had occasion to inquire which was the way to St. Anne's Lane? Upon which the person whom he spoke to, instead of answering his question, called him a young popish cur, and asked him who had made Anne a saint? The boy, being in some confusion, inquired of the next he met, which was the way to Anne's Lane? but was called a prick-eared cur for his pains, and instead of being shown the way, was told that she had been a saint before he was born, and would be one after he was hanged. 'Upon this', says Sir Roger, 'I did not think fit to repeat the former question, but going into every lane of the neighbourhood, asked what they called the name of the lane?' By which ingenious artifice he found out the place he inquired after, without giving offence to any party.

He pointed out also to each of the adversaries the good qualities of the other and the possibility of an agreement, even indeed of a warm friendship, between men of opposite parties. He propagated in society rational and moderate ideas, showing that piety need not be fanatical, and should be balanced by pleasure without profligacy, man's natural desire for amusement being satisfied by social intercourse without licence and by intellectual pleasures made accessible to the many and freed from pedantry. He proclaimed a literature free from extravagance and affectation, faithful to the teaching of the ancients and yet capable of recovering the vein of simple and unfeigned emotion which ran through the best examples of the native tradition. It was along these lines that Addison proceeded when he began to help Steele with the production of *The Tatler*. But his role did not assume its full importance until Steele, bringing the first journal to an end, founded *The Spectator* in 1711, publishing it daily, and, in concert with Addison, inventing a complete fictional framework which gave it almost the charm and variety of a novel. The 'spectator' well represents Addison himself, detached from the world but taking pleasure in looking on at it, a kind of sage judging calmly and serenely the varied aspects of the social scene. He is the centre of a circle which includes representatives of various sections of society, like the country gentleman Sir Roger de Coverley, the great City merchant Sir Andrew Freeport, a clergyman of high moral character, a shrewd lawyer, a famous soldier Captain Sentry, and a man of the world full of innocent foppishness Will Honeycomb. The authors' intention was to introduce these characters and make them discourse, and to epitomize in them a considerable part of the nation. If they had been faithful to their programme they would have produced a sort of eighteenth-century pendant to the *Canterbury Tales*. But the promise of the beginning was only partly fulfilled. Only one of the characters, Sir Roger de Coverley, attained complete lifelikeness, but he was endued with enough light and shade to rival those creations of the realistic novel of which he was the herald and forerunner.

He was the joint creation of Steele and Addison, who hoped to proceed in concert but who in fact had each a different character in mind. Steele was thinking of an old worldling of the Restoration, a man of full-blooded temperament and capable of passion who had grown philosophical as he grew older, a kind of rustic Rousseau who should praise the simple life and reveal to society what he thought of it. Addison disregarded Steele's indications and deprived the character of much of its substance. He replaced the emphatic portrait by a simple but singularly expressive pencil sketch. Himself a staunch Whig, he succeeded in portraying a very lovable Tory, full of good nature and appealing to the reader's good nature, kind, charitable, and regulating his life according to an old tradition that had much charm and value. But this excellent Tory has a whimsical head; he is full of prejudices and superstitions. His reflections are usually naïve and indicate feeble powers of reasoning. Sir Roger's ideas provoke a smile. No one would dream of taking him for a political guide. Argument is not his strong point, especially when he is compared with the Whig merchant Sir Andrew Freeport, whose views are so intelligent and forward-looking. Addison reveals at once the charm of the old England and the coming of the new. He demands sympathy for both, but his intellectual allegiance is reserved for the second. Nevertheless he wishes the two to understand each other and to live in good accord.

The creation of Sir Roger is Addison's masterpiece. The man is not only an excellent figure of comedy with his eccentricities, his peculiar expressions, his attitudes, his mental leaps, but he is foremost among those characters who are not only loved but respected even while they are laughed at. One may think his ideas fantastic and yet appreciate his good nature. Nothing could better inculcate tolerance and cordiality than such a portrait. By means of it Addison did more than any one to reconcile the extremes in his country and to soften the asperities of social life. His serene and amiable humour found benign amusement in what had been until then the object of harsh satire or ridicule.

Swift. Quite different was Jonathan Swift (1667-1745), whose pleasure in ridicule was stronger than his desire to correct. Swift displays like all moralists the faults and vices of humanity, but he does not seem to have any hope of reforming them. Instead of making, like Addison, for cordiality, he leads the reader towards misanthropy and pessimism. His habitual weapon is scorn: he jeers at what he detests and excels in exposing the absurdity of human life. He hides his mockery under an air of imperturbable gravity which for a time deceives us as to his intentions and doubles the effect of his sarcasm. In this kind of jesting he is incomparable. Swift possesses a sort of inverted enthusiasm, an embittered lyricism. Alone among his contemporaries he is animated by violent feeling, which, however, instead of warming like a flame corrodes like an acid. Capable at first of true gaiety, he grew more and more bitter in proportion as life disappointed him. But from the beginning there was harshness in his humour and until the end a strong element of the comic remained part of it.

Swift was born in Ireland. As he was without fortune, he came as a young man to England to be secretary to his distant cousin Sir William Temple. The Church was the only opening which presented itself to him and without apparent vocation he took

PLATE XIX

Paris Cher Mory's Solaria

An eighteenth-century Coffee House

PLATE XX

Gulliver in Lilliput

Robinson Crusoe on his raft

orders. He came to Temple's aid when the latter was engaged in the quarrel then raging between Ancients and Moderns and amused himself by ridiculing the Moderns in his *Battle of the Books* under the guise of an ingenious allegory. Later on the clergyman in him attacked the Papists and Presbyterians in the *Tale of a Tub* (1704). But he allowed himself to be persuaded by his mocking genius to trace the whole history of Christianity in an allegorical form, and he did it in a spirit of buffoonery which hardly spared even Anglicanism, and was well calculated to disturb pious souls of every sect. The history of the three brothers Peter (Roman Catholicism), Martin (Anglican Protestantism), and Jack (Scottish Presbyterianism) who adapt the Bible-teaching to the needs of the day and the demands of their own temperament is encumbered, in this strange book, with a whole series of prefaces, introductions, and digressions which Swift employed in order to parody erudite and controversial writers—the whole forming a rich arsenal in which all the sceptics of the eighteenth century found sharp-edged weapons.

Meanwhile Swift had engaged in politics, taking his place at first in the Whig ranks. He came to London, frequented the coffee-houses, and allied himself with writers like Addison, Steele, Halifax, and Congreve. He was now at the height of mirth and energy. He organized a famous jest directed against the astrologer Partridge. But Queen Anne, scandalized by his *Tale of a Tub*, opposed his nomination to a bishopric. Swift, disappointed and, moreover, irritated because the Whigs would not support the Church, crossed into the Tory camp in 1710. He joined Harley and Bolingbroke and became powerful, and as one born to command he enjoyed the power he exercised. He attacked the hero of the Whigs, Marlborough, in his journal *The Examiner*, and in his *Conduct of the Allies* he urged peace with France at a time when the Whigs wished to pursue the war.

The fall of the Tories in 1714 put an end to his political career. He left London to settle in Dublin, where the Deanery of St. Patrick's had been conferred upon him. Although he despised the Irish and chafed at being removed from England, he took the part of the island to which he had virtually been banished. He seized every occasion to checkmate Walpole, the Whig Prime Minister of George I. In his *Drapier's Letters* he rallied the Irish against the monopoly of minting copper money granted to the Englishman Wood. He effected the withdrawal of the monopoly, and his popularity became immense.

It was during this period of his life that he produced his most popular book, *Gulliver's Travels* (1726), in which under the cloak of fantastic stories he satirized the politics of his day, the religious quarrels, the wars of ambition, the lucubrations of science, and also the very nature of man and the whole human species. In spite of all the pessimism which burdens it, the book, especially in the first half, which relates the story of Gulliver's stay in Lilliput and in the country of the Brobdingnagians, is written with a rich and ingenious invention and unflagging spirit. Like Defoe's *Robinson Crusoe* it enjoys the privilege of amusing children while making men think. It has become popular in all languages. And considered as literature it is greatly superior to Defoe's shapeless book. The perfectly simple style has an incomparable exactness and precision. Every line, moreover, and every detail is vivified by a humour which consists in presenting the most improbable extravagances with an imperturbable gravity that procures belief for them. The presence of design and art in Swift's masterpiece raises it far above Defoe's, which was the result of a happy chance hardly looked for by its author. Reduction to the absurd is Swift's habitual method, as in the following instance, taken from his description of the Academy of Lagado:

When parties in a state are violent, he [i.e. one of the professors] offered a wonderful contrivance to reconcile them. The method is this: You take a hundred leaders of each party; you dispose them into couples of such whose heads are nearest of a size; then let two nice operators saw off the occiput of each couple at the same time, in such manner that the brain may be equally divided. Let the occiputs thus cut off be interchanged, applying each to the head of his opposite party-man. It seems indeed to be a work that requireth some exactness; but the professor assured us that if it were dexterously performed, the cure would be infallible. For he argued thus: that the two half brains being left to debate the matter between themselves within the space of one skull, would soon come to a good understanding, and produce that moderation, as well as regularity of thinking, so much to be wished for in the heads of those who imagine they come into the world only to watch and govern its motion: and as to the difference of brains in quantity or quality, among those who are directors in faction, the doctor assured us, from his own knowledge, that it was a perfect trifle.

Arbuthnot. The physician John Arbuthnot (1667–1735), a friend of Swift and Pope, was a scholar, a humanist, and a man of wit who devoted only a part of his activity to letters and showed no ambition for literary glory. But his moral qualities, his generosity, and his warm character made him the best-liked and the most respected of the circle of Tory writers to which he belonged. He was gifted with dramatic power, as is shown by his best-known work *The History of John Bull* (1712). This amusing allegory was designed to support Harley's ministry and oppose the Whigs and Marlborough who wished to pursue the war against France. Instead of a war Arbuthnot imagined a lawsuit between the draper John Bull on the one part and Lewis Baboon of France and Lord Strutt of Spain on the other part. With John Bull is associated Nic. Frog (the Dutchman), who would like the expenses of the suit to fall on England alone. The most pleasing pages of the book are those in which Arbuthnot draws the winning portrait of John Bull's mother (the Anglican Church) and that of froward Peggy (Scotland) who is in love with the Presbyterian Jack. Nowhere does he show so much tenderness and earnestness as in the first of these, nowhere so much mischievousness as in the second. The book remains one of the most famous political satires England has produced.

A good deal of Arbuthnot's prose was written in collaboration with his friends and it is not easy to tell the precise portions which belong to him. It is so with *The Memoirs of Martinus Scriblerus*, in which tradition has it that his was the principal hand. The *Memoirs* are a solemn buffoonery intended to ridicule pedants and visionaries, and contains an amusing caricature of the abuse of educational theories, the false pretensions of science being mocked much as in Gulliver's voyage to Laputa.

The Whig and Tory satirists who have just been dealt with are the special glory of the age of Queen Anne. But they represent only one aspect of the activity of the period. If they were at the centre of the world of letters there were others, theologians, philosophers, and political writers, who occupied its outskirts and shared with them the characteristic of employing a clear and facile prose which made them accessible to more and more readers.

The Deists. The controversies between Anglicans and Papists or Anglicans and dissenters which had filled the seventeenth century now gave place to a sharp polemic between orthodox Christians and Deists. The growing distrust of everything which might be styled religious enthusiasm led many minds to reject the miraculous and mysterious elements and to cling only to the rational element in Christianity. The Bible was ousted little by little, to be replaced by a kind of philosophical system at the apex of which was an abstract god possessed of every perfection with which human reason could endow him. Everything else was regarded as primitive symbolism or as superstition. Locke had set the fashion with his *Reasonableness of Christianity* in 1695. But Locke's prudence and his respect for established beliefs were no longer evident in the more aggressive work by John Toland, *Christianity Not Mysterious* (1696), nor in the pamphlets which Toland wrote towards the end of his life and which tend towards pantheism and the philosophy of Spinoza. Faith in reason and mistrustful hostility to the clergy characterize the pamphlets of Anthony Collins and even more those of Matthew Tindal, whose *Christianity as Old as the Creation* attempts to prove that Christianity is only a confirmation of natural religion and therefore superfluous.

The deism of the time was, indeed, diffuse and generalized, and is found in writers who abstained from strictly theological questions. It is the foundation of the philosophical writings of such men as Shaftesbury and Bolingbroke, though their preoccupation was with ethical and social questions.

Shaftesbury. The Earl of Shaftesbury (1671–1713), the author of *Characteristicks of Men, Manners, Opinions, Times* (1711), is one of the most original figures of the period and one of those whose ideas have made most stir in Europe. This nobleman was

an amateur, almost a dilettante, at first a follower of Locke who
had supervised his early education. Like Locke he acclaimed
the methods of rationalism, praised tolerance, and attacked and
ridiculed fanaticism (*Letter concerning Enthusiasm*, 1708). But he
himself displayed a fine ardour in research into moral laws. He
reacted against the utilitarianism of his master Locke. He combined the teachings acquired from the Stoics and Plato with a
noble Christian inspiration. From this he derived an altruistic
morality founded on the instincts which impel every man to desire
the happiness of other creatures. His optimism perceived in every
man a conscience which makes an immediate revelation to him of
good and evil, and a moral sense by means of which he perceives
the beauty of things. In his belief in man's goodness Shaftesbury
anticipated Rousseau; his transports before the sublimity of the
external world are a distant prelude to the effusions of the Romantics. The highest elements in the cult of sensibility are traceable
to him. Shaftesbury's Scottish disciple Francis Hutcheson (1694-
1746) gave a more systematic form to his scattered ideas.

Bolingbroke. Henry St. John, Viscount Bolingbroke (1678-
1751), sympathized with the Deists and poured scorn on superstition, showing no mercy to the historical elements of Christianity.
It was he who furnished Pope with the principal themes of the
Essay on Man. But he was first of all a politician. At one moment,
sharing the Tory triumphs, he had embarked upon a plan for the
restoration of the Jacobites, when the advent of the Hanoverians
forced him to fly. Thenceforward he offered an embittered opposition to the Whigs; but he produced out of his experience and his
rancour a penetrating examination of parliamentary rule. He tried
to unite good citizens in a common respect for the national ideal,
and sought to revive the principle of monarchy by making the
'Patriot king' a living symbol of the nation. In many respects he
anticipated by a century the conception of the new Toryism which
was to have its brief day of triumph under Disraeli.

Mandeville. It was with the cynicism of the Restoration and the
ideas of Hobbes that Bernard Mandeville (1670-1733) was linked.
He bitterly contradicted Shaftesbury and, far from basing the
social order on the virtues, he maintained that civilization was

founded on the vices of the individual. His famous book, *The Fable of the Bees, or Private Vices Publick Benefits* (1714–23) is designed to prove that a nation is rich and powerful only through the corruption which is inextricably mingled with all its activities. A mercantile country is necessarily a country of sharp practice and theft. The business of a good government is to harmonize the self-seeking elements which compose the nation and make them hold one another in check. It should use the vanity of individuals to make them restrain their greedily egoistic instincts.

Joseph Butler. Not all the conclusions of reason were, however, directed against traditional faith and morality. Joseph Butler vigorously attacked as a logician the logic of the Deists in his *Analogy of Religion Natural and Revealed to the Constitution of Nature* (1736), which was for a long time regarded as a decisive refutation of his adversaries and a buttress of the Christian faith.

Berkeley. The attitude of the great metaphysician of the day, George Berkeley (1685–1753), who became Bishop of Cloyne, is also very characteristic. He is famous in the history of philosophy for his absolute idealism, which went so far as to deny the real existence of matter. But this idealism had its primary source in his religious convictions and sprang from a mysticism which grew more and more obvious in his writings. The correspondences of his thought with Plato's are not more marked than the formal analogy between his dialogues and those of the Greek master. Nothing could be more admirable than the lucid prose, perfectly simple and perfectly elegant, in which Berkeley expressed his profound and subtle views.

Other Christian Writers. In all the writings which have been mentioned the intellectual element is supreme. All of them appeal to reason. But the strictly religious outlook still survived: there were Christians who concerned themselves first of all with the Christian life and who regarded the imitation of Christ as the first duty. The man who best and most vigorously expressed and directed faith in this 'age of enlightenment' was William Law (1686–1761), whose *Serious Call to a Devout and Holy Life* (1729) was then, and remained for generations, the bedside book of pious souls. He foreshadowed the Wesleyan reform, which owed much to him, and his influence bears witness to the strong current of mysticism which, soon coming to the surface, was to assist in the revival of literature.

Its effects were already visible here and there in a seeking after emotion and a musing before the face of nature, as in Lady Winchilsea's poem *A Nocturnal Reverie*, or the devotional verses of Isaac Watts, *Hymns and Spiritual Songs* (1707), and *Divine Songs for Children* (1715). The change was perhaps more striking in the theatre where, as we shall see, it led to the substitution of sentimental plays for cynical comedies. But as yet such events were exceptional, the germs of what was to come. The dominant characteristics of the classical period were the cultivation of reason and the approval of mental balance.

XXIII

THE EIGHTEENTH CENTURY (1740-70)

Poetry

It is less easy to define the characteristics of this period of letters than those of previous ones. The Restoration was primarily a cynical reaction against the restraints of Puritanism. The dominant note of the age of Queen Anne was the desire for balance and the worship of common sense. In the next third of the century, from 1740 to 1770, no definite tendency prevailed, no single personality can be put forward as truly representative. Dr. Johnson, who has sometimes been given this honour, merits it more for his services to the literary profession than for the value of his literary achievement; he represents the current of tradition, hostile to innovation, that is to say, only one of the aspects of the age.

In the realm of poetry it was a period of clever and varied, though still timid, experiments; but above all it was the period of prose, not only of the creation, but of the full blossoming, of the novel. Few works have been so widely read, not only in England but in the whole world, as *The Seasons*, the *Night Thoughts*, and Gray's *Elegy* in the realm of poetry, or as *Clarissa Harlowe, Tom Jones, Tristram Shandy*, and *The Vicar of Wakefield* in prose. But the very naming together of these works throws their dissimilarity into sharp relief; they seem to have no common factor. 'Sensibility', of which the first traces appeared at the very beginning of the century, continued to grow and develop, but without disturbing the course of classical literature, which still kept its ascendency.

Poetry, taken as a whole, clearly continued to show the influence of Dryden and of Pope. Didactic or satirical inspiration had a large part in it. The couplet, regular and symmetrically balanced, with its antitheses relieved by ingenious periphrasis, though hard-pressed by the blank verse which Thomson had revived, still formed the normal type of poetry. The classical method of criticism also persisted; if there was a difference it was that it tended to grow more dogmatic than in the past. In this respect, Samuel

Johnson (1709–84) consolidated the achievement of Pope and his contemporaries.

Dr. Johnson. As a poet, Johnson produced two satires, *London* (1738) and *The Vanity of Human Wishes* (1749), in which he modernized Juvenal as Pope had modernized Horace, and a tragedy, *Irene*, in which he observed the rules of French rhetorical tragedy. But poetry was the least part of his considerable output. Forced to do work of all sorts by the publishers on whom he depended for a livelihood, he was translator, journalist, lexicographer, commentator, novelist, biographer, and finally literary critic. To these varied tasks he brought the authority of his strong brain. Though he had not Addison's supple grace, and though his style was too consistently majestic, he yet could convey in the essays of his *Rambler* and *Idler* the results of his own personal reflection on life. His *Dictionary* of the English language has not the philological basis which would be expected to-day, but it is remarkable for the precision of its definitions and its feeling for the correct use of words: Johnson did single-handed for English what had been done for French by the *Académie Française*. His novel *Rasselas* (1759) was written under pressure of necessity in a few weeks, at the same time that Voltaire published *Candide*. Both writers make the same attack on the self-satisfied optimism which proclaims that all is for the best in the best of worlds. But it is a far cry from Voltaire's continual laughter, irreverence, and malicious wit, to the pompous solemnity of Johnson, whose restrained humour is a weak leaven for the dough which he is trying to make rise. The best of Johnson's work was done in his biographical and literary studies and in his edition of Shakespeare. Here admiration of a higher genius made him relax the rigour of his poetic dogmas. Taking up and developing Dryden's appreciation, he produced one of the wisest and sanest views of Shakespeare, while his lucid mind solved in the most plausible way many textual difficulties. But Shakespeare apart, it was the rules of classical criticism that he habitually applied in his *Lives of the Poets* (1779–81), in which he set himself up as the biographer and judge of English poets since Abraham Cowley. His interest in them as writers was balanced by his interest in them as men, and he was occasionally influenced by political or religious bias, and as a good Tory and an Anglican led to show a particular severity towards Whigs, dissenters, and deists. But taken as a whole the *Lives* display a humanity and an accuracy of judgement which have ensured them a permanent place in English criticism.

Nevertheless Johnson the man was greater than Johnson the writer. None of his own books has been so widely read or remained so much alive as that written about him by his admirer James Boswell. And the value of this book lies in the very self-effacement of the biographer, for he has succeeded in reproducing to the letter the conversation, the sallies, and the spontaneous and picturesque character of Johnson's judgements before he had stiffened and starched them for publication. The first shape of Johnson's thought was familiar and concrete. It was only after reflection that he transformed it into learned prose, abounding in Latinisms and witnessing to a constant desire for loftiness and majesty of style.

It is not only in the freshness of his talk that Boswell's pages reveal Johnson the man. He is seen with all his qualities of heart, his prejudices, and his candour. His abrupt outspokenness, his habitual good sense are not more apparent than his deep melancholy. Clear reasoner as he was, he had small faith in human reason; his profoundly religious spirit steeped itself in prayer. The clumsy giant with the seamed and surly countenance had the tenderest and most charitable heart. He is a figure full of contrasts and of a deep-set goodness, who has never since ceased to interest the English reader and to inspire for him a sympathy often refused to greater writers.

Goldsmith. Oliver Goldsmith (1730–74) was able to give a new freshness and charm to the current poetry without any change of form, by infusing it with his amiable feelings and enlivening it with his kindly smile. In his *Traveller* (1764) he records his impressions, as a traveller on foot across the Continent, of France, Switzerland, and Italy, and reflects agreeably on the character of these various countries. In 1770 he published his *Deserted Village*, an idealization of the Irish village of Lissoy in which his childhood was passed. He describes its natural beauties, the warm-hearted manners of its inhabitants, the eccentricities of the

PLATE XXI

Dr. Johnson and his circle. Dr. Johnson (left foreground) is expounding a point to Burke. Thence, going right about, the diners are: Burney, Goldsmith, T. Warton (the younger), Paoli, Garrick, Reynolds, and Boswell

PLATE XXII

RELIQUES

OF

ANCIENT ENGLISH POETRY:

CONSISTING OF

Old Heroic BALLADS, SONGS, and other
PIECES of our earlier POETS,

(Chiefly of the LYRIC kind.)

Together with some few of later Date.

VOLUME THE FIRST.

DURAT OPUS VATUM

LONDON:

Printed for J. DODSLEY in Pall-Mall.

M DCC LXV.

The title-page of Percy's *Reliques of Ancient English
Poetry*, 1765

schoolmaster, and the virtues of the village parson. His parson is the worthy companion, somewhat sentimentalized, of Chaucer's village priest:

> A man he was to all the country dear,
> And passing rich with forty pounds a year;
> Remote from towns he ran his godly race,
> Nor e'er had changed, nor wished to change his place; . . .
> His house was known to all the vagrant train,
> He chid their wanderings, but relieved their pain; . . .

Goldsmith grieves at the thought that all this is no more. The villagers have disappeared, driven out by the enclosure of the common land by the big estates which has forced them to take refuge in the towns or to emigrate. The pastoral spirit fills this graceful poem, which is nevertheless shot through with personal reminiscences and details taken from real life. One of the last fine poems written in the couplet of Pope, its idyllic view of country life was destined to provoke the gloomy and eloquent reply of George Crabbe.

Minor Poets. Among the eighteenth-century poets of whom Johnson wrote lives there are many who to-day are mere names, known only to specialists. The most neglected are, indeed, precisely those who followed the classical tradition most closely, without modifying it by a sufficiently personal contribution of their own. To them any subject seemed good provided that it were set off by a certain diction deemed poetic. Thus the physician John Armstrong described in bombastic blank verse *The Art of Preserving Health* (1774). Mark Akenside, another physician, chose a happier theme, *The Pleasures of Imagination* (1744), but produced in blank verse as a cold and correct formal dissertation what should, one would think, have been an ardent outburst. There are nevertheless notable passages in the poem which anticipate Wordsworth and were turned to use by him. James Grainger sang *The Sugar Cane* (1764) and William Falconer in the *Shipwreck* (1762) oddly mingled nautical terms with artificial diction. These are examples taken from among the many versifiers of this period when poetry was used as an elegant aid to memory by persons concerned to spread abstract doctrines or exact knowledge.

Nevertheless, active sources of inspiration, lyrical feeling, sentiment, invention, were not lacking. In fact all the poets of the time whose memory has survived were in some degree independent and original. Although none made a deliberate effort to shake off the effete diction then current, and although many passages in their works show that they adhered to the accepted creed, yet each ploughed some new furrow, each opened up some vista through which the future might be perceived.

James Thomson. Perhaps the most pregnant initiative was shown by the Scot James Thomson (1700–48). While still very young, when Pope was at the height of his fame, he came to London with the manuscript of a description of *Winter*, which he issued in 1725. Encouraged by success he produced between 1726 and 1730 *The Seasons*, a work which marks an important date in the history of the poetry of Nature. Thomson did not indeed create the feeling for Nature which had manifested itself in all times and in all countries, and nowhere with more strength and persistence than in English literature. He was not the first either to praise it or to describe it. But nobody before him had thought of basing a whole poem on the magnificence and diversity of its aspects. Neither the few characteristics with which Spenser had endowed each of the months in his *Shepheard's Calendar*, nor Milton's vivid sketches in *L'Allegro* and *Il Penseroso*, nor the local poetry of Denham in *Cooper's Hill* and Pope in *Windsor Forest* detract much from the originality of Thomson's complete concentration on this one subject: the world caressed and chastised by turns, clothed in splendour or stripped bare by the seasons. The deist in him seeing in Nature the manifestation and, as it were, the image of divinity, bound together the successive pictures and built them up into a great harmonious whole. Although a precise and minute observation of the aspects of the countryside was the source of his verse, he did not date or localize it. He does not show us one particular season, or one storm, or one sunrise, or one fall of snow in a specified place: from all that he has seen he builds up a series of canvasses in which the successive seasons are personified like so many abstractions made real—in which *the* sunrise, *the* storm, *the*

snow, and so on, are depicted in the absolute, without distinct
location in time or space:

> Through the hushed air the whitening shower descends,
> At first thin-wavering; till at last the flakes
> Fall broad and wide and fast, dimming the day
> With a continual flow. The cherished fields
> Put on their winter-robe of purest white.
> 'Tis brightness all . . .

He has recourse to the same generalizations in describing Nature
as Pope in composing his *Essay on Man*. In this respect he is
linked with writers of the classical school. Like them he hides his
personality and is reluctant to let his own feelings appear. But
his strong love of Nature is revealed nevertheless in the penetration and exactness of his pictures, and in his boldness in finding
in the smallest details of country sights an interest superior to
that of human societies, with their virtues and vices, their prosperity and their decadence.

The publication of *The Seasons* divided the classical tradition.
Thenceforward there were to be two parallel currents—a poetry
of the town and rustic poetry. Throughout the whole of the
eighteenth century these currents were of almost equal strength.
At the same time as he presented his contemporaries with a new
theme Thomson widened the scope of versification and style
by taking Milton for his chief model and writing in blank verse.
He had felt that the couplet, with its tendency to divide up periods
and to render images fragmentary, did not allow him the spaciousness which he desired and which his subject claimed. He borrowed,
therefore, from Milton his long rhythmical periods, his varied
cadences, and his way of carrying over sentences from line to line.
He also borrowed and exaggerated Milton's Latinisms and endangered the sincerity of his descriptions by excessive pomp. His
instinct drew him towards the grand style of the humanists.
Through Milton he was to return to Spenser whose archaic language
and famous stanza he reproduced with much charm in the *Castle
of Indolence* (1748), a half-humorous description of the retreat at
Richmond where he lived with a few friends in an indolence too
dear to him. He also wrote the blank-verse poem *Liberty*, an

expression of his sentiments as a patriotic Whig; some tragedies composed on the classical formula were still-born. Thomson was in no sense a rebel against the literary dogmas of his time, but it was, nevertheless, by novelty of sentiment and by the use of poetic forms of a day earlier than the time of Dryden that he achieved fame and exercised an influence which spread throughout Europe.

A contemporary of Thomson's, John Dyer (1699-1758), showed an equal though a less sublime love of the country and of contemplation in his *Grongar Hill* (1726), a very charming piece of local description; in his more ambitious work *The Fleece* (1757), a poem in four books on the wool industry, he wandered far from pure poetry. William Shenstone anticipated Thomson in his imitation of Spenser, *The Schoolmistress* (1742), a rather shapeless mixture of clowning and sentimentality. Richard Jago continued the vein of local description in his *Edge-Hill or the Rural Prospect Delineated and Moralized* (1767). These are examples among many others of the landscape or village poetry of the middle of the century.

Edward Young. Young's *Night Thoughts* was destined to even more renown than *The Seasons*. It was the first great appeal to melancholy; Young discovered an exquisite pleasure in nocturnal churchyard meditation, visiting the tombs to muse, in a kind of transport, upon the Christian conception of the vanity of earthly things. Edward Young (1683-1765) was almost an old man when he wrote his *Night Thoughts*. He had begun life as a courtier and a poet in the prevailing fashion; and had distinguished himself as a forerunner of Pope with his rhymed satires *On the Love of Fame, the Universal Passion* and *On Women*, of which the moral was that we must laugh at human folly. For the theatre he had written several successful pieces, and had shown himself less of a slave to classical forms and more passionate than Thomson. His *Revenge* (1721) in particular, coming between Shakespeare's *Othello* and Voltaire's *Zaïre*, had a long and successful career. Rather late in life Young took orders. He hoped for a bishopric but his ambition was disappointed. In addition he was afflicted by stroke after stroke of domestic calamity, losing in the space of a few years his beautiful step-daughter, his son-in-law, and his wife. It was during this period of disappointment and mourning that he published his *Night Thoughts* (1742-5), seven meditations or sermons in blank verse, which he himself described as a sequel to Pope's *Essay on Man*. Pope preached optimism and strove against the pessimists; Young harped upon the vanity of the world and directed his attack against unbelief. Pope's theme was man; Young's the immortal spirit of man. The task he set himself was to convert a worldling, an atheist, one Lorenzo, to whom his arguments and his vehement apostrophes were addressed. What most struck his contemporaries in this long and confused outpouring was the setting—the vision of the poet meditating alone in the stillness of night, his thoughts haunting newly dug graves, yews and cypresses, with the pale rays of the moon shining down upon him.

> Night, sable goddess! from her ebon throne,
> In rayless majesty, now stretches forth
> Her leaden sceptre o'er a slumbering world.
> Silence, how dead! and darkness, how profound!
> Nor eye, nor listening ear, an object finds;
> Creation sleeps. 'Tis as the general pulse
> Of life stood still, and Nature made a pause,
> An awful pause! prophetic of her end.

The modern reader is discouraged by the continual declamation and the confusion of the poem. He finds the continual mingling of pomposity and wit difficult to endure. Young kept even in sermons his taste for conceits and antitheses. His blank verse was not naturally constructed in long periods, it had the brevity of the couplet and was full of cleverly coined maxims; but on occasions it could contain long passages of real eloquence.

The *Night Thoughts* awoke more than one funeral echo. Robert Blair's *The Grave* (1743), and James Harvey's prose *Meditations among the Tombs* (1745-6), appeared almost at once. Wider and more lasting was the association that Young helped to create between the pleasures of Nature and those of melancholy, an association formally established in *The Pleasures of Melancholy* (1747) by Thomas Warton.

Melancholy was nourished also upon a yearning regret for the past, a return to the beliefs of other days, to old legends and out-worn poetic forms. It was attracted to ruins, as Young's melan-choly was to tombstones. Thanks to it, the taste for 'Gothic' took birth and a new piquancy was given to old-fashioned superstitions in the very middle of the so-called age of reason.

William Collins. This varied inspiration joined with a delicate feeling for Nature produced the scanty work of William Collins (1721–59). Though he died young, and his last years were haunted by madness, no other poet fused and harmonized the discordant influences of the mid-eighteenth century so completely as he. On the one hand, no one else offers such striking examples of that 'poetic diction' with which the Classical school was afterwards reproached, and which consists in personifications, in the refinement of far-fetched circumlocutions, in the elaboration of bold figures of style created by former poets. But if in its form Collins's work was anything but unadorned, its subject-matter showed his attraction to simple themes and medieval allegories. His ode on the *Passions* is a revival of the allegorical form. He enjoyed describing *Popular Superstitions of the Highlands of Scotland*. His love of Nature made him an admirer of James Thomson, and he wrote a noble elegy on Thomson's death. His masterpiece is his *Ode to Evening*, perhaps the most exquisite lyric of the century. These few unrhymed stanzas give a most intimate and sensitive suggestion of twilight; the poem is steeped in the evening glow. The twilight is in his verse, which is un-rhymed, for it must not be too sonorous, too sharply marked in outline and form; its task is to reflect the moment when all things fade gradually and melt into a single harmony of grey; yet it is not ordinary blank verse, which would be too rhetorical and vehement. Collins chose short unrhymed stanzas, often run-ning them together without a break, but always bringing in two short lines in which his voice seems to fall, to whisper in the shadows lest it make too much stir:

> Now air is hushed, save where the weak-eyed bat,
> With short shrill shriek, flits by on leathern wing,
>   Or where the beetle winds
>   His small but sullen horn,

> As oft he rises 'midst the twilight path,
> Against the pilgrim borne in heedless hum:
> Now teach me, maid composed,
> To breathe some softened strain.

Collins's style is made up of a charming handful of images culled from his favourite poets, above all from Milton. From an essence he distils a quintessence. His short ode is like a slighter but more lyrical *Penseroso*, a *Penseroso* changed into a musical invocation.

Thomas Gray. Collins was a lover of the poets. Thomas Gray (1716–71) was a scholar besides. His life was spent almost entirely at Cambridge, in the two colleges of Peterhouse and Pembroke, and was uneventful, enlivened only by various friendships, of which the most famous was that with Horace Walpole. He had the fastidiousness of the solitary man of letters and though with his brief and ill-sustained inspiration it cost him an exhausting effort to produce the slightest of verses, he gave England some poems which are among the most popular in the language. Ailing and melancholy, he was led to contrast the carefree games of the schoolboys of Eton with the varied ills which would befall their riper years. As he wandered at twilight in a country churchyard, he meditated upon the humble fate of those who were sleeping there and who were perhaps equal in virtue and natural endowments to the heroes whose fame had filled the world: this is the theme of the *Elegy Written in a Country Churchyard*, whose quatrains live in every English memory. To such simple themes he devoted verses more lyrical in form, more refined in style, and more melodious than those of Pope. He could raise to absolute perfection the tritest idea, e.g. that true merit is often unrecognized here below:

> Full many a gem, of purest ray serene,
> The dark unfathomed caves of ocean bear;
> Full many a flower is born to blush unseen,
> And waste its sweetness on the desert air.

However slender was the fount of poetry within him, it was essentially lyrical. Gray avoided the predominant couplet. He preferred the stanza. He was an excellent Hellenist, and in more ambitious poems, *The Progress of Poesy* and *The Bard*, he tried to acclimatize the Pindaric form, not the irregular ode made fashionable by Cowley, which had given rise to numerous shapeless compositions, but an ode of careful and learned construction. While he experimented with these difficult forms, his reading provided him with plenty of subject-matter that excited his always alert curiosity, and he was particularly interested in what literary historians were beginning to discover about the past. The subject of *The Bard* was the massacre of Welsh poets by Edward I. *The Fatal Sisters* and *The Descent of Odin* reproduced Scandinavian themes. No one was more enthusiastic than Gray about Macpherson's pseudo-Gaelic *Ossian*. Gray tried in every way to break through the bounds of the prevailing patterns of poetry. Though he was neither rich nor copious he possessed in embryo much of the taste and sentiment which was to be typical of romanticism. He kept, however, the preference of his own age for a special poetic style, unlike that of prose, fraught with ingenious circumlocutions and extenuated allegories.

To give a foretaste of romanticism it only remained for the mid-eighteenth century to provide a dash of madness. Christopher Smart reached that point in his *Song to David* (1763), a collection of extraordinary stanzas, at times hardly intelligible, at times rich in language and of mysterious beauty, inspired by an enthusiasm for the imagery of the Psalms.

Macpherson's 'Ossian'. It was, however, the successive publication of various real or supposed fragments of ancient poetry, rather than any individual performance, which was preparing the way for a poetic revival. These fragments multiplied between 1760 and 1775. First of all came *Ossian*; or rather what purported to be translations of songs attributed to a fabulous Gaelic bard of that name and published from 1760 onwards by a Scottish schoolmaster, James Macpherson. It is now established that these songs and the epic poems of *Fingal* and *Temora* were the inventions of Macpherson's imagination working on some old fragments of Erse and on memories of Homer and the Bible. They are visions of ancient battles, the lamentations of an old blind bard in the solitude of a wild but vague country of seas and mountains, recalling memories of the glories of his youth, and mournfully reflecting that good fortune in this world lasts but an hour.

I have seen the walls of Balclutha, but they were desolate. The fire had resounded in the halls; and the voice of the people is heard no more. The stream was removed from its place by the fall of the walls. The thistle shook there its lonely head; the moss whistled to the wind.

These long laments in measured cadenced prose were designed to entrance readers by rescuing them from the banality of the modern world, pouring out in floods the 'melancholy' which they craved, and offering them a setting of what purported to be primitive nature. Macpherson's *Ossian* was a fraud, but it is fitting to do justice to the original talent which the author showed in his imposture, and to the immense influence he wielded.

Percy's 'Reliques'. A less soaring ambition but greater solid worth was shown in *Reliques of Ancient English Poetry* published in 1765 by Thomas Percy, afterwards Bishop of Dromore. This was a collection of ballads or short poems with elementary versification, and in an unpolished style, which charmed by their simplicity ears weary of the monotony and the contorted language of the couplet. The collection included Percy's arbitrary remodellings as well as authentic old poems; but the total effect was genuinely archaic, and helped to evoke the medieval world, its faith, its legends, and its ways.

Chatterton. Very soon after the appearance of the *Reliques* a Bristol youth, Thomas Chatterton (1752–70), brought up in the shadow of Bristol's Gothic cathedral, succumbed to the fascination of the Middle Ages, and began to write in the old manner imitations which he ascribed to an imaginary fifteenth-century poet Rowley. His ingenuous fraud deceived only the most credulous. But his remarkable verses, some of which were felicitous and successful, and his pathetic fate—deceived in his hopes of literary fortune he poisoned himself when he was eighteen—made him a symbolic figure which lived in men's imaginations, the figure of a poet born into a hostile world and vanquished by life.

The Wartons. At the same time men of real erudition were beginning to undertake careful studies or ardent imitations of the old national poets. Richard Hurd wrote his *Letters on Chivalry and Romance* (1762); the Wartons, a family of poets and critics, were distinguishing themselves by their love for the past. The father was a Milton enthusiast. The elder son, Joseph, attacked the classical dogma in the person of Pope himself. The younger, Thomas, published between 1774 and 1781 *The History of English Poetry from the Close of the Eleventh to the Commencement of the Eighteenth Century*, which, though confused and unfinished, is full of detailed knowledge about, and fervent admiration for, the centuries so lately considered barbarous. At the same time Thomas Tyrwhitt rediscovered the long-lost secret of Chaucer's versification, and produced an edition of the poet which has been the starting-point of all modern Chaucerian criticism. The revelation of the old national texts set up another ideal over against the classical one, liberated men's minds from dictatorial and limited literary dogmas, freed the imagination and encouraged originality in preference to the art of imitation. All these ideas were in ferment before 1770, though their effect was not plainly felt until after that date. The same form apparently continued to reign as before, but interior changes were undermining it and preparing its collapse.

Prose

While poetry remained content with timid or limited experiments, prose, already so rich at the beginning of the century, went on rapidly progressing along modern paths. The middle of the century saw the first great development of the novel. It gave to the world one after the other a series of masterpieces, of various and even opposite inspiration but equal in scope and importance. The novel took the place of the theatre, which was now losing its vigour and originality, and in which tragedy had become an exercise in rhetoric and comedy had dissolved into sentiment. Many, chiefly in the middle classes, objected to going to the playhouse; they preferred to stay at home and read some story of personal adventure or descriptive of society at large. The theatre seemed to have exhausted its material. The novel with its greater spaciousness could lend itself to new developments, multiplying details furnished by observation, and grouping them by less artificial methods than those of the stage, or at least using artifices that were different and less hackneyed. These various causes contributed to the success of the great novels which appeared in succession after 1740. It is perfectly true that before this time Defoe had produced a large number of realistic novels; but Defoe was a realist only in manner and style. His subjects were strange and far-fetched when they were not downright fantastic. Many of the adventures he described simply defied credulity. Now came books in which practically everything was drawn from current everyday reality. In place of a multitude of astonishing happenings there was but one incident, and that sometimes of the most common-place kind: a master's attempt to seduce a pretty maidservant; an arbitrarily arranged marriage which drives a young girl to flight and misfortune; the hesitations of a lover between several ladies endowed with different charms—are not these the essential themes of Richardson's novels?

To replace the interest of adventures there was only the careful analysis of emotions and the portrayal of character—the two-fold task of the best modern novels, which Richardson accomplished with excessive minuteness; length, indeed, was the chief fault in works of the species which he originated.

Richardson. It was late in life and almost by chance that he set himself to original composition. Samuel Richardson (1689–1761) was a prosperous printer. Weakly and timid, he by choice sought feminine society, and being inclined to Puritanism, played the part of a lay confessor among the women and girls of his acquaintance. He guided them in the composition of their love-letters and began by writing for them little edifying tales. He was fifty when two publishers asked him for a book of familiar letters which might be of use in the conduct of life. It was with the idea of turning his readers and especially his female readers 'from the pomp and parade of romance-writing' that he wrote *Pamela, or Virtue Rewarded* (1741). From the tales of adventure he returned to the analytical method of the great sentimental French novels of the seventeenth century like Mdlle de Scudéry's *Cyrus*, but with this difference, that he was a Puritan and a realist. He adopted the

epistolary form and kept to it because of the opportunities of
analysis which it offered him. He placed foremost his purpose of
edification, but he showed a remarkable daring in the scenes in
which he described the attempts of a brutal young gentleman on
the honour of the young, pretty, and virtuous Pamela, his maidservant. The trials of the young girl are retraced by herself in two
volumes of letters in which her very sure sense of duty, her clear
conscience, her respect for her honour, are manifested as well as
her secret tenderness for her coarse persecutor. The most debatable
point in the novel is its moral, which seems to make the reward of
virtue an earthly one. The gentleman ends by marrying the girl
whom he has not been able to seduce. Nevertheless Richardson
attached particular importance to the moral, and when he produced a sequel to *Pamela* it was in order to display the perfect
virtue of his heroine, who remains gentle and deserving in spite of
her husband's infidelity.

The eight volumes of *Clarissa Harlowe* (1747–8) form Richardson's masterpiece. This is a true tragedy, with a heroine of more
dignity and culture than Pamela. Clarissa is the daughter of a rich
middle-class family; she is distinguished by her virtue, beauty,
and intelligence, and she is ambitious of becoming an improving
model to her sex without losing modesty. Though she has a weakness for the seductive Lovelace—a kind of Don Juan—she is quite
prepared to give him up, but her tyrannical family wishing to force
her into an odious marriage, she is led to throw herself on Lovelace's honour. In a vengeful spirit he carries her off and takes
advantage of her. When he wishes to repair his crime by marrying
her she rejects him, and, exhausted by moral suffering, dies an
edifying and most pathetic death.

The character of Clarissa is made up of respect for all the conventions. The sense of duty is always present in her. Her natural
instincts are, on the contrary, weak or suppressed. Everything she
does is considered, planned. She acts by principle, and to secure
the triumph of her principles makes use of the most patient diplo-
macy. Her friend Miss Howe pleases by contrast; she relieves the
reader by giving an outlet to her indignation against the Harlowe
family. As for Lovelace, he is first of all a proud man whose love

PLATE XXIII

Clarissa Harlowe alighting at the Inn at St. Albans

PLATE XXIV

TOM JONES.

A scene from Fielding's *Tom Jones*: The Gypsy Wedding

for Clarissa is mingled with hate and rancour; but he is also a virtuoso who delights in watching the emotions and palpitations of his victim. Yet, though a libertine, he is not an atheist; in theory he respects religion and virtue; and Richardson has left him enough faith to be able to depict the horror of his remorse.

The novel has a strong unity equal to that of the best classical tragedy. Its extreme length, which discourages the modern reader, did not repel its contemporaries. Its success was immense, not only in England but on the Continent. Richardson's preoccupation with morals had forced him to the most subtle and minute scrutiny of sentiments and emotions that had yet been attempted. And he had evoked a whole group of people—the Harlowe family—with such powerful brush-strokes as to give them all the relief of reality.

In his third novel *The History of Sir Charles Grandison* (1754), Richardson took a man as hero, and attempted to make of him the pattern of a Christian gentleman. He made him sensitive as well as a man of principle. He represented him as liked and respected by all women: four of them in the book are rivals for his affection. He likes two of them almost equally and weighs the matter in the scale of duty to decide which of them shall prevail. His scruples make him seem to lack blood and vitality, and his ideal, which is to preserve the conventions, is rather negative. In spite of very fine passages, this novel, lacking the freshness of *Pamela* and the tragic strength of *Clarissa*, is inferior to its predecessors.

Richardson combines a moralist's penetration with the qualities of illusion which are the result of extreme realism. But his incessant analysis of feelings grows wearisome and even a little morbid. The action is too slow and too limited. Richardson lacks the freedom of the open air; there is little that is spontaneous or cheering about his work. The inner virtues alone interest him, at the expense of the social virtues. Emotional instincts are ignored or repressed. There is no place either in his volumes for laughter, for drollery or gaiety. The whole atmosphere is charged with sentiment produced by the ever-reviving scruples of delicate, tender consciences tormented by the terror of sin.

Fielding. The lack of spontaneity, the continual self-examination which appears like calculation, and the low vitality of the characters created by Richardson provoked the mocking spirit of Henry Fielding (1707-54) and led him to produce a very different kind of fiction. Fielding came of a good family, but was without fortune; and while he studied law he began to write for the stage and the newspapers. The reading of *Pamela* moved him to attempt a parody, which turned little by little into a novel of adventure: this was *The History of the Adventures of Joseph Andrews and his friend Mr. Abraham Adams* (1742). It is hard to imagine a more striking contrast than that between Richardson and Fielding. The very opposite of the ailing little bookseller, Fielding was a sort of jolly and warm-hearted giant hugely enjoying life, generous, manly, occasionally coarse, and careless. For him men are good or bad as Nature made them. The great virtues are courage, frankness, and generosity. The detestable vices are selfishness and hypocrisy. He regards with indulgence the temptations of the senses, but he has no pity for actions which arise from calculating or conventional motives. Finally, he is a lover of laughter. The 'human comedy' entertains him immensely, and he takes few things tragically. His principal creation in *Joseph Andrews* is the figure of Parson Adams, the good man who is always imposed on, as simple as a child, travelling the roads with his cassock torn and his wig awry, often obliged to have recourse to his mighty fists and involved in comic scenes to the compromising of his cloth; not free from faults, and with all an author's vanities, but nevertheless a true scholar, to whom Greek is an open book; with all this, extremely poor, since he is but the vicar of a humble parish and burdened with a wife and children. There is something of Don Quixote in him, for he is credulity itself, living in the illusion that men are what they seem and what they should be, and not allowing himself to be disillusioned by all the mishaps of the way. The incidents of the book are designed to illustrate the various forms of social egoism.

After a fit of gloom which led him to write a cynical novel, as bitter as anything in Swift, *The History of the Life of the late Mr. Jonathan Wild the Great* (1743), the career of a vainglorious scoundrel who complacently stresses the resemblance between his villainies and the honoured actions of the great ones of this world, Fielding published in 1749 *Tom Jones*, the story of a foundling whose open, generous, and passionate nature leads him into a long series of adventures. This offered Fielding an opportunity of drawing from life many scenes of the human comedy. He gave his great novel in eighteen books the march of an epic, preserving on occasion the tone of mock-heroic parody; a sort of Homer in prose, he followed the oldest of all literary traditions. His laughter is constant and he dispels sentimentality like an unwholesome fog. Though disapproving of enthusiasm, which he regards as fanaticism, he respects religion and is very careful of social morality; he lets slip no opportunity of denouncing the abuses, cruelties, and injustices of the law. This is the eminently practical morality of the philanthropist, and indeed through his books Fielding was a collaborator in the admirable reform movement of the end of the century. On the other hand he made game of the abstract doctrines and theories of virtue of the philosophers. He made goodness spring straight from the heart.

Mr. Allworthy, the virtuous man in the book, who is without personal desires and thinks only of others—is this deliberate irony on Fielding's part?—makes mistake after mistake simply because he reasons about his duty and tries to introduce intelligence into the conduct of his life. He is unjust to the deserving and duped by the knaves. He plays the part of a blindfold Providence, and in the end it is chance alone that undeceives him.

Tom Jones, the hero, into whom Fielding has put much of himself, is wise neither as a child nor as a young man. He acts on impulse, sometimes well and sometimes ill, but though he lacks a settled idea of duty, he has something better, a good heart. Nature has endowed him with bodily beauty and happy vitality. He never acts from interested motives. If he heaps fault upon fault and misfortune on misfortune it is because he is continually falling foul of prejudices and being caught in the snare of hypocrisy. There is nothing of the Lovelace in him, and although he sins more than once in the hotness of his blood, he is the seduced rather than the seducer. He is free from Pharisaism, knowing himself to be imperfect, and the knowledge of his own weaknesses teaches him tolerance.

Sophia Western, whom he loves and who loves him, is the very opposite of Richardson's heroines. She is pure, but she has neither their punctilious fastidiousness nor their unfailing self-control. Threatened like Clarissa with a marriage she detests, she runs away from her father, but her flight is a courageous act approved by the author; her love is strong enough to make her excuse the faults of Tom Jones. In the end she reaps her reward.

In this huge comedy one of the character parts is played by Squire Western, Sophia's father. He is ignorant, coarse, a drunkard, and incapable of reasoning or any self-control, but, though he is carried away by the most absurd passions, he knows nothing of pretence or hypocrisy. So Fielding preserves some sympathy for him and condones the violences of a crazy old man. The other eccentric is Partridge, the schoolmaster, who accompanies Tom Jones as Sancho Panza did Don Quixote. Pedantic, vain, a great chatterer, superstitious, cowardly, and not too honest, he follows Jones half for love and half for interest, and brings upon him a hundred mishaps. But with all his faults he has the saving virtue of being expansive and unsophisticated.

When he published *Amelia* in 1751, Fielding had been a magistrate for two years. He had devoted himself ardently to his duties and become deeply interested in reforming judicial procedure, softening prison discipline, and limiting the effects of gin-drinking. His new novel was full of these preoccupations. In addition it was written by a man who was growing old, whose animal spirits were beginning to weaken, who had lost a little of his gaiety, and whose concern with morals was becoming more exclusive and more obvious. Fielding again put himself into his hero, Colonel Booth, a middle-aged Tom Jones whose backslidings, occurring after marriage, have more serious consequences. Booth loves his young wife Amelia, but he is weak; he allows himself to be led astray by bad company; he gambles, and reduces his household to want. But he deeply feels the remorse which was little known to Tom Jones. It is the same nature, the same man seen at different ages and in different conditions, and with a considerable loss of vitality. As for Amelia, she is a Sophia who has been tried by experience; Sophia was subordinate to Jones, Amelia throws

Captain Booth into the shade. Like Richardson's Clarissa she is the best of women, but less through the promptings of duty than through those of the heart. She is capable of every sacrifice and every forgiveness because of her love. The contrast between the two novelists persists to the end.

It is a contrast in manner not less than in ideas or characters. Fielding works through irony, and this irony, woven into every little event of the story, and sustained by many concrete details and jesting mock-heroic metaphors, develops into the richest humour.

Fielding does not bring the reader directly into the presence of his characters without himself intervening. He is always present, pointing them out to us and explaining them, in a voice almost always mocking but sometimes warmed by sympathy or indignation. He is never a true realist like Defoe, because he visibly turns the conversations he is supposed to be reporting towards the comic, cleverly twisting them if necessary, so as to throw into relief the absurdity they contain. His constant object, the unmasking of hypocrisy and stupidity, recalls Swift, but since he has less than Swift's spleen and bitterness it is most of all of Molière that he makes us think. Like Molière he excels in showing the way in which personal interest guides men's ideas or blinds their consciences.

Smollett. A new note was introduced into the novel by the Scotsman Tobias Smollett (1721–71), surgeon and journalist, who put all the violence of his temperament into his books. Need of money drove him more than once to translation ; he made versions of Le Sage's *Gil Blas* and Cervantes' *Don Quixote*. His model was the picaresque novel ; he sought success in the recital of brutal adventures and in caricature. But his work is not wanting in realism. He drew a great deal on his own life (his first book was partly autobiographical). Satirical, passionate, more capable than Fielding of poetic language—witness his *Tears of Scotland*, a burning invective written after Culloden and the bloody repression of the Jacobite rising by 'butcher Cumberland'—he displayed from beginning to end an aggressive vigour which rose more than once to true eloquence.

In 1748 he published *Roderick Random*, into which he put much

of himself, of his experiences as a child, of the misery of his beginnings as a writer, of the scenes he witnessed as a ship's surgeon
during the abortive attack on Cartagena. His hero is a victim of
brutality who himself becomes brutal in his turn. He is hard,
violent, rancorous, with but small capacity for affection in his
nature, and hardly better than the swindlers and knaves who
surround him. He is capable of living at the expense of a humble
friend who has attached himself to him like a dog, and then of
abandoning this same friend and even being ashamed of him in
his hour of prosperity. But Roderick Random hated the vices to
which he succumbed and if the author exaggerates them it is, as
he tells us, the better to turn the mind from them. The most
striking novelty of the book lies in its sea-scenes and types of seamen. It introduces us to the hatreds of shipboard, and the officers'
cruel dealings with the men. We are present at a review of the
vessel's sick men, a picture in which ferocity in the actions is
mingled with burlesque in the details. The pages which describe
the Press, or the fright of Roderick when he is tied by the captain's
orders to the mast during the battle, are not easily forgotten.
This book gives us seamen depicted by a satirist : the captain,
a brute but not lacking in courage, and the effeminate mate ; yet
the author is not without sympathy for seafaring-men, such as
the Welsh surgeon Morgan, reminiscent of Shakespeare's Fluellen,
or Roderick's uncle Tom Bowling, headstrong and impetuous like
a child, but jovial, generous, simple, and amusing with his sea-
dog's language in which everything is put in nautical terms.

There are sailors again in *Peregrine Pickle* (1751), but their portraits tend rather to the grotesque. They are sailors on land, who
form a garrison and continue to live as if still on board their ship.
The adventures of Peregrine Pickle, less savage than Roderick's,
are more lively but more disconnected, and the central figure is
painted with less force.

Smollett was to produce one more great novel, but twenty years
later, towards the end of his life. A little mollified by success and
softened by age, and also won over to some extent by the growth
of sentimentalism, Smollett changed his tone and his manner.
Humphry Clinker (1771) is a novel in letters, but the aim is quite

different from Richardson's. There is almost no plot. The letters
are designed partly to display the individual characteristics, the
tastes, the hobbies, and even the tricks of speech, of each of the
correspondents, and partly (for they are the letters of a family on
its travels) to reproduce their different impressions of the journey
and thus to make us acquainted with the appearance and manners
of places they visit. It is a happy and original idea, this of introducing us to a Welsh family making a tour in Great Britain and
seeing Bath, London, Scotland, Edinburgh, and the Highlands.
The characters of the various members of the family are sufficiently
differentiated to ensure variety in the comments: there is an old
bachelor, rich, well-informed, crossgrained, affecting misanthropy,
but with a good heart beneath a rough exterior; his sister, a plain
and coquettish old maid, peevish and miserly, their nephew fresh
from Oxford, eager and cultured; their pretty niece, frank, affectionate, and romantic; and the aunt's stupid and good-hearted
maid, vain and pious with a tendency to Methodism. Besides the
correspondents there are drawn in the letters the portraits of two
curious persons, an eccentric called Lismahago, intelligent and
disagreeable, and full of the spirit of paradox and contradiction;
and lastly Humphry Clinker, a foundling who has become the
servant of the head of the family. He is unaffected and enthusiastic, and a convert to Wesleyan Methodism, full of sincere religious fervour, a simple and affectionate soul in portraying whom
Smollett tempers irony with sympathy.

Sterne. When *Humphry Clinker* appeared, Sterne and Goldsmith had already produced their famous novels.

Laurence Sterne (1713–68), the son of an officer, Irish on his
mother's side and born in Ireland, by mishap entered the Church,
in which he cut the figure of a frivolous priest and a philandering
prebendary. He was 47 when he began to publish his *Tristram
Shandy* (1760–7), which brought him immediate fame. It is a
strange book, reflecting an ambiguous nature, that of a man who
is weak and changeable, without firmness of character or moral
supports. Sterne had a taste for lewd anecdotes, collecting them
in the course of his reading and changing the broad rough jests of
his forefathers into sly indecencies. But he was also endowed with

very delicate and sensitive feeling. The sight of suffering was intolerable to him. His very selfishness made him revolt against it. In an age when brutality was too common he made men grow tender towards sorrows which the majority passed by with indifference and some with sarcasm or insult. In default of the strength which remedies an evil he had the sympathy which weeps for it. The gradual softening of manners and, as a result, of laws, was partly due to these emotional weepers. Moreover, Sterne knew how to smile as well as weep. Indeed it is perhaps in his smile that his most exquisite sensibility finds expression. But to be sensitive to the most minute things, to the imperceptible stirrings of man's inner nature, implies more than the capacity for being moved, it leads to a pleasure in seeing the springs of the machine laid bare, to an amused perception of man's incoherence. A soft pity accompanies the smile of discovery; the same easy indulgence that is felt for the peculiarities of an individual is extended to the whole of mankind, unconsciously controlled by a similar secret play of ridiculous motives. Sterne extends to others the indulgence, the delicate pity which he feels for himself. Thus the Shandean humourist finds everywhere a thousand occasions for irradiating with a smile the tears which flow from his eyes. He is a man of sentiment when he is not a jester; most often he is both at once.

With Sterne the novel is transformed. Adventure no longer finds any place in it. What need, when the smallest, most insignificant detail may be rich with moving or comical reflections? The book, which announces itself as containing 'the Life and Opinions of Tristram Shandy' is half-way through before the hero's birth is achieved. Anything serves as an excuse for the author to introduce an interminable parenthesis. He takes pleasure besides in disconcerting the reader by a hundred mannerisms, such as asterisks and blank pages. But through all these caprices he evokes the characters with rare penetration: Shandy senior, Tristram's father, with his pedantic ideas always belied by the facts; Uncle Toby, the old soldier with a soft heart, who plays at campaigns and who could not harm a fly; his devoted follower, Corporal Trim, as kind-hearted and generous as his master; the parson Yorick, who is a sort of idealization of Sterne himself. By little successive

PLATE XXV

Sterne

Sterne taking subscriptions for a book of his own
sermons. See p. xiv

touches these characters take on a rare life and vivacity. They make our eyes water either with pity or laughter. Sterne created the type of the Shandean, sometimes distinct from the sentimentalist, sometimes confounded with him. Shandeism stands for abrupt changes of humour, whimsicality, a taste for trifles, absent-mindedness, heedlessness, disregard of happenings, and above all good humour.

Sterne furnished another example of his manner in his *Sentimental Journey through France and Italy* (1768), in which he reads a lesson to the 'splenetic travellers', always disgruntled and peevish, like Smollett, and condemns 'inquisitive travellers' who are always seeking practical information, as Arthur Young was to do. For Sterne, the attraction of travel lay in the unlooked-for incidents and the variety of the persons met with, which serve as the starting-point of trains of reflection free from bitterness but not from mischievousness. He had no preconceived hostility to foreigners, but a benevolence very slightly tinged with irony and a pity which is extended also to animals—one of the most famous episodes in the book is the meditation on a dead donkey seen as he was leaving Boulogne. Here Sterne the humourist sheds in profusion the tears which are the 'mark of sensibility and virtue'.

Goldsmith. A special place in the series of famous novels of this period belongs to Goldsmith's celebrated *Vicar of Wakefield* (1766). Goldsmith only once wrote a novel, and then it was by what might be called chance. His talent, less powerful than that of the foregoing writers, has a peculiar charm which results from the author's own nature and the easy perfection of his style. With a humour less rich than Fielding's, less pointed than Sterne's, but exquisitely controlled, he describes the adventures of Dr. Primrose, the loss of whose fortune reduces him to the standing of the parson of a small village. How the good man bears himself in his modest office; with what resignation he supports the attacks of misfortune; then the behaviour of his family, through whose virtues we may catch many a glimpse of this world's vanities—such is the sentimental comedy which is played out in this gracious work. Sterne's sentimentality here reappears without his eccentricities. The good vicar, who himself recounts his story, attracts us both by his virtues and by his human weaknesses and artlessness. There is not perhaps much consistency in a tale in which the narrator appears to be both very clear-sighted and a blind and simple soul. But Goldsmith's charm veils the many faults which he himself recognized in his book. He made of the whole an idyll which at once charmed all hearts and still keeps much of its attractiveness.

Thus it was that in thirty years the English novel produced a series of widely differing masterpieces, the work of men of various ages and different walks of life—a printer, a justice of the peace, a surgeon, a clergyman, a journalist—of different nationalities also, for though Richardson and Fielding were English, Smollett came from Scotland and Goldsmith and Sterne from Ireland. Almost every principal form had been attempted, and almost every variation of temperament expressed, in the novel which from this time forward began to take its special place as the chief interpreter in literature of the modern world.

Hume. Looked at as a whole, the middle period of the eighteenth century is seen to be pursuing, like the beginning, its rationalistic investigations in the regions of philosophy, hampered by the same resistance of the religious-minded. The greatest British (and indeed the greatest European) philosopher of this period is the Scotsman David Hume (1711–76). Analysing more boldly than Locke the elements of knowledge, he saw in it only phenomena linked together by association but possessing no real existence or causal relations outside the human mind. He bordered on complete scepticism. In ethics, he was entirely empirical; he placed his reliance upon the instinct of benevolence and judged actions by their usefulness. Although he was less aggressive than the French *philosophes*, he was not less hostile to Christianity; he refused to accept miracles and clung to a vague deism, but he tempered his intellectual scepticism by admitting rules necessary to life. Nothing could be more tranquil and assured than the march of his thought, nothing clearer than the prose in which he pursued his most subtle analyses in lucid and sober language.

Hume also turned his calm gaze upon the past in his *History of Great Britain* (1754–61), in which he strove to disentangle the causes of events and their lessons. He led the way in including sections on the literature of the age with which he was dealing. He was, it is true, not free from prejudice, and his love of order led him into a marked preference for the doctrine of royal authority. The Whigs accused him of writing as a Tory. Nor had he, though he made use of some original documents, the scientific equipment now held to be indispensable to the historian. Moreover his intense intellectualism prevented him from sympathizing with ages regarded as barbarous. His view of the Middle Ages shows lack of imagination.

W. Robertson. Another noticeable historian of the age was Hume's fellow-countryman William Robertson (1721–93), who possessed similar virtues of good composition and clarity together with a taste for exactness and truth, and who wrote *The History of Scotland* (1759) and *The History of Charles V*. Far inferior as historians were Smollett and Goldsmith, whose histories of England have no other merit than that due to their talent as writers.

Adam Smith. By the side of history came the beginnings of political economy. Again it was Scotland which saw the birth of the first great representative of the new science, Adam Smith (1723–90). His book, *An Inquiry into the Nature and Causes of the Wealth of Nations* (1776), which owed much to the French Physiocrats, has remained a classic, thanks to its coherence, the elasticity of its system, and Smith's desire to remain in touch with reality, and also to the excellence of the form. His style bestowed order, elegance, and even grace, on a subject which stands in danger of being dry.

Letter-Writers. In order to comprehend the normal tone of this age there could be no better plan than to turn to the letter-writers, who were then numerous and of whom some were exceptionally brilliant. It is true that to confine them within the precise limits of a period is difficult, either because of the length of their lives, some of which covered almost the whole century, or because of the often late date at which the letters were published. But the spirit which moved them really belongs to the middle of the century.

Lady Mary Wortley Montagu. It is here that we must place the correspondence of Lady Mary Wortley Montagu (1689–1762), of whom Pope was at first the admirer and later the bitter detractor. Lady Mary was free from prejudices, and she had the gifts of observation, intellectual curiosity, and a very acute sense of the practical, but she reveals a certain aridity of heart and is not without cynicism. Her letters invite comparison with those of Madame de Sévigné; they are rich in matter but lack the play of form so catching in the French marquise.

Lord Chesterfield. The celebrated letters of Lord Chesterfield to his bastard son were published at the author's death in 1774. They are in effect a treatise on education, but not exactly on moral education. Chesterfield was concerned with guiding the first steps in the world of a young nobleman, initiating him into the rules of polite society, and assuring his social success. He had no wish to reform morals; he accepted society as it was; he never grew indignant. He taught the art of living well, clearly perceiving and allowing for the selfish qualities of humanity. He set forth his precepts in a flowing, polished, and constantly elegant style.

Horace Walpole. The considerable correspondence of Horace Walpole (1717–97) is one of the most significant monuments of the century. All his life Walpole was a dilettante, who attempted widely different forms of literature, always making it clear that he wrote only from lack of occupation and that he must not be confounded with the mob of professional men of letters. He was an historian, a retailer of anecdotes, on occasion a novelist and dramatic author, and even a society poet. But his correspondence is the most finished and the most vital of his work. In it the politics and literature of the century are passed in review by a lively and mocking mind which expresses with pointed wit thoughts often apparently frivolous, yet really sincere, and rich in observation based upon an extensive knowledge of European society. He approaches the universality of Voltaire more nearly than any other English letter-writer.

Thomas Gray. To these letter-writers may be added Walpole's friend, the poet Thomas Gray (1716–71), who found in his readings, in his contemplative hours, in his few wanderings, and in his erudite researches the matter for many a letter, simple in form, but always exquisitely literary, and reflecting his melancholy.

Mrs. Montagu. A little later Mrs. Montagu (1720–1800), the queen of the 'blue stockings', who in her *Essay on the Writings and Genius of Shakespeare* (1769) had shown that she could defend Shakespeare with vigour against the attacks of Voltaire, gave evidence in her numerous letters of real learning and of a caustic and biting wit, as well as of sound good sense.

Wesley. These philosophers, historians, and men of letters, are the devotees of reason and common sense. They occupy the front of the stage. But to grasp the complexity of the period it is necessary to bear in mind at the same time the growing power of the Wesleyan movement. John Wesley (1703–91), who began by desiring to re-form the morals and religious practices of Oxford undergraduates, was obliged to leave the Anglican church and founded the Methodist sect. He evangelized the working classes of Britain and revived little by little the Christian piety of the country. The fervour of the new sect soon affected Anglicanism itself and the evangelical movement roused a long-sluggish clergy. Wesley was a great reformer. He had no literary ambition. 'As for me I never think of style at all, but just set down . . . the words that come first.' But his hymns (and this is still more true of those of his brother Charles) have a gracefulness which often rises to poetry; while the prose of his *Journals* and of his sermons keeps in its perfect simplicity the correctness and elegance derived from his university education.

It is necessary to remember that men like Wesley and Hume were living at the same time, in order to form an idea of the two contrasting forces which guided men's minds from the middle of the eighteenth century onwards.

THE EIGHTEENTH CENTURY (1770-98)

Prose

DURING the last third of the eighteenth century the English outlook was disturbed by violent shocks whose repercussions were
felt in literature. The middle of the century had been a time of
national triumph and expansion. Victorious England had made
the conquest of India and Canada. She was mistress of the seas.
But her supremacy was now assailed by the revolt of the American
colonies, which declared their independence in 1776 and, after a
successful war in which they were assisted by France, obtained
the recognition of that independence in 1782. During the hos-
tilities, England was divided against itself; insular patriotism was
shaken for the first time, for many Englishmen considered that
the rebels were in the right, and hoped for their success. Parliament, which since 1771 had admitted reporters, resounded with
the noise of these internal disputes.

Some years later (in 1789) there broke out the French Revolution. Again the country was divided into two camps: the partisans
and the enemies of the Revolution. Already a strong philanthropic
movement was alive in Britain, breaking down the narrowness
and selfishness of national interests. She had taken the lead in the
struggle against the slave-trade, and arraigned Warren Hastings
on the charge of practising extortion upon the natives of India.
The subversive ideas originating with Rousseau, which challenged
the educational system and the constitution of society, had found
passionate adherents north of the Channel. Some writers took
up arms to defend Rousseau's theories, others to attack them;
all were affected by them. The first rank of prose-writers was no
longer filled by theologians or philosophers, but by writers and
orators whose concern was politics. In Parliament, the younger
Pitt, Charles James Fox, and Sheridan, succeeded Chatham, the
great artificer of victory in the previous age; while above this
group towered Edmund Burke, less successful than they as a

parliamentary orator, but by the richness of his mental equipment, the grandest figure of the closing century.

Burke. Edmund Burke (1729–97) bestowed on politics the
resources of a philosophic mind enriched by extensive reading
and ripe experience. The son of a Dublin solicitor, he read law
in the Middle Temple, but then renounced a legal career in order
to enlarge his knowledge and outlook. He began by writing a
refutation of Bolingbroke's irreligious theories, which he attacked
by reducing them to absurdity in his *Vindication of Natural
Society* (1756). Then he turned to aesthetics and wrote a *Philosophical Inquiry into the Origin of our Ideas of the Sublime and
Beautiful* (1756), basing these ideas not upon convention and
tradition but upon human feelings and emotions. After a period
of apprenticeship as secretary to various political personages,
he entered Parliament in 1766, and proceeded to show his
mastery with his *Thoughts on the Causes of the Present Discontents*
(1770), an analysis of the reasons for the conflict between the
House of Commons and public opinion over the agitator Wilkes.
He showed a profound intuitive understanding of the English
constitution, justifying both the existence and the antagonism
of political parties. At the same time he was revealed as a great
prose-writer. The oratorical prose, which in the writings of his
friend Johnson suffered too often from an excess of pomp, was
better justified in Burke by the breadth and depth of his thought.
He brought the same qualities to his discussion of all the great
questions of his Parliamentary life: to the controversies on the
revolt of the American colonies, to the famous trial of Warren
Hastings, and to the debates which were called forth by the
French Revolution.

It seems at first sight as if the close of his career contradicted
the liberalism of its beginning. The man who had demanded a
wide liberty for the American colonies, who had fulminated against
the Governor-General's alleged abuses in India, now opposed with
growing wrath the doctrines and actions of revolutionary France.
Burke seemed to ignore the evils due to despotism and wished to
remember only the dangers of breaking with tradition and of
applying abstract principles to a social organism. But even in

the height of his indignation, he cast a profoundly sagacious glance on the British constitution, the product of centuries of experience. His suspicion of abstract thinking led him to defend tradition, even to glorify prejudice. In this, he laid his finger upon the deepest element in the English character, its dislike of pure theory and its respect for facts sanctioned by usage and the lapse of time.

Paine. W. Godwin. Burke was almost alone in stating the principles of conservatism; most of the writers who threw themselves into the struggle were enthusiasts for the new ideas. Priestley the great chemist, the controversial writer Horne Tooke, Tom Paine the demagogue, who had written his *Common Sense* in order to incite the American colonists to revolt and was now writing his *Rights of Man* (1791–2) in defence of France, the Scotsman Mackintosh, author of *Vindiciae Gallicae*; all these, and others besides, were in violent opposition to Burke's ideas. The utilitarian Jeremy Bentham at the same time produced his own answer to them, rejecting compromise and the practical lessons of experience in order to found society on a principle of universal application: the greatest good of the greatest number.

The same generalizing and reforming spirit distinguished the *Enquiry concerning Political Justice* (1793) of William Godwin. This was a formal indictment of existing society and a scheme for a reasoned system of social reconstruction. In its attack upon governments it went so far as to advocate the suppression of all government and to find its ideal in anarchy, where every one would have to guide himself solely by the light of his own reason. Law, marriage, property—everything which limits individual liberty—is treated by Godwin as an obstacle to progress. Even the feelings, such as love, gratitude, and pity, are held in suspicion and proscribed by the sage because they come into conflict with pure reason. Godwin had no doubts of the power of reason, which he thought should assure to humanity a limitless perfectibility. His doctrine, ennobled by the calm serenity and tranquil stoicism displayed by the philosopher, took possession for a time of the most generous among the young Romantic poets.

Gibbon. If Godwin offers an extreme example, almost a caricature, of European rationalism applied to politics, Edward Gibbon (1737–94) displays the rationalistic temper at its best in the domain of history. Gibbon was, after Burke, the greatest prose-writer of the generation. But he detached himself from the present in order to paint a picture of the past. He took for subject *The Decline and Fall of the Roman Empire*, a vast work published at intervals between 1776 and 1788. In it the growth and development of Christianity was described as a purely human phenomenon. Gibbon's wholly logical and sceptical nature rebelled against mysticism, and he scandalized devout people by his indifference to the element of the divine, and by the hints with which he undermined the half-miraculous conception of the growth of the Christian faith held by its orthodox exponents. As an historian Gibbon was learned, truthful, and as well-informed as it was possible to be in his day. He was, moreover, an artist who could compose admirable descriptive pictures and who knew how to bring them into the narrative of events. He had profited by the efforts of the English and French historians who were his predecessors, and he excelled them in the vast scale and the importance of his chosen subject.

Gibbon's style bears the stamp of his time and also that of his French education. He had an obvious preference for words of Latin origin. The desire for dignity and nobility which is found in Johnson and Burke reappears in his pages, which lack some of the vigorous picturesqueness of Anglo-Saxon speech. But he wrote with eloquence and harmony and with such precision as results from the use of abstract terms.

Paley. Political strife and the sturdy rationalism of philosophers and historians did not prevent the continuance of the religious activities of the country. The Methodist or Wesleyan movement was growing stronger and stronger among the lower classes—an ardent fire of mysticism which glowed beneath the surface of a rationalistic century. Meanwhile the orthodox logicians of the preceding generations had a successor in William Paley (1743–1805), whose *Evidences of Christianity* is an attempt to refute deism and to establish the possibility of miracles by logic alone. A clear and 'reasonable' writer, Paley built his arguments for religion on a kind of utilitarianism according to which a man's happiness is the reward for his faith.

Poetry

The literature, properly so called, of the end of the century, echoed these political and religious passions. They hastened the movement which was to lead to Romanticism. It may well be asked whether this or that writer of the day was not already an out-and-out Romantic. There was one at least, William Blake, who overleapt at one bound the most audacious extremes of thought and form reached by the boldest of his successors. The general characteristic, however, of this third of the century is not so much open revolt against the classic tradition as a naïve independence, the result of individual temperament or of the influence of certain social and moral ideas. Most people's views tended further and further towards liberty and idealism, until a moment was reached when the violence of the Terror and still more the war with revolutionary France rallied the conservative forces of the country to the principles of order and tradition. This variety of aims marked the generation but it did not as a rule affect the style of its writers. Most of the prose-writers continued to share Samuel Johnson's preference for the noble style; while the poets usually preserved the accepted poetic diction and the classical couplet.

Satirical poets. Satire had gone on its course with Charles Churchill (1731–64), a needy clergyman whose *Rosciad* (1761), a vigorous and often coarse piece of invective against actors, had brought him money and fame. It continued to occupy public attention with the *Rolliad* (1784), a work by Whig journalists incensed against the Tory policy; with the jokes of John Wolcot ('Peter Pindar'), another opponent of George III, in his *Lousiad*; with William Gifford's *Baviad* (1794) and *Maeviad* (1795), rather mediocre attacks upon the sentimentality of bad and now forgotten poets; and with Canning and Frere whose *Anti-Jacobin* ridiculed with mordant zest the excesses of the young revolutionary poets, especially Southey and Coleridge.

Didactic verse. Didactic poetry also continued to flourish. In

1781 William Hayley published his undistinguished *Triumphs of Temper*, Samuel Rogers produced his elegant *Pleasures of Memory* in 1792, and in 1799 Thomas Campbell issued his *Pleasures of Hope*, which, classic in outward form, inwardly burned with the revolutionary ardours of his unfledged days.

Various experiments, often in unfortunate directions, were being tried about this time. The childish sentimentalities of the 'Della Cruscan School' (1786–8), ridiculed by Gifford, are the most outstanding specimens of insipidity and bad taste.

Erasmus Darwin. There is much more talent in the verse of Erasmus Darwin, whose *Botanic Garden* (1789–91) dazzled his contemporaries with its conceits, its brilliancy, and its sonorous versification. The stilted way in which he travestied the conceptions of a true science by personifying plants and writing of their loves, to-day provokes a smile and seems like a parody by a facile versifier. To relish its absurdity there is no need to have recourse to the *Anti-Jacobin's* burlesque travesty of it in the *Loves of the Triangles*.

Beattie and Bowles. Nothing in the form or the content of these works anticipates a real revival. The verses of the Scotsman James Beattie are another matter; and his *Minstrel* (1771–4), written in the Spenserian stanza, foreshadows the poetry of Wordsworth. The theme of the *Prelude* may already be half-discerned in the lines in which Beattie, under pretence of depicting the making of a medieval minstrel, describes in a charming way how he owed to Nature his own imagination and poetic enthusiasm.

Again the revival of the long-forsaken sonnet-form, well heralded by Thomas Watson, shows a characteristic return to personal effusions; the *Sonnets* of W. L. Bowles, which began to appear in 1789, must be accorded the merit of having been admired by Wordsworth and Coleridge for their meditative grace.

But there were four poets, famous in very different ways, who set their mark upon the poetry of the closing century, and whose reputation persisted and even increased after the triumph of Romanticism: Cowper, Crabbe, Burns, and Blake.

W. Cowper. William Cowper (1731–1800) had in his nature that lack of balance which was to be seen again in many of the great

European romantics. Upon one side he showed a gentle, lovable, refined character, fond of innocent distractions and capable of smiles and even laughter. Another side of him revealed a strong religious feeling which was turned by the influence of his feeble health and of the sombre Calvinist doctrine to which he adhered into a tragic terror of damnation. Delightful and good as he was, he lived under an obsession of Hell. Apart from one or two powerful and tragic poems, like *Hatred and Vengeance* and *The Castaway*, in which his torment finds expression, his poetry was but the most constant of the amusements with which he sought to turn his thoughts from the fear which haunted him. Compelled by his health to live on the fringe of active life, he passed a leisured and retired existence, soothed by several tender friendships and spending his time in little manual occupations or in walks beside the river Ouse. Cowper's poems reflect his simple pleasures, his love of nature, the stirrings of his almost feminine sensibility, even the very slightest happenings of his hermitage, and, in addition, a recluse's impressions of the political events of which the postman brought him news in his retreat. Thus it was that a gentle, familiar, domestic poetry, that is sometimes charmingly gay, issued from this sick mind and tormented spirit. It was the harvest of his moments of health and serenity.

Much preoccupied with purity and morality and not at all concerned with a change of the literary form, Cowper began in 1779 by writing hymns, and went on to produce a series of didactic poems in couplets, which satirized the vices and weaknesses of his day: *Hope, Charity, Retirement, Conversation,* &c. (1782). But his personality really revealed itself in *The Task* (1785), a long effusion in blank verse, in which he unbosoms himself of his ideas, impressions, and feelings, in various keys, and without any fixed plan, but giving much space to his love and observation of nature. Nature had been his best healer, and he anticipates the Lake Poets in the way he expresses his gratitude. He believed no less firmly than J. J. Rousseau that the country is divine and the town diabolical. He summed up his ideas in the line:

God made the country, and man made the town.

At the same time he expressed in most touching verses the pure affections of his heart, for example, the lines which he wrote *On the Receipt of my Mother's Picture*, or, better still, the exquisite lines *To Mary* in which he voices his tenderness for the woman who had acted as his Providence, who had saved him from despair and madness, and who was now herself old and ill.

> Thy indistinct expressions seem
> Like language uttered in a dream;
> Yet me they charm, whate'er the theme,
> > My Mary!
> Partakers of thy sad decline,
> Thy hands their little force resign;
> Yet gently pressed, press gently mine,
> > My Mary!

Cowper's goodness of heart led him also into enthusiasm for philanthropic causes like the abolition of the slave trade. He hailed in advance the fall of the Bastille. He was neither a profound philosopher nor a well-informed politician, but his refined sensibility told him that joy and suffering are the lot of all men, and inspired him on occasion with a generous cosmopolitanism whose tones it is pleasing to hear on the eve of the long and implacable Napoleonic wars. Cowper's playful humour was revealed particularly in the inimitable ballad of John Gilpin, the honest tradesman who was so poor a horseman and whose ride was so much longer and more impetuous than he desired.

All Cowper's works display an unfaltering gift of style and versification, a purity and elegance inherited from the best classic writers, but usually free from their conventions. The perfect simplicity of Cowper's letters—he was one of the most exquisite of English letter-writers—is found in almost all his poems. He reformed literary style not, like Wordsworth, by set precept but spontaneously by giving free expression to his nature.

G. Crabbe. George Crabbe (1754–1832) to all appearance faithfully continued the tradition of the classical writers. Like them he used the couplet, and he preserved their style, their diction, their antitheses, and their periphrases. After a few pieces of small importance he first made his name with *The Village* (1783), a poem in which he appealed to truth against romantic fiction, one might almost say against poetry itself. He set himself against the pastoral tradition, against that illusion of rustic happiness and innocence which had captivated so many minds in ancient times and since the days of the Renaissance—the tradition so recently revived by Goldsmith in his *Deserted Village* and at this time made almost a commonplace of European literature by the famous writings of Rousseau. No, against such lies and such prettinesses reality must protest. The son of a poor family at Aldborough, on the bleak east coast of England, Crabbe had practised medicine for some time and struggled painfully to gain a livelihood before he took orders; he thus knew at first hand the wretchedness and the vices of the people, especially the agricultural labourers and fishermen of Suffolk. He was indignant that real miseries should be thus travestied in agreeable and cruelly optimistic pictures. He would show the sores—the bitter existence of the villagers, the desperate struggles with a stubborn soil, the sordid condition of their cottages, their foul poverty, the neglect with which they were treated by the doctors when they were reduced to the hospital, and by the clergy when they sought the consolations of religion. He showed them living beneath an unfriendly sky in desolate places where that nature which townsfolk vied in praising offered nothing but its harshness. With an implacable realism he described one after another the scenes of their everyday existence and demanded in indignant tones that an end should be put to this long falsehood.

> No; cast by Fortune on a frowning coast,
> Which neither groves nor happy valleys boast;
> Where other cares than those the muse relates,
> And other shepherds dwell with other mates;
> By such examples taught, I paint the Cot
> As Truth will paint it, and as Bards will not.

In his ardent desire to see the lot of these poor people bettered Crabbe joined forces with the philanthropists, and he hoped to serve this cause by unveiling the evils of which they were the victims. As it was part of his plan to depict weaknesses and vices, the satiric spirit remained uppermost in him. Thus in form he was

a descendant of Pope but with a difference due to the very humanity of his subject; he was, as has been said, a 'Pope in woollen
stockings'.

During the whole of the rest of his life, which covered the early
period of Romanticism, Crabbe persevered with a surprising regularity in the path he had entered at 29. Since, however, his later
poems were not so definitely controversial and combative in character, he could allow the tone of his painting to be less unbrokenly
dark, and he found more and more space (though without forsaking
realism) for lives woven of mingled good and evil, for average
people who were sometimes good and sometimes bad. This is seen
in his *Parish Register* (1807), in which a clergyman reviews the
happenings in his parish in the course of a year, in his *Borough*
(1810), in which instead of a village he describes the life and the
people of a small town with their more varied habits and occupations, and in his *Tales in Verse* (1812) and *Tales of the Hall* (1819),
in which he finds room for people of less humble rank. But his
melancholy view of life and mankind persisted through these
changes. Crabbe's native pessimism is never transfigured by
soaring transports or the vision of beauty. The picture of the
world which he presents is precisely a picture that is not coloured
by poetic illusion. Crabbe's verses themselves, often vigorous,
always full of sense, have no charm of delicacy. He gives his
readers only painful emotions and tarnished visions; he saddens
both ear and eye. In short Crabbe might well be described as the
most unromantic of men, and yet the very boldness of his realism
made him a kind of revolutionary. He reacted against a long-
lived poetical convention, he proclaimed the necessity of a change
of attitude. He led literature back towards truth, and by his interest in humble people he anticipated Wordsworth, though he
left to the later poet the task of glorifying their humility. On the
other hand he escaped the extravagance of an arbitrary philosophical conception, and one often feels the need of returning to
him from the Romantics in order to tread once more on solid
earth.

Burns. Another poet during the same period was teaching
poetry, but by altogether different means, 'to build a princely

throne on humble truth'. He was a real peasant who drove the plough as he hummed his songs, and who knew all the wretchedness of the countryman's life but knew as well its joys and mirth. The young Scotsman Robert Burns (1759-96), the son of a farmer and a farmer himself, published in 1786 a collection of lively spirited verses which, though based on no premeditated theory, were destined to shape the path towards the poetic revolution. The mere fact that Burns was a peasant poet writing in the language of his country was enough to cause the break with conventional poetry. Although Burns was full of respect for the English classical school, Pope and his disciples, whose manner and style he imitated in the poems in which he did not use his native speech, he freed himself from this tutelage in the rest of his work, where he followed the course of popular Scottish poetry, which consisted mainly of songs, ballads, and short and vigorously realistic poems. His great admiration was reserved for the collections of Allan Ramsay, and especially for the idiomatic verses, full of spirit and humour, of his compatriot Robert Fergusson, who had died mad at the age of 23. Burns's great originality lay in the fact that he expressed his own nature directly in his poems with a frankness to which literature was unused. He put into them his passions, his joys, and his sufferings; his revolts against Presbyterian tyranny; a whole personal poetry in contrast with the usual cold and timid formality of the century. His Scottish tongue brought into play a multitude of words and phrases that were picturesque, familiar, and racy of the soil, and seemed all the more vivid because the poetic convention of the day tended to discard more and more of the concrete vocabulary which appeals directly to the senses. The clear, fervent blood that ran in Burns's veins, warming and colouring his poems, threw into contrast the pallor and insipidity of the pseudo-classic muse. Didacticism was no more: a man of strong and often irregular passions, who felt pleasure and remorse intensely and suffered tumults of conscience, grief, and agonies of spirit, was revealing his heart without scruple or reticence, singing aloud his love and hatred.

This was rebellion in a country weighed down by a harsh religious constraint, of which, indeed, Burns knew the virtue, for

PLATE XXVI

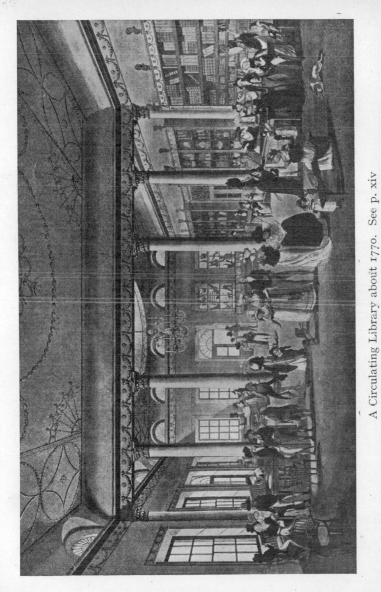

A Circulating Library about 1770. See p. xiv

LYRICAL BALLADS,

WITH

A FEW OTHER POEMS.

LONDON:

PRINTED FOR J. & A. ARCH, GRACECHURCH-STREET.

1798.

P O E M S,

CHIEFLY IN THE

SCOTTISH DIALECT,

BY

ROBERT BURNS.

THE Simple Bard, unbroke by rules of Art,
He pours the wild effusions of the heart :
And if inspir'd, 'tis Nature's pow'rs inspire;
Her's all the melting thrill, and her's the kindling fire.

ANONYMOUS.

KILMARNOCK:

PRINTED BY JOHN WILSON.

M,DCC,LXXVI.

PLATE XXVII

See p. xiv.

there has never been drawn a nobler picture of a god-fearing rustic family than his *Cottar's Saturday Night*:

> The priest-like father reads the sacred page,
> How Abram was the friend of God on high.

But he loathed the vice of hypocrisy to which this severity led, and many were his attacks on the sect of the 'Auld Lichts' and his sarcasms directed against the 'unco' guid':

> O ye wha are sae guid yoursel,
>   Sae pious and sae holy,
> Ye've nought to do but mark and tell
>   Your Neebours' fauts and folly!

For the same reasons he felt himself attracted towards those reprobates, those outcasts from a self-righteous society, those good-for-nothings who found the means of forgetting their miseries in some convivial drinking-bout and in the common sharing of misfortunes (*The Jolly Beggars*). Or else he amused himself with the adventures and superstitions of the common people like those of his *Tam o' Shanter*, who after an evening at an inn had a strange ride home, tormented by the pranks of wicked witches. For drinkers Burns had a ready indulgence. He was pleading his own cause. He sang with a good will the praises of John Barleycorn, whose seductions he knew too well, for his convivial habits helped to shorten his life.

All Burns's work reveals an alert and agile genius. In the exactness and soberness of his drawing this peasant was a true classic. He could command a clear-cut, rapid, frank style, as easily when he jested as when he was expressing his hot emotions, his lover's transports, or his feelings of pity for human beings or animals or flowers: for the mouse or for the mountain daisy he had overturned with his plough. Nothing could serve better than his short poems to make the Romantics feel where lay the true lyric fire.

Blake. In the same generation there lived a poet who went far beyond all others along new paths, foreshadowing and out-distancing the most determined Romantics in his self-abandonment to pure imagination and faith in the power of the seer. By the end of the eighteenth century William Blake (1757–1827) already was so violent and spontaneous a revolutionary in poetry that for many years, treated as an eccentric, he remained on the outskirts of the literary world. The most isolated and undisciplined of poets, he appeared a little too early to find his public, exercised hardly any immediate influence, and was only recognized years later as the supreme visionary.

Blake was an engraver, an extraordinary artist who left illustrations which reveal the same unfettered genius as his poems. Many of his verses were nothing but accompanying commentaries for his drawings. He gave up nearly the whole of his life to composing prophetic works in which the most intrepid reader can make out little but flashes of light against a background of obscurity. Happily, however, Blake started more modestly with short songs and brief lyric poems, *Poetical Sketches* (1783), *Songs of Innocence* (1789), and *Songs of Experience* (1794), which make him accessible to a wide range of readers and have a unique charm.

After a series of sketches inspired by the poets of the Renaissance, he dedicated to childhood his *Songs of Innocence*, expressing through the mouths of little children his feelings of piety and joy and naïve tenderness at the beauty of the world. Everything in the collection is an expression of love and tender feeling and of belief in the goodness of nature. The symbol of it is *The Lamb*, which is at once the embodiment of gentleness and the child Jesus, the God of children:

> Little Lamb, who made thee?
> Dost thou know who made thee?
> Gave thee life, and bade thee feed,
> By the stream and o'er the mead;
> Gave thee clothing of delight,
> Softest clothing, wooly, bright;
> Gave thee such a tender voice,
> Making all the vales rejoice?

These poems are tuneful lispings rather than reasoned and studied verse: it might truly be said that they proceed out of the mouths of babes. Wordsworth was to see the child from outside, making use of him philosophically rather than becoming a child himself. With Blake the assimilation is perfect. The whole collection is pervaded with the breath of simplicity and fancy. The sweetest of the poems are true cradle-songs. The melody is simple, apparently artless, and yet exquisite.

The *Songs of Experience* are the counterpart, so to speak, of the *Songs of Innocence*. Between the two came the French Revolution, of which Blake was for a time an enthusiastic partisan. His eyes were opened to the evils and vices of a doomed world which must be transformed. Religious and moral tyranny weigh down childhood, curtail its flights, mutilate its joys. The earth is unhappy; she lacks love and gaiety. The baleful priest interposes himself between man and God. Religion is poisoned by rancour and hatred The symbol of life is no longer the lamb but *The Tiger*, marvellous, no doubt, but an object of terror whose existence bears witness that not all creation is good:

> Tiger, tiger, burning bright
> In the forests of the night,
> What immortal hand or eye
> Dare frame thy fearful symmetry?
>
> In what distant deeps or skies,
> Burnt the fire of thine eyes?
> On what wings dare he aspire?
> What the hand dare seize the fire?

Throughout his life Blake was groping towards the symbolic expression of his mystical philosophy. He postulates as a principle that science is evil. He tolerates only religion; but his religion is even more heterodox than Milton's and intensely personal. Science, founded on analysis, is an ill-omened power which goes on its way splitting and defacing the primitive unity which imagination alone can rediscover and restore. 'Bacon, Locke, and Newton are the three great teachers of atheism or Satan's doctrine.'

The same ideas can be dimly seen through the thick gloom of Blake's long poems: *The Marriage of Heaven and Hell* (1790), *The French Revolution* (1791), *The Book of Urizen* (1794), *The Book of Los* (1795), *Jerusalem* (1804), and *Milton* (1804), where we will not attempt to follow him.

Blake for his own purposes changed the form no less thoroughly than the matter of poetry. He eschewed the couplet. In his songs he used short rhyming lines in stanzas which are often very irregular. Anapaestic rhythm he employed freely. In his prophetic poems he was inspired by Ossian and the Bible: he used no rhyme, but a blank verse with very long lines that was a kind of rhythmical prose. The regularity of Miltonic blank verse was repudiated by this great admirer of Milton. Hardly anything of the eighteenth century survives in either his thought or his expression. From the very first a despiser of simple logic, he pushed imagination to the point of extravagance. He was a fanatic who lived in a world which existed for him alone, like that of madmen, and to which other minds had no access. His genius, indeed, was not sane. Nevertheless amid the facile banality of contemporary poetry his strangeness, even though it is the strangeness of hallucination, is psychologically and poetically more impressive than the ordinary good sense of other men. If he lost his way in mystery, it was because he at least attempted to explore it.

The Novel from 1780 to 1800

The conflict between tradition and the new tendencies is no less evident in the novel than in poetry, and it leads to an extreme variety in the works produced. Though the period does not offer us any name equal to those of the masters of the middle of the century, it is interesting in its diversity and shows with what suppleness this literary form, still so new, could be bent to every need. Some of the novelists are in the direct line of their predecessors. Sterne's sentimentalism reappears in an aggravated form and quite unmixed with comedy in Henry Mackenzie's *The Man of Feeling* (1771). Never has virtue shed so many tears, or the heart suffered more palpitations.

Miss Burney. Very different in its energy and strength is the work of Frances Burney, especially her first two novels, *Evelina* (1771) and *Cecilia* (1782). Miss Burney adopted Richardson's epistolary method, but she rejected melodrama for comedy. *Evelina* relates the adventures of a well-bred young girl on her entrance into the world. She is poor and is thrown into a vulgar circle of City people whose manners arouse her scorn and awaken her ridicule. Miss Burney's talent for realism is unrivalled: Smollett's comic figures are mere caricatures beside her life-like portraits. She herself has less delicacy than Jane Austen was to display, but a richer humour and more animated scenes. Admired by Johnson and his circle, Miss Burney as Mme D'Arblay makes her contemporaries live again for us in a diary which covers fifty years (1768–1818); she also gives a picture of the life at court, where she was for fifteen years a lady-in-waiting—Keeper of the Robes—to Queen Charlotte. The diary and letters abundantly justify the epithet 'little character-monger' which Dr. Johnson once laughingly bestowed upon her.

An observant mind and a gift of presenting things in a comic light are the outstanding merits of Miss Burney. She has no moral or utilitarian preoccupation, and in this she is distinguished from the majority of her contemporaries.

Rousseau's Influence. Richardson had already conceived of the novel as affording a moral lesson by the force of example, but towards the end of the century the didactic tendency became more decided under the influence of Rousseau. One of Rousseau's ideas, expressed in *Emile*, was that all fiction should be withheld from the child. Fiction is a lie and all lies should be proscribed. Rousseau excepted only *Robinson Crusoe*. He would not have children read any other book. It was therefore against his desire, though in accordance with his doctrine, that a whole literature for children began to grow and multiply, banishing the romantic and the marvellous, and designed to replace the stories with which youth had until then been nourished. Away with Jack the Giant-killer, banish Goody Two-Shoes! This change, which was to fill the Romantics, Lamb, Coleridge, and Wordsworth, with consternation, is marked by the appearance of a multitude of books devoid of all fancy, in which the authors had set themselves the task of inculcating practical moral advice or exact knowledge, and especially copious lessons in natural history. It was the period of the educationalist Mrs. Trimmer, of Dr. Aikin and his sister Mrs. Barbauld with their *Evenings at Home* (1792–6), and of Hannah More, who, however, availed herself chiefly of the theatre for her teaching. The most popular novel of the type was that of Thomas Day, a fanatical admirer of Rousseau, who published his *Sandford and Merton* in 1783–9. His books heralded those of

Miss Edgeworth, whose talent was to eclipse the efforts of her predecessors.

Revolutionary Novelists. The same didactic tendency frequently reappears in the novels meant for grown-up people. The writers' object is to indicate the vices of a wicked world and to oppose to a corrupt civilization the virtues of the natural man. When the French Revolution broke out the reformatory or subversive effect of the novel became more intense. Among the works in this group must be placed those of Robert Bage the free-thinker, *Man As He Is* (1792), and *Hermsprong, or Man as He Is Not* (1796), which combine with Rousseau's influence that of Voltaire and Diderot; those of Thomas Holcroft, who divided his attention between plays and novels and preached liberty, equality, and fraternity in his *Anna St. Ives* (1792), and *Hugh Trevor* (1794). Of more lasting merit are the *Caleb Williams* (1794) and *St. Leon* (1799) of the philosopher William Godwin who in the first of these built up a story of terror simply out of the oppression of the law. More discreetly Mrs. Inchbald attacked social conventions in *A Simple Story* (1791), and *Nature and Art* (1796).

Mrs. Radcliffe. Meanwhile there was the novel of mystery and thrills. It had been rather clumsily inaugurated by Horace Walpole in 1764 with his *Castle of Otranto*, which combined the appeal of the Gothic and of the marvellous. In 1777 appeared the *Old English Baron* of Clara Reeve, who borrowed from Walpole chiefly medieval atmosphere; but this type of novel attained its zenith in the work of Anne Radcliffe (1764–1822), whose books *The Romance of the Forest* (1791), *The Mysteries of Udolpho* (1794), and *The Italian* (1797) agitated with delicious terrors a whole generation not only in England but throughout Europe. The ordinary theme of Mrs. Radcliffe's novels is the trials and persecutions inflicted on the heroine by a mysterious traitor or atheist in some wild place or ancient castle full of strange passages and terrifying dungeons. The mysteries, always explained in the end in such a way that no mystery remains, the terrors, always terminated by the heroine's love-match, are presented with real art and with a feeling for wild nature which implies a very pronounced romantic taste. These half-poetic romances heralded the less intellectual part of the literature which followed them. Matthew Gregory Lewis had neither the moral scruples of Mrs. Radcliffe nor her care in eluci-dating the mystery. Influenced by German romances, he went to the utmost extremes of horror and murder in his *Monk* (1796), in which he indulges as well in the most licentious pictures. His extra-ordinary success is an indication of the tastes of his time.

Beckford. There is more true Romanticism in the *Vathek* (1784) of the young William Beckford, written originally in French and later translated into English by another hand. Although it was partly inspired by the exotic romances of Voltaire, whose irony it preserves, *Vathek* is distinguished from them by the terrible gran-deur of its conclusion, the description of the Hell of the hall of Eblis. Beckford himself, with his misanthropy, his despair, his inability to procure satisfaction for himself with his immense fortune, his vain search for happiness, is a most striking prototype of many a Byronic character. His hero, Vathek, pursues a career of criminal extravagance, and vows himself to the service of Eblis, the spirit of evil, in the hope of attaining omnipotence. He and the beautiful Nouronihar, his consort, are the victims of their insatiable thirst for the absolute. This short novel presents the most curious mixture of the grotesque and the terrible, of satire and impassioned imagination. The style preserves the artistic rhetoric of the eighteenth century enriched with a picturesqueness which foretells the new era. The Oriental colour recalls the Arabian Nights. The only work of Beckford's which is of any account, it is memorable in itself, and even more so because of its date.

With Blake, Beckford, and Mrs. Radcliffe the change to Roman-ticism is not merely brought nearer, but is actually accomplished.

THE EIGHTEENTH-CENTURY DRAMA

IT has seemed better to take a general view of the drama in the eighteenth century than to divide it up into periods. It has not sufficient literary value to merit detailed study, but it is interesting on account of the diversity of the currents which cross and re-cross it throughout the century.

On the whole, the drama lost vitality; or rather, for it continued in appearance to be very active, it lost originality and talent. The genius of the century had passed from it to the novel. It was the novel which had become truly representative; free from most of the conventions which burdened the theatre, it succeeded better in depicting life, manners, and ideas. It attracted those serious spirits who since Puritan times had looked upon plays with suspicion. The theatre public nevertheless remained large, but it was chiefly drawn to the theatre by the fame of the actors or actresses. It is very remarkable that the names of the great players of this age have remained more familiar than those of most of its dramatic authors. How many people are ignorant of the very existence of Aaron Hill, Murphy, Kelly, Colman, who preserve the memory of Macklin, Mrs. Siddons, Kemble, and above all Garrick, whose personality even to-day equals in prestige that of the most eminent men of letters? The playing of such-and-such an actor was in many instances the looked-for treat. The enthusiastic revival of many of Shakespeare's plays helped to confirm this attitude. People went to the theatre, no doubt, to see *Hamlet* or *Macbeth*, but it was the interpretation of the prince of Denmark by Garrick or of Lady Macbeth by Mrs. Siddons which was the novelty and the principal attraction. This revival of old works came in part from the impotence of the stage to show 'the verie Age and Bodie of the Time, his forme and pressure', and it hindered the creation of new plays. The interest was becoming historical and retrospective. At a time when Shakespeare was being carefully re-edited by Rowe, Pope, Theobald, and Johnson, his

PLATE XXVIII

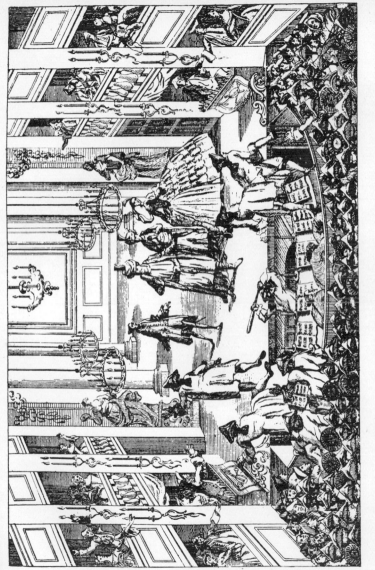

Covent Garden Theatre, 1763. The engraving commemorates the destructive riot in that year.
See p. xiv

plays, more or less remodelled, provided actors with their most
sensational parts. The quest for more elaborate and more striking
costumes and scenery was another factor which took off the
attention of the audience from what should be the essential
part of a truly living stage. Moreover, it should be noted that the
great success of the Shakespearian performances remained for a
long time almost without effect on the form of the new plays,
which as a rule bore the stamp of the classical tradition.

Tragedy. The taste for literary correctness and regularity which
distinguished the reign of Queen Anne drove English drama away
from the national tradition to follow the fashion of France, where
for more than half a century a theatre had reigned which was subject to the unities, simplified, allowing of only one plot, banishing
comedy, and making all the action take place in one psychological
crisis. The doctrine had produced masterpieces; on it Corneille
and Racine had built a series of plays worthy of the highest
admiration. But they were addressed to a select few and did not
claim to attract a very wide public. They were alien to the habits
of mixed English audiences who cared less for analyses of feeling
than for action, movement, and variety, and who were interested
in strongly individual characters rather than in finely and logically-
drawn motives. The English authors who tried to acclimatize
French tragedy were thus putting themselves in opposition to the
genius of their country and, one might add, to their own secret
tastes, for most of them remained convinced of the pre-eminence
of Shakespeare. The plays they produced have now no more than
historical interest, but some of them had in their own time a lively
success with a limited audience. This was the case with the adaptation by Ambrose Philips of Racine's *Andromaque* under the title
of *The Distressed Mother* (1712) and with Addison's *Cato*, a
tragedy in the manner of Corneille, which made a great stir in 1713
for reasons, it is true, rather political than literary. Poets of
reputation, like James Thomson and Young, were trying their
hand at this type of play round about 1720–50, Thomson with cold
correctness, Young with more freedom and spirit; his tragedy
Revenge is reminiscent of *Othello* and is distinguished by its
declamatory vehemence. Samuel Johnson produced in 1749 his

unlucky tragedy *Irene*. In 1750 the poet laureate Whitehead adapted his *Roman Father* from Corneille's *Horace*. Aaron Hill and Arthur Murphy in turn adapted Voltaire, who had himself tried to introduce into the framework of regular tragedy a little of the movement and spectacular interest of the English theatre.

The tragedy which had the most renown in the eighteenth century was the *Douglas* (1756) of the Reverend John Home, based on the old ballad of *Childe Maurice*, which redeems its dramatic mediocrity by an attempt to give an impression of primitive times and by some touches of Scottish colour.

Domestic Drama. The true tendency of the serious theatre of the century is better expressed by its essays in the field of middle-class or domestic drama.

Domestic drama is based on the idea that the destiny of ordinary men is as capable of affecting the emotions as that of heroic or legendary characters. It is of democratic origin and realistic in expression. George Lillo (1693–1739) initiated this type of play when his *London Merchant, or the History of George Barnwell* was produced in 1731. It was the story of a London apprentice who let himself be drawn by a courtesan into committing murder, and expiated his crime on the scaffold. In fact, Lillo had had precursors in Elizabethan times in certain works of Dekker and Heywood and more directly in the anonymous *Arden of Feversham*. But he had a more decided bias and narrower limitations than the Elizabethans. He set out to find strong emotions, terror and pity, in prosaic life, without the help of poetry or any recourse to verse. His realism is unfortunately impaired by stylistic conventions and he is deficient in true dramatic talent. With more energy, Edward Moore, another tradesman, wrote in 1753 his *Gamester* in which the tragedy of the gambler and the ruin caused by his passion are presented with a pathos which is often of great power. The influence of Lillo and Moore, although they had no immediate imitators in England, was considerable on the Continent. Diderot was inspired by them in his drama and derived from their work a new dramatic system, a revolution in literature which heralded the social revolution.

Comedy. These domestic tragedies were edifying works. They inculcated virtue by depicting the consequences of vice. They underlined their moral lessons by many a declamatory tirade. From the beginning of the century, comedy itself began to follow a similar path. It was becoming sentimental and began to replace the cynical malice of the Restoration, the amused satire of men's weaknesses, egotism, and hypocrisy, by the stirring of virtuous emotions. Sentimental comedy was founded on a belief in the goodness of human nature, which succeeded the belief in that same nature's perversity and grossness. It tended less to provoke smiles than to cause the easy tears of sensibility to flow. It went so far in this direction as to abdicate its own original genius.

Colley Cibber in his *Careless Husband* (1704), and Richard Steele in his *Tender Husband* (1705) and *Conscious Lovers* (1722), were the first to give this direction to comedy. Shaftesbury's optimistic philosophy was anticipated in the first of these plays and lent its support to those which followed. Later in the century Rousseau's influence brought strong reinforcement to this type of play. Man is good at heart. He does good by instinct. His virtues excite tender and virtuous emotions. Meanwhile the comic spirit had taken flight. There appeared many comedies good enough, as Fielding said, to be sermons. Farce was condemned as 'low'. The plays of John Kelly, Whitehead, Mrs. Sheridan, and Isaac Bickerstaffe are among the most notable specimens of this prolific species.

The new comedy and the domestic tragedy, both equally moralizing, joined forces to encourage the development of a kind of play which is the forerunner of melodrama. In it are to be found a plot abounding in incident and startling happenings, great store of pathos, some comic scenes for contrast, and every now and then long speeches designed to edify and to display the attractions of honesty and well-doing. The best-known representative of writers of this kind of hybrid play is Richard Cumberland with *The Brothers* (1769), *The West Indian* (1771), and *The Fashionable Lover* (1772).

However, true comedy was not resigned to its end. The spirit of the Restoration, which had extended its influence over Farquhar, survived in the still very free plays of Mrs. Centlivre, *The*

Wonder! A Woman Keeps a Secret (1714) and *A Bold Stroke for a Wife* (1717). Many people still went to the theatre for amusement rather than instruction. A few authors preserved the gift for mocking irony and humour. John Gay, the friend of Pope and Swift, cast ridicule upon the beginnings of sentimentalism in his *Beggar's Opera* (1728), the dry, trenchant humour of which recalls Swift. The play was very successful, but owed that success chiefly to the sprightly songs with which it abounded; it was a first attempt at comic opera rather than a true comedy.

Fielding. Henry Fielding, before he became a great novelist, devoted himself at first to comedy, even, indeed, to farce. He made clever adaptations of Molière's *L'Avare* (*The Miser*) and *Le Médecin malgré lui* (*The Mock Doctor*). But it was in parody and political satire that he obtained his most personal successes, in his *Tragedy of Tragedies or The Life and Death of Tom Thumb the Great* (1731), a caricature of heroic drama, and his *Pasquin* (1736), and *The Historical Register for the Year 1736-7*. His raillery at the fashions of the time, his banter of well-known people, especially people in high places and members of the government, disturbed the authorities to such an extent that they re-established the censorship.

Fielding had lightened the drama by writing several short pieces in three acts instead of five. The actor Samuel Foote (1720–77) followed his example and presented a whole series of brief, satirical, and amusing sketches which are hardly distinguishable from farce. About the same time George Colman (1732–94) was pursuing Fielding's campaign against the sentimental mania of his time, as in his comedy *Polly Honeycombe* (1760), although later on he was drawn along by the current, and had to make sufficient room for the tender emotions in his masterpiece *The Clandestine Marriage* 1766), written in collaboration with Garrick.

Goldsmith. It was to protest against the flood of sentimentalism and 'genteelness' which was invading the stage that Goldsmith put on his comedies *The Good Natur'd Man* (1768) and *She Stoops to Conquer* (1773), of which the latter is the only play of this period, except those of Sheridan, which has survived and continues to be acted at regular intervals. The other dramatic works enumerated in this chapter are for the most part only historical curiosities. *She Stoops to Conquer* was not exactly an original work; it derived from Farquhar's *Beaux' Stratagem* in subject as in good humour. But it was born in a propitious hour, and Goldsmith lent it some of his own natural charm and embellished it with his excellent literary style.

Sheridan. Richard Brinsley Sheridan (1751–1816) had a striking success while he was still very young with his *Rivals* (1775), *The School for Scandal* (1777), and *The Critic* (1779). Endowed with more sparkling and exhilarating wit than Goldsmith, he revived the comedy of Vanbrugh and Congreve without their coarseness and cynicism. Like them he divests himself of all concern with moralizing. He attacked the hypocrisy of the sentimentalists although he himself gave high credit to the good heart hidden beneath a dissipated exterior. He excels at epigram; no author is more witty. But if he deserves to remind us of Congreve, he cannot be placed in the same rank. His characters are remarkable for their dramatic qualities, but they have no reality off the stage. They are not the expression of an existing society; the retorts of the fools show as much of the author's wit as those of the intelligent characters. The figures are traditional rather than taken from life. But their repartee amuses and dazzles us so long as they are on the boards. Thanks to his verbal talent and his sense of the theatre, Sheridan produced a most brilliant display of fireworks.

After him followed only dramatists who are now forgotten. Really amusing comedies were rare, but one may nevertheless single out *The Belle's Stratagem* (1780) and *A Bold Stroke for a Husband* (1783) of Hannah Cowley, and *The Way to Get Married* (1796) and *A Cure for the Heartache* (1797) of Thomas Norton. What distinguished the theatre of the last quarter of the century was the success of plays of philosophical or revolutionary tendency. Hannah More made the stage serve her humanitarian teaching in *Percy* (1777) and *The Fatal Falsehood* (1779). The novelists whom we have mentioned, like Thomas Holcroft and Mrs. Inchbald, expressed in their plays the same ideas as in their books. George Colman the younger framed his theses in an exotic setting in

Inkle and Yarico (1787) and brought them back to England in *The Heir-at-Law* (1797). At the same time Lewis was exploiting terror in the theatre and producing a dramatic version of his *Monk* in *The Castle Spectre* (1797). The end of these various experiments was melodrama, which was reinforced by foreign importations. The work of the Austrian Kotzebue triumphed in England as it did on the Continent. It is remarkable that Sheridan himself became Kotzebue's adapter in 1799 with his *Pizarro*. It was a kind of abdication of the national genius and the prelude to a long eclipse.

ROMANTICISM 1798–1830

Poetry

FROM the European point of view the eighteenth century had been Great Britain's first great literary century. She had made large exchanges and for the first time had given perhaps more than she received. It is true that since the Restoration of 1660 these exchanges had been made almost entirely with France. Italian influence had ended with the Renaissance and German influence was still to begin. England had in general accepted the neo-classic doctrine from France but she had enriched it with her own genius. Her deists, her humorists, her novelists, and her poets had aroused on the Continent an admiration which had induced a violent current of Anglomania. Voltaire had originally constituted himself the interpreter and champion of the new faith. However strongly he was later to oppose the infatuation for Shakespeare, he had done more than any one else to popularize Shakespeare's name. He had never ceased to pay homage to Pope and Swift. Diderot had rendered almost fanatical adoration to the novelist Richardson and the dramatist Lillo. The Encyclopaedists had drawn largely upon Locke's philosophy and upon the irreligious armoury of the deists. On the other hand, all the early symptoms of romanticism in English literature had aroused a prompt response in Europe: Young's *Night Thoughts* for example, Thomson's *Seasons*, Macpherson's pseudo-*Ossian*, and the melancholy of Gray.

In return France had towards the close of the century paid her debt by giving back to their native country the ideas of the English philosophers, developed by more passionate and bolder combatants. Through Jean-Jacques Rousseau especially she had powerfully stirred up the ideas which helped on a revolutionary movement in literature not less than in politics and education. The Revolution of 1789 itself had in its beginnings violently shaken English thought and won the approval and even roused the enthusiasm of many minds across the Channel.

But little by little from 1800 onwards opinion in England began to set almost unanimously against republican France, and still more against Napoleonic France. In the nineteenth century Great Britain turned away from the enemy nation, from its literature as from all else, and transferred her sympathy to Germany, who had for a quarter of a century been giving the world great thinkers and great poets, who were, moreover, admirers and indeed imitators of her own literary past—of Shakespeare, Milton, and of the forerunners of Romanticism. However revolutionary France might have shown herself, she had, on the whole, remained attached to the literary formulas of the classical age, against which there was in her no reaction with any force until nearly 1830. It was Germany that supplied the new impulse and indeed the philosophical doctrine that made Romanticism conscious of its aspirations: and English Romanticism, in so far as it was nourished by foreign thought, went to school in Germany. But England found there only a confirmation of her own tendencies, a theoretical basis for her instincts, a justification for her revolt against a literary convention whose yoke she had always borne with difficulty.

It is customary to fix the initial date of English Romanticism in the year 1798, when the *Lyrical Ballads* of Wordsworth and Coleridge appeared. It is a date justified by the fact that this rousing call was the first articulate protest against the matter and form of the predominant type of poetry. Blake had already gone much further, but he was an eccentric, suspected of madness, whose genius was not to be recognized until well into the nineteenth century. The authors of the *Lyrical Ballads*, on the other hand, knew clearly what they had done and what they wished to accomplish. They belonged to that generation, born about 1770, which was in the full flower of youth in 1789, which had trembled with joy at the fall of the Bastille, but which, gradually becoming alienated from the Revolution and disgusted with its excesses, was to end by formally condemning the rationalist movement of the eighteenth century and taking refuge in uncompromising conservatism. Since the following generation of the great romantics, that of Byron and Shelley, which came to manhood about 1815, was to set itself in opposition to the earlier one and to show itself as

intrepidly liberal as that had become conservative, it is not possible
to base the unity of Romanticism on the identity of its political
principles. Romanticism was first and foremost a literary movement and it was a common faith in poetry which bound together
these two opposing generations. The supreme faculty of the poet
is imagination, which must take the place of reason for the solution of the riddle of life and nature. The function of the poet is
essential. Now, as at the Renaissance, he regains the lead, but
this time after a crisis which had brought experience and revealed
the insufficiency of abstract philosophy. Wordsworth and Shelley,
politically as far asunder as the poles, agree in seeing the poet as
the guide, the prophet, and the seer. Romanticism is thus essentially poetic.

It took up the study of man with the means proper to the poet
and applied itself to that aspect of light and shade in the soul
which the philosophers had thought negligible. The mysterious
regions of instinct, of feeling and the senses, and the subtle relations between man and Nature, were the chosen objects of its
scrutiny. In his first prefaces Wordsworth describes himself as
before all else a psychologist who has returned to the study of
reality and desires to enrich those too poverty-stricken ideas,
incomplete and therefore misleading, which in the belief of the
eighteenth century had summarized the whole of the human soul
and of social life. Nothing reveals the change more clearly than
a simultaneous reading of the preface to Pope's *Essay on Man* and
the definitions of poetry put forward by Wordsworth and Shelley.
Pope saw in poetry a superior mnemotechnic method of engraving
in the mind the thought of the philosophers; Wordsworth and
Shelley saw in it philosophy itself, the highest and profoundest
philosophy. So Romanticism, as M. Lanson has well expressed it,
is 'shot with metaphysics' ('tout traversé de frissons métaphy-
siques'). The Romantics, relying on imagination, and convinced
of the absolute truth of poetic intuitions, substituted for the cold
mechanism of cause and effect a vision of mysterious forces which
they called divine. They repudiated deism for a faith which is
sometimes pantheism, sometimes mysticism.

To express their fervent passions they sought a more supple and more lyrical form than that of Pope, a language less dulled by convention, metres unlike the prevailing couplet. They renounced the poetic diction of the eighteenth century, created a fresh set of poetical associations of words, and drew upon unusual images and varied verse-forms for which they found models in the Renaissance and the old popular poetry. They refashioned, indeed, the language of poetry as much as its matter; and this was the cause of the long resistance of the public; its habits were upset and it was disconcerted by something that appeared to it either formless, obscure, or puerile. But the Romantic campaign ended in so complete a triumph that towards 1830 the same public had become unjust to the eighteenth century and could hardly bear to read its verse any longer.

Wordsworth. The poet who expressed the deepest aspirations of English Romanticism was William Wordsworth. He saw Nature and man with new eyes, and his whole work is an attempt to communicate that new vision. In his youth he had been an enthusiast for the French Revolution, but towards the age of 28 he gave up his dreams of political regeneration in order to devote himself entirely to the task of bringing to the world the largest possible measure of happiness by the disturbance of old habitual ways of thought and by seeking in the cultivation of sensibility and imagination the sources of the most general and the healthiest enjoyment, that might be had by all, 'in widest commonalty spread'. He had to show that men had put happiness where it did not exist; that they had created for themselves a false idea of poetry; and that they had forsaken simultaneously the true ways of beauty and of joy. To attain this object Wordsworth had something better than abstract precept; he relied on his experience. He examined himself; he recalled the ups and downs of his youth, the joy he had then known, and the wrong turnings that his thought had taken, bringing unhappiness upon him; and he described the means by which he had at last recovered his serenity of mind.

Born in 1770 on the edge of the Lake District and educated at the little grammar school of Hawkshead in the heart of that picturesque country, Wordsworth had spent happy years in daily communion with Nature. After some years at Cambridge he made in 1792 a stay in France and became seized with enthusiasm for the Revolution and love for France. These feelings were to persist in him for a time after his return to England, but first the Terror and then even more effectively the spirit of conquest which displayed itself in the French Republicans, shook his hopes of immediate felicity on earth. He devoted himself to the construction of abstract political systems like a good disciple of the 'philosopher' William Godwin, whose out and out rationalism has been considered. These purely intellectual exercises led only to endless doubts and contradictions. He reached a sort of moral despair from which he gradually emerged only by returning to the study of Nature and the cultivation of poetry. By 1798 he had recovered his first joyousness, and his association with the young Coleridge, who had passed through a crisis very like his own, confirmed him in the wisdom thus acquired—a wisdom of which all his verse henceforward was to be the expression.

In the poems which he wrote, in a concrete and often semi-dramatic manner, for the *Lyrical Ballads* of 1798, he broke with tradition, seeking his subjects in the small happenings of country life, in the talk of countrymen and children, in the doings and the feelings of humble people, or in the emotions aroused in his own heart by the various aspects of the countryside. For these new subjects he employed a new language. He strove to prove that the purest poetry was written in the simplest words. He took for his model the speech of the country people, freed of its dialect and its grammatical mistakes.

His poetry, stripped of all the ornaments of style hallowed by usage, and almost devoid of built-up story, depended therefore for its effect solely upon his strength of feeling and imagination:

> The moving accident is not my trade;
> To freeze the blood I have no ready arts;
> 'Tis my delight, alone in summer shade,
> To pipe a simple song for thinking hearts.

> O Reader! had you in your mind
> Such stores as silent thought can bring,
> O gentle Reader! you would find
> A tale in every thing.

Wordsworth's most beautiful verses are those which he wrote when he was between 28 and 35 years old; when his sensibility was fresh, his imagination powerful, and his capacity for joy still unimpaired. During this period the short poems contained in *Lyrical Ballads* were augmented by fresh collections which contain his purest gems of poetry and his boldest experiments, the product of that very familiarity of expression and that homeliness of subject which were for a long time to provoke the ridicule of the witty. It was during this period also that Wordsworth was cogitating *The Recluse*, designed to be a great philosophical poem in blank verse in which he would expound his views on life, mankind, and society. Destined never to write more than mere fragments of it, he began with *The Prelude* in which he analysed the growth of his poetic genius during his childhood and youth and recalled the lessons he owed to Nature, his first and greatest teacher.

From 1805 until 1815, when the poet's vitality was being sapped by domestic misfortunes, his optimism shaken by the establishment of the French Empire and the victories of Napoleon, and his imagination fatigued by the demands he had made upon it, he found a noble inspiration in moral poetry, in the thought of duty and in the energy with which he attacked the Emperor. He had already written some fine patriotic sonnets; he now wrote many more, and composed his great poem *The Excursion*, in which he expounds his faith by the device of making a philosophical pedlar refute the pessimism of a recluse who has turned misanthropist because he has seen his dreams of social regeneration shattered by the set-back of the Revolution.

Unfortunately, after the fall of Napoleon Wordsworth found no noble cause to serve. A new tyranny weighed upon Europe, that of the Holy Alliance, which suppressed by force the liberal aspirations of the peoples. Wordsworth himself had become a conservative and was frightened by the most legitimate attempts at reform. His poetry reflects his fear of change and is stamped with mistrust. Its inspiration grew colder and more rare, but at intervals until his death in 1850 some noble sonnets scattered through his work or included in the series called the *Ecclesiastical Sonnets* and *The River Duddon* still recall his better years.

PLATE XXIX

Dove Cottage about 1805. See p. xiv

PLATE XXX

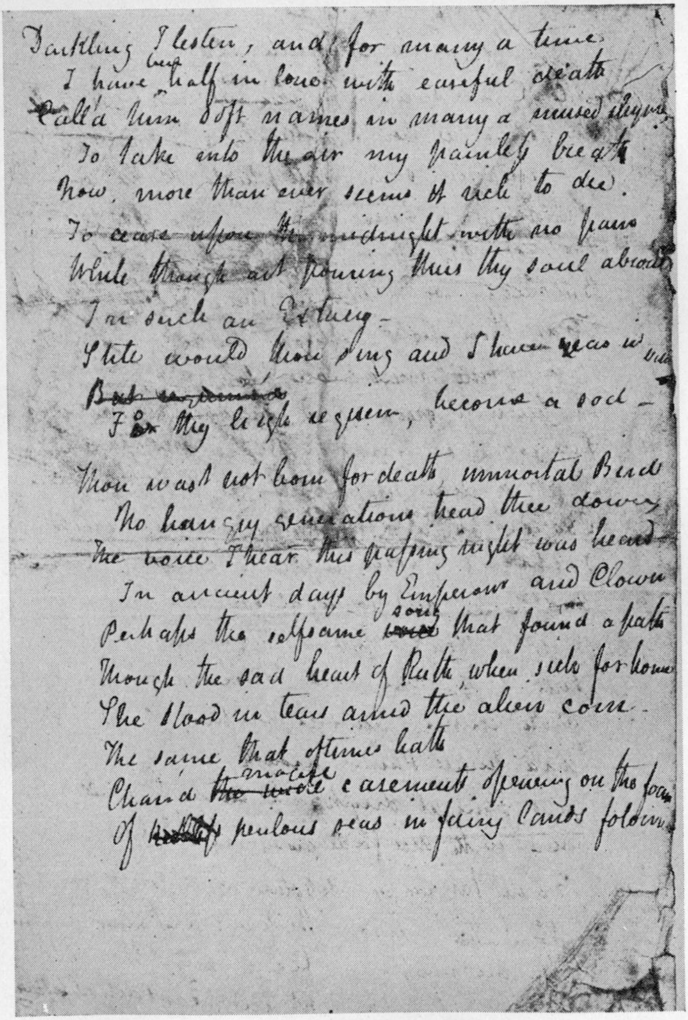
Darkling I listen, and for many a time
I have been half in love with easeful death
Call'd him soft names in many a mused rhyme
To take into the air my quiet breath
Now more than ever seems it rich to die
~~To cease upon the midnight with no pain~~
While ~~thou art~~ pouring thus thy soul abroad
In such an Ecstasy—
Still wouldst thou sing and I have ears in vain
~~But requiem~~
For thy high requiem, become a sod—

Thou wast not born for death, immortal Bird
No hungry generations tread thee down
~~The voice I hear this passing night was heard~~
In ancient days by Emperor and Clown
Perhaps the selfsame ~~voice~~ song that found a path
Through the sad heart of Ruth, when sick for home
She stood in tears amid the alien corn—
The same that oftimes hath
Charm'd ~~the wide~~ magic casements, opening on the foam
Of ~~keelless~~ perilous seas in faery lands forlorn.

Stanzas from Keats's 'Ode to a Nightingale' from the author's manuscript now in the Fitzwilliam Museum, Cambridge. See p. xiv

It was only by degrees that his poetry captured public opinion. It impressed at once some chosen spirits, who were transformed by it, but it was not until 1830 that it was widely recognized by his compatriots, or that England found in it the mirror of her inmost feelings. In the interval she had listened chiefly to the epic tales of Walter Scott and the sombre violence of Byron. But Wordsworth's careful reading in the book of Nature, his lessons in sentiment and imagination, finally took first place. It was a well-deserved triumph. Few lives have been so entirely and undividedly consecrated to poetry and through poetry to the education of the spirit as Wordsworth's. He had not been content merely to possess imagination himself but had held it his duty to awaken and to clarify the imagination of his readers: he tried to direct their steps towards poetry. Perhaps no man has played so well, so constantly, and so nobly as he the part of poetic guide.

Coleridge. Coleridge, who was Wordsworth's friend, 'his spirit's brother', and at one time his collaborator, presents as many contrasts with him as analogies. Both guided their lives by the same philosophy. Both passed from a revolutionary temper to conservatism and from a kind of poetic pantheism to religious orthodoxy. In poetry also they believed at first that they could bear each other company, but they soon perceived that they must take separate paths. When they wrote *Lyrical Ballads* they were obliged to partition the field of poetry between them. While Wordsworth set himself to shed the light of the imagination over real life, over the most ordinary incidents and people, Coleridge took the supernatural for his province; his plan was to project a human interest into romantic themes, and 'a semblance of truth sufficient to procure for these shadows of imagination that willing suspension of disbelief for the moment, which constitutes poetic faith'. While Wordsworth was rhyming his ballad of *Goody Blake and Harry Gill*, in which is seen the effect of a poor woman's curse on a miserly young farmer who beats her because she robs his hedge of sticks, Coleridge was telling the strange adventures of an *Ancient Mariner*, one of those who first sailed the Pacific, who, because he slays an albatross, suffers terrible hallucinations, seeing the approach of a spectral vessel in which are Death and 'Life-in-

Death', and is brought back to his native country by the dead
sailors of his own ship, a crew of ghosts. This fantastic poem is as
full of marvellous invention as Wordsworth's of homely details.
It has besides a perfection of style and rhythm and a refinement
of sound and cadence of which Wordsworth was not capable:

> The fair breeze blew, the white foam flew,
>   The furrow followed free;
> We were the first that ever burst
>   Into that silent sea.

> Down dropt the breeze, the sails dropt down,
>   'Twas sad as sad could be;
> And we did speak only to break
>   The silence of the sea!

Coleridge 'was an epicure in sounds', and in this poem he reached
the highest point of verbal beauty ever attained by the English
lyrical genius, basing itself on the old popular ballads. From these
ballads Wordsworth borrowed their simple and often prosaic
phrasing, Coleridge their strangeness, which he transfigured by his
exquisite art. He was to produce again, in his mysterious and
never-finished *Christabel* and in that strange fragment *Kubla
Khan*, born of an opium dream, unrivalled specimens of his poetic
gifts. But he fell, a victim of opium, into premature discourage-
ment (*Dejection: an Ode* 1802), relieved only by some contemplative
poems. He had lost his 'shaping spirit of imagination'. The rest of
his life was devoted to prose, to sketches of a philosophic doctrine
inspired by German thinkers and the mystics, and to lectures on
literary criticism, themselves fragmentary but so new and suggestive that they stimulated a whole generation and are still re-
sorted to to-day for some of the most penetrating judgements ever
delivered on English poets.

Coleridge's talk possessed an incomparable richness. From his
youth up he had read book after book, and for preference books
of the most abstruse kind. His inspirations came to him from the
library, as those of Wordsworth from observation of the countryside. His imagination was inflamed by the words and pictures of
old tales which would have made no impression on other people.
The extraordinary *Ancient Mariner* is a kind of cento compiled

from twenty old books of travel, whose very phrases reappear in Coleridge's verse transfigured by his arrangement of them and the magic of his metre.

With Wordsworth absorbed chiefly in the present, these memories of a distant past made Coleridge the representative of another aspect of Romanticism. No work fulfils so well as his the definition of Romanticism as 'the renascence of wonder'.

Southey. The chief characteristic of the poetry of Robert Southey (1774–1843) is its preference for outlandish settings. As a young man and a revolutionary he took for his themes *Wat Tyler* and *Joan of Arc*; but in after years he preferred to lead his readers into the most distant countries and through civilizations as different as could be from those they knew. Southey had conceived from the start the project of 'exhibiting all the more prominent and poetical forms of mythology which have at any time obtained among mankind, by making each the ground-work of an heroic poem'. He partly realized this ambitious design in the writing of *Thalaba* (1801), *Madoc* (1805), *The Curse of Kehama* (1810), *Don Roderick* (1814), evoking in turn Arabia, Mexico, India, and Spain in the time of the Visigoths. All these works are remarkable for the ease and copiousness shown by the poet, for the richness of description and variety of verse-forms that he employs. Thus in *Thalaba* he makes use of irregular blank verse, in *Kehama* of irregular rhymed stanzas. Yet in spite of the talent spent upon them these poems had only a passing fame. Southey's historical and geographical instinct was chiefly for the framing. Far-fetched mythologies seemed to him picturesque subjects; what he knew about them he learned from the books in his library; he did not penetrate to the heart of them. His heroes retain a British code of morals: Southey himself in every clime remains, in Professor Herford's phrase, 'the decorous English protestant'. Such epics had their day. They have a superficial vastness but no depth. The most human of them is the last, *Roderick*, for Southey knew Spain and his memories of the Spanish resistance to the Napoleonic invasions gave some life to the exploits of a hero less unreal than the others.

Southey, like Wordsworth and Coleridge, had early taken an

interest in the popular ballads. He himself wrote a fair number of short poems in this manner, some of which have survived in anthologies. His ballads are marked by their mixture of impressive terror and humour; they opened a new field.

Southey did not make a name in poetry to be compared with those of Coleridge and Wordsworth. But he was a great man of letters, a voracious reader, at home in libraries (see *My days among the Dead are past*), and an inexhaustible writer in prose as well as verse. His easy, limpid, and level style served him well in writing not only innumerable articles, but the history of Brazil (in 1810–19) and the lives of Wesley and, above all, of Nelson. His *Life of Nelson* (1813) remains a classic.

Wordsworth, Coleridge, and Southey are the 'Lake poets', so called because their lives were spent partly in the Lake district. Only Wordsworth was born there, but all three lived there for a shorter or longer period. Linked together by friendship, they were still further united by the mutual ardour of their revolutionary ideas in youth, and by the common reaction which followed in their riper years. They held many points of poetic dogma in common, however much their most characteristic verses may differ. Some of their productions are almost interchangeable.

Walter Scott. A common interest in popular ballad poetry may be taken as the link between the Lake poets and the Scottish writer Walter Scott (1771–1832). In 1796 Scott translated the *Lenore* of the German Bürger, but he had no need to go abroad for his inspiration. There were ballads in plenty in southern Scotland, and in 1802–3 he published a collection of them, *The Minstrelsy of the Scottish Border*, which is comparable with Percy's *Reliques*. He soon turned to original composition and produced in quick succession *The Lay of the Last Minstrel* (1805), *Marmion* (1808), *The Lady of the Lake* (1810), *Rokeby* (1813), and others. These were not ballads but long poems half epic, half lyrical, in which history was presented in the colours of romance, and they gained a rapid popularity. Scott's chief Romantic quality was his affection for the past, for the Middle Ages and the days of chivalry. He did not, like Southey, scatter his poetical energies in distant fields, but devoted himself chiefly to Scotland, and his great know-

PLATE XXXI

JOHN KEATS
National Portrait Gallery

PERCY BYSSHE SHELLEY
National Portrait Gallery

GEORGE GORDON BYRON
In the possession of Sir John Murray

CHARLES LAMB
British Museum

PLATE XXXII

Scott's library at Abbotsford, built 1812. See p. xv

ledge of his own country enabled him to bring an element of fact
into legends full of romantic character.

Scott was distinguished from the Lake poets by his martial
spirit; he loved to depict scenes of war and heroic single combat,
and his strongly accented verse lent itself to such themes:

> The English shafts in volleys hailed,
> In headlong charge their horse assailed:
> Front, flank, and rear, the squadrons sweep,
> To break the Scottish circle deep,
>   That fought around their king.
> But yet, though thick the shafts as snow,
> Though charging knights like whirlwinds go,
> Though bill-men ply the ghastly blow,
>   Unbroken was the ring; . . .
>   (The battle of Flodden in *Marmion*).

He also excelled in quiet description of scenery, but showed
classical restraint in the way he subordinated pictorial passages
to the narrative. The sudden rise to fame of Byron made him turn
to prose; and the reputation of his verse was soon to be over-
shadowed by that of his novels; but from 1805 to 1813 he was the
most widely-read of British poets.

The second generation of the great Romantic poets unites the
names of Byron, Shelley, and Keats; beside them must be placed
the names of Thomas Moore, Leigh Hunt, W. S. Landor, and
Thomas Hood.

The first three are linked together in the dates of their lives
and in their common fate of an early death. Their short careers
fit one within another, Byron (1788–1824) dying at the age of 36,
Shelley (1792–1822) at 29, and Keats (1795–1821) at 26. But if
they did not live long they lived intensely, and each of them left
work marked by supreme qualities.

Byron. Lord Byron was the only one of them to know fame in
his lifetime. He began as a disdainful nobleman and wealthy
dilettante with his *Hours of Idleness*, published in 1807 at the age
of 19. Scornfully criticized in the *Edinburgh Review*, he revenged
himself with his *English Bards and Scotch Reviewers* (1809). But his
fame burst like a thunder-clap upon the world when he published
the two first cantos of *Childe Harold* (1812) on his return to England

after a journey in Spain and the East. With *Childe Harold* Byron introduced into English literature the figure of the disillusioned man, the hero sated with pleasures and debauches, despising mankind, living on the edge of society and in revolt against its laws. He struck off several copies of this portrait between 1813 and 1816 in poems which have an exotic setting: *The Giaour, The Bride of Abydos, The Corsair, Lara, The Siege of Corinth, Parisina*. It is in these that English romanticism expressed the *mal du siècle* as Goethe had done in *Werther* and Chateaubriand in *René*. Under all these various names Byron painted his own portrait, exaggerating for effect the violence of the passions and the eccentricities of the characters. His heroes were distinguished by pride and scorn, but they all kept a tender place in their hearts for some woman, who was always gentle, loving, and impassioned.

All this poetry contained much that was conventional and repetitive, but it gave an impression of power that made the verse of the Lake poets appear over-refined and a trifle bloodless.

Byron was to rise above his earlier manner when misfortune attacked him; in 1816, his wife left him on account of his immorality and he, who had been the idol of English drawing-rooms, became an object of scandal and condemnation. He exiled himself from England for ever, and took up an ironical and arrogant attitude towards his native country. He lived for a time in Switzerland, and there composed his drama *Manfred* (1817). He then settled in Italy, where he lived mostly in Venice, making a great show of leading a dissolute life. He finished his *Childe Harold* (1816–18), and wrote a series of plays which were not destined to be performed—*Cain, Marino Faliero, Sardanapalus*; and then he found his true bent in the poetry, now lyrical or passionate, now careless or satirical, of his *Don Juan* (1819–24). He met a premature and glorious death from illness at Missolonghi, whither he had gone to fight for the independence of Greece.

Byron's political attitude was that of a liberal opponent of the Holy Alliance. He scoffed at the reactionary spirit which moved the Lake poets. Before going to the help of the Greek revolt he had supported the Italian *Carbonari*. He arraigned England for her responsible share in the tyranny which weighed on Europe after

Waterloo, and Castlereagh in particular as the minister who in his eyes personified that policy.

But his satire was not only political. His lively powers exercised themselves upon the English cant of which he felt he had been a victim and of which he became in the eyes of foreigners the great denouncer. He enjoyed giving cause for scandal by his cynical maxims and by the licence of his descriptions. He indulged his passion against religion in making a hero of the first murderer Cain, who refused to bow to the laws of a God that had admitted evil into the universe. In *Don Juan*, written in the eight-line stanza or *ottava rima* of the Italian mock-heroic poets, Byron's method is principally ironic. At a time when wit was divorced from poetry, he spread a rich banquet of witty sallies, mocking everything, even his own verse, and making room for puns and jokes in the midst of passages full of pathos or true poetry. Don Juan's ship is wrecked in a tempest. Thirty passengers escape in the long-boat, nine in 'a poor little cutter'. The latter is 'quickly swamped':

> Nine souls more went in her; the long-boat still
> Kept above water, with an oar for mast,
> Two blankets stitch'd together, answering ill
> Instead of sail, were to the oar made fast:
> Though every wave roll'd menacing to fill,
> And present peril all before surpass'd.
> They grieved for those who perish'd with the cutter,
> And also for the biscuit casks and butter.
>
> *Don Juan*, ii. 61.

To-day this unique poem remains the most vital and the most important part of the great mass of his work, the earlier half of which has lost most of its freshness.

A headlong improviser, little given to remodelling and polishing his lines, Byron was an unequal writer. He affected to disdain the stylistic innovations of the Lake poets and to admire Pope and the English classical school. But he had not Pope's care for artistic finish; many of his lines are harsh, rugged, and unrhythmical; on the other hand, he has energy and vigour. He excelled all his contemporaries in the gift of choosing effective subjects and making a powerful appeal to men's minds. His immorality did him ill-service during the Victorian age, and his faults as a versifier have harmed his reputation in his own country. But his poems, which all embody some sensational romance, lose less in translation than those of his rivals. He has been incontestably the most popular of the English romantic poets in Europe and his influence, particularly in France, has been immense.

Shelley. Byron's great motive-impulse was pride; Shelley's was love. Though of a titled family, and rich, he gave up his life to the struggle against all that he felt to be a cause of human misery. He revived again the ideas of the 'philosopher' William Godwin some twenty years after they had for a brief space aroused the enthusiasm of Wordsworth and Coleridge. Shelley in his turn saw in established institutions, in kings and priests, all the diverse forms of evil and obstacles to happiness and progress. His imagination took wing towards the new world which would come into existence when all these forms of error and hatred had disappeared. The essence of his work is his prophecy of a new-born age: it is the spirit of the eighteenth century transmuted by lyric ardour. Into an irreligious philosophy Shelley put all the fervour of religion. In his youth he proclaimed himself an atheist: at 21 he wrote *Queen Mab*, which is a formal profession of atheism. At 26 he published *Laon and Cythna*, which became, after revision and under the new title of *The Revolt of Islam*, a sort of transfigured picture of the French Revolution. In 1820 appeared *Prometheus Unbound*, the hymn of human revolt triumphing over the oppression of false gods. He also published the drama *Hellas* in honour of Greece risen against the Ottoman yoke. Shelley's life was full of such challenges, which he maintained with a passion more single-hearted than Byron's and less undermined by scepticism. Where Byron was inspired by a dislike of mankind, Shelley was inspired by love: a love not limited to mankind, but extended to every living creature, to animals and flowers, to the elements, to the whole of Nature. The poet holds passionate communion with the Universe. He becomes one with the lark (*To a Skylark*), with the cloud (*The Cloud*), and the west wind (*Ode to the West Wind*):

> Make me thy lyre, even as the forest is:
> What if my leaves are falling like its own!
> The tumult of thy mighty harmonies

> Will take from both a deep, autumnal tone,
> Sweet though in sadness. Be thou, Spirit fierce,
> My Spirit! Be thou me, impetuous one!

He is not content, like Wordsworth, merely to love and revere Nature: his very being is fused and blended with her.

Shelley's other great poems are *Alastor* (1816), in which he recounts his pursuit of an unattainable ideal of beauty; *Julian and Maddalo* (1818), in which he draws his own portrait contrasted with that of Byron; *The Cenci*, a retelling in dramatic form of the terrible story of Beatrice, who, the victim of a father's lust, takes his life in revenge; *Epipsychidion*, in which he sings of his love for a beautiful young Italian girl; *Adonais*, an elegy dedicated to the poet Keats, and the unfinished poem *The Triumph of Life*, which has remained a mysterious fragment with the promise of a master-piece. The lyrical rapture of all these works is unique. In all English poetry there is no utterance so spontaneous as Shelley's; nowhere does the thought flow with such irresistible melody. He achieved an ease and flexibility of rhythm that is quite astonishing in every form of verse he used—whether blank or rhymed verse, couplets (*Julian and Maddalo*), stanzas (the Spenserian stanza in *Adonais* and *The Revolt of Islam*), *terza rima* as in *To the West Wind* and *The Triumph of Life*, iambic verses as in the preceding poems, or anapaests as in *The Cloud* and *The Sensitive Plant*. His style contains a unique mixture of abstractions and visual images. To the decipherment of the text of Nature Shelley brought a subtlety that surpasses Wordsworth's; penetrating the mystery and perceiving 'the warm light of life', it seems to see into truths that are beyond utterance. Such subtlety implies, no doubt, an exceptional sensibility which can appeal only to a small elect band of readers, and is not universal like the visions of Wordsworth. The contrast between the thought, which never ceased to be youthful and rash, and the infallible sureness of the great lyric flights, is the distinguishing mark of Shelley's incomparable poetry.

John Keats. John Keats, the Adonais of Shelley's song, whose life was yet briefer than Shelley's, nevertheless presents us with a like miracle, different and even opposite as were his qualities. Swift, impetuous, soaring movement was the supreme characteristic

of Shelley (*Ode to the West Wind, Ode to Liberty, Ode to Naples*),
an impulse that turned him away from a past where tyranny and
evil ruled, and from a present which all noble spirits must detest,
to take flight to regions where love and liberty will reign in triumph.
He longed for change and progress and saw the Golden Age before
him, not behind; the west wind that sweeps away the dead leaves
is the symbol of his poetry. The substance of his verse is light,
liquid, airy. Phantoms and the impalpable essence of reality are
the only freight of his winged vessel, for its flight must be un-
burdened. In contrast with this the verse of Keats moves with the
slow pace of a march burdened with treasures; it has the full, close
richness of the teeming earth, the 'mellow fruitfulness' which Keats
ascribes to autumn, the autumn that conspires with the sun:

> . . . how to load and bless
> With fruit the vines that round the thatch-eaves run;
> To bend with apples the moss'd cottage-trees,
> And fill all fruit with ripeness to the core.

Keats found fault with Shelley for the thinness of his verse and
urged him to 'load every rift with ore'. For Keats was in no haste
to reach the future. He lingered in thoughtful contemplation of
all the beauty there had been in the past of mankind and all the
charms displayed by Nature in the present. His pole-star was
beauty, in Nature, in mankind, in art. He seized upon beauty
wherever it had been plentiful on earth—in Greek mythology,
in medieval legend, in great poetry. Far from prophesying about
it as a thing of the future, he found it had come to pass but was
already distant, and he mourned its disappearance. It was with
profound sadness that he thought of Ruth 'in tears amid the alien
corn' or evoked the palaces of faërie. The future seemed to him
to menace that beauty which was the sole object of worship, the
only higher truth. The analytical science which destroyed the
lovely legends seemed to him horrible. Why then hasten, and
towards what goal? The poet's role is to glean what remains of
beauty in the world. Poetry for Keats is neither rushing wind
nor headlong current, but a lake with wooded and flowery shores;
sky, flowers, and woods are reflected in its deep waters, motionless
in that strange mirror.

Born in London in 1795, the son of a livery-stable keeper, John Keats was intended for medicine and received only a scanty education, which included no Greek. But his poetic vocation asserted itself against all obstacles. Save for some short journeys, of which one was a walking-tour in the Lake district and Scotland, Keats was never to know much more of Nature than what he could see of it on the outskirts of the capital. He knew of Greek mythology only what he could learn from a classical dictionary and the marbles in the British Museum. Perhaps this very deprivation was partly the cause of the yearning quality in his feeling for Nature and his passion for Hellenic beauty. After a few juvenile verses already full of rare touches, in 1818 Keats published his poem *Endymion*, written in couplets free of structural constraint, a veritable chaos of images and legends. Some pages of it are admirable, but its confusion drew down the sarcasms of the *Quarterly Review*. There is a rich strangeness in it, and much true poetry tainted with mannerisms for which Keats was the first to blush the moment it was finished. The growth of his powers was so rapid that by 1819 he had published a volume which included such masterpieces as *Lamia*, *Isabella*, *The Eve of St. Agnes*, and a fragment of the *Hyperion* in which he designed to tell the downfall of the primitive gods of Greece before the advent of younger gods endowed with supreme beauty. Besides these, he had already written the odes (*Ode to a Nightingale*, *Ode on a Grecian Urn*, *To Autumn*, *Ode to Psyche*, &c.) which are the most exquisite expression of his genius. But his health was undermined by consumption, and he had given the world only these marvellous foretastes when he died at the age of 26.

Other poets who have died young have owed some part of their fame to their untimely end. But Keats's work as he left it has a beauty that is absolute and wholly individual. The influences of Spenser, of Shakespeare, and especially of Milton can be felt in it, but they do not dominate it. His memories of the great poets of the Renaissance do not enslave him; they enrich him. Whatever he borrows reappears transmuted; it becomes his own. Except in *La Belle Dame Sans Merci*, where in the briefest possible space he achieved the highest perfection of the ballad, Keats cultivated that wealth of detail which loads every word and every note of his poetry. Shelley's is not the only verse that seems fluid and unsubstantial beside his. No other English poet brings together so many riches in a single line or a single stanza. Keats must be read slowly, so heavily is each syllable charged with associations and echoes. Apparently free from all moral dogma, his poetry has the most compelling enchantment for lovers of pure beauty.

Thomas Moore. Intervening between the two generations that have just been dealt with, Thomas Moore (1779-1852) came nearer than any other poet at the beginning of the nineteenth century to rivalling the successive reputations of Scott and Byron both in Great Britain and on the Continent, for the Lake poets were still either unknown to, or scorned by, the public. Like Scott and Byron, Moore had the gift of telling romantic stories in verse. *Lalla Rookh* (1817) was one of the most famous of Oriental poems, and the spirited prose of its setting and the varied interest of the verse tales can still charm and captivate the reader. With less success and against his natural bent, Moore tried, in *The Loves of the Angels*, to imitate Byron's irreligious effrontery. His chief title to poetic fame rests, however, on the *Irish Melodies*, in which, as an Irish poet, he did for his native land what Burns had done for Scotland. Patriotic themes alternate with sentimental ones in this collection. The union of the verse and the music is accomplished with rare ease. It is true that Moore lacked Burns's picturesqueness and his lively humour. He is often artificial, and he wrote for London drawing-rooms, not Irish cottages. His verse is glutted with scents and melodies, and sometimes they are too cheap; but the best of his songs have an undeniable elegiac charm.

Moore was a droll and a wit as well as an elegiac poet. With Byron he waged war against the reactionary government in *The Two-penny Post-bag* (1812-13), letters purporting to have been intercepted in the post. They are full of spirit and satire, but now require to be read with an elaborate commentary because of their allusions to the events of the day. *The Fudge Family in Paris* (1818), on the other hand, in which Moore records, after the manner of Smollett in *Humphry Clinker*, the travel impressions of various members of an English family, is still amusing; the subject is a stay in Paris after the peace in the days of the Holy Alliance. The verse is animated and shows the spirit of true comedy, and the satire is softened by humour. Thus the wit of the eighteenth century survives in Moore's work mingled with various romantic influences. Moore's talent, less profound than that of the great poets, was more readily appreciated, but has lost its freshness more rapidly than theirs.

Samuel Rogers. Samuel Rogers (1763–1855), who had produced in *The Pleasures of Memory* a didactic poem of pure classical form, borrowed a slight romantic tinge from *Childe Harold* for his poem *Italy* (1822), a mixture of verse and prose which, although it lacks vigour and concentration, is still pleasant reading. But Rogers's chief link with the romantic movement is to be found not in his verse but in his friendships.

Campbell. Thomas Campbell (1777–1844) is another link between the two ages of poetry. His *Pleasures of Hope* had shown romantic aspirations invading the domain of Pope's couplet. Later he attempted, with little success, a verse romance, *Gertrude of Wyoming* (1809), in the manner of Scott, but using the Spenserian stanza. He is remembered, however, almost solely by one or two martial ballads from among many that are either sentimental or melodramatic. His name instantly calls up some of the most popular of battle poems: *Ye Mariners of England* (1801), *Hohenlinden* (1803), and *The Battle of the Baltic* (1809). Their patriotism is often aggressive, but they have a straightforward style and an inspiriting rhythm.

Landor. Walter Savage Landor (1775–1864) and Leigh Hunt (1784–1859) are primarily prose-writers; but their verse has a claim to notice, especially that of Landor, who opposed the often verbose and shapeless romanticism of his contemporaries in the name of classic art—the classic art not of Pope but of Greece and Rome. Landor was isolated in his generation both by his political convictions, which were those of a republican aristocrat of the Miltonic type, and by the character of his poetry. He laid down as a principle the necessity for condensation and restraint—qualities which conflicted in Landor with a natural exuberance and abundant rhetoric, to which his prose bears witness. They are deliberately and it seems wilfully adopted. But sometimes in this kind of poetry he succeeds admirably; he is the English master of the epigram in the Greek sense—the poem in a few lines with the relief and the repose of sculpture. Similar merits are apparent in the poem *Gebir* (1798), in which the Eastern story is often rendered obscure by extreme conciseness, and the plays *Count Julian* (1812) and *The Siege of Ancona*. The *Hellenics*—translations into English of heroic idylls which he had originally written in Latin—published in 1867, approach nearer to perfection.

Leigh Hunt. Leigh Hunt had less poetic talent, but was more deeply involved in the romantic movement. He was to exercise an early and not always happy influence on Keats. He occasionally admitted into his poetry a familiarity that bordered upon vulgarity, for which he was not undeservedly scoffed at as the head of 'the cockney school'. His best-known work is *The Story of Rimini* (1816), in which he once more gave the couplet the varied rhythm (the looseness too) it had had in the time of Elizabeth, and freed it from the monotonous symmetry of Pope: but it is by a few short poems in the anthologies that he survives.

Thomas Hood. One of the most highly gifted poets at the beginning of the century was Thomas Hood (1799-1845), who at the age of 23 produced *Lycus the Centaur*, a striking piece of description, and of great imaginative daring. To it he soon added the graceful and melancholy fantasy *The Plea of the Midsummer Fairies*, and the sombre and dramatic *Dream of Eugene Aram*. But all his life Hood had to struggle against ill health and poverty. In order to live he had to renounce serious poetry and to exploit his rich vein of comedy, overflowing with puns and nonsense. It was by his *Odes and Addresses to Great People* (1825) and by his *Whims and Oddities* that he made an impression on the public. Nevertheless he continued to produce from time to time poems of a loftier type, sometimes, as in *Miss Kilmansegg and her Precious Leg*, concealing profound sentiment and powerful satire beneath a grotesque exterior, sometimes achieving the most poignant descriptive poetry, as in *The Haunted House*. More popular than any of the others to-day are *The Song of the Shirt* and *The Bridge of Sighs*, in which Hood managed to express, without lapsing into mere sentimentality, the misery of a poor sweated sempstress and the pity felt at the suicide of a lost woman. He found for these poems, and especially for the second of them, most original metres and rhymes, which heightened their pathos.

Minor Poets. The feeling for social misery that here inspired Hood appears again in Ebenezer Elliott (1781–1849), a simple Sheffield labourer, who in his *Corn Law Rhymes* (1828) made the cry of hunger ring forth with a bitter strength that makes us overlook his excess of rhetoric and his often antiquated style. Elliott also had a sincere love of the countryside, which is conveyed in more than one poem not unworthy for exactness of observation and feeling to be put beside those of Wordsworth.

Robert Bloomfield (1766–1823), who began life as a farm-servant and who in 1798 published *The Farmer's Boy*, was nearer to Crabbe than to Wordsworth. Like Crabbe, he held to the couplet and the style of the eighteenth century; but the tone of *Rural Tales* (1810) is as joyful as that of the author of *The Village* was gloomy.

Another peasant poet, John Clare (1793–1864), owed his reputation in part to the very humbleness of his lot. His *Poems Descriptive of Rural Life and Scenery* (1820) show that he possessed qualities of sympathetic observation.

There are many secondary poets in this period who show a feeble reflection of the masters. Mrs. Hemans (1793–1835), copious, tuneful, and sentimental, is clearly under the influence of Wordsworth. Hymns, pleasant easy descriptive pieces, and appeals to simple and pure affections are the best part of her abundant, rather superficial verse.

The Christian sentiment which inspired her appears at full strength in *The Christian Year* (1827) of John Keble (1792–1866), who put a tender feeling for nature into his hymning of the rites of the English church.

James Hogg (1770–1835), 'the Ettrick Shepherd', may be linked with his fellow countryman Walter Scott. He took his inspiration from the ballads of his native land, and wrote some

very fine ones himself in his *Queen's Wake*, while Scottish Jacobite
poetry inspired his *Jacobite Relics of Scotland* (1819–21). To Burns
is due a little of the inspiration of Robert Tannahill (1774–1810),
who has left us some love-songs, and to Scott much of that of
William Motherwell (1797–1835), author of some stirring martial
ballads on Viking themes.

The son of the great Coleridge, Hartley Coleridge (1796–1849)
inherited his father's poetic gifts but also his weakness of character;
and intemperance ruined a talent full of promise. Among his work,
which includes some remarkable prose criticism, may be singled
out his *Sonnets* (1838). They bear witness to a rare culture and
reflect Wordsworth's influence rather than that of his father.

The most original of the poets who may be grouped with Shelley
and Keats is Thomas Lovell Beddoes (1803–49). Beddoes combined
an admiration for their poetry with that of the most gloomy
Elizabethan tragedians, Webster and Tourneur. He has all the
extravagance of the Renaissance and mingles the playful with the
gruesome. *The Bride's Tragedy* (1822) and *Death's Jest-Book*
(finished in its first form in 1826) contain lovely songs, full of
originality and pathos.

A few years after the afore-named, Richard Harris Barham
(1788–1845) a priest in ordinary of the chapels royal, was to
triumph in the comical and whimsical manner. His *Ingoldsby
Legends* first collected in 1840, were a unique series of burlesque
tales in surprisingly dexterous verse. No parodies in the mock-
heroic style had a more lasting and popular success through the
Victorian age.

George Darley (1795–1846), also a keen student of the older
English literature produced in 1827, *Sylvia, or the May Queen*,
but his best poem, *Nepenthe*, circulated privately in his life-time.
This difficult but beautiful allegory of man's life only appeared
in print in 1897.

The Romantic period, from 1799 to 1830, is chiefly distinguished
by a lofty gravity and imaginative ambition, but it was far
from indifferent to wit and gaiety. We have seen that these
qualities abound in the poetry of Byron, Moore, and Hood. They
appear almost alone and without alloy in that of James and

Horace Smith, whose *Rejected Addresses* (1812) are parodies of contemporary poets as just as they are amusing; and in that of W. M. Praed (1802–39), a master of light society verse which shows an adroit mixture of elegance, fancy, and banter.

Prose

The Novel from 1800 to 1830. The novel of terror, embodying one of the characteristics of romanticism, continued to prosper until it was eclipsed by the triumph of Sir Walter Scott. To Mrs. Radcliffe succeeded Matthew Gregory Lewis, who imported from Germany some of the more superficial and grosser elements of the literary revival. After *Ambrosio, or the Monk*, which had caused great excitement in 1795, he wrote his *Tales of Terror* (1800), *Tales of Wonder* (1801), and *Romantic Tales* (1808), attempting no more than effects of melodramatic violence. Charles Robert Maturin, an Irish clergyman, was more sincere in his use of terror, and more serious in the employment of the supernatural; in 1807 he produced *The Fatal Revenge* and in 1820 the masterpiece of this class of literature, *Melmoth the Wanderer*, in which he was not at pains to explain the mystery in the fashion of Mrs. Radcliffe, but prolonged the horror to the very end. Mrs. Shelley, Godwin's daughter, and the poet's wife, enhanced the tale of marvels with a philosophical idea in *Frankenstein*, in which she imagined the creation by human science of a monstrous being devoid of all feeling.

Jane Austen. The novel of terror had its opposite in the work of Jane Austen (1775–1817), who delightfully made fun of the passion for Mrs. Radcliffe's horrors. A direct literary descendant of Addison, Goldsmith, and Miss Burney, and an admirer of Cowper and Crabbe, she produced between 1796 and 1816, during the wars against the French Revolution and Napoleon, work that for calmness, delicacy, exquisite touch, and miniature grace has no rival in the whole of English literature. In the half-dozen novels she wrote, this daughter of a Hampshire rector set herself to study the ways of feminine affection, the delicacies and distresses of young and sensitive but not passionate hearts, their mistakes and their sorrows in first love. Around these young ladies she placed, with a lively though restrained sense of comedy, and with perfect exactness of touch, the various figures of the gentlefolk of a country neighbourhood. She did not seek to instruct her readers; her aim was to draw a picture that would amuse them. Within the narrow limits which she set for herself, she achieved a finished realism, with qualities of the highest wit and elegance.

Her quizzical spirit shows itself at its liveliest in the first novel she sketched as early as 1797 *Pride and Prejudice.* Delicacy of analysis and a more serious mood are increasingly characteristic of her other works, *Sense and Sensibility, Northanger Abbey, Emma, Mansfield Park,* and *Persuasion.* But all her work bears a unique imprint. Not troubled like the Romantics by the desire to prophesy, Jane Austen knew neither their heights nor their depths. She kept firmly to the middle path, and, knowing as she did how to set bounds both to her talent and to her field of observation, she was better able than they to produce work of consummate art without blemish or excess, illuminated in all its parts with a delicate and equal light.

Miss Mitford. Miss Mary Russell Mitford (1786–1855) wrote no novels, but she fondly depicted the village of Three Mile Cross, near Reading, with its landscape and the life and customs of its people, in *Our Village: Sketches of Rural Life, Character, and Scenery* (1819–32). The minuteness of her drawing equals that of Miss Austen, but it was principally the countryside that interested her. The rustic setting is the chief element in her picture; in the novels of Miss Austen it is barely touched. In a series of detached sketches she succeeds in giving with slight successive touches a true and yet attractive impression of her village. More fortunate in her pleasant model than Crabbe had been, she was able to be realistic without ceasing to find savour in life.

Educational novels, so numerous in the previous generation, reach their zenith with Maria Edgeworth (1767–1849), who enlivens her moral purpose with a multitude of vivid observations, both in the books she intended for children, in her novel, *Belinda* (1801), and in her *Tales of Fashionable Life.* She did not limit herself entirely to the didactic field, and she showed that she was equally capable of depicting the people and the countryside of

PLATE XXXIII

FANNY BURNEY

JANE AUSTEN

CHARLOTTE BRONTË

GEORGE ELIOT

her native Ireland. Her local sketches are full both of penetrating satire and of sympathy. *Castle Rackrent* (1800), *The Absentee* (1810), and *Ormond* (1817) are remarkably truthful studies of a unique people.

At almost the same period another Irishwoman, Lady Morgan, was also producing lively pictures of the manners of her country in novels, of which the best known are *The Wild Irish Girl* (1806) and *The O' Briens and the O' Flaherties* (1827).

Walter Scott was generously to confess that Miss Edgeworth's books had given him the idea of doing for Scotland what she had done for Ireland. In fact Scotland hardly needed a foreign example. Before Scott's time there had appeared the domestic novels of Elizabeth Hamilton and Mary Brunton, and Jane Porter's historical novel *The Scottish Chiefs* (1810). Parallel with Scott's novels appeared Miss S. E. Ferrier's books, *Marriage* (1818), *The Inheritance* (1824), *Destiny* (1831), and the more important works of John Galt, *The Ayrshire Legatees, Annals of the Parish* (1821), and *The Entail* (1823), microscopic local studies, confined to some Scottish village but seasoned with the most simple and charming humour.

Walter Scott. It was from this lineage that the novels of Walter Scott were, in part, derived; but every feature in them was ennobled by the genius that could give an epic scope and movement to his stories. Scott's novels betray the same original impulse as his poems, the same imaginative joy in the re-creation of the past; but the novel offered him a more adaptable and wider field than the narrative poem. It gave him better opportunity for the display of his varied gifts, his antiquarian knowledge, his observation of life and character, his delight in popular as well as courtly scenes, and his rich humour. He and Byron, alone in their generation, were destined, for very different reasons, to fill the world with their fame. Although in England the first place in the English romantic movement is not given now-a-days to Scott and Byron, there is no doubt that they have always occupied that place, and still keep it, in the opinion of the rest of Europe.

Scott's first novel, *Waverley*, begun about 1805 but not completed and published until 1814, goes back for its theme only to the eighteenth century. In a sense it was as much a geographical as an historical novel, and it delighted the public by its pictures of Highlanders and the Highlands. He came even nearer to his own day in his next two novels, *Guy Mannering* and *The Antiquary*, the action of which is laid in the time of Scott's own youth. It was only with *Old Mortality* that he really turned to the past, and told how the Covenanters took up arms and were defeated in the days of Charles II; and he returned to the eighteenth century immediately afterwards with *Rob Roy* and *The Heart of Mid-lothian* (1818). In *The Bride of Lammermoor* and *The Legend of Montrose*, although he went back to the seventeenth century, he still kept strictly to Scottish soil. These, his first and finest novels, have the advantage of being placed in the country he knew best and in the historical periods with which he was most intimately familiar. Without sacrificing verisimilitude, he could to a large extent combine tales of historical happenings with descriptions of scenes and manners based on his own direct observation, particularly of the common people, whose essential characters had changed little during the previous hundred years. He thus brought Scotland into European romanticism, of which it may be said to have become one of the essential elements.

It was thus, by such prudent degrees, that Scott advanced to-wards the historical novel proper. In 1819 he surprised the public with *Ivanhoe*, in which he abandoned Scotland for England, and tried to paint a picture of the twelfth century, of the regency of John Lackland, and the half-legendary figure of Richard Cœur de Lion. Here, helped by his acquaintance with the literature of the age of chivalry, he produced what was, in spite of many conven-tional and romantic traits, the first plausible picture of the Middle Ages to stir the imagination both of the public and of historians.

He did not abandon Scotland altogether, for he returned to it in order to describe the reign of Mary Stuart in *The Monastery* and *The Abbot*; but he now set to produce a whole series of purely English novels; he threw himself into the England of Elizabeth in *Kenilworth*, the England of James I in *The Fortunes of Nigel*, and in *Peveril of the Peak* into that of Charles II, to whom he had already devoted *The Legend of Montrose*. He brought Cromwell on to the scene in *Woodstock* (1826). He changed his ground in 1823 with *Quentin Durward*, which has for its scene the France of Louis XI, and in 1825 with *The Talisman*, in which he deals once more with Richard Cœur de Lion, this time in the Holy Land, warring against the chivalrous Saladin.

The range of Scott's subjects is even greater than this incomplete enumeration would lead one to believe. The quality of the novels is doubtless unequal, and the Scottish novels have a solidity and truth which have enabled them to withstand the assaults of time better than those in which Scott pictured foreign lands or the very remote past. On the other hand it was the latter, particularly *Ivanhoe* and *Quentin Durward*, which gave the strongest active impulse to the development of the great historical novel, both in England and on the Continent.

To the accomplishment of this huge task Scott brought varied gifts which have rarely been found in combination in his imitators. His knowledge of history had been increased by copious reading since his earliest youth. His own contribution was the zest of the story-teller; his natural heartiness made him love life in all its manifestations. He had an innate sense of the picturesque, developed by his passion for antiquarianism and collecting. His Tory sentiment, which had from the beginning turned him from the revolutionary enthusiasm that for a time at least inflamed almost all his contemporaries, gave him a natural sympathy with the days of chivalry. On the whole he respected history more scrupulously than most of his successors. The romance in his tales involves as a rule only the characters of his own invention and leaves almost unchanged the historical figures: Claverhouse, Louis XI, Charles the Bold, Mary Stuart, James I, Cromwell, Prince Charles Edward, and the rest.

Scott is not without his faults and his limitations. His love interest is apt to be insipid and monotonous; his heroes and particularly his heroines, with their conventional natures and their correct behaviour, are at variance with the passionate and violent background of the old stories. His fluent style is not very artistic and the effect is often heavy and dragging. But in the end objections and criticisms are swept away by the broad powerful current of his narrative genius. Scott was one of the greatest of all who

have enriched the popular imagination, the rival of Homer and
Shakespeare in fertility. He was a Romantic in his love of the
picturesque and his interest in the Middle Ages. But he had
but little sympathy for the romantic cult of mystery, and his
vast literary output is in the rational and realistic style of the
eighteenth century.

Reviewers and Critics

Other Prose-writers. Poetry and the novel were not the only
forms of literature to be invaded by the romantic spirit at this
time. The widespread influence of the new Renaissance made
itself felt in almost every realm of thought, transforming literary
criticism and the essay, and planting the first seeds of revival in
philosophy, theology, and history.

The spirit of the eighteenth century and the great rationalist
movement did not, indeed, vanish suddenly. On the contrary,
this was the period of the development of the Utilitarian doctrines
which Jeremy Bentham had enunciated before the French Revolution. Their vehicle, the *Westminster Review*, was founded in 1824.
The Utilitarian creed was applied to political economy by David
Ricardo in his *Principles of Political Economy* (1817), which
extolled Free Trade, and by Thomas Robert Malthus (1766–1834),
who saw the remedy for pauperism in the restriction of the birth-
rate. These were the two Radical thinkers who shepherded the
country into the paths of democracy. Again, the Scottish philosophy of common sense originated by Thomas Reid (1710–96)
continued to be upheld by Dugald Stewart (1753–1828), who
based his doctrine on intuition and experience. His disciple Sir
James Mackintosh (1765–1832) began with a brilliant refutation
of Burke in *Vindiciae Gallicae*; but little by little he absorbed the
ideas of his great adversary and ended by defending the British
Constitution in the name of the very doctrines of liberty and progress upheld by the Radicals who attacked it.

The wittiest spokesman of the Whigs at this time was the
clergyman Sydney Smith (1771–1845), one of the founders of, and
principal contributors to, the *Edinburgh Review*, who conducted
a most active and amusing campaign against the conservative

spirit of the Tories. Sydney Smith was the promoter of most of the humanitarian and political reforms at the beginning of the century. His most celebrated campaign is the one he undertook for Catholic emancipation in his *Letters of Peter Plymley* (1809). He put liveliness and good humour at the service of good sense. Entirely free from Romantic mysticism, he recalls Swift without the latter's bitterness and with a love of his fellow men that hardly ever showed itself in his great predecessor.

In 1812 William Cobbett (1762–1835) founded the *Weekly Political Register* which became the organ of popular Radicalism. As the son of a countryman he knew how to talk to the people and especially to farmers. Free from all doctrine and theory, inconsistent, vacillating between Whigs and Tories, he had a direct grasp of facts and relied on his personal experience and observation (*Rural Rides*, collected in 1830). His career as an agitator did not prevent him from loving the English countryside and describing its scenery as well as its life. Cobbett's work, which was considerable in extent, sometimes vulgar but always strong and healthy, made him one of the most active promoters of the parliamentary reform of 1832.

Political and religious Romanticism found an interpreter in Coleridge who, turning towards the Germans, and especially Kant and Schelling, took as his basis the Kantian distinction between pure reason and practical reason in order to trace the limits of the Understanding and to maintain the cause of that higher Reason which he describes as intuition, spiritual vision, poesy. Small fragments only of his ideas are expressed in the journal *The Friend* (1809) or in essays like that *On the Constitution of Church and State* (1828). But Coleridge effected much more by conversation than by his books, and according to the testimony of John Stuart Mill he did more than any one else 'to shape the opinions among young men who can be said to have any opinions at all'.

Such were some of the aspects of English thought during the first third of the nineteenth century. The works of which we have spoken belong rather to philosophy or politics than to pure literature. The great development of prose writing in this period showed itself chiefly in the literary criticism and in the essay, and it was here that, outside the novel, it attained its most striking effects.

It must not be supposed that all criticism at this time was 'Romantic'. On the contrary, the great reviews founded at the beginning of the century, the *Edinburgh Review*, a Whig organ started in 1802, and the *Quarterly Review*, which arose in opposition to it in 1809 as the Tory organ, agreed in denouncing the new poetry. The spirit of the eighteenth century still dominated their literary criticism. Francis Jeffrey (1773–1850), though he gave high praise to *Childe Harold* and the Waverley Novels led a lively attack upon the Lake poets, especially Wordsworth, and it was his review, the *Edinburgh*, that ridiculed Byron's first poem. Gifford in the *Quarterly* did cruel execution on Keats's *Endymion*. It was the same with the earlier numbers of *Blackwood's Magazine*, where J. G. Lockhart devoted himself from 1817 to 1825 to violent assaults on the Romantics, and where only Walter Scott, his future father-in-law, was spared. To find a champion with the public the innovators had to wait until John Wilson ('Christopher North') succeeded Lockhart as chief writer for *Blackwood's*. Thus the renown of the Lake poets only spread slowly, after a long period of hostility and ridicule. Nevertheless, certain Romantic poets like Wordsworth set forth their ideas in the prefaces to their collections, and, moreover, they found brothers-in-arms, friends, and disciples, ready to defend their verse and reveal its aims and its beauties; to reverse the literary judgements of the preceding century, explore the national past, rehabilitate the despised ages, and in a word reform the public's idea of poetry. And some of these critics— Lamb, Hazlitt, De Quincey, and Leigh Hunt—were also remarkable writers.

It is significant that the very style of these men showed a reaction against the so often abstract prose of the eighteenth century, with its short and balanced sentences. They had, like the poets, a rich imagination, and they searched after singularity and individuality in style. Some of them went back to the age of Milton, Sir Thomas Browne and Jeremy Taylor, and cultivated the periodic style. They needed parentheses to express the shades of a thought more complex than that of their immediate predecessors.

Coleridge. In the new criticism it was again Coleridge who took the lead. His own tendencies were strengthened by the German criticism of Lessing, Schlegel, and J. P. Richter, who led with a sometimes unjust violence, a reaction against the doctrines of the classical age, and especially against the French theatre, finding their ideal in Shakespearian drama. This had long been admired for its life and its poetry, but it had been taken for granted that Shakespeare was ignorant of all artistic rules: that he had genius but lacked art. The Romantics, on the other hand, believed that Shakespeare possessed supreme art, art no longer mechanical but organic like a work of Nature, and, like it, able to fuse all sorts of different elements into a harmonious whole, to combine tragedy and comedy, realism and idealism, instead of keeping them separate. It was on these principles that Coleridge resumed the study of Shakespeare in his lectures of 1811–12. The same spirit informs his comments, often disconnected but new and suggestive, though sometimes excessively subtle, on English authors. In his *Biographia Literaria* (1817) he applied his marvellous analytical faculty to Wordsworth's poetry, stating both its merits and its defects with such exactness that at the first attempt he produced a final judgement on his contemporary.

Lamb. Coleridge's school-friend Charles Lamb (1775–1834), without his philosophical ambition, possessed an easier and more attractive way of writing. He helped the general public to widen the field of its reading and reconsider the pronouncements of the eighteenth-century critics. Charles Lamb was a friend of the Lake poets, but he passed his life as a clerk in a London office, far removed from natural scenes. He was an ardent student of the Elizabethan dramatists. In 1807 he and his sister Mary published their *Tales from Shakespeare*, which have passed through numerous editions and have brought the plays of the great poet within the reach of children. In his *Specimens of the English Dramatic Poets contemporary with Shakespeare* (1808), he selected the finest scenes from the unequal plays of the Renaissance theatre, and brought out their merits by means of commentaries that were equally remarkable for their justice and for their warmth of sympathy. Little by little he covered the field of English letters, now dealing with the prose writers of the age of Milton, now with the comic authors of the Restoration, and illuminating with his imaginative genius periods and authors neglected or despised for more than one hundred years.

Lamb was not only a critic, but a poet, some of whose touching lines, like *The Old Familiar Faces,* have lived. Above all, however, he was a refined humanist, whose smile could be both satirical and tender. He revealed his own tastes and memories in his prose *Essays of Elia* (1820 onwards). Here he did for London what Wordsworth was doing for the mountains, finding in it boundless sources of delight for mind and heart, studying its people, its beggars, its chimney-sweeps, as Wordsworth studied the shepherds of Westmorland. The great mass of humanity amid which he lived inspired a kind of writing in which drollery was mingled with affection. In the very streets of the city he found an inexhaustible source of instruction and enjoyment, just as the Lake poets found it in their valleys and streams. Though he did not write of them in verse, his exquisitely wrought prose, with its rich literary tone, preserves the poetic history of words, and enriches them with echoes, scarcely less than does Keats's poetry. A fancy which in daily life and in his *Letters* ran readily to jests and puns gives a lively gaiety to his pages, and counterbalances their bookish pedantry. The whole forms one of the most palatable compounds in English literature.

Hazlitt. William Hazlitt (1778–1830) was a friend of Lamb, knew the Lake poets in their early days, and began his career with a great admiration for Coleridge. He brought to literary criticism a temperament harsher and more passionate than Lamb's. His revolutionary opinions, which he preserved to the end of his life, brought him at first into sympathy with the Lake poets, only to alienate him from them when they cast into the flames what they had once worshipped. Hence came grudges and indignation, which repeatedly disturbed the impartiality of Hazlitt's judgement. But these causes of injustice were present only when he discussed his contemporaries. Usually he can be followed with perfect safety when he studies the past, as in his *Characters of Shakespeare's Plays* (1817), *Lectures on the English*

Poets (1819), *Lectures on the English Comic Writers* (1819), and *Lectures on the Dramatic Literature of the Age of Elizabeth* (1820). These studies have a particular character of their own. Hazlitt cared nothing for history or biography. He seized on a play or a poem and gave in a direct vigorous manner a reader's impressions of the work or the characters. He expressed himself in a series of incisive, brilliant, and surprisingly acute statements. He goes straight to the core of the matter without preamble or deviation, and each shaft of his light penetrates to the very heart of his subject. He showed no less power of intuitive perception in his *Spirit of the Age* (1825), in which he reviews the writers of his own time, but here allowances must be made for his animosities. Since Coleridge left only fragments of criticism, and Lamb confined himself to the role of editor and commentator, Hazlitt was really the leading Romantic critic, and it is one of his titles to the name that he was able to do justice to Pope and the eighteenth century evenwhile he glorified the Renaissance and appreciated the value of some innovations of his own age.

Like Lamb he was as much an essayist as a critic. In *The Round Table* (1817), *Table Talk* (1821–2), and *The Plain Speaker* (1826), he produced his equivalent of the *Essays of Elia*. His essays show less charm of personality and style but have a frankness and virility, and also a touch of misanthropy, that are all his own.

Leigh Hunt. Beside Hazlitt, the figure of Leigh Hunt (1784–1859) is more or less eclipsed. A poet, novelist, and a dramatist, Hunt had less power of concentrating his efforts. He was above all a journalist, and as such was long held in suspicion for his liberalism and for his attacks on the Prince Regent. There is a certain diffuseness in his work, which rarely attains the first rank. But he had spirit, humour, and fancy. He was an originator in theatrical criticism and helped to restore to a place of honour more than one undeservedly forgotten page from the past. His many volumes have lost the freshness of their appeal, but a selection of his miscellaneous essays can still be read with pleasure, and his *Autobiography* is attractive because it retraces his troubled career and makes the Romantic generation live again.

De Quincey. Thomas de Quincey (1785-1859) was as prodigal of his talents as Leigh Hunt. Two books which have kept their interest stand out, happily for him, from his copious and varied work: *The Confessions of an English Opium-Eater* (1821), and the *Reminiscences of the English Lake Poets*. The first of these is memorable by reason of the strange visions it calls up of the gorgeous and terrible nightmares suffered by the opium-eater. In these passages De Quincey's prose attains a lyrical, sonorous, and melodious eloquence, the equal of which is not to be found elsewhere. It would be verbose declamation but for the majesty of the visions that are evoked and for the incomparable volume of his reverberating organ-notes.

De Quincey was himself the victim of the opium whose effects he describes. Hence the failures of his intellectual energy. His work is chaotic and inconsistent. Although he was well-read, and one of the first Englishmen to initiate himself into German philosophy, ephemeral articles were the only result of his learning. He displayed his gifts, which were those of a psychologist rather than a literary critic, to better advantage in his reminiscences of the Lake poets, in whose neighbourhood he had spent several years. No writer has penetrated further into the mind and personality of these poets or displayed less scruple in revealing the less worthy features of their characters and their lives. Mischievous gossiping is here as evident as the desire for truth.

De Quincey's prose, which is often highly poetical, is a remarkable creation, slightly spoiled by an art that is too obvious and comes very near to artifice.

Landor. Landor, remarkable as a poet, was a great prose-writer. The *Imaginary Conversations between Certain People of Importance in their Day*, written between 1824 and 1829, are of a quite different order of beauty from the pages of De Quincey. The latter had from the Romantics a taste for mystery and for morbid psychology. Landor, in spite of his eccentric and violent character, was a disciple of the classical school. He strove for lucidity of style and in his most vehement passages still took the rhetoric of ancient writers for his guide. His *Imaginary Conversations* consist of dialogues between characters of every age, from distant Graeco-

Roman antiquity to his own nearest contemporaries. It cannot exactly be said that he revealed the soul of his personages, for whether he lends them his own sentiments or puts into their mouths the very ideas he wishes to attack, they are the interpreters of his own opinions, which were often capricious and blinded by passion. He was tending towards the monologues in which Browning was to exercise his moral activity in attempting to probe the minds of the most varied personages, but he is too full of himself to have the impartiality which this kind of composition requires. Thus it is chiefly on account of their often admirable language that the *Imaginary Conversations* occupy a high rank in the English prose of the first third of the nineteenth century.

Peacock. Landor, classic though he might be in form, was linked with the Romantics by the warmth of his temperament. During the full flow of the Romantic movement it was left to Thomas Love Peacock (1785–1866) to play the part of the intelligent and ironic observer of its excesses. His mocking spirit, on the watch for every prejudice, recalls that of Voltaire. He attacked the Romanticists with irony or with parody, not only ridiculing the Lake poets whom he detested, but poking fun at Shelley whom he liked. For this satire he used the form of the novel, if the name of novel can be given to those eccentric works *Headlong Hall* (1816), *Melincourt* (1817), *Nightmare Abbey* (1818), *Maid Marian* (1822), *Misfortunes of Elphin* (1829), *Crotchet Castle* (1831), and *Gryll Grange* (1860). They are amusing fantasies with scarcely any plot; the characters are merely outlines. Peacock was a learned Hellenist and his style would be pedantic were it not for the humorous use he makes of it. He had his share of enthusiasm for Nature and love of old legends, but he represented in his age the protest of a sceptical mind against the various idealisms of his great contemporaries.

XXVII

THE VICTORIAN ERA (1830–80)

General characteristics of the Period

STRICTLY speaking, the Victorian age ought to correspond with the reign of Queen Victoria and extend from 1837 to 1901. But literary movements rarely coincide with the exact year of a royal accession or death. Without ignoring the personal influence for dignity and propriety that the Queen exercised over an important part of English society, we must think mainly of the social and economic factors which so greatly changed the politics, the customs, and the daily life of the nation. Thus Catholic emancipation (1829), Parliamentary reform (1832), the suppression of slavery in the Colonies (1833), and the construction of the first railway (1830), preceded by some years the coronation of the Queen. On the other hand, after two generations which themselves differed perceptibly from one another, a new spirit of discontent and of bold criticism manifested itself, particularly after 1880, and gave to the end of the long reign an aspect of stronger and stronger re-action against the characteristics which we have grown accustomed to range under the name of Victorian.

From the literary point of view this great age appears at first as a continuation of Romanticism, but with distinct features which grow gradually more defined and more pronounced, and impart to it its particular character. It was the period in which the conflict between religious feeling and the scientific spirit, between mysticism and rationalism, became intense and wide-spread. Opposite those who detached themselves from dogma were ranged those who, haunted by regret for the age of Faith, hoped to revive primitive orthodoxy and the practices, rites, and ceremonials of the past. This great debate was, however, chiefly inward and individual, although few consciences escaped it, and a good many were troubled or bruised by it[1]; nevertheless the

---

[1] The best-known expressions of this inward conflict were published after 1880, but they refer, as far as the actual period of the conflict goes, to the preceding epoch. Such are the *Autobiography of Mark Rutherford* (1881–5)

characteristic feature of this period in comparison with the following one is the prudence and reserve with which novel ideas on the subject of faith and morality were ordinarily expressed. There was general agreement in avoiding scandal, and the few who transgressed were black-listed by public opinion.

The prophetic spirit of the great Romantics still survived; but it had passed from the poets to the prose-writers. The guides to whom men turned when uncertain of their path were, apart from the scholars proper and the philosophers, such thinkers as Carlyle or Ruskin, and later, for a more limited public, Matthew Arnold. The poets still held a high rank and a large audience, but it cannot be said that they exercised an influence on thought and conduct equal to that of the writers above-mentioned.

Carlyle. We may begin the study of the Victorian era with Thomas Carlyle (1795–1881), not only because he was in the van but because his voice resounded in his generation with more force and aroused wider echoes than any other.

Carlyle's start in life was difficult: the son of a master-mason in a Scottish village, he was born into an uncultured family with a father who was upright and hard and a rigid Calvinist. He fought for his first education with obstinate toil. Destined at first to be a Presbyterian minister, he studied at the University of Edinburgh, where he cut himself loose from orthodoxy. After a crisis in which his ideals threatened to founder, he at length recovered his true course when he began in 1821 to devote himself to German studies. He had had forerunners here, among others Coleridge and De Quincey, but the intense labour with which he translated and analysed German writers established a closer link between himself and Germany. Though he was sensitive to Schiller's idealism and attracted by the mysticism of Novalis and the humour of Jean Paul Richter, he nevertheless understood the superiority of Goethe. Goethe became his supreme master in spite of the essential difference between their natures, and of the contrast between Goethe's Olympian serenity and the torment of a soul which had remained in its depths Calvinistic and haunted by the problem of Good and

of W. Hale White, Mrs. H. Ward's *Robert Elsmere* (1888), Samuel Butler's *Way of All Flesh* (1903), and *Father and Son* of Sir Edmund Gosse (1913).

Evil. This period closed with an original book which was both very Germanic in its method and very personal, a sort of allegorical autobiography, *Sartor Resartus* (1833–4). The hero is supposed to be a German professor who has written a philosophical treatise on clothes, their origin and their influence. The idea comes in fact from Swift, but Carlyle makes use of it to express the doctrines of German transcendentalism. He is concerned to pierce through the clothes, which are veils and disguises, to the secret essence, proceeding from the outward to the inward, from appearances to reality. The whole book is written in a tone of intense, massive, and imaginative irony; in it Carlyle employed for the first time the forceful and bizarre style, the tormented and poetic prose, which were to become characteristic of him.

Down to this point Carlyle had been chiefly an interpreter. Now he became an historian. The work of his maturity consists of three considerable historical studies, *The French Revolution* (1837), *Cromwell's Letters and Speeches* (1845), *Frederick II* (1858–65), and on the fringes of these, a biography, *The Life of John Sterling*, and various essays on social politics: *Chartism* (1839), *Heroes and Hero Worship* (1841), *Past and Present* (1843), *Latter-Day Pamphlets* (1850).

All these works, even the historical ones, are animated by the same spirit, filled with the same ideas. Carlyle was both satirist and prophet. He vehemently denounced the evils of the present, even while he dealt with the past. He expounded his doctrines on the conduct of individual man and the organization of society. Although he had freed himself from dogma he remained very religious. He represented Calvinism secularized; he rejected the letter of Christianity but retained the spirit. There was a mystic ardour in him, a violent spirituality which helped on the transition of pious England towards a new state of independent morality.

He fought against materialism and against the Utilitarians who considered only material progress. He grew wrathful against an age entirely given over to the winning of money and the pursuit of pleasure. He branded alike the worship of Mammon and dilettantism. He scourged the sanctimonious optimism of his generation. Present society was evil; beneath the veil of a deceitful prosperity it concealed frightful pauperism. Life was serious and should be employed in bringing order into a chaotic world.

But Carlyle, who had at first been a Radical and had later sympathized with Chartism, became in the course of the years more and more hostile to democracy, which he feared and flouted. To the equalitarian idea he opposed that of hero-worship; he lauded the heroes of the past, the magi, prophets, and priest-kings; he lauded them in the present in their new form, men of letters on the one hand, captains of industry on the other. The only way to emerge from anarchy is for the people to find their heroes and obey them. Their distinguishing mark is strength. They are able to overthrow shams; decrepit powers must give way before young powers. Carlyle even while he acclaims aristocracy is not therefore a Conservative. He has no respect for inherited or for transmitted power. He arrives at, or comes very near, the worship of mere strength: 'might is right'. He seems at times to see in success the proof of right, especially in his *Frederick II*. In some respects, he has been one of the inspirers of British Imperialism, the precursor of Froude, Henley, J. R. Seeley, Lord Rosebery, and Rudyard Kipling.

These passionate ideas are expressed in an eccentric and powerful style into which enter several elements borrowed from German, but which on the whole is entirely personal. This vehement style, recalling that of the Hebrew prophets, surprises by its lyrical turn, its continual coining of new words and expressions, its personifications of abstract qualities, and its singular figure-heads. It is endowed with an intense life, animated by a rugged humour and by the gift of comic exaggeration. We feel that the writer is carried away by his verbal inspiration and that he exults in hitting hard. Carlyle's imaginative vision, rich in concrete details, contributes even more than his conscientious documentation to the value of his historical works. He re-creates, nay, re-lives the past. His *French Revolution* is perhaps his literary masterpiece. In it he has given expression to a vision of flames and smoke, of night shot with lightning. It is a grinning and hallucinating, a gloomy and lurid picture, exhibiting the passion, the tumult, and the frenzy of those terrible years.

Carlyle excels in violent antitheses, for example in *Past and Present*, where he contrasts the religious society of the Middle Ages, idealistic and well-organized, with the materialism and anarchy of modern times.

Naturally this intemperate and aggressive writer aroused as much distaste as enthusiasm. His continuous tension grows monotonous and harassing. He shakes and overrides the reader; but he leaves no one indifferent. He is, of all the writers of the nineteenth century, the one who bears most plainly the mark of strength.

Ruskin. Carlyle made an appeal for energy. What awoke his indignation in the society of his time was its cowardice, its lack of moral resilience, its flabbiness in the struggle against vice and poverty. The indignation of John Ruskin (1819-1900) was caused by the ugliness of the industrial world, the lack of beauty and art. Ruskin's campaign for reformation was complementary to that of Carlyle, whom he hailed as his master.

Born in London, but of a family three-quarters Scottish, brought up by a rigidly pious mother, whose influence, however, was balanced by that of a father who loved art and poetry, Ruskin combined both strains in his own nature. He kept his mother's moral stiffness even when he abandoned her orthodoxy, and he made himself the champion of that artistic culture of which his father had sown in him the first seeds. He was a spiritualizing critic of art before he became the apostle of the social doctrine whose object is to spread throughout the community the taste for, and the possibility of, a beautiful and harmonious life free from the slavery of the machine.

After an individual and original education, which residence at the University of Oxford did not succeed in turning back into the ordinary paths, he began with a series of studies, *Modern Painters* (1843-60), devoted to painting, of a kind almost entirely new in his country. In it he eulogized modern landscape painters at the expense of the old, gave enthusiastic praise to Turner, and opposed the spiritual view of art to the view that it is merely a matter of the senses. He completed this series with architectural studies, *The Seven Lamps of Architecture* (1849) and *The Stones of Venice* (1851-3), in which he proclaimed both his admiration of Gothic art, the work of a sincere faith, and his scorn for Renaissance art, the artificial and irreligious product of an imitation of Paganism.

However partial this view of the past might be it was a revelation to his contemporaries. Ruskin founded art on faith, on sincerity, on the truth and justness of the symbol. Similarly he raised an enthusiastic hymn to Nature and demanded faithful and scrupulous interpretation of it by the artist. He taught people to see. He aroused the admiration of Charlotte Brontë and George Eliot: the latter proclaimed him 'one of the greatest teachers of the age'.

Ruskin's ideas were expressed in a magnificent poetic and decorative prose whose descriptions rivalled in richness the pictures of which he wrote (for example Turner's *Slave Ship*); sometimes they were themselves pictures acting directly on the imagination in the manner of those of the great painters (*The Roman Campagna*). If his books erred by too great looseness of construction and if his superb style may now and again be thought over-weighted in its magnificence and excessive in its splendour, it furnished many examples of that beauty which Ruskin extolled to his generation. He had already enlarged his aesthetic doctrine in studying the relations between the work and the artist, declaring that its composition should be compatible with a happier life in the worker. From 1857 onwards he devoted himself to the preaching of the economic doctrine he had arrived at. This made him the emphatic adversary of the Utilitarians, the denouncer of an industrialized society which spread ugliness abroad through the world and was itself founded on abject poverty, on a soulless labour that desolated human life. He sacrificed his fortune in practical efforts to realize his ideals which were disappointing in their immediate results; but his propaganda, through the numerous lectures that he gave throughout the country, and books like *Unto This Last* (1862), *Sesame and Lilies* (1865), *Fors Clavigera* (1871), *Munera Pulveris* (1872), and others, stirred public opinion. Indeed, Ruskin founded in England what was really a new religion, wherein the quest for beauty in the daily life of all, even the most humble, became a sort of duty. His efficient preaching helped little by little to embellish English life, as they embellished English letters.

Matthew Arnold. Another writer, shortly after Carlyle and Ruskin and sometimes in agreement with, but more often in opposition to, them, undertook to implant in England the practice of neglected but necessary virtues. This was Matthew Arnold (1822–88), an inspector of schools. He was not, like the two others, only a prose-writer; he made his mark in poetry, but we are at present concerned with his prose. Carlyle had desired to strengthen in his fellow countrymen the true Anglo-Saxon virtues; he had turned them towards their Germanic origins. He had professed to scorn the Latin nations and their attributes. He had incited the strong to redouble their strength. Without subscribing to the literal teaching of the Bible he poured out to his countrymen the tumultuous and passionate eloquence of the Hebrew prophets. Ruskin for his part had commended the Middle Ages to their admiration, and had turned them away from the Renaissance and the characteristic beauty of classical antiquity. But, according to Arnold, it was exactly the classical qualities that the Englishman has need of in order to attain harmonious perfection in morals and in literature: England was exaggeratedly insular and must acquire a cosmopolitan outlook; it was crude and lacked delicacy of taste and urbanity. Nor was it interested enough in abstract ideas. It took pleasure in hazy conceptions instead of seeking the pure clarity of the intellect. It was not to the Hebrews or the Germans or the men of the Middle Ages that England could with advantage look for teaching, but to the Greeks or to that people which among the moderns had imbibed most of Hellenic culture, the French. Even in the elements which composed the population of Great Britain we must not see only the Anglo-Saxon dough, solid without doubt but heavy and lumpish. It was only right to remember also all that the Celtic leaven had imparted to it of grace, of suppleness, and of fantasy.

There was another point: in her past England had reason to be proud of the literary splendour of the Elizabethan period, or of the glories of her Romantic movement. But she had too long condemned or disdained 'the indispensable eighteenth century'. In fine, it was the classical spirit that Arnold strove to rehabilitate and to propagate in his country. From 1855 onwards he consti-

tuted himself 'the detector-general of the intellectual failings of
his own nation'. All his prose works are directed to this end:
On Translating Homer (1861), *The Study of Celtic Literature* (1867),
Essays in Criticism (1865 and 1888), and *Culture and Anarchy*
(1869) in which he declared that 'culture is the minister of
the sweetness and light essential to the perfect character'. A
poet himself, he saw in poetry mainly 'a criticism of life', and
reverenced it for the part it played in the formation of character
and the guidance of conduct. This was apparently a Utilitarian
doctrine; but, contradictory though it might seem, he never
ceased to attack 'the Philistines', by whom must be understood
a middle class indifferent to the disinterested joys of pure intelligence.

Such a teaching could not reach an audience as large as Carlyle's
or even Ruskin's. But though it was more restricted it was
destined to be scarcely less fruitful. If Arnold's teaching was
known chiefly to the lettered classes, it spread through them to
an ever-widening public, and passing from the Universities to the
schools it prepared the way for the desired reform.

Arnold, moreover, was not content with a purely literary and
intellectual culture. He never ceased to be a religious man,
although he held himself aloof from any definite creed, and he
attempted to eliminate the dogmatic element from Christianity
in order to preserve its spirit and permit it to come into line with
the conquests of science and the progress of liberal thought. It
was in this temper that he wrote *St. Paul and Protestantism* (1870),
Literature and Dogma (1873), and *God and the Bible* (1876).

His elegant and lucid prose, relieved by a delicate irony, combining polish with veiled satire, and abounding in phrases which
have achieved familiar currency, was at once the mirror of his
nature and the handmaid of the varied causes which he pleaded.

Rationalism. If the writers who have been discussed were the
most original of the Victorian era they were so by virtue of the
novelty of their point of view, midway between the predominant
rationalist outlook and the still persistent Christian sentiment.
They did not represent the majority. The widest current of the
period is that of complacent utilitarianism, happy in the increase

of prosperity, in man's victories over Nature, in the steady growth of liberalism, in the tolerance of religion, and in the wider dissemination of precise knowledge throughout the nation. The eighteenth-century optimism, created by the triumphs of reason, persisted in many of the Victorian writers. The progress of their own age led them to hope for further advances, definite or vague, in the future.

The majority of these writers, philosophers, historians, or scholars, remained outside or only on the outskirts of literature, although some are among the greatest names of the era: Charles Darwin (1809–82), whose patient studies of animal species gave currency to the doctrine of transmutation and to that theory of evolution which refashioned the whole of human thought; John Stuart Mill (1806–73), who threw a clear intellectual light on the processes of logic, on the principles of political economy, on political liberty, and on the problem of the status of women; Herbert Spencer (1820–1903), who co-ordinated ideas drawn from various sciences into a coherent and comprehensive system of thought; Thomas Huxley (1825–95), who, himself a learned physiologist, served the cause of science with tireless vigour in the great war it was then waging with theology; Henry Buckle (1821–62), who traced the progress of rationalism through the ages in his *History of Civilization in England*; the historians, E. A. Freeman, William Stubbs, James Anthony Froude, S. R. Gardiner, W. E. H. Lecky, who between them covered the field of English History, J. R. Green who summarized the whole of it in his deservedly popular book *A Short History of the English People*; these men, representing as they did diverse tendencies, were often good writers; but they cultivated fields of knowledge which tended to become more and more specialized on account of the ever-growing technical or documentary demands of science or history.

On the other hand, and almost alone among the historians of the century, Thomas Babington Macaulay (1800–59) displayed in a high degree the especial qualities of the man of letters. He was a poet and an essayist as well as an historian. His *Lays of Ancient Rome* (1842), *The Armada*, and *The Battle of Ivry* were among the most frequently recited verses belonging to the middle of the century; no ballad surpasses them in animation and vivacity of narrative. In his *Essays*, as in his vast but unfinished *History of England from the accession of James II* (1849–61), he not only displays the learning of a voracious reader served by a prodigious memory, but carries to the highest point the rhetorical virtues of composition, of order, of logic, and of sequence which make him perhaps the most easily and immediately understood of English authors. To all this he added the brilliance of a crisp antithetical style, with short, balanced sentences and sharp clear-cut outlines. Its fault lies in an excessive symmetry which runs the risk of becoming at length monotonous, and in a continuous glitter which tires the eyes and makes them long sometimes for the shade. But as one whispers this complaint one marvels afresh. Macaulay, although he is disparaged by subtle and fastidious minds, is still to-day the author to whom the reader turns with relief when, baffled by obscure analyses or jerky impressionism, he yearns for unclouded light. Through these qualities of supreme clarity as well as through the oratorical nature of his talent, he is related on one side to the previous century and on the other to the literature of the Latin peoples. Thus he presents the most perfect contrast with his contemporary Carlyle.

He differed from Carlyle in matter as in manner. A decided and self-confident Whig, he could not be impartial. He had as much enthusiasm, as Carlyle had scorn, for liberty, for individualism, for the progress of industry and the growth of material prosperity, and for parliamentarianism. Macaulay had no desire to descend into the often-clouded depths of minds or of problems. He retained only what was lucid and also superficial. His wide luminous pictures of the reign of William III contrast with the thunderous visions of the historian of the French Revolution.

The Religious Revival. Although it went on its way spreading and gaining ground, rationalism did not triumph without opposition. It did, indeed, invade the most advanced party in the Anglican Church, which, under the name of the Broad Church, inclined more and more towards a deistic or unitarian doctrine. But a purely religious revival, steeped in Romantic influences, showed itself about 1830. It was as far removed from the deism of

the Broad Church as from the spirit of the Evangelicals who constituted the Low Church, who were predestinarians and violently
anti-papist, and resembled the Dissenters in the bareness of their
forms of worship.

The 'High Church', on the contrary, sought to revive the ancient
rites, with all their pomp and symbolism. It exalted the principle of
authority, the hierarchy and dogmatic teaching. Instead of being
inspired by the doctrines of liberalism it resumed its connexion with
the medieval tradition. It was favourable to mystery and miracles
and appealed to the sensibility and imagination which during the
eighteenth century had been crushed by the supremacy of intellect.
It corresponded to that mystical tendency which on the Continent
had caused the conversion to Catholicism of Friedrich Schlegel and
led the free-thinking Chateaubriand to write his *Génie du Chris-
tianisme*. The germ of it is to be found in 1822 in Wordsworth's
Ecclesiastical Sketches, which are a sort of timid 'Génie de l'anglican-
isme'. Although Wordsworth here showed himself a good Anglican,
he insisted on the traces of the Catholic past which survived in
English Protestantism. There is a marked tenderness mingled
with melancholy in the sonnets in which he speaks of the dissolution of the monasteries and of the end of the worship of the saints
and the Virgin. He was moved by the thought of mutability. He
regretted the too numerous suppressions in the ritual, lamented
the disappearance of the ancient abbeys, and admired the
splendours of the old cathedrals.

It was one of Wordsworth's disciples, John Keble, professor
of poetry at Oxford, who some years later started the 'Oxford
Movement'. The first impulse towards reaction was given by his
sermon on the 'national apostasy' in 1833. But his ideas had
appeared as early as 1827 in his *Christian Year*, a series of pious
effusions appropriate to the religious festivals of the year, a sort
of commentary on the Anglican liturgy, full of gentle emotion and
beautified by a feeling for nature. As pure poetry these poems are
not of the first order, but they had a considerable success and were
soon to be found in the majority of English homes.

In the Oxford Movement which Keble heralded there were two
phases. At first there was the High Church revival in the bosom

of Anglicanism, distinct from Roman Catholicism and independent, but approaching it in its ceremonial, its dogmatism, and its attachment to the past. This spirit displayed itself in Oxford in the pamphlets called *Tracts for the Times* (1833–41), whence its name, the 'tractarian movement'. Apart from Keble it was inspired by E. B. Pusey (1800–82), who originated 'Puseyism', the form of Anglicanism which came nearest to Rome without being merged into Romanism.

Newman. Then came John Henry Newman (1801–90) who was to go to the length of breaking completely with Protestantism and returning to the bosom of the Roman Church. Newman, the most important personality of the 'Oxford Movement', is also its most conspicuous writer. He was driven to take the decisive step by his dislike of liberalism and his indignation against political interference with the clergy. He dreamt of a free and powerful church, and aspired to a return to the spirit of the Middle Ages. At first he believed that this reform could be accomplished by Anglicanism, but he was disturbed by the lack of 'catholicity' of this insular church. He found universality and the principle of authority only in Rome. After a period of hesitation passed in retreat he was converted to Roman Catholicism in 1845. He became a Cardinal in 1879.

In the course of his career he revealed himself as a great writer in verse and prose. He set forth the reasons for his conversion in his *Apologia pro Vita Sua* (1864), in reply to Charles Kingsley who was an Anglican canon and had imputed lack of frankness to Rome and to Newman himself. He also wrote a novel, *Callista*, the story of a beautiful Greek artist, a carver of idols, who at first resists Christianity, then is converted, and finally dies a martyr. In poetry he produced in 1865 his *Dream of Gerontius*, a vision of the invisible with a chorus of angels in the manner of *Faust*; and in 1868 *Verses on Various Occacions*.

The nature of his work in prose limits the number of his readers, for it is largely theological. The duel between faith and science interests a great many minds, but the question whether the religion of Rome or that of England is the more apostolic only appeals to adepts. Newman contented himself with condemning the spirit of the century for its liberalism, which he regarded with horror. He never argued against this liberalism; he rejected it. His interior struggle is less moving than it might be because it appears to be entirely intellectual; it is a matter of orderly arguments drawn up in line, and the author's indignation only shows itself in flashes.

In spite of all, Newman was a great writer. He used an extraordinarily simple prose, supple, distinguished, essentially aristocratic, and deeply imbued with the culture of Oxford.

His conversion was to be followed by that of others. Cardinal Wiseman, author of the novel *Fabiola* (1854), was always a Catholic; but Cardinal Manning only became one at the age of forty-three in 1851. Also connected with Rome are the poets Gerard Manley Hopkins, Coventry Patmore, Francis Thompson, and Mrs. Meynell, who will be dealt with later.

The Novel

Only four years separate the last novels of Scott from the appearance of Dickens's first novel in 1836; and yet the transition is like a change of worlds. But the belief should be guarded against that Scott's influence was suddenly extinguished and, more generally, that romanticism in the English novel abruptly came to an end.

In fact when Victoria came to the throne the variety of works of fiction which were well known and popular throughout the country was very great. Frederick Marryat (1792–1848) was producing his sea-stories, read especially by the young, *Peter Simple* (1834), *Jacob Faithful* (1834), and *Midshipman Easy* (1836). A milder successor of Smollett, Marryat happily combines precise technical knowledge with lively narrative and humorous incidents and characters.

Again, the versatile Edward Bulwer Lytton (1803–73) was making his debut with a series of novels steeped in the Byronic spirit; their heroes were brilliant dandies (*Falkland* (1827) and *Pelham* (1828)), or attractive criminals (*Paul Clifford* (1830) and *Eugene Aram* (1832)). After Byron, Scott was Bulwer Lytton's inspirer. He wrote historical novels with striking subjects: *The Last Days of Pompeii* (1834), *Rienzi, the Last of the*

Tribunes (1835), followed after an interval by *The Last of the Barons* (1843), and *Harold* (1848). Later, in response to the change in public taste, he turned to the domestic novel in *The Caxtons* (1849), and *My Novel* (1853). This is but a glance at a copious and picturesque output to which the Utopian *The Coming Race* was added in 1871. It always succeeds in stimulating curiosity, but it is spoilt by its lack of sincerity, its theatrical tone, and the false glitter of a style which smacks too much of rhetoric.

The novels of Benjamin Disraeli, the future Earl of Beaconsfield (1804–81), have offered more resistance to time. Perhaps this is due to the dazzling political career of their author; for they have the advantage of drawing from life the character of a man who, when he became Prime Minister, was to put more than one of his ideas into execution. Like Bulwer Lytton, Disraeli began with the portrait of a dandy, *Vivian Grey* (1826–7), a young adventurer with more brains than scruples. In the novels which followed his entrance into Parliament, he gave more and more space to his views as a democratic Tory and founder of the 'Young England' movement, and to the Oriental visions of an imaginative Jew, proud of his race, who became a great promoter of British Imperialism. In *Coningsby* (1844), *Sybil* (1845), and *Tancred* (1847), Disraeli was among the first to point to the amelioration of the wretched lot of the working class as a social duty of the aristocracy. His faults are like Bulwer Lytton's; he is often pretentious and artificial. But there are eloquent pages in his books, and a gift of witty expression which seems to have been quite natural to him, and still keeps its fascination. The movements of English politics under Queen Victoria can be studied better in Disraeli's novels than anywhere else. They are, however, novels with a purpose; the characters are created with a view to the thesis and retain a certain air of unreality. They stand a little outside the great line to which belong Dickens and Thackeray, who began to write some years later than Bulwer Lytton and Disraeli.

Dickens. Charles Dickens (1812–70), has perhaps enjoyed a wider and more fervent popularity than any other English writer. He is also one of the most original in type. Not that his novels refuse to enter recognized categories: he began, though he was hardly aware of it, in the picaresque manner with *Pickwick* (1836–7), then he attempted the historical novel in *Barnaby Rudge* (1841) and *A Tale of Two Cities* (1859). In *Oliver Twist* (1837), *A Christmas Carol* (1843), *Hard Times* (1854), &c., he devoted himself to the novel of social conditions with a reforming purpose. In *David Copperfield* (1849–50) he produced a sort of autobiographical romance. But whatever he wrote he set so personal a stamp on his books that at every turn he seemed to be an innovator.

Half of the novelty consisted in the field of observation which was the outcome of his own experiences. His youth had been passed in London and had brought him into contact with the working and lower-middle classes. He had been familiar with the most humble surroundings, and the most wretched districts, and he made the description of them his habitual subject. A new and vivid realism enters into his pictures, but it is a realism humorous and tender by turns, the opposite of that which was to triumph later in the century, gloomy, cynical, and overwhelming. Dickens's realistic scenes are now lit up by laughter, now warmed by pity. They are either distorted by lively caricature, or transformed by a curious fantasy, even by a truly poetic imagination. The observation, which is abundant, piercing, swift, and cinematographic, as we should now say, is at the same time iridescent with humour and tears.

Dickens's manner is even more original than his matter. He had received a very incomplete education and had been moulded neither by school nor university. His mind was formed by fitful effort, a little by disconnected reading, a great deal by familiarity with popular speech, the pithiness of which he excelled in reproducing. The concrete and imaginative quality of this speech appears in his often ungrammatical style, in which the words and even the syntax are animated with a singular life. No one has derived so much effect from the elliptic ways of common talk and those vivid prepositions which in English can so successfully be manipulated to underline actions and gestures and describe attitudes. He is constantly creating burlesque or comic expressions, unhindered by any fastidiousness or by fear of exaggeration or bad taste. If he is not supported by a classical education, neither is he embarrassed or overawed by it.

These characteristics appear in their best light in his first books. Gradually his style, which had been entirely spontaneous, grew mannered, strained, and forced. The influence of Carlyle became apparent in it as it became apparent in his thought itself (*A Tale of Two Cities, Hard Times*). He strained after a sort of philosophical irony and social criticism in which many personified abstractions and satirical symbols are mingled with a rhetoric and lyricism which resemble the prophetic utterances of Carlyle.

Dickens aroused the enthusiasm of his contemporaries both by his irresistible comedy and by his exuberant pathos. His comic spirit is still active to-day, while for many of his readers his pathos has lost its original effectiveness. The Bardell-Pickwick case still remains a comic masterpiece; the death of Little Nell (*The Old Curiosity Shop* 1840-1), to-day appears overcharged with sentimentality and almost artificial in its appeal to our tears. A comparison of the latter pages with the surer and more sober touches of the moving passages of Thackeray (as, for example, the death of Colonel Newcome) is very unfavourable to Dickens. But it would be profoundly unjust to class him among the purely comic writers and to reject everything in him which appeals to feeling. His charm lies in the gift he possesses of allying sincere and overflowing tenderness with comedy. His comic figures are dear to him; at first he is amused by them, then he begins to love them for the pleasure he finds in depicting them. His Pickwick, who is purely ludicrous to begin with, is little by little adorned with virtues which transfigure him. Without ceasing to be amusing he becomes the object of affection much more than of ridicule. Dickens can seize the grotesque aspect of a character without withholding his sympathy from him. He loves and makes us love all the strange creatures he brings on the scene if he finds them in the smallest degree good-hearted.

With his impulsive liveliness Dickens is excellent at sketches but weak in composition. Writing for periodicals in which his books appeared serially, he often proceeded at haphazard. His Pickwick was created from day to day without a previously drawn-up plan. When Dickens tried to compose a plot he was constrained and embarrassed, as, for example, in *A Tale of Two Cities* or *Hard Times*. He succeeded better when he retraced a life, childhood, or a career, as in *David Copperfield*, recounting successive happenings in simple chronological order. He cannot mark progress by the analysis of character, for his characters have no development. They are susceptible of sudden conversions but as a rule they are fixed from the start in attitudes which do not vary. The repetition of mannerisms and grimaces is Dickens's favourite method. It is thus that his characters give the illusion of life; they are recognizable and strongly individualistic, but they have no deep inner life. They recall Ben Jonson's 'humours' rather than the really human creatures of Shakespeare.

There are thus serious reservations to be made in praising Dickens. But he is none the less a novelist of genius who has created a whole world of beings stamped with a distinctive mark and animated with the movement of life. He was able to spread over his loosely constructed books an atmosphere which is his own and unique. He has peopled men's imaginations with unforgettable scenes and figures. In spite of the satirical spirit which rules in his work and is brought to bear on institutions, laws, and the severities and hypocrisy of the sanctimonious, his warmth of heart makes life good and pleasant. He displays the faculty for joy and heartiness among the very wretches whose misery he paints. He does not deny them tender emotions, good humour, or the relaxation of laughter. His morality is summed up in a general appeal to goodness, generosity, and loving-kindness. It puts into action the great precept 'Love one another'. It helps men's hearts to open and expand.

Thackeray. Dickens was magnificently successful in depicting the life of the people; he was ill acquainted with the upper classes and painted them without verisimilitude. It was William Makepeace Thackeray (1811–63) who was the penetrating analyst of both the upper middle class and aristocratic society. He brought, moreover, to his pictures a realism of a very different kind from that of Dickens, more exacting and less mingled with fantasy and lyricism. Thackeray's peculiar quality is his resistance to the

PLATE XXXIV

'The Rival Editors' from E. K. Browne's ('Phiz') illustrations
to *Pickwick Papers*. See p. xv

PLATE XXXV

CHARLES DICKENS

WILLIAM MAKEPEACE
THACKERAY
National Portrait Gallery

ALFRED TENNYSON

ROBERT BROWNING
National Portrait Gallery

romantic spirit which filled literature, especially in his youth. He repudiated it as false and impeached it as immoral.

His career was at first that of a satirist and parodist in prose and verse. Across the first third of the nineteenth century he stretches out his hand to the writers of Queen Anne's reign. His great masters are Addison, Goldsmith, and, above, all Fielding. As well armed with classical knowledge, as well informed in French and German literatures as Dickens was ill furnished, a chastened and elegant writer, and, moreover, capable of imitating every style and reproducing various jargons, he revealed himself at first as a master of irony. His first compositions were newspaper articles and humorous essays for *Punch*. From these there was to grow a curious book, *The Book of Snobs* (1846-7), in which in a very marked democratic spirit he ridiculed, sometimes with gaiety and sometimes with bitterness, the national tendency to fawn on the nobility, and to copy its manners, its faults, and even its vices. Under the same heading of snobbishness he denounced the false idols of the day, the vanities and affectations, the selfishness and brutality that are often hidden beneath a magnificent exterior, and the real vulgarity that is masked by a cloak of state.

Between whiles in the *Yellowplush Papers* he copied the ideas and talk of footmen in a great house, the better to display the caprices of their masters. His curiosity ranged abroad in the *Paris Sketch Book* (1840) and *Irish Sketch Book* (1843). Then he attempted the novel proper and produced a very powerful work, *The Luck of Barry Lyndon* (1844), where he makes a blackguard cynically recount the hundred infamies of a life of shifts and vices which he believes to be perfectly normal and justifiable. Here he was working in the vein of Swift and still more in that of Fielding's *Jonathan Wild*.

But it was not till 1848 that he attained real fame with his pictures of contemporary life: *Vanity Fair* (1847-8), soon followed by *Pendennis* (1848), and *The Newcomes* (1853); and his historical novels *Henry Esmond* (1852), and *The Virginians* (1857-9). The first three of these books are the work of an observer combined with a moralist. In reaction against romanticism Thackeray re fused to put heroes on the stage, to glorify passion or transfigure life. He knew how to amuse by depicting eccentricities and whims, but he did not stop there: he displayed the weaknesses and failings of the best people, and the cruelties of life. He was to draw upon himself the accusation of cynicism because of his ironic revelations of the human soul, for whose miseries he did not propose any remedy. His ever present morality was perfectly orthodox, but it never ceased to sadden and discourage. Thackeray often tended to oppose intellect and virtue as incompatibles. Becky Sharp (in *Vanity Fair*), all energy and intelligence, has the career of a heartless and unscrupulous adventuress. Amelia Sedley in the same book has an excellent heart but is a foolish creature. Colonel Newcome has the noblest qualities of generosity and goodness of soul but he walks with childlike unconsciousness through society and politics.

At the same time these studies of imperfect or indifferent characters display an admirable sureness of touch. The springs of action, the impulses of sentiment or egotism, are revealed with a clear-sightedness impossible to Dickens. Thackeray's characters may not have all the outward vitality that Dickens could communicate, but they are studied far more deeply within.

In his historical novels, and particularly in *Esmond*, Thackeray adopted an altogether new method, and did not allow himself to be dominated like the majority of writers by the genius of Scott. *Esmond* purports to be the autobiography of a man who attained maturity in the reign of Queen Anne, took part in Marlborough's campaigns, conducted an intrigue designed to re-establish the Pretender on the throne, and was on speaking terms with the greatest writers of the time, Swift, Addison, and especially Richard Steele. For such an undertaking Thackeray was prepared by a rare knowledge of the history and literature of the eighteenth century. He was writing at the same time lectures on *The English Humourists of the Eighteenth Century* (1853); he was soon to write *The Four Georges* (1860–1). He not only knew the facts, but he had been able to assimilate in a remarkable degree the very style of the period, showing that strange suppleness which had already enabled him to reproduce with amusing fidelity the very turn of speech of people of every class and also of foreigners, both Germans and, above all, Frenchmen. Thus he succeeded in producing the illusion of the past. But all this is only the frame for a psychological novel of a new and daring type in which the successive loves of the hero are analysed with the most delicate subtlety: his blind passion for the dazzling Beatrix, and his tenderness, at first filial, for the mother of Beatrix, Lady Castlewood, which changes gradually into true love. This book, freed from some rather narrow restraints of morality which had hitherto shackled him, shows a degree of artistic force and freedom in the study of passion which Thackeray had not before reached. It would be sufficient by itself to reveal the genius of a writer who did not always realize all the possibilities of his strength, either because of a certain natural indolence, or because of his too obvious taste for preaching, or through fear of shocking too violently the conventions and scruples of his time.

The Brontës. The romanticism ridiculed and opposed by Thackeray was still alive and active, and it was an admirer of *Vanity Fair* who afforded the most striking proof of this. She returned to the depiction of those strong passions generally avoided by both Dickens and Thackeray. There was a Byronic strain in Charlotte Brontë (1816–55), refined, it is true, by religious training and moral discipline, and mixed with those realistic elements which were now beginning to prevail. This daughter of a Yorkshire parson, who had grown up in the harsh and dreary solitude of the moors, brought lyrical warmth and the play of strong feeling into the novel. *The Professor* and *Villette* were based on her own personal experience, a stay which she made in a boarding-school in Brussels. Her dreams and her resentments kindled the fiery pages of her masterpiece, *Jane Eyre* (1847); in *Shirley* (1849), she set a story of intimate emotion against a background of Yorkshire in the time of the industrial disturbances. Charlotte Brontë was a mistress of wit, irony, and accurate observation, but an impassioned eloquence expressed in a style that is often abstract was her distinguishing mark.

Even more original was her sister Emily Brontë (1818–48) who before she died at the age of 30 had written fearless poems which disclosed her fiery stoicism, fervent pantheism, and entirely independent spirituality. She left a strange novel, *Wuthering Heights*, wherein among her passionately loved moors she set a tragedy of love at once fantastic and powerful, savage and moving, a nightmarish story which strangely blends virginal ignorance with lightning-like intuition. There is no other book which contains so many of the troubled, tumultuous, and rebellious elements of romanticism.

Towards the middle of the century novelists began to be absorbed in the presentation of social problems rather than in analysis of personal emotion. Dickens had given the initial impulse to this movement with *Oliver Twist* in 1838, in which he attacked the wretched lot of foundling children ill-treated in the workhouses. In the *Christmas Books* (1843-8), his genial fancy called charity to the aid of the poor. Disraeli devoted *Sybil* (1845) to the sufferings of working people. Charlotte Brontë gave much space to the same problems in *Shirley*.

Mrs. Gaskell. Social problems occupied these novelists intermittently; they were almost the sole concern of Mrs. Gaskell (1810-65), the biographer of Charlotte Brontë. She lived for many years in Manchester, and knew at first hand the evils of the intensively industrialized districts. Her novels, *Mary Barton* (1848) and *North and South* (1855), show very close observation; they are packed with concrete details and at the same time full of pity for the working-class victims of financial self-seeking. In *Ruth* (1853) Mrs. Gaskell showed the same sympathy for unfortunate girls. She also proved herself to be a tender, gentle and amused humorist in *Cranford* (1853). This was a novel without a purpose, a delicate picture of the society of a small provincial town, which recalls Jane Austen and Miss Mitford, and at a greater distance Addison and Goldsmith.

Charles Kingsley. Charles Kingsley (1819-75) was an Anglican minister, the founder of the Christian Socialists, and actively interested in the co-operative movement. He embodied his generous ideals of reform in the novels *Yeast* (1848) and *Alton Locke* (1850), books which suffer as works of imagination, notwithstanding their force and eloquence, from the too large amount of space occupied in them by theorizing and preaching. But he was also an historical novelist. In *Hypatia* (1853) he returned to the earliest days of Christianity; in *Westward Ho!* (1855) he commemorated the adventurous spirit of the Elizabethan navigators, and that of the descendants of the Vikings in *Hereward the Wake* (1865). He was the apostle of energy, of what has been called 'muscular Christianity', and a defender of Protestantism, particularly in the poem *The Saint's Tragedy* (1848), against the Romish tendencies of the tractarian movement. He wrote some vigorous ballads. An energetic writer and remarkable for his descriptions of Nature, which he passionately loved, his lack of stricter artistic standards prevented him from reaching the first rank.

Charles Reade. Artistic scruples are, on the contrary, manifest in the work of Charles Reade (1814–84), combined moreover with a strict scheme of documentary exactness. Reade, who all his life in spite of indifferent success had dramatic ambitions, turned rather late to the novel in 1853. Using in every case the same quasi-scientific method, he wrote novels with a social purpose like *It is Never too Late to Mend* (1853), a picture of the horrors of prison life, *Hard Cash* (1863), depicting the abuses to which lunatic asylums gave rise, and *Put Yourself in his Place* (1870), directed against trade unions; pathological studies like *Griffith Gaunt* (1866) and *A Terrible Temptation* (1871); also a famous historical novel, *The Cloister and the Hearth* (1867), on the life of the father of Erasmus, in which he showed the transition from the Middle Ages to the Renaissance in process of taking place. The very conscientiousness of his documentary preparation, his diligence in having recourse in every instance to real facts, cools the heat of his imagination. He was the first in date of the conscious, resolute realists.

Wilkie Collins. In the same period Wilkie Collins (1824–89) attained in *The Woman in White* (1860), *The Moonstone*, &c., to a hitherto unknown mastery in the rather mechanical art of plot-construction. He excelled in arousing the sense of terror and in keeping in suspense the explanation of a mystery or the revelation of a crime. He influenced Dickens's last novel, *Edwin Drood*, and anticipated by nearly half a century the detective novels of Conan Doyle.

Trollope. Anthony Trollope (1815–88), without making use of documents like Reade, produced a whole series of studies in novel form which give the impression of being drawn from real life, neither distorted nor idealized. Eschewing the violent and dramatic effects in which Reade delighted, he presented without poetical feeling but not without humour, and with a moderation which seems to be truth itself, many a scene of provincial life, especially of the ecclesiastical world of a cathedral town, in *The Warden* (1855), *Barchester Towers* (1857), *The Last Chronicle of Barset* (1867), &c. He wrote with ease and regularity, without fuss, and in a uniform and almost impersonal style. The illusion which he creates depends in part on the temperateness of his artistic ambition. He has told how he imposed on himself a daily task of so many pages and passed from one book to another without allowing himself any break. But his characters are lifelike and shrewdly drawn, and he knows how to tell a story. He made his various sketches into a sort of summary of middle-class life in England; as he himself said of one of his novels: 'no heroism and no villainy. . . . Much Church but more love-making'.

George Borrow. It is convenient to place George Borrow (1803–81) among the realists although his stories about gipsies carry the reader into a world which seems romantic. But the most authoritative critics vouch for the exactness of his pictures. *The Bible in Spain* (1843), *Lavengro* (1851), *The Romany Rye* (1857), *Wild Wales* (1862), are snatches of autobiography or travel notes rather than novels. No other writer of the middle of the century possesses to such an extent the freshness of the open air and the taste for adventure. Borrow was a strange two-sided man. There was a fanatical Protestant in him, always ready to denounce Romish idolatry, and there was also the lover of the open road, the fighter who enjoyed using his fists, and made friends with the vagabonds of the earth. His Romany *chals* are in no danger of being forgotten any more than his scenes of Spanish life, which he knew at first hand when he travelled from place to place in Spain as a pedlar for the Bible Society. Nothing could be more alert or more breezy than the prose of this eccentric.

A place should be made by his side for two men who were not

novelists but opened their countrymen's eyes to unknown scenes and modes of life: A. W. Kinglake (1809–91) with his fascinating pictures of the East in *Eothen* (1844), and Richard Burton (1821–90) with his *Pilgrimage to El Medinah and Meccah* (1855–6).

However interesting the writers of whom we have just spoken may be for various reasons, we must pass on to George Eliot and Meredith in order to find names worthy to be placed alongside those of Dickens and Thackeray. In date both belong entirely to the second half of the century, the novels of George Eliot having appeared from 1857 to 1876 and those of Meredith from 1856 to 1895. In reputation and popularity George Eliot succeeded the great masters of the middle of the century, while Meredith, whose fame came later, shared the succession to her with Stevenson and Hardy.

George Eliot. It would hardly be possible to exaggerate the fame which George Eliot, whose real name was Mary Ann Evans, (1819–80) enjoyed in her lifetime. With the rich humour of her great predecessors she seemed to combine a deeper philosophy than they had been capable of. In her hands the novel gained in depth while it preserved all its width of range. When she took up imaginative writing she was a woman already mature who had acquired a deep and masculine culture. Brought up during her youth in austere and ardent piety, she had broken free from religion and had adopted the philosophy of Auguste Comte and Herbert Spencer. Yet she retained in her new liberty an emotional reverence for the beliefs she had discarded and, even in the free union which she contracted with George Henry Lewes, an acute, poignant, and obsessing sense of moral issues. She could make even her entertainment instructive, and knew how to appeal to both the imagination and the reason.

That, at any rate, was the effect achieved by her first novels: *Scenes of Clerical Life* (1857), *Adam Bede* (1859), *The Mill on the Floss* (1860), which are the flower of her genius. Her realism brings her into relation with Thackeray, but she chose an entirely different field of observation. Instead of the aristocracy she studied rural society: the farmers, small landowners, and clergy of Warwickshire, her native county. Like Thackeray again she

was constantly probing the minds of her characters, but instead
of the irony which made people call Thackeray a cynic, she showed
an emotional sympathy and a tender pity. She was as much alive
as he to hypocrisy and weakness; indeed, she unmasked them even
more pitilessly. She had a gift for demonstrating the connexion
between faults of conduct; with merciless determination she laid bare
the consequences of a first mistake leading on to error and even to
crime. But all the time she preserved a keen sense of the humanity that is common to all, and she suffered at the thought of the
sufferings of the guilty. She found another kind of pathos in the
efforts towards a good life, towards well-doing, towards an ideal,
which have ennobled many a heroic spirit that has remained
obscure. She reached her highest emotion in contemplating the
power of an intimate grief to purify and hallow commonplace people.
No writer of fiction excels George Eliot in her direct appeal to the
conscience or in forcing the reader to question and examine himself.

And yet her work is full, at any rate in her first books, of
concrete and picturesque touches, and characters who abound
in natural wit and racy speech, like Mrs. Poyser in *Adam Bede*, or
who amuse us by the lively play of their prejudices and whims,
like the Tulliver family in *The Mill on the Floss*. These early
novels are rich also in descriptions of the English countryside
drawn not merely with exactness but with that intimate charm
that love alone can give.

Scenes of Clerical Life and *Adam Bede* are the novels which best
preserve the balance between the author's gifts, observation,
humour, and pathos blending into one harmonious whole. There-
after, even in the admirable *Mill on the Floss*, and still more in the
later masterpiece *Middlemarch* (1872), some parts are overwhelmed
beneath the weight of a too ponderous psychology which smacks
more of study and research than of inspiration. George Eliot
wearied even her admirers by her historical romance *Romola*
(1862–3) and by her novel with a purpose, designed to rehabilitate
the Jewish race, *Daniel Deronda* (1874–6). In the end her novels
sank under the weight of reflection which clogged their action. The
'pale cast of thought' which Hamlet said destroyed resolution

choked George Eliot's vitality. The novel became altogether too much of a laborious and painful inquiry into moral questions; the philosophy oppressed and killed the imaginative part of the work. But George Eliot must be judged by the books in which she gave the full measure of her whole nature, and the century produced no novels which surpassed, few that equalled them.

Meredith. At about the same time as George Eliot, George Meredith (1828–1909) began a series of novels which was to continue until the end of the century. He, like her, was filled with intellectual ardour and the passionate desire to understand; but he expressed a very different mood: irony, not sentiment, was his dominant characteristic. His muse was inspired by the spirit of comedy; his realism was mixed with fantasy. He began with a sparkling and witty Oriental tale, that might have been taken from *The Thousand and One Nights*: *The Shaving of Shagpat* (1856). When, in *The Ordeal of Richard Feverel* (1859), he undertook a direct study of English society, it was towards the aristocracy that he turned; and in this he recalls Thackeray rather than George Eliot. His manner was epigrammatic; he passed from aphorism to aphorism. Methodical analysis and strict logic gave place to a manner that was from the first impressionistic, though less noticeably so than it afterwards became. His theme in *Richard Feverel* was education, or rather a satirical study of doctrinaire educationalists who set out to play the role of Providence without calculating the forces of Nature. The father of Richard blasts and desolates the life of the son whose happiness he seeks according to his own ideas. Not that he is without wisdom or sagacity, witness the striking maxims ranged in his book: *The Pilgrim's Scrip*. Against this background of irony stand out passages of rapturous poetry like that of the first meeting of Richard and Lucy, and of intense pathos like that which describes her death.

Meredith later attempted historical romance in *Vittoria* (1866), the subject of which is the Italian uprising of 1848 against the Austrian occupation; while *Beauchamp's Career* (1876) is a political novel which traces the life of a young aristocrat who makes himself the champion of radicalism and social reforms.

Later on, in *The Egoist* (1879), *Diana of the Crossways* (1885), *One of Our Conquerors* (1891), &c., it was to the emancipation of woman, the victim of masculine egotism, that he chiefly devoted himself.

Everywhere Meredith displays a rare penetration into the characters of men and women. He excels in laying bare, particularly in men, the springs of egotism. *The Egoist* is his masterpiece and one of the great works of the century. He incited woman to defend herself against masculine tyranny and to that end to cultivate her wit, to see clearly and to understand life: 'More brain!'

His ideas found expression in a style of rare vivacity and of singular subtlety, although it often lacks the lucidity of the great masters. Neglected for a long time by the public, Meredith seems to have written more and more for his own satisfaction, taking pleasure in setting the average reader at defiance. His obscurity increased with the years. Filled with allusions not easy to grasp, his prose (no less than his verse) requires an often painful effort. Certainly it is worth the effort, but the radiance of the writer is obscured. Meredith attained belatedly in the last ten years of his life a fame which has grown a little dim, though no doubt only temporarily, since his death. But the rich substance of his books, their healthy philosophy free from sentimentality but tonic and invigorating, and the keen air of intelligence that blows through them, assure us of their survival.

Samuel Butler. The rationalism of George Eliot was permeated with sympathy for the religious temperament; Meredith's intellectual outlook did not embrace organized religion which had no place in his work. Samuel Butler (1835-1902), the son of a clergyman and destined for the church, was a rebel against clerical discipline and attacked it with bitter irony. His aggressive spirit ranged itself against current morality and tradition; and he was just as irreverent towards science and learning. He had much of the destructive critical spirit of Swift and Voltaire. His *Erewhon* (1872), a sort of inverted Utopia, at first achieved only the success of a curiosity. His posthumous novel *The Way of all Flesh* (1903) is a kind of autobiography in which the evils of an

ecclesiastical upbringing are set forth, and in which the author
attacks family life as it is. The boldness of Butler's thought made
him dear to the subversive generation which followed him. His
dry humour was particularly appreciated after his death. His
role was eminently that of a forerunner.

Poetry

The poetry of the period was still full of beauty and richness,
though more restricted than contemporary prose in its effect upon
thought, and more limited in inspiration and novelty than during
the romantic era. Two names dominate it in the middle of the
century, those of Tennyson and Browning. Their parallel achieve-
ments presented a striking contrast to their contemporaries, who
became accustomed to define each by comparison with the other.
In both poets, it is true, the influence of romanticism persists,
Tennyson being related to Byron and Keats, while Browning was
inspired at first by Shelley but subsequently took a completely
different path.

Tennyson. Alfred Tennyson (1809–92), the son of a Lincolnshire clergyman, enjoyed the earlier and wider popularity of the
two. His first poems, published in 1830, were, it is true, entirely
unsuccessful, but when twelve years later, in 1842, he published two
volumes which included revised, embellished, and also new poems,
he became famous at a stroke. In the first place they revealed an
astonishing technical mastery and a versification that was as
supple and varied as it was melodious. Tennyson was eclectic, he
profited by the successes of all his forerunners; he was aiming at
exquisiteness of style and metre perhaps even before any ideas
had begun to interest him as much as his art, and until the end of
his long career artistic concern was uppermost in him. His purified taste led him to reject what had been affected and mannered
in his first poems. Besides developing and improving his own
style he did something towards refining and polishing the poetic
manner created by his great predecessors of the last generation.
These had too often, in their reaction against the eighteenth century
and in the rush of their creative power, given free play to their
temperament and produced some shapeless outpourings. But in

Tennyson a classical sense was allied to the romantic temperament. He had that sense of measure which had distinguished
Pope and Gray. Thus he was to leave a remarkable number of
poems whose beauty is without flaw or rift and which owe their
enduring appeal to the balance of various talents and the perfection of their form.

This success was as frequent in the blank verse poems as in the
rhymed lyrics. It is evident, for example, in the soft languor of
The Lotos Eaters:

> But, propt on beds of amaranth and moly,
> How sweet (while warm airs lull us, blowing lowly)
> With half-dropped eyelid still,
> Beneath a heaven dark and holy,
> To watch the long bright river drawing slowly
> His waters from the purple hill—
> To hear the dewy echoes calling
> From cave to cave thro' the thick-twin'd vine—
> To watch the emerald-colour'd water falling
> Thro' many a wov'n acanthus-wreath divine!
> Only to hear and see the far-off sparkling brine,
> Only to hear were sweet, stretch'd out beneath the pine.

And it is no less striking in the severe beauty of *Ulysses*:

> Tho' much is taken, much abides; and tho'
> We are not now that strength which in old days
> Moved earth and heaven; that which we are, we are;
> One equal temper of heroic hearts,
> Made weak by time and fate, but strong in will
> To strive, to seek, to find, and not to yield.

Both reveal the same care for elegance of style and harmony of
sounds. An equal beauty distinguishes the long or short poems
of his sixty years of poetic composition. Those weaknesses, those
crudities, those prosaic passages, which detracted from the work
of Wordsworth for example, and which were to spoil half of that
of Browning, are not to be found in the poetry of Tennyson. As an
artist, he ranks among the greatest of his race.

The value of his work did not, indeed, lie merely in its qualities
of form. He experienced in his own being the intellectual movements of his century, he shared its aspirations, its troubles, its

anxieties, and reflected them in his verse.   Beneath its half-jesting, mock-epic form, *The Princess* (1847) is occupied with the dawning question of feminism. The poet appears at first to be amused by it but gradually grows warmer and concludes in all seriousness a poem which opened in a tone of bantering irony.

In *In Memoriam* (1850), moved by grief at the premature death of his friend Arthur Hallam, Tennyson sets down his thoughts on life and death, revealing the anguish of the search after grounds for belief in immortality, and the torment of the modern soul oscillating between the hopes offered by Christianity and the negations of science. Deliberately quiet and even in its tone, and made up of short stanzas all in octosyllabic quatrains (*a b b a*), it is one of the most beautiful elegies in the language; it is also Tennyson's most truly philosophical work, in which his heart unbosoms and questions itself to find at last in religious meditation a tremulous peace:

> Our little systems have their day;
>   They have their day and cease to be:
>   They are but broken lights of thee,
> And thou, O Lord, art more than they.
>
> We have but faith: we cannot know;
>   For knowledge is of things we see;
>   And yet we trust it comes from thee,
> A beam in darkness: let it grow.

Nevertheless, Tennyson had a vehemence, even a certain tinge of Byronic revolt, which had early found vent in *Locksley Hall* and to which he gave full expression in *Maud* (1855). This is a lyrical narrative with a number of different scenes, in which every sort of verse-form is employed in turn; it tells of the passionate love of a young man embittered by a harsh fortune, a pessimist who loathes the venality and corruption of society; kept from his beloved by the pride of her family, he becomes almost wild with grief, and does not find solace again in life until he responds to the call to arms that suddenly resounds through his country—it is the time of the Crimean War. In spite of the great beauty of the songs scattered through the poem it did not find favour with the public: it illustrates the limitations which the Victorian mind imposed on writers. Violent satire and exalted passion disquieted the poet's contemporaries; and Tennyson returned to a more temperate poetry, to a more healthy and normal philosophy.

He satisfied the demand with *Enoch Arden* (1864), a poem concerned with heroism and virtue in a setting of the life of the people. Admirable in execution and finish, it is a picture by a master in which exception can be taken only to a certain excess of varnish in the painting and of sentimental sweetness in the life described. He satisfied the same demand even better with his last great work, which occupied him until his old age, *Idylls of the King* (1859–85). Here, with extreme adroitness, he drew from the Arthurian legend a series of scenes, many of them faithfully borrowed from the old sources, and sometimes, as, for example, in the *Morte d'Arthur*, almost transcribed from the work of Malory. The Idylls have grace, wit, pathos, and poetry. Tennyson did not try to reproduce the manners of the past in their rough truth, or to preserve its savagery and licence. With the help of some hints that were still quite vague in Malory, he converted the old and still half-barbarous epic into a highly civilized poem of dainty moral refinement in which the manners tend toward an ideal as pure as that of the severest circles of Victorian society. The result was a series of excellently told and much transformed tales, directed towards a noble moral end.

During the same period he turned to dramatic writing, and produced several plays which were well received but not triumphantly successful. They show his powers as a writer, but they lack the true dramatic inspiration.

When he died in 1892 he had long reigned unopposed on the throne of poetry, although his last years had seen growing in his shadow a rival whom an increasing number of admirers placed beside or even above him.

Browning. Robert Browning (1812–89) was in almost every respect Tennyson's opposite. What chiefly interested him was the study of the human soul. He was a psychologist first of all; art with him took second place. From the very start he discussed, in monologue or dialogue, problems of life and conscience. In *Pauline* (1833), the dramatic disguise was thinner than it later became; the poem was in effect a fragment of personal confession. In *Paracelsus* (1835), he described the strange career of the Renaissance physician, in whom true science and charlatanism were combined. This poem already revealed Browning's peculiar gifts; using his hero as mouthpiece, he poured forth with inexhaustible eloquence his own ideas and his aspirations. Paracelsus is the victim of his high ambition, which is to attain truth and transform the life of man. For the sake of this ideal he commits the blunder of rejecting emotion and eschewing love. Too late he understands his mistake. His failure is glorious, but he fails. This enormous poem by a young man is astonishingly spirited and deeply imbued with philosophy. As a work of art it suffers from its very richness and redundance and from its lack of controlling form and outline. Browning did not have an assured success until he disciplined his dramatic talent within stricter limits. But from the first his work contained a sort of challenge to his readers' powers of attention and understanding. *Paracelsus* was followed in 1840 by *Sordello*, in which the story of the life of a little-known Italian poet is wrapped in obscurities of expression that have become proverbial.

At intervals Browning attempted the drama proper. In 1837 he published *Strafford*, which was followed by other plays, six in all, between then and 1846. In spite of their merits these plays, overburdened with argument, did not succeed with the public. Their action was sacrificed too much to the study of the characters.

His limited dramatic power showed to better purpose in the isolated scenes which make up *Pippa Passes* (1841). Here Browning imagined the effect of the songs of a little working-girl, strolling about during a holiday, on the destiny of the very different persons who hear them in turn. The ingenious but quite external link that unites these successive pictures allows free play to all of them, and the poem reaches the height of grim tragedy in the scene of the murder of the old husband by the two lovers Sibald and Ottima. But as a rule Browning was content to collect a series of disconnected studies, chiefly monologues, into volumes: *Dramatic Lyrics* (1842), *Dramatic Romances and Lyrics* (1845), *Men and Women* (1855), *Dramatis Personae* (1864), *Dramatic Idylls* (1879–80). With keen, tireless curiosity he brings the most

varied personages to make their confessions to us, some drawn
from history, others imaginary, some good, some bad—all unravel-
ling, thanks to the clear-sighted poet, the tangled skein of their
emotions and actions. Browning appears to give them wide scope
and let them say what they like, but in fact he guides their confi-
dences in the direction of his own philosophy of energy and freedom, and towards that faith in life, in the spiritual essence and
immortality of the soul, which is the basis of his generous optimism :

> The year's at the spring,
> And day's at the morn ;
> Morning's at seven ;
> The hill-side's dew-pearled ;
> The lark's on the wing ;
> The snail's on the thorn ;
> God's in his heaven—
> All's right with the world!
>
> (*Pippa Passes.*)

After 1850 Browning returned more than once to the long poems
on a single theme which had marked the beginning of his career.
Christmas Eve and Easter Day (1850) contains the clearest
definition of his religious sentiments, of his sympathy for the
various creeds each of which performs its work here below, and
of his own more liberal Christianity which includes and transcends
them. His masterpiece is *The Ring and the Book* (1868–9). Here
the story of the trial of Pompilia, accused by her husband Guido
of adultery with the young monk Caponsacchi, is set forth in ten
long successive monologues by the principal actors, witnesses, and
bystanders in the drama. Each section repeats the story of
the same events, varying it according to the different interests or
prejudices of the speaker : the poem shows, indeed, a startling
defiance of moderation. The repetition justifies itself by the light
it throws on the various characters and also by its psychological
purpose, which is to show the distortion of facts and motives as
they are interpreted by a group of human beings. But it is impossible to deny either the fault of prolixity which results from such a
process, or the amazing virtuosity of the poet and the magnificent
effects he achieved in the principal depositions.

A whole series of long poems followed this master work until Browning's death, but with less success; they betray the enfeeblement of his genius and exaggerate the defect which mars all his work, obscurity. This blighting obscurity derives in part from the subtlety of the poet, from his taste for brief and abrupt allusions, from the richness of his learning which he assumed (with a touch of pedantry) to be shared by the reader. It proceeds also from incomplete development of the style, which leaves too much of the work to be done by the reader.

To sum up, it was the excess of thought over art which imperilled Browning's poetry. But we must beware of supposing that his gifts were solely those of the thinker. If it were so, Browning would have no existence as a poet. On the contrary, he was almost stupendously endowed as a writer and versifier. He had at his command a vocabulary of rare extent which included many technical terms of all descriptions. He employed blank verse with an ease that might be called excessive, and no other poet has been able to juggle so dexterously with simple, double, or triple rhymes. Thus his verse effects are most varied, ranging from the tragic to the comic, and indeed to the grotesque. But he could restrain his exuberance on occasion, and replace it by a surprising compactness. His lyrical faculty burst forth in admirable short songs. One may cite as perfect masterpieces, in blank verse monologue *My Last Duchess*, and in rhymed stanzas the marvellous *A Woman's Last Word*, so weighted with sense and feeling in its inimitable brevity.

From a distance his distinctively poetic gifts stand out in greater relief against the background of a philosophy that is vigorous but no longer able to provide solutions as satisfying to the generations which have followed him as they seemed to his own.

Mrs. Browning. Elizabeth Barrett (1806 61) became Mrs. Browning in 1846. She was a few years older than her husband, and had begun by writing poems which were rather old-fashioned in form, and showed a curious mingling of the influences of the Bible, the Greeks, Byron, and Shelley. She turned with greater success to an imitation of Coleridge in her impressions of the Middle

Ages; then she gave voice to sensitive pity in *Cowper's Grave* and to passionate indignation in *The Cry of the Children*, an eloquent protest against the employment of children in factories. But her best work was done after she knew Browning. Her *Sonnets from the Portuguese*, written just before she married, tell of her love for Browning who found her ill and lonely and cured her with his tender care. In return she vowed a passionate gratitude to him: she had felt the shadow of death upon her, she had been brought back to life, and in complete self-surrender she won an ecstatic happiness.

> Then love me, Love! Look on me—breathe on me!
> As brighter ladies do not count it strange,
> For love, to give up acres and degree,
> I yield the grave for thy sake, and exchange
> My near sweet view of Heaven, for earth with thee.

Though her diction was far from pure, and her sense of rhythm uncertain, her sonnets abound in vivid phrases, in strong new images, in trenchant brevities. The narrow frame of the sonnet-form kept her habitual exuberance within bounds, and it is here, in *Sonnets from the Portuguese*, where her passion was most intense, that she best submitted to the discipline of art.

Her other great work, *Aurora Leigh* (1857), is as vast as an epic; indeed, it is a kind of domestic and contemporary epic on a romantic theme. It is in blank verse, and Mrs. Browning's blank verse was very unequal. Often in its extreme looseness it comes so close to prose as hardly to be distinguishable from it. Long stretches are dry without any beauty of form, and are besides spoilt by a pedantic wordiness, a sort of inflated utterance and affectation of masculinity. But there are many pages where sentiment and style alike are admirable, in passages both of irony and of lyrical emotion. Then the verse takes wing and soars with rare ease, and with a nervous strength that is characteristic of Mrs. Browning, showing her to be not only original but an equal of the greatest. It is to be regretted that this wide-flung and generously conceived poem could not be sustained to the end by a firmer artistic technique.

Arthur Hugh Clough. Wordsworth's influence is perceptible in almost every poet of this period: it is particularly strong in Clough and Matthew Arnold. Arthur Hugh Clough (1819–61) developed, indeed, in the opposite direction to Wordsworth; he moved from the narrow piety of his early years towards a religious faith freed from all dogma. He sought with great sincerity a moral law that could be conciliated with the great intellectual developments of the century. He attempted, especially in *Dipsychus*, 'the double-souled', (1850), to reconcile the sceptical and the idealistic tendencies of the soul. His best work, however, *The Bothie of Tober-na-Vuolich* (1848), is a gay and spirited account of an excursion of Oxford students in the Highlands, in which the purifying and spiritualizing power of Nature manifests itself as in Wordsworth. What Clough lacked was a surer art; his importance lies chiefly in the quality of his thought and the frank and noble vitality of his character.

Matthew Arnold. In Clough's friend Matthew Arnold (1822–88), we meet with the same search for a rule of life and a law of thought expressed with much greater lucidity. Arnold's importance as a prose-writer has already been discussed. His poetry is entirely reflective: he does not shine in constructing a story. Beside Arnold, even Wordsworth seems rich in narrative and in concrete details to bear the weight of his symbols. The comparison shows Arnold as too starkly intellectual. He lacked action and movement, which are necessary even to lyric poetry. But as a reflective writer he is often exquisite. He can express melancholy feeling with rare purity and, when he chooses, even with an emotion that is sometimes poignant. A great humanist, nurtured in the ancient literatures and a lover of Greek art, Arnold had a classic moderation and exactness of thought. When, indeed, he attempts tragedy, as in *Merope* (1858), or the epic manner, as in *Sohrab and Rustum*, he is only a poet of the second rank. His eminent quality is a deep-searching pensiveness; he expresses the turmoil of his soul in its regret for vanished faith and its anxious search for a new wisdom:

> The Sea of Faith
> Was once, too, at the full, and round earth's shore
> Lay like the folds of a bright girdle furl'd.

But now I only hear
Its melancholy, long, withdrawing roar,
Retreating, to the breath
Of the night-wind, down the vast edges drear
And naked shingles of the world.

(*Dover Beach.*)

His greatest or profoundest poems are *Tristram and Iseult,* the elegy *Thyrsis* on the death of his friend Clough, *The Scholar Gipsy, Dover Beach, The Forsaken Merman, The Church of Brou, Stanzas from the Grande Chartreuse,* and *Obermann.* The classic spirit reveals itself in the lucid style, the absence of violent effects, and the abandonment of those decorative graces which Arnold blamed Tennyson for abusing. But the romanticism against which he strove manifested itself in his disillusion and discontent with the present. Disciple of Wordsworth as he was, he sometimes betrayed the influence of Byronic disenchantment, though he substitued a melancholy resignation for Byron's mood of revolt.

The pre-Raphaelites. The simplicity of style cultivated by Arnold also had its place in the original programme of the pre-Raphaelites who, however, diverged from him in their refusal to load their verse with philosophy. The pre-Raphaelites were above all artists: art was their religion. Their very name bears witness to the relation which established itself at this time between poetry and painting. It belonged at first to a group of painters who had grown enthusiastic over the Italian primitives before Raphael. They admired the Middle Ages, and thus their reform led to the reappearance of one of the principal elements in the earliest Romanticism. It was also in harmony with the aesthetic ideas of Ruskin, the scorner of the Renaissance, who hailed the beginnings of the pre-Raphaelite movement. The first and greatest of the pre-Raphaelites, Rossetti, was a painter as well as a poet; and Morris also could use brush as well as pen.

The pre-Raphaelites worshipped beauty above everything. They echoed the American poet, the aesthete Edgar Allan Poe. Keats's love of beauty as an ideal made him their great inspirer among the Romantics. They found their favourite models in the

PLATE XXXVI

The Towers of Oxford from the south-west as Matthew Arnold may have seen them when he wrote 'The Scholar Gipsy'

poems he wrote in a medieval setting, such as the ballad of *La Belle Dame sans Merci, Isabella*, and *The Eve of Saint Agnes*. But they cultivated also the old Italian poets, Dante and his contemporaries, the old French poets like Villon, and the verse-romances of France, Great Britain, Germany, and Scandinavia.

D. G. Rossetti. Such are the general characteristics of this movement; but each poet left his own individual mark upon it. At their head was Dante Gabriel Rossetti (1828–82), the son of an Italian refugee in England, who produced his first pictures and his first poems in 1849. He translated Dante's *Vita Nuova* and fragments of old Italian poets. He sang of *The Blessed Damozel* in exquisite verse, while he made her the subject of one of his most characteristic canvasses:

> The blessed damozel leaned out
>   From the gold bar of Heaven;
> Her eyes were deeper than the depth
>   Of waters stilled at even;
> She had three lilies in her hand,
>   And the stars in her hair were seven. . . .
>
> It was the rampart of God's house
>   That she was standing on;
> By God built over the sheer depth
>   The which is Space begun;
> So high, that looking downward thence
>   She scarce could see the sun.

His chief poems, written in his youth, appeared in 1870 and were violently attacked for their sensuality by Robert Buchanan, who condemned 'the fleshly school of poetry'. His work consisted of sonnets and ballads. In the sonnets of *The House of Life* he poured out his love for his young and beautiful wife, whose loveliness he never tired of celebrating. These sonnets are rich to the point of excess, and subtle to the point of obscurity; in place of the medieval allegory they contain a sort of mystic symbolism which is unlike anything that had gone before it in English literature.

Rossetti drew inspiration for his ballads from the popular poetry of the Middle Ages but he transformed them by his artistic

refinement. He strove after simple strength and dramatic movement, making continual use of the refrain and obtaining striking
effects, but he could not hide the artificiality of such imitations of
a rude and simple poetry.

Rossetti's work is extremely individual and original. It is
distinguished in English literature by its rich Italian colouring
and its warm sensuous quality. Its peculiar characteristic is the
symbolic use of details to suggest a whole complex of feelings, like
the emblems used by the primitive Italian painters. This symbolism is as successful in intimate and familiar scenes, like the
admirable *My Sister's Sleep*, as in those mystic conceptions like
The Blessed Damozel, which are the very essence of pre-Raphaelite
spirit.

His sister Christina Rossetti (1830–94) in a sense represented
more perfectly the ideal of simplicity that was at the root of the
new movement. A woman of deep piety, passionately devoted to
her beliefs (she belonged to the Anglican Church), Christina lived
the life of an ascetic, refusing to marry a man with whom she was
in love, because he did not share her faith. Her poetry was pre-
dominantly religious. She showed a lyrical gift, a pure sense of
melody, and remarkable powers of versification in her short poems
upon the thought of death, the longing for the everlasting rest,
and the vanity of earthly things. But she possessed also a fanciful
imagination and a love of the country, and revealed them in the
most popular of her child poems, *Goblin Market*, a charming fairy
story which points a moral with light-hearted gaiety. Elsewhere,
though she avoided the 'conceits' of metaphysical poetry, she
often recalls the religious poets of the seventeenth century, such
as Herbert or Vaughan, in their most pure and crystalline verses.

Morris. William Morris (1834–96) found his earliest inspiration
in the Middle Ages. He loved everything Gothic; he fed his
imagination on the pages of Froissart, of Chaucer, and of Malory,
and there found the picturesque framework of his stories. When
he turned to antiquity it was in the spirit of the story-tellers of the
fourteenth century. Later on when he came to know the literatures
of Scandinavia and Iceland he treated them in the same manner.
But all the great legends as he told them are wrapped in a

PLATE XXXVII

"Buy from us with a golden curl"

Illustration designed by D. G. Rossetti as frontispiece to his sister Christina's volume, *Goblin Market and other Poems*, 1862

PLATE XXXVIII

ROBERT BRIDGES
Photograph by Percy Withers

THOMAS HARDY
Photograph by Walter Thomas

GEORGE BERNARD SHAW
Photograph by Raphael

RUDYARD KIPLING
By permission of Mr. Kipling

dreamy atmosphere; they have the air of vast frescoes in which characters move with expressive gestures; his poetry is like an immense tapestry. Although Morris saluted Chaucer as his master and turned his back on the Renaissance, it is Spenser whom he recalls and whom he resembles. Although he became prominent as a teller of famous stories he remained essentially lyrical; he never brings the reader close to reality like Chaucer or Walter Scott. These characteristics run through all his great compositions, *The Life and Death of Jason* (1867) and *The Earthly Paradise* (1868–70), which have the colour and soft air of the Mediterranean, and *Sigurd the Volsung* (1876), which is stamped with the ruggedness and virility of the North.

A prolific dreamer in love with beauty, delighting himself and his contemporaries with so many old tales grown precious with time; a translator besides of many a Scandinavian saga, of the *Aeneid* and of *Beowulf*, Morris showed surprising fertility and variety of rhythm, a rare flow of language, and on occasion a striking use of archaism. Yet no poet played a more active part in the life of his time. Like Ruskin he undertook to lead back to beauty a civilization made ugly by utilitarian industry. He strove to bring art into everyday life. He was an artist himself; a painter, and a designer of stained glass, tapestries, fabrics, wall-papers; the founder of a printing-press for editions-de-luxe; a reformer of English and, perhaps it might be added, of European furnishings. From this fine enterprise he passed on to a decided socialism which finds expression in his prose works, *A Dream of John Ball* and the charming utopia *News from Nowhere* (1891), a vision of a regenerated society from which the constraint of law and politics has almost disappeared, where pain and sorrow survive, but lessened, and where passion is still felt but in gentler shape, all in the peaceful setting of a Nature that is free to all.

William Morris's true genius, his lyrical quality tinged with sadness, is revealed in his shorter pieces perhaps more fully than in his longer poems and at least as fully as in his novels; this is true both of his earlier collection *The Defence of Guenevere and other Poems* (1858) and his final *Poems by the Way* (1891). The monotony which mars his most ambitious poems does not extend to his short pieces, which are likely to achieve a more permanent popularity.

Swinburne. Algernon Charles Swinburne (1837–1909) was the spoilt child of the pre-Raphaelite group, at once its prodigy and its embarrassment. But unlike the other members of the group he was a musician rather than a painter. However exquisite its musical qualities may be, the poetry of Rossetti or of Morris is primarily pictorial. It has line and colour. Swinburne's poetry lacks firm contours and sure outlines. The sonority of the rhymes or of the modulations is that which links the verses together. Vowels call to vowels, and consonants to consonants, and these links often seem stronger than the links of thought or imagery. From his youth upwards Swinburne manifested an unheard-of skill in versification, a gift for imitating the most widely differing rhythms, not only those of English poets but also those of the Latins, the Greeks, and the French. With this gift he would have surpassed all lyric poets if it were not that the noblest passages of melody result from the subtly-changing harmony between thought and rhythm. Swinburne did not wholly avoid the danger of betraying the incredibly perfect mechanism of his technique, and thus 'unsouling' his versification.

His subjects were the great romantic themes, Shelley's and Landor's revolt against society, the hatred of kings and priests, and the struggle against conventional morality; here he was inspired also by the French romantics, Victor Hugo on one side and Baudelaire on the other. The influence of the *Fleurs du Mal* is predominant in *Poems and Ballads* (1866), that of Hugo's *Châtiments* in *Songs before Sunrise* (1871). Swinburne's passion was sincere enough, but it was neither very personal nor very new. It was in the form of his poems, in his extraordinary lyrical onrush, that his mastery shone forth. For he was essentially lyrical even when he attempted drama, as he did at the start of his career. The success of *Atalanta in Calydon* (1865) was due to the beauty of the choral and dithyrambic passages. Dramatic movement and the creation of characters were outside his range.

The boldness of the tone of sensuous pleasure in *Poems and Ballads* provoked a scandal. But it was also a revelation of splendid audacity which aroused the enthusiasm of the younger generation, a thunder-clap like the appearance of *Childe Harold* fifty years earlier. This violent paganism broke in upon Victorian reserve; it was the first far-heard signal of a revolt that was not to become general till a generation later. It was passion's claim to express itself without reticence: it was the cult of Venus opposed to the cult of the 'pale Galilean'.

These songs of love were succeeded by poems dedicated to national liberty, especially that of Italy, for Swinburne was an ardent admirer of Mazzini. The vagueness and even emptiness of his rhapsodies are compensated for and veiled by his unfailing lyric ardour.

Swinburne returned to Love, his favourite theme, in two later series of *Poems and Ballads*, those of 1878 and 1889. He challenged Tennyson, opposing the decorous restraint of the *Idylls of the King* by the boundless passion of his *Tristram of Lyonesse* (1882) in which the ancient legend is retold by a poet unhampered by any moral considerations. This poem again is entirely lyrical; its merit lies not in the depiction of character, but in the richness of the descriptions, especially those of the sea, for which Swinburne had the passion of the English race, already manifest in the obscure but impressive *Sea farer*.

If upon the whole the substance of his poems seems slender beside the magnificence of the form it must not be concluded that his intelligence was uncultivated. He was an avid reader of wide knowledge, and in general was a good judge of the writers he admired. He was an abundant prose-writer and in several respects an original critic. The dithyrambic fervour poured out in more than one sonnet or elegy manifested itself also in the prose-pages of his *Blake* and of his studies in the Elizabethan dramatists. He revealed Blake's genius that had long lain in oblivion. He resumed Lamb's campaign on behalf of the contemporaries of Shakespeare. Undoubtedly his lyrical prose often errs in excess both of praise and blame. His abuse of superlatives not only wearies and repels the reader but tends to lessen the gaps between writers of very unequal merit. Nevertheless, his criticism more than once has a revealing power. It is founded on real and direct knowledge and on warmly sympathetic reading; and it abounds in appreciations that are more penetrating and judicious than might have been expected from his unbalanced temperament.

Meredith. Of an entirely different order from the poetry of Swinburne is that of George Meredith, whose genius as a novelist we have discussed. In Meredith thought is master and the often ill-matched form is sacrificed to it. Although he had some contact with the pre-Raphaelites, Meredith followed a separate path. He was not absorbed in the worship of art. He had a philosophy to express. Like Wordsworth he wished to communicate his comprehension of life and his particular view of morality. He began, it is true, with a poem of pure analysis of which the theme was love, the relations of husband and wife, their dissensions, misunderstandings, and their mutual infidelity which is ended by the death of the wife. This is *Modern Love* (1862), a series of fifty short poems each of sixteen lines rather like an extended sonnet. As mysterious as Shakespeare's *Sonnets*, as obscure as many of Browning's monologues, this collection has moments of singular beauty and an energy, a strangeness, a compactness of expression, which are peculiar to Meredith.

The rest of his poetry, apart from several generous political outbursts like the *Odes in Contribution to the Song of French History* (1898), is almost entirely occupied with the riddle of the world and the lessons of life to be drawn from it. Meredith attacks asceticism; he will shut out no instinct, even though it be founded in our animal nature; but his aim is to lead mankind through continuous evolution to a state of gradually widening intelligence and more refined spirituality. His ideas, more subtle than Wordsworth's and much less clear and communicable, are expressed with very unequal success in *Poems and Lyrics of the Joy of Earth* (1883) and *A Reading of Earth* (1888) in which his most beautiful verses are undoubtedly those dedicated to Nature, like *Love in a Valley*, *The Woods of Westermain*, *The Lark Ascending*, *The Thrush in February*, &c.

Meredith's poetry is rich in sense and substance, with short passages of unsurpassed loveliness, but its command of rhythm is imperfect, though it attempts the boldest experiments in versification. It remains a closed book to many readers and yields up its emotion or wisdom only to a small number of the elect.

Contemporary with the pre-Raphaelites but detached from them are Coventry Patmore and Fitzgerald. Coventry Patmore (1823–96) was a religious poet, at first a member of the Church of England, but converted in 1864 to Roman Catholicism. *The Angel in the House* (1854–60) describes the betrothal, the wedding, and the joys of a devout marriage in which the hearts are in accord. Its simplicity is sometimes exquisite, but it does not altogether avoid prosaic passages. Patmore's lyric talent shows to better advantage, less mingled with alloy, in *The Unknown Eros* (1877), a collection of irregular odes in a more sustained and majestic style.

Edward Fitzgerald (1809–83), an amateur of letters and a translator, achieved fame with his free poetic version of the Persian quatrains of *The Rubaiyat of Omar Khayyam* (1859). This is a poem full of pessimism, Oriental in tone, yet classical in its poise, which startled a century of self-satisfied prosperity, and fascinated it by its unfamiliar features, and by its insistence on the vanity of life. To this piece of ironic pessimism disguised under the cover of a translation was shortly afterwards added the work of James Thomson (1834–82), author of the most sombre and despairing poetry in the language. His masterpiece is *The City of Dreadful Night* (1874), a portrait of London by night as the seat of all human misery. Here Thomson puts into words the agony of life, in dark and powerful stanzas thronged with symbolic visions. This poem at the end of a self-confident age is like a prelude to the gloomier literature which was to come. It serves as a preface to the work of a Hardy or a Gissing: in itself it is the supreme song of despair.

To sum up, the rich, diversified, and prolific Victorian age continued the Romantic tradition, rounding it off and sometimes also contradicting it, if only by the greater and greater share allowed to Realism. In general its very prosperity made it complacent even in its satire and only towards the end of the period did there appear a pessimistic spirit which was to gather strength in the following age. Similarly, the Victorians had in general a great respect for the established code of morality, and in their imaginative writing refused to touch on questions which seemed likely to shake it. A sometimes rather narrow idea of propriety limited their excursions even into the realism on which the age prided itself, and this timid reserve provoked in following years a sarcastic protest that was excessive and that ignored the vast and splendid conquests of the Victorians. But it is clear that even during the last years of Queen Victoria's reign a reaction had set in, though some of the great men who have just been passed in review were still alive and still writing. Already some poets and some prose-writers, such as Rossetti, Swinburne, Meredith, and Samuel Butler, had set an example and formed a taste for new adventures, for freedom and daring, untrammelled by the reigning conventions. This movement, gradually quickening in pace, characterizes the literature which remains to be dealt with, that which belongs to the years between 1880 and the present day.

XXVIII

FROM 1880 TO THE PRESENT DAY

General Characteristics

THE literature of the period from 1880 to the present day can be neither studied in all its parts, nor viewed from a great enough distance to appear in its true proportions. All that is possible is to note the various currents flowing through it, the features of the past that it preserves, and the new trends which distinguish it.

The most striking thing about the last half-century is perhaps the rapidity and nervous excitement of its progress. A single generation has seen year by year marvellous inventions emerge to transform everyday life and give it a strangely quickened rhythm. Men who are middle-aged to-day were alive at the birth of the gramophone, the telephone, wireless telegraphy, and the cinema. They witnessed the first experimental beginnings and the marvellous development of the bicycle, the motor-car, and the aeroplane, and they still wonder at things which younger people accept without surprise as a part of their natural heritage. In the sphere of social ideas, feminism developed so vigorously that every chain which had fettered women was suddenly snapped, and they became at one blow electors to Parliament and eligible for it ; nearly every career reserved hitherto for men was opened to them. Socialism passed from theory to practice, and organized a party growing in strength and numbers which before the end of the period was to be called in its turn to govern the country.

Meanwhile a World War, surpassing all previous wars in extent, massacre of human beings, and heaped-up ruin, carried off the flower of a generation and left behind economic disturbances of which the end is not yet in sight ; but at the same time it prepared men's minds, which had been momentarily overwhelmed, for the setting up of a League of Nations designed to prevent all future wars. What had been the noble and impracticable dream of rare thinkers seemed to become for the first time a conscious determination and a generalized effort for peace and unity.

All these great changes were bound to find their echo in contemporary literature. They made it very different from what had gone before, they intensified the break with tradition, and at the same time they promoted a sort of literary anarchy which in poetry went so far that some writers cast aside the age-old forms of versification and attempted verse without fixed rules, called 'free verse'. Even in prose an extreme impressionism makes many recent works disconcerting to those still accustomed to the old rhetoric and to the logical and connected sequence of ideas.

Most of these features are characteristic of Europe, indeed, of the whole world, rather than of England alone. The following are more particularly English. The often desperate struggle between faith and science may be said to have been the mark of the preceding period: by 1880 this conflict was, on the whole, ended. For most writers Christianity was no longer an active force; instead of opposing the church, they ignored it. There were exceptions to this tendency, but they were too few to carry weight. The attitude which became general was rather that of the indifferent Meredith than that of the aggressive Swinburne. Not that religious sentiment had ceased to exist; after a period below the surface it reappeared in the most unexpected places, and in original shapes, as, for example, in the work of George Moore, Shaw and Wells. Meanwhile the abandonment of the old beliefs and the silent refusal of science to respond to the deepest questionings of mankind, led more than one writer into a pessimistic ethical philosophy which had hitherto made only an isolated appearance. The realistic method applied to a study of the condition of humanity cast a gloom over the novel at the end of the nineteenth century. From that deadly atmosphere it freed itself by bold attempts to reconstruct society on new lines, attempts which imply condemnation of the previous ideal. Social criticism was henceforward carried on with an unprecedented frankness, vigour, and power of attack. What had seemed the very foundations of English thought and life were denounced as if before a revolutionary tribunal. The last vestiges of feudal life were indicted in the name of Justice and

Socialism. Even the idea of the 'gentleman' was submitted to ironical analysis; and, above all, Victorian reticence with its refusal to depict passion and the excitements of sense gave place to a more and more daring representation of the realities of life. Cynicism was an accepted doctrine; for some time, under colour of aestheticism, a certain decadence was the fashion. Concern with morality was held by some people to be incompatible with the liberty of the mind and the truth of representation.

Side by side with this great alteration in the general point of view in England there was a cosmopolitan development in literature without parallel in the past. Since the beginning of the nineteenth century England had acknowledged no ascendancy but that of Germany, and even that was rather in the world of philosophy and scholarship than in that of literature. But now she was turning again towards France, whither Arnold and Swinburne had led the way. In fiction she welcomed the doctrines of the naturalistic school of novelists, and in poetry those first of the French Parnassians and then of the Symbolists. Scandinavian and Russian influences made their way, and England grew enthusiastic over Ibsen and Tolstoy. The whole career of an eminent man of letters like Sir Edmund Gosse (1849–1928) was filled by the sympathetic study of these foreign literary currents. On the other hand, the extraordinary growth of the literature of the United States had a marked effect; for the identity of language made possible a continuous literary commerce. Whitman found imitators of his democratic fervour and his irregular versification. Under the influence of both America and France the short story multiplied exceedingly, and the three volume Victorian novel came to an end. The subject-matter of literature became less and less insular: the colonies, the dominions, and foreign countries all began to come within its range. A half-foreigner like Lafcadio Hearn or a Pole like Conrad was to be found taking his place among leading writers.

The intense nationalism of Kipling was, no doubt, a reply to this intellectual cosmopolitan movement, but Kipling himself, being the great champion of imperialism, spread his curiosity over the Seven Seas and no one tried harder to make his books the mirror of the whole globe. Following Carlyle's lead, Kipling glorified the energy of his race, but in so doing helped powerfully to widen the field of English literature.

There were others who tried to withstand the subversive thrust. Orthodoxy found defenders like Chesterton. The novels of Shorthouse, of Mrs. Humphry Ward, of Father Hugh Benson, the verses of Mrs. Meynell and Francis Thompson, were answers to religious indifference. And so the harmony of the whole music is made up of a hundred diverse and often discordant voices. Meanwhile the Celtic revival foreseen by Matthew Arnold produced remarkable works. It disturbed and enriched current conceptions of aesthetic beauty: Ireland had cut herself off from literary union even before her political separation.

Finally a striking event is the rebirth of the theatre, which, after vegetating for a century with an antiquated repertory and no few borrowings from abroad, awoke again to an independent, active, and original life.

Criticism

A glance first of all at literary criticism will help us to distinguish some of the principal currents of our time. We must begin by noticing how in criticism itself the scientific spirit has encroached on the domain of letters. Literary history, like history in general, becomes more and more the object of learned research which in its methods, in its study of documents, in its statistics, and in its attempt at impassivity is related rather to science than to letters properly so called. Scholarship pursues its task in specialist books and articles, using an often highly technical vocabulary for the benefit of the initiated. It employs thousands of humble and sometimes anonymous workers. If it produces general surveys they are usually co-operative works in which various specialists have collaborated. The belief that historical truth is attainable only by these means has brought a certain discredit on individual and personal criticism which does not bear clearly enough the mark of erudite scholarship. But the need for such criticism persists, even though its authority be diminished. It continues to exist and resigns itself to the charge of possessing only temporary value; for it is conscious of performing an indispensable task. Those who practise it exhibit their own tastes and preferences of temperament, and so are nearer neighbours of the purely imaginative writers. They exercise a more direct effect on their readers' minds. They usually have views of their own and a style marked with their personality; and they may themselves become real literary figures.

These two opposite tendencies are well illustrated by the parallel careers of two men whose work appeared round about 1880.

Leslie Stephen. The first, Sir Leslie Stephen (1832–1904) wrote biographical and critical essays: *Hours in a Library* (1874–9) and *History of English Thought in the Eighteenth Century* (1876). He carried on the study of the latter subject to produce in 1900 *The English Utilitarians*. His vast learning led to his being entrusted from 1882 onwards with the editorship of the *Dictionary of National Biography*, a task which fatigue obliged him to hand over to Sidney Lee in 1891. Leslie Stephen was first and foremost a biographer and a historian. As a rationalist and agnostic, he was particularly interested in the eighteenth century, with its belief in reason and its characteristic features of lucid thought and style. Stephen's main qualities as a critic were self-repression, and a genuine desire to get at the truth by a careful study of events and books. In so far as the spread of well-ascertained and precise knowledge was his principal object, he may be regarded, in spite of striking individual differences, as first of the line of critics of the last half-century who have been both scholars and men of letters, such as Edward Dowden, A. C. Bradley, W. P. Ker, George Saintsbury, C. H. Herford, Oliver Elton, and H. J. C. Grierson, to cite only a few of the most distinguished of those who have concentrated on the study of English literature.

Walter Pater. Meanwhile, a contemporary of Leslie Stephen, Walter Pater (1839–94), a fellow of Brasenose College, Oxford, published in 1873 *Studies in the History of the Renaissance*, which was followed after a long interval by *Imaginary Portraits* (1887), *Appreciations* (1889), *Plato and Platonism* (1893); and by the novel *Marius the Epicurean* (1885). Pater taught a literary doctrine, that of 'art for art's sake'; and a moral doctrine, that of hedonism, or the quest for the greatest or most refined pleasure.

He invited the reader to taste among all possible joys those which he himself considered most exquisite; and the most exquisite, he thought, were those which came from art or from the reflection of the past. He enjoyed analysing the passionate, ingenious, and accomplished figures of the Renaissance. He did not write in order to instruct, but amused himself in elaborating a style capable of expressing the subtleties of a complex mind. He achieved a prose that was both rich and subtle, musical, full of delicate shades, but always held in check by a firm classical sense; it takes rank among the most refined of English prose styles. It is wrought with as much care as highly polished verse. The product of finished craftsmanship, it can hold its own with poetry as a medium for purely poetical effects.

A similar tendency is displayed in John Addington Symonds (1840–93), who specialized even more than Pater in the study of the Renaissance: *The Renaissance in Italy* (1875–86), *Shakespeare's Predecessors in the English Drama* (1884). These books are written in a richly figured style which suffers from being overburdened with ornament.

About 1890 the group of aesthetes of whom Oscar Wilde was the most brilliant representative were actively formulating doctrines and applying them. Oscar Wilde will be discussed later as a novelist and a dramatist; but he could also be a theorist when he chose, as in *Intentions* (1891). He spiced the doctrine of 'art for art's sake' with a certain cynicism; wit, paradox, and mocking humour give a keen edge to his beautifully wrought prose.

'Art for art's sake' soon roused opposition from the national genius. It was accepted but at the same time modified by R. L. Stevenson, a great stylist whose prose was nevertheless vigorously full of fresh air and the spirit of adventure; but it was bitterly opposed by William Ernest Henley (1849–1903) in *Views and Reviews* (1890–1901) who assumed the old dogmatic tone and whose trenchant judgements had their effect upon the younger generation. Sir Walter Raleigh (1861–1922), in his vivid studies of Shakespeare, Milton, Johnson, and Wordsworth, was concerned with the problems of his subjects' characters and the motive principles of their lives rather than with pure aesthetics; and it was to his psychological boldness and penetration that Lytton Strachey owed his success in his striking evocations of the recent past: *Eminent Victorians* and *Queen Victoria*.

These are only a few aspects of the enormous critical output of the last half-century but they will help us a little to find our bearings among the still confused mass of imaginative writers, poets, and novelists.

Poetry

Since Swinburne there has been no startling poetic apparition. The poems which have made a stir are for the most part the work of authors who were first and foremost writers of prose: Stevenson, Kipling especially, and Hardy. Not that poets have been rare, they have never been so numerous; not that they have indolently followed the beaten tracks, for many of them have been inspired by the spirit of novelty and rebellion against admitted rules. But prose has gained the ascendancy and absorbed the attention of the public even more completely than in the Victorian era. Beside the prolific and often vigorous output of novels, and the revival of the theatre, pure poetry seems slender, dispersed, and lacking in volume of utterance.

The Poet Laureate who succeeded Tennyson, Alfred Austin (1835–1913), is a forgotten figure. The Laureate who followed him, Robert Bridges (1844–1930), stands out more clearly; like Sir Edmund Gosse, Watts-Dunton (1832–1914), and Sir William Watson (born in 1858) he was distinguished by an exquisite and scholarly classicism and by the polished form of his verse. His collected *Shorter Poems* (1890) marked him as a lyric poet of high rank. In 1929 he published, at the age of 85, *The Testament of Beauty*, a long poem written in 'loose Alexandrines', to use his own term. It is a philosophical poem of remarkable vitality and energy, and is interspersed with beautiful passages of natural description and human wisdom. C. M. Doughty (1843–1926), the explorer of Arabia, was distinguished by an epic imagination, austere to an excess in *The Dawn of Britian* (1906–7), *The Titans* (1916), and *Mansoul* (1920).

Kipling. But the real sensation in the last decade of the nineteenth century was undoubtedly the poetry of Rudyard Kipling.

It roused some people to wild enthusiasm, others to protest, and it surprised every one. Deliberately intended to appear rugged and vulgar, it was a clever combination of the folk-song and the music-hall chorus, with a command of rhythm worthy of Swinburne. Into this rough mould were poured heroic themes and sentiments. It resounded like a drum-beat or a bugle-call among the exquisite refinements of chamber music. It progressed like a military march with growing dignity from the *Barrack-Room Ballads* of 1892 to the *Seven Seas* of 1896 and the *Five Nations* of 1903. It was the hymn of Imperialism, taken up by thousands of voices; it contained an entire popular philosophy, a whole national policy. The poems were roughly-hammered, sinewy, without delicate graces; but with a powerful and compelling swing. Sometimes the language is pure slang, sometimes it is largely Biblical. With these different means Kipling achieved a volume of effects which made him the English counterpart of the American Walt Whitman.

The same imperialistic theme was handled by W. E. Henley, another apostle of energy who preached to the languid the duty of adventure and of taking risks in *The Song of the Sword* (1892) and *For England's Sake* (1900). He strove in his forceful verse to set down his sensations directly; he showed himself an impressionist in *In Hospital* (1903) and in *London Voluntaries* (1893). His violence and his real strength exercised an undeniable influence on his contemporaries.

The Decadents. Opposite these poets of effort and action were ranged the aesthetes whose doctrine was 'Art for art's sake' and who bore the name of decadents. The periodical *The Yellow Book*, illustrated by Aubrey Beardsley, which appeared from 1894 to 1897, was their rallying point. With its daring subjects and crude realism this publication caused a scandal like that aroused by Swinburne's *Poems and Ballads*. The representative poet of this movement was Oscar Wilde; but he would have left behind nothing but the memory of a decadent elegance if crime and imprisonment had not matured his utterance and inspired him with the poignant verse of *The Ballad of Reading Goal* as well as the prose of *De Profundis*.

Pessimists. In addition to the decadent aesthetes there were the pessimists. Pessimism filled the poems of John Davidson (1857–1909), *Fleet Street Eclogues* (1893–96), and *Ballads and Songs* (1894), and the verse of Ernest Dowson (1867–1900). The latter shows the influence of the French poet Verlaine, the Villon of the nineteenth century. The pessimistic impulse found a classical and crystalline expression in the *Shropshire Lad* (1896) and *Last Poems* (1922) of A. E. Housman (born in 1859) who admitted into his miniature volumes nothing but the quintessence of the exquisite. The great novelist Hardy, discouraged by the unfavourable reception of his novel *Jude the Obscure*, devoted himself entirely to poetry after 1898 when he published his *Wessex Poems*. At the age when most poets veer towards prose he revealed himself a poet. In spite of the effort which it cost him to master the forms of verse, in spite of a certain prosaic awkwardness, Hardy's sincerity and frankness produced poetry that was both musical and highly individual. He was the poet of disillusionment. From the short lyric pieces of his *Wessex Poems* he passed to the ambitious undertaking of *The Dynasts* (1903–8), the vastest poetical work of modern times. It describes Napoleon's struggle against Europe, combining historical realism with the symbolism of a new mythology. Supernatural spectators of the great conflict comment on each catastrophe and draw from it a lesson of bitter resignation; but the distant hope of a less evil world is allowed to survive.

Religious Poets. Religious faith held its own chiefly among Roman Catholics, such as Mrs. Alice Meynell (1850–1922); and it was magnificently expressed in the work of Francis Thompson (1859–1907) who may be looked on as a successor of Coventry Patmore, though his talent was of a very different order. *Love in Dian's lap* and *Sister Songs* were followed by some flamboyant odes, the most famous being *The Hound of Heaven*. Francis Thompson recalls the metaphysical poets of the seventeenth century, especially Crashaw. His descriptions are extraordinarily rich and colourful; his eloquence is passionate, but sometimes too rhetorical.

The strange and obscure poems of the Jesuit, Gerard Manley Hopkins (1844–89), a nineteenth-century Southwell, were not conveniently available until 1918, when they impressed themselves on readers by virtue of their technical novelty and subtle under-currents of emotion.

The Celtic Revival. Among the poets produced by the Celtic revival an honourable place must be given to G. W. Russell (Æ.): but W. B. Yeats (born in 1865) holds an unchallenged pre-eminence. He was born in Ireland, and Irish, English, and Continental influences met in him. Some of his work is pervaded with a Celtic mysticism that is based on ancient Irish traditions but modified and completed by the symbolism of the day, by pre-Raphaelite refinement, and by the strange visions of Blake. Yeats's youthful poems have an airy grace; they deal with imaginative, ideal love and are written in a smooth, simple manner which contrasts strangely with the vaporous subtlety of the matter. As he progressed he became more intellectual; his poetry has proved more masculine but a little of its first charm has vanished.

Numerous poets have appeared since the beginning of the twentieth century whose work remains unfinished. A place apart must be given to those whose career was cut short by the world war; of these the best known is Rupert Brooke (1887–1915). His precocious gifts had already attracted attention; he seemed to be a fanciful follower of the aesthetes; but war gave his verse an impressive gravity, strength, and pathos.

Other poets. We cannot do more than name a few of the living poets who have shown something more than promise. Alfred Noyes (born in 1880) early achieved popularity without straying from the traditional paths. The present Poet Laureate, John Masefield (born in 1878), a vigorous, talented, but uneven writer, has made an original contribution to the complex mass of modern poetry, with his forcible style, strong, concrete vision, and vivid, penetrating realism. He follows Kipling in his love of physical energy, Walt Whitman in his joyful sense of human comradeship. He has experimented in various kinds of poetry without settling down to any one of them, and it is not easy to summarize his character as a poet. Classical inspiration is felt in the work of T. Sturge Moore, Laurence Binyon, James Elroy Flecker, and John Drinkwater. Walter de la Mare's poetry is distinguished by a subtle symbolism. Edmund Blunden has renewed in English verse the heavenly dreams of Vaughan, but clouded by the sad modern knowledge of the Great War. Lascelles Abercrombie, in his verses narrative, dramatic, or directly philosophic, inquires into the nature of things, as in *Emblems of Love* (1912), a poem on the possibilities of romantic love, and the *Sale of St. Thomas* (1930), based on the old legend of St. Thomas as the Apostle of India and containing a noble effort to express the consummation of human experience. Several younger writers have adopted the 'imagism' developed in America and France. This consists in the pursuit of spontaneity, in the effort to capture sensations and images in advance of the process of considered reflection. The imagist shuns abstract terms and logical constructions: he is content simply to suggest. A characteristic representative of this manner is James Stephens, an Irish poet and story-teller whose slight fragments of verse are as natural and musical as the song of birds.

T. S. Eliot, who is by birth American, has been adopted by many recent poets as their leader and symbol. His *Collected Poems* are perhaps the finest example of the allusive, indirect, modern style, intellectual and learned, in which the poet's consciousness of his emotions finds expression rather than the emotions themselves. *The Waste Land* (1922) was hailed by some as the greatest modern poem. Since then Eliot's verse has sought to express a return towards Catholicism. He has no less distinguished himself as a literary critic and ethical thinker.

Plain simplicity, delicate refinement, realism, symbolism, impressionism continue to be developed side by side. Many writers have shown that they possess great powers of various kinds; some have attempted reforms in versification that are bold almost to rashness. But there is no central personality, no clear dominating tendency. It is hard to predict what the next developments of English poetry will be, though we cannot deny that its vitality is as great as ever.

The Novel

Hardy. If poetry is plentiful, novels are yet more so; and they reflect the age with its various tendencies of thought and feeling more clearly and directly.

A gloomy realism pervades many of the outstanding books of the end of the nineteenth century. One of the leading novelists of the period is Thomas Hardy (1840–1928). His work is tinged with the pessimism of Schopenhauer, and presents striking analogies with the French naturalistic writing of Flaubert and Zola, due not to imitation but to community of atmosphere. Hardy lived an isolated life in his native district, Dorsetshire and the surrounding region, the 'Wessex' of his novels; and his work is, therefore, devoted to provincial and still more to rural life. His concern is for the bonds which unite men with the countryside in which they live, and their present lives with the distant past. The setting has a poetry of its own; the land itself, with its woods and fields, heaths and downs, is a character in Hardy's novels. Descriptions are never put in merely for decorative effect; places are made to exert a deep and constant influence on human beings. Hardy's country is rich in memories, scattered with Roman camps and barrows that go back to prehistoric times. This dim past still presses upon the life of to-day; action and destiny are controlled by an inexorable heritage. Thus the freedom of the living is curtailed, apparently even destroyed. Fatalism is dominant. Mysterious, all-powerful forces and blind chance guide the affairs of mankind. Victorian optimism with its belief in responsible liberty gives place to an infinite bitterness—a bitterness which shows no trace of revolt, but the calm of fate and resignation.

This philosophy emerges from the series of novels which Hardy published between 1870 and 1896. They are related to one another both in their setting and in their fatalism. The best of them are *Far from the Madding Crowd* (1874), *The Return of the Native* (1878), *The Mayor of Casterbridge* (1885), *The Woodlanders* (1887), *Tess of the d'Urbervilles* (1891), and *Jude the Obscure* (1896). Hardy's success grew steadily and reached its climax in *Tess*. The bold coarseness of certain scenes in *Jude* caused a scandal, but this opposition is a thing of the past. The public was eventually conquered by the author's strong sincerity and harmony, and when Hardy died in 1928 he was acclaimed as the patriarch of English letters, the greatest literary figure of his time.

Hardy exhibits in his books elemental passion, deep instinct, the human will struggling against fatal and ill-comprehended laws, a victim also of unforeseeable chance. His mastery lies in the creation of the natural surroundings, and here he shows himself to be a great nature poet, who can make discoveries through close observation and acute sensitiveness. He notices the smallest and most delicate details, yet he can also paint vast landscapes, particularly of his own Wessex in its melancholy or noble moods. Everything conspires to leave an impression of disenchantment in the reader's mind; to throw into relief the great ironies of life, just as the small ones are brought out in the striking collection of short stories, *Life's Little Ironies* (1894).

Gissing. The beauty of nature, even when she is indifferent or hostile, sheds a consoling charm over Hardy's realism. The work of George Gissing (1857–1903) was also realistic, and in the absence of this beautiful setting, it produces an effect of overwhelming and absolute dejection. Chance and distress forced him to undertake ill-paid hack work, and he knew more of the poor districts of London than of the country. The scenes of Gissing's books resemble those of many of the novels of Dickens; he was an admirer of the great novelist and published a remarkable study of him, *Charles Dickens*, in 1898. But he has no trace of the humour which lights up Dickens's pictures of London; he knows nothing of the gaiety which shines forth in so many of the poor wretches created by his predecessor. Gissing had experienced the misery of life in London, and did not forget its bitterness and horror. The resemblance to the extreme naturalistic writers of the French school is far stronger in him than in Hardy. He has no hope of setting right the evils which he describes, he seems not to believe in any vision of social betterment. In *The Unclassed* (1884) he describes the tragedy of those who have gone down in the world; *Demos* (1886) deals with the uselessness of socialist agitation; *The Nether World* (1889) with the degradation of the slums; *New Grub Street* (1891) with the penniless writer's hopeless effort to make his way; *Odd Women* (1893) with the dreary lot of the unmarried woman struggling to live in a society that cares nothing for her.

The desire for complete objectivity prevented Gissing from attempting any lyrical effects, any transformation of ugly features, in his gloomy and oppressive work, made sordid by its very subject-matter: he curbs on principle a sensitiveness that might easily become sentimental. He is deliberately 'shorn of his beams' except in the rare moments when his restrained passion rises to eloquence. Yet in spite of appearances he is a true humanist, an ardent Hellenist, and his bare, unaffected, sober, and lucid prose is among the best of the period.

Stevenson. The English temperament could not yield entirely to pessimism. The love of action and energetic life were too deeply ingrained in it for it to indulge persistently in a state of inert despair. The antidote was found in a revival of the novel of adventure and the open spaces. The first great writer to satisfy the national craving during this period of gloom was Robert Louis Stevenson (1850–94). This young Scot would have had more excuse than most people if he had given way to despair, for his life was a perpetual struggle against an incurable malady, a respite won from death. But as life slipped from him, he laid hold on it with redoubled strength, writing by choice for the young, for readers who love tales of travel and adventure better than morbid analyses of states of mind. In *An Inland Voyage* (1878) and *Travels with a Donkey in the Cevennes* (1879), he described his wanderings in France. *The Silverado Squatters* (1883) is an account of the Far West of America. In *Treasure Island* (1883) Stevenson supplied the younger generation with a prime favourite. With *Kidnapped* (1886), *The Master of Ballantrae* (1889), and *Catriona* (1893) he returned to the Scottish novel of Sir Walter Scott, giving it a rapid energetic pace.

He ventured once outside his usual limits, in *The Strange Case of Dr. Jekyll and Mr. Hyde* (1886), a symbolic tale of man's dual nature, good and evil; but it owes its peculiar force less to its psychology than to bold outline and to the ingenuity with which it is told. In addition to this imaginative work he also produced a number of essays on morals and literature, in particular *Virginibus Puerisque* (1881), and some delightful poems of which the best known are *A Child's Garden of Verses* (1885). He was obliged to emigrate for health's sake to Samoa in the Pacific, and produced a number of vivid and detailed descriptions of these regions, which were then almost unknown to literature. He died in Samoa at the age of 44.

In all his work Stevenson combines the old delight in story-telling and romance with modern realism. These antagonistic forces are reconciled in his style, which is amazingly successful, a natural gift carefully cultivated. By a triumph of art it achieves complete clarity without losing vigour and picturesqueness and often delights the reader with a sense of classic perfection. Stevenson's skill and ease in composition are as remarkable as his style. He takes a foremost place as a short story writer: *The Pavilion on the Links*, *Thrawn Janet*, and *The Beach of Falesa* are leading examples; and not less so as a novelist, in respect of most of his work, whether it be pure fiction like *Treasure Island* or partly historical like *Kidnapped*. His qualities give him a unique distinction among the prose writers of his time.

His cultivation of style—in which he was influenced by France, as he himself recognized—did not, however, range him with the aesthetes who pursued art for art's sake. Though he broke away from the strong religious traditions of his Scottish upbringing, and though his life was typically Bohemian, those traditions reappear in him under the form of a concern—chiefly, indeed, negative—for morality, which made him exclude from his work anything that might offend young readers, and preserve a clear distinction between right and wrong even in his most outspoken passages. In fine, we may look back at Stevenson as a vital and attractive writer whose reputation is less likely than those of many of his contemporaries to be disturbed by passing fashions in philosophy or politics.

Kipling. A few years later Rudyard Kipling followed Stevenson with his stories of Indian life—*Plain Tales from the Hills* and *Soldiers Three* (1888). At first they seemed in comparison with the highly artistic tales of Stevenson to have a certain taint of vulgarity. Kipling was a journalist, born in Bombay in 1865; he told stories of the country of his birth, the natives, the English officials, and above all the soldiers whom he had known. The brutality in his manner was excused by the force and flavour of the telling. Gradually he evolved a new and really artistic technique, and applied it in the next series of tales—*Life's Handicap* (1891),

Many Inventions (1893), and *The Day's Work* (1898), in which the short story reached its highest point of realistic or imaginative intensity. We have discussed Kipling's poetry: the poet in him showed again in the prose of his marvellous animal epic, the two *Jungle Books* (1894 and 1895). Kipling had already attempted a regular novel in *The Light that Failed* (1890); he now produced the incomparable *Kim* (1901) and a whole series of stories for children, including *Captains Courageous* (1897), *Stalky and Co.* (1899), *Just So Stories* (1902), and *Puck of Pook's Hill* (1906), to name only the most popular.

Kipling loved pioneers, adventurers, abnormal people suspected because they were too independent or looked down on because they were vulgar, simple soldiers on foreign service, black sheep who make up for their faults by their bravery; but he discovered a peculiar vein of instruction which distinguished him from Stevenson, who was primarily an entertainer. Under a superficial appearance of cynicism Kipling possessed a highly consistent philosophy influenced by Carlyle's doctrine of energy and resembling the temperament of W. E. Henley. He made himself, as has been said, the spokesman of Imperialism. He thought not merely that happiness was to be found in action, but that the ideal of ethics consisted in the sacrifice of the individual to the interests of the tribe. He claimed that leadership was the right and the duty of the white man, and particularly of the Anglo-Saxon. He loved to depict the fierce struggle against natural or savage forces. He glorified the bond that linked Englishmen of the dominions and colonies to the mother country. He laid stress on the deep common emotions which made them one even though dispersed. He showed how the worst errors could be redeemed by unostentatious service to the community.

Pride in energy and joy in effort stretched to breaking-point gives Kipling's work its significance: and the energy he praises belongs to his own genius. It is visible in his forceful concentrated narrative and in his tense style. He has a unique power of concrete vision. With a phrase, a single word, he evokes a scene or a country: and at the same time he is at home in the mysteries of every craft, master of every kind of technical language, every sort of soldiers' or sailors' slang.

With all these harsh and violent qualities, Kipling is a lover of children. No one has understood them better than he, and no one has written more delightful books for them. For very small children there is nothing to rival the fantastic humour of *The Just So Stories*; and alone of modern writers he has created an entire mythology for older boys and girls in the *Jungle Books*, which are the most truly imaginative works of the nineteenth century just as *Pickwick* is the most exhilarating.

This imaginative power and also the exotic scenery of many of his books gained for Kipling, the supremely and aggressively nationalist writer, an instant and boundless popularity all over the world. Kipling is even more responsible than Stevenson for the growth of a vast literature whose theme is action and the open-air life, even in countries which had been handled roughly by his material vigour.

In his own country, on the other hand, his ascendancy has waned since imperialism ceased to be the ruling religion. The growth of socialism and the spread of international pacifism have checked his popularity, clashing as they do with his feudal idea of a military order of society based on personal loyalty alone. But the literary value of his work remains unimpaired, and Kipling is more certain to survive than almost any of his contemporaries. Some of them show more delicacy or greater subtlety, but no one equals him in the vigour of his grasp or can pack so much within the narrow compass of a short story.

Kipling's work is, in fine, a glorification of the genius of England, of the instincts and the practical opportunism of his race through-out the ages. It was to be countered by a group of writers who won popularity at about the same time or very shortly afterwards, and who shared in common the characteristic of being determined critics of English society as it was, and hostile to its traditional ideals. These writers were Shaw, Wells, and Galsworthy.

H. G. Wells. The first of these three will be considered as a dramatist. H. G. Wells, born in 1868, was first a draper's assistant and then a pupil of Huxley, the biologist. He began his literary career by writing stories with a semi-scientific flavour, based on the imaginative development of some fact of science; such were

The Time Machine (1895), *The Island of Dr. Moreau* (1896), *The Invisible Man* (1897), *The War of the Worlds* (1898), and *The Food of the Gods* (1904). Here he uses the special kind of marvel which can be suggested by modern science. These ingenious tales, told in simple, vigorous language, thrill and disturb the reader with their deliberate harshness and cruelty; of all his books they have had the widest circulation at home and abroad.

From physics and biology Wells passed on to social problems. For a time he was a member of the Fabian Society, and wrote treatises like *Anticipations* (1902) and *Mankind in the Making* (1903) in which he gives an imaginative picture of society in the future reformed by socialism. With the new century he began a series of novels on social themes, of which the best known are *Love and Mr. Lewisham* (1900), *Kipps* (1905), *Tono-Bungay* and *Ann Veronica* (1909), *The New Machiavelli* (1911), and *Marriage* (1912), sarcastic pictures of social life as he saw it, with glimpses of life as it might be and as, according to him, it should be. Few men have been so little hampered and checked as he by the sense of tradition and the weight of heredity; he seems to have no sentimental links with the past. English life as he sees it, with its remains of a graded social hierarchy, is represented by the 'Bladesover System' for which he has nothing but scorn and irony. The material life of England is backward like its social organization. Wells cheerfully makes a clean sweep of existing institutions, finding them out of date, silly, and unreasonable. The root of the evil lies in the confusion produced by the universal rule-of-thumb methods of living, in 'muddling through'. What is needed is a reformation on the lines of that scientific progress which has so far had but little effect on English life.

Born in the lower middle rank of society and uninfluenced by the classical type of education, Wells resembles Dickens in origin, but unlike Dickens he is not content merely to make the social system more tolerable: he is ready and anxious to abolish it. He sifts all conventional values and boldly reconstructs the world. To the biologist society is nothing but a field for experiment, and the experimenter is restrained by no prejudice and no instinct: he can launch himself unhampered upon the career of sociological inventor.

PLATE XXXIX

The library of the British Museum: the great circular Reading Room, opened in 1857.
See p. xvi

PLATE XL

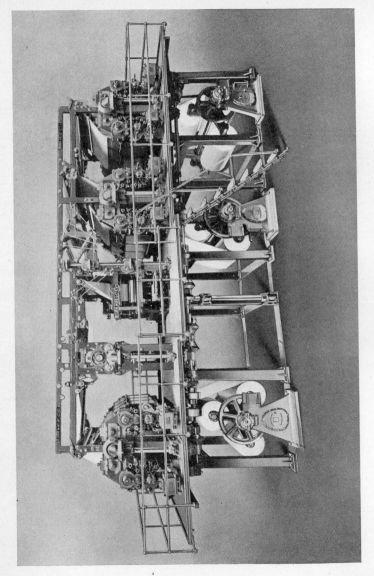

A modern newspaper printing machine. See p. xvi

Moreover, in painting a picture of this past which he condemns, Wells has been able to draw upon memories of his early years, upon his own knowledge of the failures and injustices of society. He has turned to his own experience of life, to the spectacle of absurdities which he himself has witnessed. His best novels, like *Kipps* and *Tono-Bungay*, are rich in direct observation and impression. Later on his theories and ideas about reform have entered more and more into the pictures he draws and the characters he presents. His novels have lost their firm outlines; the action halts and languishes; the teller of tales forgets his story. His style also grows uncertain, becoming impressionistic, abrupt, and jerky. The penalty of Wells's astonishing fecundity is weak, inartistic construction and too many improvisations of style.

On the other hand, in his later novels written after the outbreak of war in 1914, there appears a new mysticism which has disconcerted those who accepted his uncompromising worship of science. The most remarkable of these novels are *Mr. Britling Sees it Through* (1916), *Joan and Peter* (1918), and *The Undying Fire* (1919). Like *God the Invisible King* (1917), they bear witness to the continued restlessness of a self-examining spirit which cannot remain satisfied with any of the positions it has previously attained and which is always moving on and always searching, however self-confident it may seem to be in each of its successive phases.

H. G. Wells advances towards a goal which constantly recedes and which even he himself does not clearly perceive; but he hastens towards it with a vivacity, a dash, and a decisiveness which are in themselves a surprising sight. He has outstanding gifts of a purely literary kind but they are mixed with faults which make the survival of his work a matter of doubt. Yet the great stir which his books have made in the world is already a sufficient success. Wells writes for immediate effect and he has known better than any other writer how to make social problems obvious, close, and tangible. It matters little to him apparently that he has left few characters who force themselves upon the mind by their own merits, independently of the ideas and doctrines which they illustrate. It is an achievement to have interested and stirred one generation.

Galsworthy. Artistic conscience is always prominent, on the contrary, in the work of John Galsworthy (1867–1933), another keen critic of national prejudices, but of a different type from Wells, with a dissimilar point of view. Galsworthy came not from the lower-middle class but from the landed gentry, and he was able to pass judgement upon a section of society of which Wells knows little. His training was classical, not scientific, and he had a wide knowledge of Continental literature, being especially influenced by that of France and Russia. He always kept a literary ideal before him; the concise and noble realism of Turgenieff served him for a model. With deep roots in his native soil, Galsworthy achieved by sheer effort of will an intellectual detachment which allowed him to observe and judge his own country as though he were outside it; in this he was a successor of Matthew Arnold, Meredith, and Samuel Butler. He is entirely clear-sighted and astonishingly impartial, but his satire contains a quivering sensitiveness foreign to Wells, and also an acute perception of the charm and merit of the dying order of society which he is attacking.

His realism also shows, moreover, a sort of revival of the Romantic spirit in the respect and place which he gives to strong emotion. The characteristics that he condemns most readily in his fellow countrymen are, in the first place, their attitude of hostile suspicion towards open, genuine, and violent passion unrestrained by social convention: and, secondly, their distrust of unfettered intellectual activity, and of the fearless search for truth.

After a few tentative novels he found himself in *The Island Pharisees* (1904). Here, by contrast with the bold revolutionary ideas of a Continental anarchist, he throws into relief the stagnation of thought in the English privileged classes, with their rejection of any emotion which seems to them too strong, new, or disturbing, and their preference for dull settled conformity. He shows how even when they have good intentions they are shackled by their egoism and terrified both by emotional impulse and by audacity of thought.

The five works entitled *The Country House* (1907), *Fraternity* (1909), *The Patrician* (1911), *The Dark Flower* (1913), and *The Freelands* (1915), reveal a similar philosophy. Here he brings his penetrating criticism to bear in various surroundings, dealing with country squires, the aristocracy, and artists; and he carries forward his sympathetic study of fierce passions, splendid and irregular.

Galsworthy's masterpiece, however, is the work eventually known as *The Forsyte Saga*, continued by *A Modern Comedy*, the whole being a collection of six novels, the earliest of which is *The Man of Property* (1906). It is a sort of natural history of a rich upper-middle class family, the epitome of English conservatism. Galsworthy's object is to describe the successive generations and their attitude towards the history of the last half-century and to such recent events as the Great War, the growth of socialism, unemployment, the coal strike. Though the entire work exhibits the same quality of irony in its treatment of social prejudices and of the possessive instinct, Galsworthy's views do not remain fixed and unalterable. From the start of the *Saga* he shows that he admires grand Victorian figures like old Jolyon; but he gradually begins to display a tardy indulgence, even a kind of growing sympathy, for the character who was originally the central object of his satire, Soames Forsyte, 'the man of property', who first appears as a selfish, brutal husband, grasping and covetous, but shows that he can be a strongly affectionate father, full of self-denial and ready to sacrifice himself, and dies almost as a hero. In this change we can see Galsworthy gradually drawing closer to the characteristic English standpoint, and returning more or less to traditional paths, without, however, losing the warmth of impulse which marked his attacks upon social customs and institutions.

With its ample sweep the *Forsyte Saga* recalls the ambitious structure of Balzac's *Comédie Humaine* or Zola's *Les Rougon Macquart*; or still more, in its extreme modernity, the series of scenes of contemporary life created by Anatole France around the figure of 'Monsieur Bergeret'. Every section of it is distinguished by subtle analysis, by truth and diversity of character-drawing, both in men and women, by the poetical quality of the descriptions of natural scenery, above all by a sensitive, flexible, and delicate style which remains artistic even when it is audaciously colloquial.

A. Bennett. Arnold Bennett (1867–1931) wrote a large number of novels of different sorts; several of them are of the type of realistic social studies. Their setting is the pottery district of Staffordshire, from which Bennett himself hailed; they are *Anna of the Five Towns* (1902), *The Old Wives' Tale* (1908), *Clayhanger* (1910), *Hilda Lessways* (1911), and *These Twain* (1916). They present a detailed, unadorned picture of life in an industrial district in the provinces: it is a grey-toned picture of an unheroic people, but their obscure struggles, joys, and sufferings are studied with unobtrusive sympathy. Bennett's realism links him with the French naturalistic writers, but he does not share their taste for cynicism and indecency. Like them he effaces himself behind his characters, and his method is to build up with small strokes a convincing picture of a peculiar, limited society—a picture without much radiance or easy charm, and admirable for exactness rather than for poetical quality.

Chesterton. Society has had its defenders against these attacks. The most prominent and original of them is G. K. Chesterton (born in 1874), who has stood forth as the champion of tradition and common sense in discussions like *Orthodoxy* (1908) and in fantastic novels like *The Napoleon of Notting Hill* (1904), *The Man who was Thursday* (1908), &c. He answers the sarcasm of the critics with jests. He laughs at the depressing conclusions of science and defends the simple joy of life. Chesterton believes that the age-long experience of mankind is the best part of man's wisdom and that the bond of religious authority is still the best link between man and man. He goes back beyond Luther, the innovator, and contrasts the scattered condition of the Protestant sects with the strong unity of the Church of Rome.

He makes his defence of common sense attractive by clothing it in the outward form of paradox. His method is to deliver a raking fire of unexpected arguments supported by an unfailing wealth of vigorous imagery and comparison. To protect and defend his much-loved ideas of order and discipline he does not hesitate to play the buffoon, hoping to win his point through laughter. He is a humorist who amuses and dazzles his reader but wearies him in the long run by constant repetition of the same

tricks. He has made platitudes sparkle. Though he has often been
too much a journalist, yet his critical studies of Browning and
Dickens deserve lasting reputation.

Other novelists. His best companion in arms has been Hilaire
Belloc (born in 1870). He has written novels, including *Emmanuel
Burden* (1904) and *Mr. Clutterbuck's Election*, but he is better
known as an essayist and controversialist with a talent less
mannered than Chesterton's but also less strongly individual, and
dissipated in an enormous output of written matter.

Mrs. Humphry Ward (1851–1920), a niece of Matthew Arnold,
stands midway between the reformers and the traditionalists. In
1888 she had an immense success with *Robert Elsmere*, in which,
with some independence, she drew a pathetic picture of a clergyman's spiritual conflict between literal faith and historical
knowledge. The many novels, however, which followed her
masterpiece place her rather among the defenders of established
order and traditional respectability. She was distinguished for
industrious workmanship rather than for creative imagination;
her style is sober and abstract, not concrete and picturesque, and
in both its good and its bad qualities quite unlike the impressionistic manner of most of her contemporaries.

During this period historical novels continued to appear, but
they had diminished in both importance and number. The most
artistic of them was *John Inglesant* (1881) by Joseph Shorthouse
(1834–1903), a narrative of religious life in England in the seventeenth century, at the time when the High Church was tending
towards Roman Catholicism. It gained a deserved reputation
through the glowing idealism which pervades it and the strange
atmosphere of mysticism which enwraps it.

Maurice Hewlett (1861–1923) went back to the age of chivalry
in imaginative stories like *The Forest Lovers* (1898) and *The
Queen's Quair* (1904), in which he seems to be trying to escape
from the present that has lost the charm of poetry.

But in recent years these survivals of an overworked type of
fiction, to which Stevenson alone in his day could give any real
vitality, have proved less popular than the novels with an unusual
foreign flavour in which Stevenson himself and Kipling were so

prolific. The period is marked much more by a growing curiosity about distant parts of the world than by any return to the past: and this is proved by the success of the work of Lafcadio Hearn and Conrad.

Lafcadio Hearn (1850–1904), was born in the Ionian Islands, of Irish and Greek parentage. After extensive wanderings he became a professor at the University of Tokio and married a Japanese wife. His books are not so much novels proper, as descriptions of strange countries. In 1890 he wrote *Two Years in the French West Indies*, and then devoted himself to Japan, revealing it to English readers in admirable analytical studies of the character of the people like *Glimpses of Unfamiliar Japan* (1894) and *Kokoro* (1896). For the conventional idea of Japan he substituted a picture of the true Japan, heroic beneath its smiling courteousness. He learned to respect, even to admire, the moral character of the Japanese no less than their art.

Conrad. Joseph Conrad (1857–1924), a Pole born in Ukraine and educated in France, became an Englishman only when he was 28 years old. At first English was a foreign language to him, and to the end of his life he retained a foreign accent. Deep sympathy with the British character was not his by birth; he acquired it gradually, in the course of many years spent first as a common sailor and later as the master of a vessel in the English merchant service. The depths of his nature and the foundation of his philosophy remained Slav; he shared the Russian novelists' sense of mystery, their tragic obsession with the unknown, their haunted preoccupation with human misery. His work is steeped in pessimism. He proclaimed that he desired to be first and foremost an artist, and his art is related to Continental realism. It therefore cost him a long struggle to overcome the resistance of the English public, and his great popularity was achieved only towards the end of his career.

With a few exceptions Conrad's novels are concerned with the sea: in most of them, and the best, the scene is the bridge of a ship or some far-off coast. *The Nigger of the Narcissus* (1897), *Youth* (1902), *Typhoon* (1903), *Lord Jim* (1900), are leading instances. Though English literature was already rich in tales of the sea and though Kipling was writing at the same period, Conrad was able to contribute something fresh, not merely because of his expert knowledge of a sailor's life but because he had an uncommon angle of vision. Nor was he less original in his narrative craftsmanship. His characters are brought before the reader not directly but through the conflicting and fragmentary images of them formed by various witnesses. He makes, as it were, a preliminary sketch and then proceeds to fill it in and enrich it. Perplexity, apparent contradictions, a kind of mystery, are the result of this method. Even the explanation of the action may be deferred for a long time and the story keeps to the end a certain air of strangeness. The Nigger of the 'Narcissus', for example, is a curious indefinite person about whom the crew have different ideas, changing their opinions during the voyage; no one knows whether his inertia is due to laziness or to illness, or whether he is sincere or pretending, and the doubts are hardly dispelled when the story closes.

These strange foreign tales are a background for the display of native English character. Conrad admired British sailors for their coolness, for the discipline which ruled aboard their ships; he was not blind to the English habit of empiricism and scorn of exact knowledge but he showed in *Typhoon* how they were redeemed by imperturbable tenacity and will-power. The 'muddling through' so much ridiculed by Wells has a powerful attraction for Conrad. He was equally fascinated by English as a language, and by the possibilities which it holds for narrative and description; but he enriched it with his characteristic foreign qualities. His full, rich prose, more highly coloured and more sensuous than would be natural to an Englishman born, has a place to itself in modern fiction. Conrad's work is the most striking illustration of the merits and possibilities of cosmopolitanism in literature.

Some more. The many different kinds of novel already enumerated do not exhaust the list. They give a very incomplete idea of the changes through which the novel has passed during the last fifty years. The influence of the aesthetic and decadent movement already noticed in poetry may be traced also in fiction. Its best-known representative is Oscar Wilde with his *Picture of Dorian Grey* (1897), in which he makes a study of his own dilettantism, and describes people who look for nothing but pleasure and, denying the existence of any other standard of conduct, try to turn living into a game or an art. The sentimental, improving type of realistic novel, which had been so successful in the Victorian Age, was still popular. It was represented by the productions of the Scottish 'Kailyard School' and most delightfully by Sir James Barrie (born in 1860) with his *Window in Thrums* (1889), *The Little Minister* (1891), *Margaret Ogilvie* (1896), &c., which paint tender, sensitive, and charming pictures of simple and ordinary folk. These are novels of provincial life: a variety of the same type is the novel of colonial life, developed by Olive Schreiner (1855–1920) with her popular *Story of an African Farm* (1883) and her picturesque descriptions of South African life.

This tendency of writers to specialize is one of the curious characteristics of this age. They have specialized not only in particular districts but in particular races; an outstanding example is Israel Zangwill who has written a large number of novels, including *The Children of the Ghetto* (1892), about the world of Jewry. Sir Arthur Conan Doyle (1859–1930) after producing a few historical novels gained great popularity as a writer of detective stories with *The Adventures of Sherlock Holmes* (1891), creating thereby a new type which has had many offshoots.

A place apart is required by George Moore (1852–1933) who during forty years was the connecting link between English and French literature. His early novels *A Mummer's Wife* (1885), *Esther Waters* (1894), *Evelyn Innes* (1898), were all influenced by the French naturalist school. In his later periods he was no less French though in a different way, adopting a Gallic precision of language and a love of literary form which have dominated his works ever since. His autobiography *Hail and Farewell* (1911–14) is an intimate account of his own mind and his experiences of others, in Ireland, Paris, and London.

In quite recent years new novelists of high quality have appeared to continue the work of their forerunners or to explore fresh paths. W. S. Maugham (born in 1874) began with novels of the naturalistic type but his scenes of life in the Pacific mark him as a follower of Stevenson and Conrad. E. M. Forster (born in 1879),

D. H. Lawrence (1885–1930), May Sinclair, Hugh Walpole, Frank Swinnerton, J. D. Beresford, R. H. Mottram, Katherine Mansfield, Virginia Woolf, Clemence Dane, Aldous Huxley, J. B. Priestley, James Joyce—to name only a few of the best-known writers—give proof of the marvellous suppleness and vitality of the novel, which the changing fashions and preoccupations of each successive generation can modify but not exhaust. Nearly all of the last named writers deserve an ample study.

The Theatre

Throughout the XIXth Century. Since 1880 fiction has developed vigorously and brilliantly; the drama has practically been reborn. Not that theatres in the country of Shakespeare have ever been deserted, except during the Commonwealth. But for many generations the middle class looked on them with suspicion and disfavour. The puritanically inclined held aloof from them, regarding them as profane or frivolous, and tolerating them only when the piece was an established classic, especially a play of Shakespeare. The history of the theatre in recent times has been an affair of great actors rather than great dramatists. John Philip Kemble and Mrs. Siddons were followed in the romantic period by Kean and Macready, and closer to the present day by Henry Irving and Ellen Terry. Each of them brought a new and individual touch to the interpretation of famous and popular parts. The life of the theatre maintained itself in them, but nothing was added to the old repertory except a few mediocre plays of passing interest. From the very beginning of the eighteenth century we can trace a progressive decline in originality and literary merit, due exception being made for the isolated brilliance of Goldsmith and Sheridan. In the nineteenth century the falling off becomes still more marked. There is, indeed, a whole series of works in dramatic form, many of them by distinguished writers, but these, written in ignorance or in contempt of stage conditions and often not even intended to be played, scarcely belong to the history of the theatre. Wordsworth's *Borderers*, Coleridge's *Osorio*, Byron's numerous tragedies, like *Marino Faliero* and *Sardanapalus*, Shelley's *The Cenci*, must be studied purely as literature. The same criticism holds good, with increased force, for *Joseph and his Brethren* (1824) by Charles J. Wells, for *The Bride's Tragedy* (1822) and *Death's Jest Book* (begun 1825, published 1850) by Beddoes, and for *Mary Tudor* (1847) by Aubrey de Vere. The *Mirandola* (1821) of Proctor (Barry Cornwall), Sir Henry Taylor's *Philip van Artevelde* (1834), and T. N. Talfourd's *Ion* (1835)—all works of considerable poetic quality— were presented on the stage and applauded by a group of literary people, but their success was short-lived. Browning's youthful tragedies, *Strafford* (1837), *A Blot in the 'Scutcheon* (1843), *Colombe's Birthday* (1844), &c., had a similar fate; and if some of the plays which Tennyson wrote in his maturer years, such as *Queen Mary* (1875), *The Cup* (1881), and above all *Becket* (1893) were more successful, they owed their success mainly to their excellent production by Irving. As for Swinburne's trilogy on *Mary Stuart*, his *Marino Faliero* (1885), and his *Locrine* (1887), they are obviously intended to be read rather than acted.

All these plays are worth reading as poetry but they do not belong to the repertory of the theatre. The real tradition of drama was supported only by a few very mediocre writers. One of the most expert of them was J. S. Knowles (1784–1862) who produced a series of tragedies in verse, like *Virginius* (1820), which have no real poetry in them but are vigorously constructed; and some popular comedies, the best of which is *The Hunchback* (1832). About the same time the prolific and talented Bulwer Lytton had a great success with *The Lady of Lyons* and *Richelieu* (1838), melodramas without permanent value but with real dramatic qualities.

As the century advanced the theatrical production grew more and more impoverished. Old plays, chiefly Shakespeare's, were revived: plays were borrowed from abroad, and were inartistically adapted or toned down to suit the sentimental, optimistic taste of the public. Originality seemed to have deserted the stage altogether.

The popular writers of the day were the actor Dion Boucicault (1820–90), who adapted innumerable pieces to the prevailing taste, and H. J. Byron (1834–84), also an actor, who sometimes, as in *Cyril's Success* (1868), *The Corsican Brothers* (1869), and

Our Boys (1875), gave proof of a more individual talent in his construction of plot, though his dialogues were most artificial. Almost
the only author to attempt a comedy of contemporary manners
reflecting the intimacies of Victorian life was another actor, T. W.
Robertson (1829–71), who has been called the leader of the 'tea-
cup and saucer School'. He wrote *Society* (1865), *Ours* (1866), *Caste*
(1867), and *School* (1869), his usual method being to place a sentimental couple in a coarse environment.

But from 1880 onward signs of revival grow more numerous
and more significant. Gradually the stage began to profit by the
freedom and boldness which was being recovered for literature.
W. S. Gilbert (1836–1911) crowned an extensive and prosperous
dramatic career with comic operas like *H.M.S. Pinafore* (1878)
and *The Mikado* (1885), where lively political and social satire
puts an edge on long passages of comic doggerel. *Breaking a
Butterfly* (1885) and *Saints and Sinners* (1884) by Henry Arthur
Jones, and *The Second Mrs. Tanqueray* (1893), *The Gay Lord
Quex* (1899), and *Iris* (1901) by Sir Arthur Pinero, not uninfluenced
by Alexander Dumas *fils*, showed an attempt to overhaul the
conventional technique of the stage and to introduce more strongly
realistic scenes. At the same time Sheridan's sparkling wit seemed
to live again in the comedies of Oscar Wilde, *Lady Windermere's
Fan* (1892), *A Woman of No Importance* (1893), *The Importance
of being Earnest* (1895). The first two of these are marred by
artificial sentiment, but all three of them abound in repartees full
of verbal polish and cynical elegance. They are light pieces; with
more seriousness and substance they might be called subversive
of moral order.

The Revival. These are all products of a transitional age: they
lack depth, their audacities are narrowly limited, they are still too
much bound by convention to be really novel. A more vigorous
and loftier impulse, however, was given by the drama of Ibsen,
with its rich flow of ideas and its daring views on moral and social
questions. The great Norwegian writer was introduced to England
by a group of admirers, including Sir Edmund Gosse, Bernard
Shaw, and the dramatic critic William Archer, who translated and
discussed his work and forced people to admire it. The emptiness

and insipidity of the degenerate English drama at once became apparent. The result was a reform in acting and also in stage-setting. In 1904 Harley Granville Barker and Vedrenne, in management at the Court Theatre, started the movement and set the example, and plays themselves began to exhibit a realism, energy, and intelligence which had long been absent. Here we can only mention Somerset Maugham's *Mrs. Craddock* (1902) and *Lady Frederick* (1907), Harley Granville Barker's *The Voysey Inheritance* (1905) and *Waste* (1907), and St. John Hankin's *The Return of the Prodigal* (1905) and *The Last of the De Mullins* (1908).

Bernard Shaw. One man, however, took the lead and dominated the scene with his extraordinary talents, demoniac energy, and aggressive wit—Bernard Shaw, born in Dublin in 1856, who, previously a critic, began his sensational dramatic career with *Widowers' Houses* in 1892.

Fundamentally Shaw's place is beside the novelists who at the same period were attacking social traditions. As a socialist, he disapproves of existing institutions; as an Irishman, he speaks of England as a foreign country and shows no respect whatever for her beliefs; as a logician, he pursues his ideas unperturbed to their extreme conclusions, and revels in paradox. He delights in ridiculing, upsetting, scandalizing, astonishing his public. He challenged it, laughed at its tender feelings, mocked at every English ideal, went to the English anarchist Samuel Butler for spiritual nourishment, and drew inspiration from the foreign and most unorthodox ideas of Schopenhauer, Ibsen, Nietzsche, Wagner, and Karl Marx. In spite of all this Shaw succeeded by sheer zest and wit in gaining not only a hearing but applause in the very place where it is most difficult to introduce ideas which oppose the existing ones—the theatre.

Shaw found an entirely new form for his plays. They are really dialogues in which revolutionary views are developed. The plot is usually sacrificed and has little importance. The characters have no great reality; they are simply the means of putting forward disconcerting ideas. But Shaw manages to produce amusing and laughable situations, and his irreverences are excused and redeemed by humour. The plays collected in 1898 under the

title of *Plays Pleasant and Unpleasant* (*Mrs. Warren's Profession,
Arms and the Man, Candida, You Never can Tell*), those collected
in 1901 as *Three Plays for Puritans* (*The Devil's Disciple, Caesar
and Cleopatra, Captain Brassbound's Conversion*), together with
Man and Superman (1903), *John Bull's Other Island* (1904),
Fanny's First Play (1911), &c., make up a solid and homogeneous
group in their diversity of subjects; they set forth a social philosophy and under their cloak of farce are often simply pieces of
propaganda. Shaw is a humorist who likes pretending to be a
charlatan; but he gives plenty of food for thought, for with all
his mountebank tricks he is felt to be somehow in earnest.

In *Man and Superman*, with its long introduction at the
beginning and its 'Revolutionist's Handbook' at the end, Shaw
gave a general view of his leading ideas and a summary of his
philosophy of the Life Force, which urges man on through continual evolution towards an ever deeper and more enlightened
state of consciousness. Since the War, without abandoning his
sarcasm or his humorous fantasy, he has given an almost religious turn to his work; that is to say, he has tended more and
more to take up the problem of life after death, to try to learn
something of that God whom he regards as the Force hidden in
evolution. In the play, or series of plays, called *Back to Methuselah*
(1921) he imagines a man who lives long enough to attain, by
successive stages, to perfect wisdom; in the end he becomes a being
liberated from bodily functions, a pure intelligence.

In *St. Joan* (1924) he interprets the career of Joan of Arc in a
new and individual way. He shows her able, by sheer good sense,
to break through the barrier of creed and to raise herself above
the beliefs of her time. He makes her 'the first protestant', who,
guided by her inner light, unconsciously frees herself from, and
shakes off, the tutelage of the church. The humorist in Shaw
amuses himself by showing the working of modern ideas on Joan
and those around her, and making them say what they would have
said if they had realized the meaning of what they were doing—a
flagrant violation of the traditions of the theatre and the historical
novel, which do their best to avoid anachronism. The great
characteristic and novelty of Shaw's work, taken in the mass, is

that it has proved by its noisy success that England can applaud plays whose interest is chiefly intellectual while confirming her good-natured tolerance of sarcasm levelled at herself.

Galsworthy. Another dramatic critic of social life is John Galsworthy, who from 1909 onwards, when he produced *The Silver Box*, has alternated plays with his novels. In *Strife* (1909), *Justice* (1910), *The Pigeon* (1912), *Loyalties* (1922), *Escape* (1926), &c., he holds in check the humour and fantasy which overflow in Shaw's work. With intense seriousness and strong controlled emotion he presents some aspect of the evil or injustice that is born of laws and prejudices. He deliberately keeps his plays widely unlike his novels, which are so rich in subtle shades of meaning. He deals with many social problems with remarkable soberness and clarity, although his well-balanced mind is for ever weighing the pros and cons. He avoids Shaw's long tirades; his dialogue is crisp and vigorous; if he has a weakness, it lies in a certain failure to fill out his characters or to develop the action, both of which sometimes seem to be left too much in outline.

Other dramatists. Sir James Barrie, unlike Shaw and Galsworthy, at first conformed to the national tradition of mingling humour with sentiment, as for example in *The Little Minister* (1897), an adaptation of the story of one of his exquisite novels of Scottish life. Subsequently the spirit of satire gained the upper hand, or at least shared the field with humour and fantasy, in *The Admirable Crichton* and *Quality Street* (1902) and *Dear Brutus* (1917). Always a popular author, Barrie had an unbounded success with his fairy play *Peter Pan* (1904) which so pleasantly combines the simplicity of childhood with the fascination of the strange and mysterious.

Poetical drama continues to flourish: it was nobly represented in Stephen Phillips's *Paolo and Francesca* in 1899. John Masefield, the poet, wrote a vigorous play in prose, *The Tragedy of Nan*, in 1909, but then turned to verse in *Pompey the Great* (1910), *Philip the King* (1914) and *A King's Daughter* (1923): but he has not had the success on the stage which his poetic talent deserved. John Drinkwater (born in 1882) has been more fortunate: his art consists in presenting lifelike pictures of the characters of famous historical personages and of the principal events in their careers. His plays include *Abraham Lincoln* (1918), *Mary Stuart* (1921), and *Cromwell* (1921), the first being his best.

All these plays have been produced on the London stage, but London is no longer the only centre of the drama. The revival of provincial life has produced the Manchester Repertory Theatre, where Lancashire dialect and humour are to be heard once more; and about 1921 an interesting series of native Scottish plays was produced in Glasgow. The earliest and the most important production of 'local' drama took place, however, in Ireland, under the influence of the Celtic Revival.

For the theatre in Dublin which he founded, Yeats, the poet, wrote a number of plays which show the same delicate beauty as his poems. They include *The Countess Cathleen* (1892), *The Land of Heart's Desire* (1894), *Cathleen ni Houlihan* (in prose; 1902), *Deirdre* (1907), and others. Their merit consists not so much in presentation of character as in a tender or tragic symbolism enveloped in an atmosphere of dreams.

J. M. Synge (1871-1909) had a more vigorous and more truly dramatic talent. He was sensitive alike to the element of magic so dear to the Irish imagination and to the homely, realistic comedy and farce mingled with that magic. He developed a poetical, archaic style based on the speech of the Aran Islands. These were the main features of a highly original drama in which racy unusual comedies like *The Tinker's Wedding* and *The Playboy of the Western World* (1907), full of irreverent farce, alternate with the grim despair of *Riders to the Sea*.

More recently Irish drama has shown vigorous life in the strictly realistic but strong and thoroughly local work of Sean O'Casey, whose play *The Silver Tassie* refers to the Great War while his *Juno and the Paycock* (1925) and *The Plough and the Stars* (1926) belong to the period of the tragic conflict from which emerged the Irish Free State.

We see, then, that the dramatic genius which was formerly the greatest glory of English letters has revived with new formulas. It has adapted itself to modern conditions, and holds up the mirror to nature and society much as it did in the sixteenth century. Had it produced no other Renaissance than this, the age in which we

live would have deserved well of literature. But, as we have seen
elsewhere, this very age has furnished, both in poetry and above
all in fiction, abundant proof of the intellectual vitality of the
country.

The fecundity of the present age seems to give assurance of a
splendid future; beyond that it would be vain to prophesy. We
cannot foretell what the years will bring; we may more fittingly
conclude this too rapid survey of a twelve-hundred-year-old literature by glancing at its marvellous expansion, which has followed
the political fortune of the country and the spread of the English
tongue over the world.

We have seen how English literature was born within the confined limits of the small Germanic tribes that had established
themselves in Great Britain, speaking the dialects of the Angles
and the Saxons. At the start nothing could be more narrowly
isolated. The clergy may have maintained a link with the rest of
Christendom but this link consisted entirely in borrowings from
abroad for the native language, and communication between
England and the outer world took place solely by means of Latin.
All that was really original in her output remained pent up in
the vernacular without any possibility of expansion.

This state of things persisted throughout the Middle Ages and
even during the Renaissance. French and Italian joined Latin
as media of communication and through them England shared
largely in the culture of Europe, being moulded and enriched by
it but gradually assuming an ever more individual form until she
began to produce literature so great that it is still her chief pride.
But it was composed in a language unknown abroad, and long
remained a treasure which other nations could not share. It was
not until the beginning of the eighteenth century that full communion was established between Great Britain and the rest of
Europe. It was only then that perfect 'give and take' began. The
great English writers of the past, whose influence and fame had
until then been confined to their own country, at last entered into
possession of the universal renown to which they were entitled.
Whether or not they knew it or desired it, English writers from

that time onward would address themselves to a cosmopolitan public.

English thought and the leading ideas of the English novel, the English theatre, and English poetry had their immediate influence in the whole of the Western civilized world. They became one of its chief intellectual and imaginative forces. For two centuries this expansion has gone steadily forward. As the nation has developed politically the seed sown among the primitive tribes has taken root, and has become a great tree whose branches cover half the globe—not only those vast spaces of the earth that are England's colonies and dominions, but also foreign countries, and among them those which sowed the seed in the beginning.

Throughout this time the native home of free trade has continued to import as much as she has exported. Like her mixed language, which is Germanic in its origins but hospitably welcomes French, Latin, and Greek words, her literature has borrowed freely from those of antiquity and of foreign countries, without losing its insular individuality. It has shown, perhaps, a greater capacity than any other literature for combining a love of concrete statement with a tendency to dream, a sense of reality with lyrical rapture. It is characterized by loving observation of Nature, by a talent for depicting strongly-marked character, and by a humour that is the amused and sympathetic noting of the contradictions of human nature and the odd aspects of life. Just as the English language has given an English accent to foreign words which marks its entry into possession of them, so literature has everywhere set a deep and individual stamp even upon the ideas and stories which have come to it from without.

INDEX

PRINTED IN GREAT BRITAIN AT THE UNIVERSITY PRESS, OXFORD
BY JOHN JOHNSON, PRINTER TO THE UNIVERSITY